Lecture Notes in Computer Science

Lecture Notes in Artificial Intelligence   14113

Founding Editor

Jörg Siekmann

Series Editors

Randy Goebel, *University of Alberta, Edmonton, Canada*
Wolfgang Wahlster, *DFKI, Berlin, Germany*
Zhi-Hua Zhou, *Nanjing University, Nanjing, China*

The series Lecture Notes in Artificial Intelligence (LNAI) was established in 1988 as a topical subseries of LNCS devoted to artificial intelligence.

The series publishes state-of-the-art research results at a high level. As with the LNCS mother series, the mission of the series is to serve the international R & D community by providing an invaluable service, mainly focused on the publication of conference and workshop proceedings and postproceedings.

Henrik Legind Larsen · Maria J. Martin-Bautista ·
M. Dolores Ruiz · Troels Andreasen ·
Gloria Bordogna · Guy De Tré
Editors

Flexible Query Answering Systems

15th International Conference, FQAS 2023
Mallorca, Spain, September 5–7, 2023
Proceedings

Springer

Editors
Henrik Legind Larsen (iD)
Legind Technologies
Haslev, Denmark

Maria J. Martin-Bautista (iD)
University of Granada
Granada, Spain

M. Dolores Ruiz (iD)
University of Granada
Granada, Spain

Troels Andreasen (iD)
Roskilde University
Roskilde, Denmark

Gloria Bordogna (iD)
Consiglio Nazionale delle Ricerche
Milano, Italy

Guy De Tré (iD)
Ghent University
Gent, Belgium

ISSN 0302-9743 ISSN 1611-3349 (electronic)
Lecture Notes in Artificial Intelligence
ISBN 978-3-031-42934-7 ISBN 978-3-031-42935-4 (eBook)
https://doi.org/10.1007/978-3-031-42935-4

LNCS Sublibrary: SL7 – Artificial Intelligence

This Springer imprint is published by the registered company Springer Nature Switzerland AG
The registered company address is: Gewerbestrasse 11, 6330 Cham, Switzerland

Paper in this product is recyclable.

Preface

This volume constitutes the Proceedings of the 15th International Conference on Flexible Query Answering Systems, FQAS 2023, held in Palma de Mallorca, Spain, 5–7 September 2023, collocated with EUSFLAT 2023. The biennial FQAS conference series has been running since 1994, starting in Roskilde, Denmark, where it also was held in 1996, 1998 and 2009; in 2000 it was held in Warsaw, Poland; in 2002 in Copenhagen, Denmark; in 2004 in Lyon, France; in 2006 in Milan, Italy; in 2011 in Ghent, Belgium; in 2013 in Granada, Spain; in 2015 in Cracow, Poland; in 2017 in London, UK; in 2019 in Amantea, Italy; and in 2021 in Bratislava, Slovakia.

FQAS is the premier conference concerned with the very important issue of providing users of information systems with flexible querying capabilities, and with easy and intuitive access to information. More specifically, the overall theme of the FQAS conferences is the modelling and design of innovative and flexible modalities for accessing information systems. The main objective is to achieve more expressive, informative, cooperative, and productive systems which facilitate retrieval from information repositories such as databases, libraries, heterogeneous archives, and the web.

Supporting these aims, FQAS is a multidisciplinary conference drawing on several research areas, including information retrieval, database management, information filtering, knowledge representation, computational linguistics and natural language processing, artificial intelligence, soft computing, classical and non-classical logics, and human-computer interaction.

The sessions, including the special sessions, comprised a total of 26 submissions, and at least two double-blinded reviews per paper contained in these proceedings. The sessions covered advances in the following mainstream fields: Data and Text Mining, Disinformation Detection, Flexible Queries over Semantic Systems, Methods and Applications in Natural Language Processing, Artificial Intelligence Law and Regulation, and Applying AI to Social Science and Social Science to AI. Each session is introduced in the following Table of Contents.

An important contribution of the conference has been that it has greatly facilitated a deeper discussion on the papers presented, which has resulted in new collaborative works and further research progress in the areas.

We hope that the collection of main contributions presented at the conference will provide a source of much-needed information and inspiration on recent trends in the topics considered. To this aim, the conference further provided three inspiring keynote speeches, given by leading researchers in particular topics of interest to the conference theme, namely: Identifying Misinformation Online: Open Issues and Challenges, presented by Gabriella Pasi, OpenWebSearch.eu, Building an Open Web Index for an Open Web Search Ecosystem, presented by Michael Granitzer, and Survey of Readiness Levels Methodologies, presented by Hassane Essafi.

We wish to thank all authors for their excellent papers and the referees, publisher, sponsors, and local organizers for their efforts. Special thanks go to the organizers of the special sessions, the keynote speakers, members of the Advisory Board, members of the Program Committee and, not least, EUSFLAT for hosting FQAS 2023 collocated with EUSFLAT 2023.

September 2023

Henrik Legind Larsen
Maria J. Martin-Bautista
M. Dolores Ruiz
Troels Andreasen
Gloria Bordogna
Guy De Tré

Organization

General and Program Co-chairs

Henrik Legind Larsen	Legind Technologies A/S, Denmark
Maria J. Martin-Bautista	University of Granada, Spain
M. Dolores Ruiz	University of Granada, Spain

Local Organizing Committee

Karel Gutiérrez-Batista	University of Granada, Spain
Carlos Fernandez-Basso	University of Granada, Spain
Roberto Morcillo-Jimenez	University of Granada, Spain
J. Angel Diaz-Garcia	University of Granada, Spain
Andrea Morales-Garzón	University of Granada, Spain
Bartolome Ortiz-Viso	University of Granada, Spain

Steering Committee

Henrik Legind Larsen	Legind Technologies A/S, Denmark
Troels Andreasen	Roskilde University, Denmark
Gloria Bordogna	National Research Council of Italy, Italy
Guy De Tré	Ghent University, Belgium

International Advisory Board

Carlos D. Barranco González	Spain
Jesus Cardeñosa	Spain
Henning Christiansen	Denmark
Hendrik Decker	Germany
Jorgen Fischer Nilsson	Denmark
Norbert Fuhr	Germany
Hélène Jaudoin	France
Janusz Kacprzyk	Poland
Donald Kraft	USA
Frederick E. Petry	USA

Olivier Pivert	France
Henri Prade	France
Giuseppe Psaila	Italy
Zbigniew W. Ras	USA
Grégory Smits	France
Sotir Sotirov	Bulgaria
Nicolas Spyratos	France
Adnan Yazici	Turkey
Slawomir Zadrozny	Poland

Program Committee

Troels Andreasen	Roskilde University, Denmark
Ignacio J. Blanco	University of Granada, Spain
Fernando Bobillo	University of Zaragoza, Spain
Gloria Bordogna	National Research Council of Italy, Italy
Antoon Bronselaer	Ghent University, Belgium
Henning Christiansen	Roskilde University, Denmark
Alfredo Cuzzocrea	University of Calabria, Italy
Ernesto Damiani	University of Milan, Italy
Bernard De Baets	Ghent University, Belgium
Guy De Tré	Ghent University, Belgium
J. Angel Diaz-Garcia	University of Granada, Spain
Carlos Fernández Basso	University of Granada, Spain
Sébastien Ferré	Université de Rennes, CNRS, IRISA, France
Karel Gutiérrez-Batista	University of Granada, Spain
Allel Hadjali	LIAS/ENSMA, France
Petr Hurtik	IRAFM, Czech Republic
Helene Jaudoin	IRISA-ENSSAT, France
Etienne Kerre	Ghent University, France
Donald Kraft	Louisiana State University, USA
Marie-Jeanne Lesot	LIP6, Sorbonne University, France
Antoni Ligeza	AGH University of Science and Technology, Poland
Trevor Martin	University of Bristol, UK
Andrea Morales-Garzón	University of Granada, Spain
Roberto Morcillo-Jimenez	University of Granada, Spain
Jørgen Fischer Nilsson	Technical University of Denmark, Denmark
Andreas Nürnberger	Otto von Guericke University Magdeburg, Germany
José Ángel Olivas	University of Castilla-La Mancha, Spain

Bartolomé Ortiz-Viso	University of Granada, Spain
Frederick E. Petry	Naval Research Lab, USA
Olivier Pivert	IRISA-ENSSAT, France
Henri Prade	IRIT - CNRS, France
Giuseppe Psaila	University of Bergamo, Italy
Zbigniew Ras	UNC Charlotte, USA
Marek Reformat	University of Alberta, Canada
Francisco P. Romero	University of Castilla-La Mancha, Spain
M. Dolores Ruiz	University of Granada, Spain
José M. Serrano-Chica	University of Jaén, Spain
Miguel-Angel Sicilia	University of Alcalá, Spain
Andrzej Skowron	Warsaw University, Poland
Grégory Smits	IRISA/University of Rennes, France
Peter Vojtas	Charles University Prague, Czech Republic
Jef Wijsen	University of Mons, Belgium
Adnan Yazici	Middle East Technical University, Turkey
Slawomir Zadrozny	Systems Research Institute, Polish Academy of Sciences, Poland

Special Session Organizers

Fernando Bobillo	University of Zaragoza, Spain
José Antonio Castillo Parrilla	University of Granada, Spain
J. Angel Diaz-Garcia	University of Granada, Spain
Julio Amador Díaz López	Imperial College London, UK
Carlos Fernandez-Basso	University of Granada, Spain
Matija Franklin	University College London, UK
Jesica Gómez-Sánchez	University of Granada, Spain
Karel Gutiérrez-Batista	University of Granada, Spain
Ignacio Huitzil	University of Milano-Bicocca, Italy
David Lagnado	University College London, UK
Guillermo Lazcoz Moratinos	Centro de Investigación Biomédica en Red, Spain
Andrea Morales-Garzón	University of Granada, Spain
Roberto Morcillo-Jimenez	University of Granada, Spain
Bartolomé Ortiz-Viso	University of Granada, Spain
M. Dolores Ruiz	University of Granada, Spain
José M. Serrano-Chica	University of Jaén, Spain
Francesca Tassinari	European Commission, Belgium
Javier Valls-Prieto	University of Granada, Spain

Sponsoring Institutions

- University of Granada
- Universitat de les Illes Balears
- Govern Illes Balears, Consejería de Fondos Europeos, Universidad y Cultura
- Ajuntament de Palma
- EUSFLAT: European Society for Fuzzy Logic and Technology
- Fundació Universitat Empresa de les Illes Balears

Keynote Speakers

Identifying Misinformation Online: Open Issues and Challenges

Gabriella Pasi

Abstract. In the World Wide Web and on social media, a large amount of content of different nature and origin is spread without any form of reliable external control; in this context, the risk of running into misinformation is not negligible. In recent years, an increasing awareness of the possible risks of running into fake news, fake reviews, or health misinformation has emerged. This has motivated a considerable amount of research finalized at defining systems that are able to predict if a piece of information is truthful. Several approaches have been proposed in the literature to automatically assess the truthfulness of content disseminated online.

Most of them are data-driven approaches, based on machine learning techniques, but recently also model-driven approaches have been studied, based, in particular, on the Multi-Criteria Decision Making (MCDM) paradigm, and also based on the use of Knowledge Bases. Both categories of approaches make use of prior knowledge related to the problem under consideration, which is injected into the decision process.

This talk will present an overview of the approaches to coping with the problem of misinformation detection, with particular emphasis on model-driven approaches, their open issues, and current challenges. Among these approaches, those based on the aggregation of salient features related to misinformation will be considered. Their application to specific problems will also be addressed, as well as the problem of evaluating these systems.

Building an Open Web Index for an Open Web Search Ecosystem

Michael Granitzer

Abstract. Web search has become an essential technology forming the backbone of our digital economy. A rather small number of gatekeepers dominate Web search, which creates a biased, one-sided information access centred around economic success. This one-sided ecosystem puts pressure on small contributors requiring them to optimize their content towards these gatekeeper a vicious cycle resulting in locked-in effects and a closed search engine ecosystem.

In this talk, I will present the recently started OpenWebSearch.eu initiative, which aims on developing an Open Web Index (OWI) to promote an open search engine ecosystem and to provide true choice for users. I will discuss the principal of an Open Web Index, the technical challenges for developing it and how the research community could benefit from an open web search ecosystems that enables to conduct experiments at scale.

Survey of Readiness Levels Methodologies

Hassane Essafi

Abstract. In our digital world, R&D activities play fundamental role in the progress and the prosperity of our societies. The European commission, local authorities are financing and supporting academic and industrial organizations to develop breakthrough R&D activities. In return, they are expecting from the R&D labs to produce breakthrough results. For this purpose, they are more and more pushing to use Readiness Level scales (i.e. TRL: Technology Readiness Level) in order to allow the decision-makers evaluating maturity and consistency of the produced outcomes.

In this presentation I will relies on the work we done in the MultiRate project (https://www.multirate.eu/, topic: HORIZON-CL3-2021-SSRI-01-01 – A maturity assessment framework for security technologies) to give an overview of different works (methodology and frame work) proposed to assess different aspects of Readiness Levels. The aim of this presentation is to raise awareness concerning the importance of using Readiness Levels (such as TRL). During this presentation we will discuss some key Readiness Indicators proposed to assess the maturity the R&D outputs. Indeed the TRLs offer means to appreciate the maturity of research results. By assigning a TRL to a given technology or research outputs, researchers and evaluators can gauge, with acceptable accuracy, the maturity and pertinent of the engaging development, considering factors such as feasibility, proof of concept, and experimental validation. This assessment helps determining the readiness of the research results for progress development or implementation.

We will mainly focus on TRL but we cover others existing established readiness level approaches and methodologies used to evaluate the different aspects of products/systems/processes. It include, beside Technology Readiness Level (TRL) scale, Integration Readiness Level (IRL), Commercialization Readiness Level (CRL), Manufacturing Readiness Levels (MRL), Security, Privacy and Ethics Readiness Level (SPRL) and Societal Readiness Level (SRL).

Contents

New Advances in Disinformation Detection

Data and Text Mining

Applying AI to Social Science and Social Science to AI

Flexible Queries Over Semantic Systems

On Reducing Reasoning and Querying in Natural Logic to Database Querying

Troels Andreasen[1]([✉]), Henrik Bulskov[1], and Jørgen Fischer Nilsson[2]

[1] Roskilde University, Roskilde, Denmark
{troels,bulskov}@ruc.dk
[2] Technical University of Denmark, Kgs. Lyngby, Denmark
jfni@dtu.dk

Abstract. This paper outlines a systems architecture for deductive querying of knowledge bases in a natural logic. The natural logic may be conceived as an extension of formal ontology languages featuring multiple quantified relationships between classes in addition to the subclass relation. It is proposed to obtain deductive querying by computation and storing of relevant logical consequences in a preliminary step. The paper explains how then subsequently query answers within the natural logic can be computed through plain relational database querying using ordinary query languages.

Keywords: deductive querying · natural logic · explainability · database reduction

1 Introduction

This paper outlines principles and systems architecture for deductive querying of knowledge bases in natural logic. Natural logics are forms of formal logic that resemble a fragment of stylized natural language [2,3,6,10,11]. Logical deduction systems for natural logic are developed e.g. in [7,9]. Here we describe a simplified form of natural logic called NATURALOG suited for knowledge base content and its computational querying. As a key advantage natural logics make knowledge bases comprehensible for domain experts having no training in formal logics. This aspect is of course crucial when scaling up to knowledge bases for practical use.

NATURALOG admits arbitrary relationships between the introduced classes comprising combination of quantifiers. As such NATURALOG may also be viewed as a relational generalization of syllogistic logic, and also in this respect as a generalization of description logic. Indeed, NATURALOG may be understood as a fragment of predicate logic in disguise. However, unlike predicate logic there are no explicit variables in the sentences in the knowledge base itself, only in the NATURALOG query forms posed to the knowledge base.

The deductive query facility is the *raison d'être* of the system. This facility enables computational retrieval with sentences and relationships that are only implicitly present in the targeted knowledge base. This relies on logical consequences of the knowledge base. Such computed derivatives reflect the sentences that humans more or less effortlessly would conclude from the knowledge base.

© Springer Nature Switzerland AG 2023
H. L. Larsen et al. (Eds.): FQAS 2023, LNAI 14113, pp. 3–14, 2023.
https://doi.org/10.1007/978-3-031-42935-4_1

Computational deductive querying is known from logic programming. However, whereas in logic programming obtained answers are at the level of individuals, in NATURALOG the answers are obtained in the form of concepts. In order to achieve computation with concepts rather than just individuals, we perform an encoding of the NATURALOG sentences into terms in a metalogic. This is an alternative to a resorting to logical type theory. As metalogic we have introduced DATALOG, see e.g. [1]. This is outlined in [8] and then further developed and described in more detail in a number of publications, to mention in particular [4,5]. As a key point, in this paper we implement the metalogic setup in a relational database query language. Thereby we can take advantage of efficient implementations in available relational database systems.

We compute the relevant logical consequences of the knowledge base in a pre-step with inference rules in Sect. 5. The various common deductive queries then reduce to database search and can therefore be computed as database queries fetched from a library as explicated in Sect. 6. The computations grant full explainability of the output results by their coming about through a chain of inferences rooted in the knowledge base sentences.

In this way step-by-step computation of inferences is replaced by *en masse* computation driven by equi-join. The present paper follows up on EJC [5] explaining and demonstrating these principles on a tiny knowledge base. It serves as preparation for subsequent scaling up necessary for validating scalability and hence the usefulness of the entire approach.

2   NATURALOG **in a Nutshell**

In the NATURALOG methodology a domain is modelled as a collection of concept classes connected by relationships. This is also known from entity-relationship models. NATURALOG focuses on the concept classes rather than individual entities within the classes.

Fundamentally, NATURALOG offers sentences in the form of subject-predicates. Linguistically, they take the form of a noun phrase followed by a transitive verb followed by a noun phrase. In common cases a noun phrase is simply a common noun preceded by (a possibly implicit) quantifier (determiner) some or every. Accordingly, the general form of NATURALOG sentences is simply the linguistic subject-verb-object form

> ([every] | some) *concept verb* (every | [some]) *concept*

The common form in a knowledge base is every *concept verb* some *concept*. The indicated defaults for quantifiers implies that this common form can be written

> *concept verb concept*

Consider the sample sentences

> pancreas isa endochrine_gland
>
> endocrine_gland isa gland

The isa relationship (sometimes written 'is' instead of 'isa') expresses the fundamental inclusion relationship between classes. The first sample in the full form becomes

> every pancreas isa some endochrine gland

An example utilizing an *ad hoc* verb in NATURALOG is

    pancreas produce insulin

being the short form of every pancreas produce some insulin

Concepts/classes are introduced to the knowledge base by being mentioned in a knowledge base NATURALOG sentence. The inclusion relationship becomes a partial order by appropriate "built-in" inference rules for the natural logic stated outside NATURALOG. As such they form the ontology part of a knowledge base. Often the partial order approaches or forms a hierarchical structure.

Generally the concept terms may be count nouns or, as in the following example, mass nouns

    insulin isa hormone

This may be construed more strictly as "every (amount of) insulin is (an amount) of (some) hormone".

3 Compound Concept Terms

NATURALOG also features compound concepts where a head common noun is attached qualifications, say, in the form of prepositional phrases and restrictive relative clauses, adjectives and noun compounds. Examples

    cell in pancreas

    cell that produce insulin

    cell in pancreas that produce insulin

One observes that this recursive language "productivity" leads beyond a simplistic ontology framework comprising only a fixed inventory of concepts.

As a leading principle in NATURALOG the various restrictive qualifications of compound terms may preferably be seen as variants of underlying restrictive relative clauses. Accordingly, in this, somewhat simplistic, view the "canonical" form is

    simple_concept that *verb concept*

exemplified by cell that produce insulin.

Logically, the verb denotes a binary relation, giving in predicate logic for this example $\lambda x.(cell(x) \wedge \exists y(produce(x, y) \wedge insulin(y)))$, see further [4]. We stress, however, that NATURALOG sentences in the knowledge base are not converted to predicate logic. Indeed, the logical inference is to take place directly on the NATURALOG sentences.

Also for prepositional phrases the preposition functions as a binary relation although the relation does not come from a verb. However, one may conceive of a prepositional qualification as a shorthand for a restrictive relative clause. For instance, cell in pancreas may be thought of to stand for cell that reside-in pancreas.

3.1 Proxy Concept Terms

In the present approach to implementation of NATURALOG the compound concept terms are disassembled recursively into the simple constituent sentences in Sect. 2. This gives rise to introduction of auxiliary proxy concept terms, connected by means of additional isa sentences. As an example, suppose that the compound cell in pancreas that produce insulin appears in the knowledge base in some sentence. The compound is decomposed giving the following collection of knowledge base sentences:

> cell-that-produce-insulin isa cell
> cell-that-produce-insulin produce insulin
> cell-in-pancreas isa cell
> cell-in-pancreas in pancreas
> cell-in-pancreas-that-produce-insulin isa cell-that-produce-insulin
> cell-in-pancreas-that-produce-insulin isa cell-in-pancreas

introducing the three proxy terms cell-that-produce-insulin, cell-in-pancreas and cell-in-pancreas-that-produce insulin. The point is that these concept terms are internally treated logically as "petrified" simples irrespectively of the applied compound naming with hyphens. This decomposition approach serves to facilitate reasoning and eventually deductive querying.

4   Graph Visualisations

In previous papers on NATURALOG we introduced an distinguished graph form [4,5]. In the knowledge base graph concept terms including proxies form the nodes, while the sentences form the directed arcs. The arcs are labelled with quantifiers subjected to the mentioned default conventions.

As examples consider first the following three sentences visualized in Fig. 1(a)

> betacell isa cell
> betacell produce insulin
> insulin isa hormone

Then consider the following sentence

> betacell isa cell that produce insulin

being decomposed with a proxy as visualized in Fig. 1(b).

A given concept term is uniquely represented across the sentences in which it may appear in the knowledge base. This holds also for proxy terms. So there is one large "interwoven" graph for the entire knowledge base. The sentences with 'isa' form the ontology subgraph. This graph is a partial order where the transitive isa connections are left implicit. So are the active-to-passive-voice arcs being present at all arcs in opposite directions. At the bottom of the ontology there are the atomic concepts, that is concepts having no subordinate concepts. These may be simple or compound.

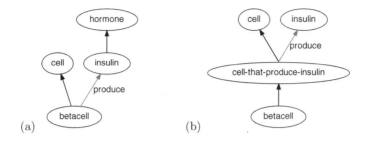

Fig. 1. Two sample knowledge base graphs.

5   Inference Rules

We introduce inference rules that enable computing of logical derivatives. These derivatives may generally contribute to query answers. However, before we describe the proper inference rules we consider the so-called subsumption rule, explicated in [4]. This rule is to ensure proper definition of the proxies.

The subsumption rule may infer additional sentences that are introduced relative to sentences in the entire knowledge base. Suppose that in the knowledge base there is betacell isa cell and betacell produces insulin. Moreover, suppose that the term cell-that-produce-insulin is present somewhere in the knowledge base together with the pair of sentences that support this proxy. Then, by the principle of subsumption the derived sentence betacell isa cell-that-produce-insulin is to be added to the knowledge base as illustrated in Fig. 2(a). This is because the considered proxy is to be established logically as if-and-only-if by the general sentence-generating requirement

IF X isa cell AND X produces insulin
THEN X isa cell-that-produce-insulin

for all concepts X in the knowledge base.

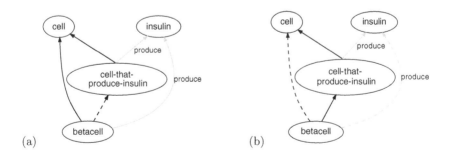

Fig. 2. Subsumption and monotonocity example. Dashed relations are inferred.

Conversely, suppose there be given only betacell isa cell-that-produce-insulin with the defining pair cell-that-produce-insulin isa cell and cell-that-produce-insulin

produce insulin. Then betacell isa cell and betacell produces insulin follows logically
and are established by means of the monotonicity rules as illustrated in Fig. 2(b).
The subsumption principle adds sentences only, no new concepts (nodes).

Now we return to additional inference rules used for forming logical consequences. We consider here the following rules for computing additional derived
sentences in the knowledge base:

1. **Weakening** turns every into some, resting on the assumption that all mentioned concepts in the knowledge base as well as their super-ordinates be non-
   empty. This is the so-called existential import principle. From the sentence
   [every] betacell produce insulin the rule infers some betacell produce insulin.
2. **Inversion** gives the dual passive voice form of a sentence, thereby contributing with opposite directed arcs for all given arcs. For the sentence betacell produce insulin the inversion rule will provide the sentence some insulin
   is_produced_by betacell.
3. **Monotonicity** specializes the subject term or generalizes the linguistic object term, as exemplified in Fig. 3(a), pancreas isa endocrine_gland
   and endocrine_gland produce hormone yields pancreas produce hormone and
   Fig. 3(b) betacell produce insulin and insulin isa hormone yields betacell produce hormone.

These inference rules generate additional deduced sentences being materialized in the knowledge base. In [4] we further introduce a concept materialisation
rule that adds additional concepts (nodes) with concomitant sentences linking to
existing concepts. The generated concepts are generalisations of given concepts.

In addition to the concept qualifications, the main verbs of sentences may be
attached adverbial qualifications in the form of prepositional phrases as described
in [4].

6   Deductive Querying via Database Querying

In [4,8] we devised a scheme where NATURALOG be encoded and embedded in
a logical layer in the form of the DATALOG logical database language. Query
answers are obtained formally as instantiations of metalogical variables ranging over terms. Queries presented to the knowledge base take the form of a

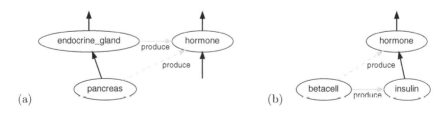

Fig. 3. Monotonicity rules: (a) inheritance and (b) generalization

NATURALOG sentences, where concept terms may be replaced with metalogic variables.

Here we pursue a variant of this embedding proposed in [5] amounting to using SQL as metalogic instead of DATALOG. Deductive querying of the natural logic knowledge base stored in a relational database is achievable by conventional database querying, taking advantage of the generally available efficient algorithmizations.

As detailed in [5], the relevant parts of the deductive closure of the entire knowledge base is computed in advance using the inference rules re-expressed as database queries. In this way deductive querying reduces to ordinary database querying. The price to pay is the cost of inferential pre-computation of the knowledge base and a possibly significant increase of the amount of stored sentences. What is saved is single-step use of the inference rules in the query processing. Effectively, the common single step deduction (generally resorting heavily to backtracking) is replaced by mass processing with efficient equi-joins and caching. This aligns well with path-exploration graphs algorithms.

As a tiny sample knowledge base in the following we use:

> betacell isa cell
> alphacell isa cell
> insulin isa hormone
> glucagon isa hormone
> pancreas isa gland
> betacell isa cell in pancreas that produce insulin
> alphacell produce glucagon
> cell that produce hormone reside-in gland

The graph of the above knowledge base is shown in Fig. 4. The subsumption rule adds sentences as explained in Sect. 5, in this case, as it appears in the graph with a dashed arc

> cell-that-produce-insulin isa cell-that-produce-hormone

In addition, besides contributions from weakening and inversion, the monotonicity rules would add (not included in Fig. 4)

> betacell produce insulin
> betacell produce hormone
> alphacell produce hormone

The materialization rule would add additional concepts such as cell that produce insulin being situated below the given concept cell that produce hormone, cf. [4].

6.1   Specialisation and Generalisation Concept Queries

The main forms of querying in NATURALOG considered here are

> X isa φ and φ isa X

where φ is a NATURALOG term. In the below exposition we consider the three cases of concept terms

$$\varphi = \begin{cases} class \text{ (i.e. simple term, name)} \\ class \text{ that } r \ \varphi \\ class \text{ that } r_1 \ \varphi_1 \text{ and } r_2 \ \varphi_2 \end{cases}$$

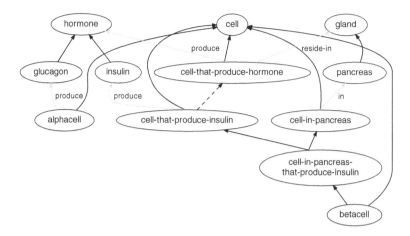

Fig. 4. Knowledge base example extended with a sentence (dashed) due to subsumption

For instance, φ may be cell, cell that produce insulin, cell that produce hormone and in pancreas.

The first query form, X isa φ, is to yield all knowledge base concept terms ontologically below (that is, subordinated) φ, formally computed as instantiations of the metalogical variable X. Conversely, the second query is to compute all concepts above φ in the considered knowledge base.

For the knowledge base we assume here the simple database relation form kb(sub,rel,obj) being a tripartition of the common NATURALOG sentences. In linguistic parlance the partition is: subject, verb, object. For the sake of the exposition here we consider only the prevailing every-some default quantifier form in the encoded NATURALOG sentences. The triples in this knowledge base relation consists of constants due to the proxying described in Sect. 3.1.

Let us first consider the "extensional" downwards query forms X isa φ, which are to be computed with $\boldsymbol{Down}(\varPhi)$, where $\varPhi$ is the proxy form of φ. This yields SQL queries according to the following cases:

1. For the NATURALOG query case 'X isa $class$' we calculate $\boldsymbol{Down}(class)$ by
        SELECT sub FROM kb
        WHERE rel = 'isa' AND obj = $class$ It is necessary that the relation 'isa' is made reflexive at least for all atomic concepts, that is concepts without subordinate concepts in the knowledge base. Example: insulin isa insulin.
2. For the case 'X isa $class$ that r φ' we construct $\boldsymbol{Down}(class\text{-that-}r\text{-}\varPhi)$ as
        SELECT sub FROM kb
        WHERE rel = 'isa' AND obj = $class$
        AND sub IN
            (SELECT sub FROM kb
            WHERE rel = r AND obj IN $\boldsymbol{Down}(\varPhi)$)

This query is parameterised with *class* and with r and with Φ. The embedded expression $Down(\Phi)$ is expanded to its resulting SQL expression in the pre-query evaluation phase. This recursive expansion reflects the syntactical structure of the encoded NATURALOG sentence. This purely "syntactic" expansion that follows the static structure of the query term precedes computing of the query answer with the SQL expression.

3. For the NATURALOG query case 'X isa *class* that r_1 φ_1 and r_2 φ_2' we form

    SELECT sub FROM kb
    WHERE rel = 'isa' AND obj = *class*
    AND sub IN
        (SELECT sub FROM kb
        WHERE rel = r_1 AND obj IN $Down(\Phi_1)$)
     AND sub IN
        (SELECT sub FROM kb
        WHERE rel = r_2 AND obj IN $Down(\Phi_2)$)

As a simple example, consider the NATURALOG query 'X isa cell that produce hormone'. Case 2 above with $Down$(cell-that-produce-hormone) yields

    SELECT sub FROM kb
    WHERE rel = 'isa' AND obj = 'cell'
    AND sub IN
        (SELECT sub FROM kb
        WHERE rel = 'produce' AND obj IN $Down$(hormone)

where $Down$(hormone) envokes case 1 to give the final query

    SELECT sub FROM kb
    WHERE rel = 'isa' AND obj = 'cell'
    AND sub IN
        (SELECT sub FROM kb
        WHERE rel = 'produce' AND obj IN
           (SELECT sub FROM kb
           WHERE rel = 'isa' AND obj = 'hormone'))

With the considered knowledge base the result is {cell-that-produce-hormone, cell-that-produce-insulin, cell-in-pancreas-that-produce-insulin, betacell}. The conspicuous absence of alphacell in the answer would be remedied by the mentioned materialization principle that would add a node cell-that-produce-glucagon in analogy to betacell.

The corresponding "intensional" (that is upwards) query forms φ isa X, are computed with analogous data base query forms $Up(\Phi)$.

6.2 Commonality Queries

The property commonality queries referring to two concepts φ_1 and φ_2 are realized as a query intersection using

    $Up(\Phi_1)$ INTERSECT $Up(\Phi_2)$.

Looking downwards with $Down$ instead of upwards one can get the "extensional" overlaps, that is the common subconcepts.

Conversely, for selecting the differences in properties between two stated concepts there are

$$Up(\Phi_1) \text{ EXCEPT } Up(\Phi_2)$$
$$Up(\Phi_2) \text{ EXCEPT } Up(\Phi_1)$$
$$(Up(\Phi_1) \text{ EXCEPT } Up(\Phi_2)) \text{ UNION } (Up(\Phi_2) \text{ EXCEPT } Up(\Phi_1))$$

6.3 Connection Queries

There are of course open-ended possibilities for deductive query forms besides the above up and down queries. Straightforwardly, there are queries that explore relations between two given concepts such as

SELECT rel FROM kb
WHERE sub = 'betacell' AND obj = 'hormone'

This suggests considering logical connections between two given concepts via more than one connecting relation, that is with intervening concepts. In other words exploration of logical pathways along paths in the knowledge base graph conception.

6.4 Exploring Pathways

The graph conception of the knowledge base invites pathway exploration. Logically pathways are formed simply by sentences having the proper matching quantifiers. For instance a row of every-some sentences. However, from an application point of view the relations along the path must make sense for instance as relevant chemical or causative pathways.

As a preliminary case of pathway exploration of a NATURALOG knowledge base we consider paths of length two between two stated concepts, $c1$ and $c2$, $Path2(C1, C2)$, where the pair is supposed to be connected via third (unknown) concepts, c.

A simplistic solution of $Path2(C1, C2)$ is obtained with

SELECT a.rel, a.obj, b.rel
FROM kb a, kb b
WHERE a.sub = $C1$ AND a.obj = b.sub AND b.obj = $C2$

In principle this solution extends readily to paths with three relational steps etc. However, realistically, solutions have to take into account that paths higher in the ontology are significantly less informative than paths remaining deeply in the ontology. Recall that all sentences have a dual voice form in the reverse direction. This implies that every connection can be traversed in both directions.

6.5 Analogies

In the knowledge base betacell associates to insulin and alphacell in parallel associates to glucagon. Such analogy constellations invites the formulation a general query expression that computes an unknown in a partially given analogy constellation. As an example we may ask for the missing fourth component given betacell, insulin and alphacell expected to compute glucagon as answer:

    SELECT b.obj

    FROM kb a, kb b

    WHERE a.sub = 'betacell' AND a.obj = 'insulin' AND a.rel =b.rel

        AND b.sub='alphacell'

More generally we envision the development of libraries of such general purpose canned query expressions for deductive querying and exploration of logical knowledge bases.

7 Concluding Summary

We see natural logic as a meeting place for practical use of knowledge bases and computational logical reasoning. We depart from the referenced works in natural logics [2,3,6,10,11] by enabling deductive query capabilities through a metalogic setup implemented in SQL. Furthermore, we promote a graph conception of natural logic knowledge bases facilitating the comprehension of logical deduction.

The above deductive query techniques are subject to computational testing in the first stage on the tiny sample knowledge base. Then as a next step scaling to significantly larger knowledge bases. Clearly, the viability of our approach to deductive querying in practical applications hinges on its scaling capabilities. In this paper we have suggested a pre-computation of relevant parts of the deductive closure. This enables replacement of single step inferencing during query evaluation with mass computation relying on efficient relational database operations. In this respect we appeal to sophisticated optimization algorithms in available database environments.

References

1. Abiteboul, S., Hull, R., Vianu, V.: Foundations of Databases: The Logical Level, 1st edn. Addison-Wesley Longman Publishing Co., Inc, Boston (1995)
2. Abzianidze, L.: Langpro: natural language theorem prover. In: Conference on Empirical Methods in Natural Language Processing (2017)
3. Abzianidze, L.: LangPro: natural language theorem prover (2021). https://naturallogic.pro/LangPro/. Accessed 31 May 2021
4. Andreasen, T., Bulskov, H., Jensen, P.A., Nilsson, J.F.: Natural logic knowledge bases and their graph form. Data Knowl. Eng. (2020)
5. Andreasen, T., Bulskov, H., Nilsson, J.F.: A natural logic system for large knowledge bases. In: Tropmann-Frick, M., Thalheim, B., Jaakkola, H., Kiyoki, Y., Yoshida, N. (eds.) Information Modelling and Knowledge Bases, vol. 333, pp. 119–133. IOS Press (2021). https://ebooks.iospress.nl/volumearticle/56439
6. Karttunen, L.: From natural logic to natural reasoning. In: Gelbukh, A. (ed.) CICLing 2015. LNCS, vol. 9041, pp. 295–309. Springer, Cham (2015). https://doi.org/10.1007/978-3-319-18111-0_23
7. Moss, L.S.: Syllogistic logics with verbs. J. Log. Comput. **20**(4), 947–967 (2010)
8. Nilsson, J.F.: In pursuit of natural logics for ontology-structured knowledge bases. In: The Seventh International Conference on Advanced Cognitive Technologies and Applications (2015)

9. Pratt-Hartmann, I., Moss, L.S.: Logics for the relational syllogistic. CoRR, abs/0808.0521 (2008)
10. Valencia, V.M.S.: Studies on Natural Logic and Categorial Grammar, Categorial grammar. Universiteit van Amsterdam, Amsterdam (1991)
11. van Benthem, J.: Essays in Logical Semantics. Studies in Linguistics and Philosophy, vol. 29. D. Reidel, Dordrecht (1986)

Diversifying Top-k Answers in a Query by Example Setting

Grégory Smits[1], Marie-Jeanne Lesot[2(✉)], Olivier Pivert[3],
and Marek Z. Reformat[4]

[1] IMT Atlantique, Lab-STICC, 29280 Plouzané, France
`gregory.smits@imt-atlantique.fr`
[2] Sorbonne Université, CNRS, LIP6, 75005 Paris, France
`marie-jeanne.lesot@lip6.fr`
[3] University of Rennes – IRISA, UMR 6074, Lannion, France
`olivier.pivert@irisa.fr`
[4] University of Alberta, Edmonton, Canada
`reformat@ualberta.ca`

Abstract. For a given data base T and a user query Q, the top-k answers are the k tuples from T that best match Q. The integration of a diversity constraint aims at avoiding returning redundant tuples, that are too similar one to another. This paper addresses the diversification question in the Query By Example setting, especially for approaches that can deal with possibly very different representative examples provided by the user. It proposes a new definition for diversity that depends on the query, in order to guarantee that the result set illustrates the diversity of the representative examples provided by the user, covering all components of the query. The paper proposes a numerical measure to assess diversity in that sense, an algorithm to identify such a diversified top-k set, optimising both the query satisfaction and the diversity measure, as well as its integration into a flexible querying approach.

Keywords: Querying by example · diversified top-k answers

1 Introduction

In order to exploit information stored in Data Bases (DB), users need to interact with the underlying Data Base Management System (DBMS) that relies on a query algebra and a, generally declarative, formal query language. Now most end users are not computer scientists and cannot express their information needs using formal languages. The Query By Example (QBE) paradigm, as introduced in [13], alleviates the query formulation step as the query is only expressed through a few examples of answers the user expects: from these representative examples, the QBE mechanism infers a formal query that can be submitted to the DBMS. This principle can be enriched to allow taking as input some counter-examples as well, i.e. an additional set of unwanted answers [2]. This expression of an information need through several representative examples means that different kinds of answers are acceptable. This implies that the query inferred from the user-provided examples should be of a disjunctive nature.

© Springer Nature Switzerland AG 2023
H. L. Larsen et al. (Eds.): FQAS 2023, LNAI 14113, pp. 15–26, 2023.
https://doi.org/10.1007/978-3-031-42935-4_2

Providing users with a set of diversified answers generally means that the underlying querying system has to identify k tuples from the DB, k being a hyper-parameter, that best match the query and are not too similar one to another, see e.g. [12] for an overview of this research issue. The objective is to provide a complete view on the possible interesting answers the DB may contain by constraining them to differ one from another. A diversified top-k result set is classically defined as a set of answers that maximizes a pairwise dissimilarity among the returned answers.

This paper addresses this question of diversifying the result set of a query in the case where it has been inferred from representative examples of expected answers. It argues that a QBE setting requires a new definition of the notion of diversity, that has to take into consideration the query and not only the set of candidate answers. More precisely, a result set to a disjunctive query is said to be diversified if it covers all the user-provided representative examples from which the considered query has been inferred. The objective is so to provide users with answers covering all the different examples of answers they are willing to accept.

The contribution of this work are:

- an adaptation of the notion of diversity in a QBE setting,
- an algorithm to provide users with a diversified top-k result set, optimising both the query satisfaction and the diversity measure,
- the technical integration of this approach in a flexible QBE setting that explicitly models the disjunctive component of the user information need.

The paper is structured as follows. After positioning the research issues addressed in this paper wrt. existing works in Sect. 2, it details in Sect. 3 the proposed approach, discussing both the underlying notions and an algorithmic solution. Section 4 experimentally shows how this diversification strategy takes place in a QBE implementation, namely the DCQ strategy [7], additionally illustrating the relevance of the results it allows to obtain. Section 5 concludes and draws some perspectives for future works.

2   Related Works

This section positions the proposed approach wrt. existing QBE systems and result diversification strategies.

2.1   The Query-By-Example Paradigm

The QBE strategy, introduced by Zloof [13] in the 70's, aims at easing the interaction of a user with a DBMS [10]: it takes as input i) one or several example tuples provided by the user or ii) user-defined positive or negative evaluation of prototypical examples reflecting the content of the database. This paper focuses on the first case.

Formally, the QBE paradigm considers a queried table T, that may be the result of a join query, whose schema is $\{A_1, \ldots A_p\}$. T stores a set of tuples $T =$

$\{t_1, \ldots, t_n\}$ where $t_{i=1..n} \in D_1 \times \ldots \times D_p$ and D_j is the domain of attribute A_j. This paper focuses on the case where the user provides a set $\mathcal{E} = \{e_1, e_2, \ldots, e_m\}$ of examples to illustrate what he/she is looking for. The examples from $\mathcal{E}$ may be taken from T or be non-obesrved tuples. The QBE system then computes for each candidate tuple $t \in T$ a satisfaction score denoted $s_\mathcal{E}(t)$ that quantifies how much t matches the query Q implied by $\mathcal{E}$. As detailed below, existing approaches differ in the way the satisfaction degrees are computed. Without loss of generality, it can be considered to output scores in $[0, 1]$. Two hyper-parameters are used to control the result set: an integer k specifying the number of expected results and $\alpha \in]0, 1]$ a qualitative threshold regarding the satisfaction degree. For any query Q, the result set is defined as $\Sigma_Q^\alpha = \{t \in T / s_\mathcal{E}(t) \geq \alpha\}$. Finally, $\Sigma_Q^{k,\alpha}$ denotes the subset of Σ_Q^α containing at most k tuples that best match Q, i.e. with maximal satisfaction degrees. It may happen that $|\Sigma_Q^{k,\alpha}| < k$ when there are less than k answers that satisfy Q with a score of at least α. In the QBE case, the notation is slightly revised as Q is replaced by $\mathcal{E}$, leading to sets of results denoted $\Sigma_\mathcal{E}^\alpha$ and $\Sigma_\mathcal{E}^{k,\alpha}$ respectively.

Existing approaches to QBE may be categorized into three groups. The first one does not explicitly infer a formal query and considers that the user provided examples are independent one from another: it looks for the tuples in the database that are similar to at least one example (wrt. all the attributes) and, if provided, dissimilar to all counter-examples (wrt. at least one attribute). The approach by De Calmès et al. [2] relies on a case-based reasoning system to identify the candidate answers. It defines the satisfaction score $s_\mathcal{E}$ as a combination of similarity with positive examples and dissimilarity with counter-examples. In the case where only positive examples are available, Zadrozny et al. [11] propose a k-NN based QBE strategy to identify the tuples that are close to the provided expected answers.

A second, related, category does not infer a formal query either, but exploits dependencies between the provided examples, so as to extract from them an appropriate similarity measure that learns correlation from attributes: the Disjunctive Concept Querying (DCQ) strategy [7] relies on the Choquet integral to build a satisfaction score $s_\mathcal{E}$ that allows to interpret the provided examples as different types of expected results. More precisely, it allows to identify subsets of somewhat similar representative exemplars that emphasize the importance of shared combinations of values but without discarding more outlying examples that do not look like any other member of $\mathcal{E}$.

A third type of approach builds a formal query from the provided examples and counter-examples: in [4], the positive examples are analyzed as a whole to identify their most representative (i.e. most frequent) fuzzy predicates, seeing to it that these predicates do not also cover one of the unwanted answers. In [11], the inferred search condition is composed of fuzzy terms taken from a pre-defined vocabulary that discretizes each attribute domain in the DB. An interesting aspect of this approach is that it provides users with a linguistic description of the values shared by positive examples that are not shared by counter-examples.

2.2   Diversified Search

Combining the notion of satisfaction with that of diversity is a research question that has received a lot of attention, starting from the recommendation system framework [9]. It is now used in many application contexts, still including content recommendation [1], but also AI explanation [5] and DB queries [12] to name a few. Focusing on DB querying, it may be the case that many very similar tuples fully satisfy the submitted query, thus leading to a top-k result set containing one type of answer, hence the need for answer diversification strategies.

Diversity is defined and assessed in most existing works as a the result of a pairwise comparison of the candidate answers: denoting Σ a set of candidate answers and $dist$ an appropriate distance measure, it is basically defined as

$$div(\Sigma) = \sum_{t,t' \in \Sigma} dist(t,t') \tag{1}$$

Given a set of candidate answers Σ_Q^α, i.e. tuples associated with a sufficient satisfaction degree, a diversification mechanism aims at finding the subset denoted by $\tilde{\Sigma}_Q^{k,\alpha}$ that contains k answers as diverse as possible, i.e.:

$$\tilde{\Sigma}_Q^{k,\alpha} = \arg \max_{\substack{\Sigma \subseteq \Sigma_Q^\alpha, \\ \text{s.t.} |\Sigma| = k}} div(\Sigma) \tag{2}$$

Some approaches perform a post-processing clustering step on the set Σ_Q^α to determine its structure as groups of somewhat similar answers [8]. The diversified result set is then composed of the most representative tuples taken from each of these clusters. This clustering strategy obviously leads to an overall increase of complexity of the querying system and a significant computation time overhead, or a non-relevant partition if the clustered result set is too small.

To the best of our knowledge, the question of result diversification in the QBE setting has not been studied. The next section thus proposes a definition of a diversified result set dedicated to QBE systems where diversity is defined with respect to the provided set of examples and not only depending on the set of answers, so as to guarantee a complete coverage of the examples that have been used to infer the query.

3   Result Diversification in the QBE Paradigm

This section describes the proposed strategy for diversifying result sets in a QBE setting and an algorithm that allows to identify an optimal set of answers, where optimality depends both on the satisfaction score and the diversity measure.

3.1   Diversity wrt. a Set of Representative Examples

Given a set of representative examples $\mathcal{E}$, diversifying $\Sigma_\mathcal{E}^{k,\alpha}$ takes a definition that differs from existing approaches dealing with this issue, as reminded in

Sect. 2. Instead of maximizing the dissemblance between pairs of tuples in $\Sigma_{\mathcal{E}}^{k,\alpha}$, the presented approach aims at guaranteeing that the returned set of answers covers as much as possible the set of expected answers the user has specified.

Definition 1. *Given a similarity measure sim and η a similarity threshold, a set Σ of candidate answers is said to be a* **diversified result set** *with respect to the set of expected answers $\mathcal{E}$ if it covers each example in $\mathcal{E}$. The notion of coverage refers to a minimal similarity to at least one of the candidate answers. Formally, Σ is diversified with respect to $\mathcal{E}$ iff.:*

$$\forall e \in \mathcal{E}, \exists t \in \Sigma \ st. \ sim(e,t) \geq \eta,$$

where sim is an appropriate similarity measure (see e.g. [3]).

Given $\Sigma_{\mathcal{E}}^{\alpha}$ a set of candidate answers, the question is to find a subset of k candidates, subset denoted by $\tilde{\Sigma}_{\mathcal{E}}^{k,\alpha}$, that are diversified considering $\mathcal{E}$. Depending on $\mathcal{E}$, the queried table T and the parameter values (k, α, η), it may obviously be the case that such a subset does not exist.

The aim of a diversification approach is to find the optimal subset $\tilde{\Sigma}_{\mathcal{E}}^{k,\alpha}$ wrt. a numerical criterion of diversity. We propose to define diversity in a QBE setting as related to a fair coverage of the representative examples in $\mathcal{E}$. In other words, each user-provided example of expected answer e should be covered by the same number, $\lfloor \frac{k}{|\mathcal{E}|} \rfloor$, of tuples in $\tilde{\Sigma}_{\mathcal{E}}^{k,\alpha}$ that are sufficiently close to it. Denoting by $S_{\Sigma}^e = \{t \in \Sigma, \ st. \ sim(t,e) \geq \eta\}$ the set of tuples in Σ that are sufficiently close to e, we propose the following diversity criterion:

$$div(\Sigma, \mathcal{E}) = \frac{1}{\lfloor \frac{k}{|\mathcal{E}|} \rfloor} \times \sqrt{\frac{1}{|\mathcal{E}|} \sum_{e \in \mathcal{E}} \left(|S_{\Sigma}^e| - \left\lfloor \frac{k}{|\mathcal{E}|} \right\rfloor \right)^2}. \tag{3}$$

Note that, according to that definition, a candidate answer t may cover several representative examples e simultaneously. Indeed, it may belong to several sets S_e when it is sufficiently similar to several e. The aim is then to find, from a set of candidates $\Sigma_{\mathcal{E}}^{\alpha}$, the subset with cardinal k that maximises diversity. This diversified result set is denoted by $\tilde{\Sigma}_{\mathcal{E}}^{k,\alpha}$ and its definition is identical to Eq. 2 but instantiated with the proposed definition for diversity.

3.2   Diversification Strategy

This section introduces the algorithmic strategy we propose to compute the diversified result set $\tilde{\Sigma}_{\mathcal{E}}^{k,\alpha}$ that provides the best diversity wrt. $\mathcal{E}$. The first, preliminary, step consists in retrieving the set $\Sigma_{\mathcal{E}}^{\alpha}$ of the tuples from T that have a sufficient satisfaction degree with respect to $\mathcal{E}$. Algorithm 1 provides the pseudo-code of the proposed approach that is commented below.

To determine the set of tuples from $\Sigma_{\mathcal{E}}^{\alpha}$ that will belong to the diversified set of answers $\tilde{\Sigma}_{\mathcal{E}}^{k,\alpha}$, an empty list l_e is initiated for each element $e \in \mathcal{E}$. Then, $\Sigma_{\mathcal{E}}^{\alpha}$ is scanned in a decreasing order of the score $s_{\mathcal{E}}(t)$ and each candidate t is

Input: Candidate answers $\Sigma_{\mathcal{E}}^{\alpha}$; similarity measure sim; similarity threshold η; number of desired answers k

Output: Diversified answers $\tilde{\Sigma}_{\mathcal{E}}^{\alpha}$

1 $\tilde{\Sigma}_{\mathcal{E}}^{\alpha} \leftarrow \emptyset$
2 $l_e \leftarrow []$ for each $e \in \mathcal{E}$
3 $maxle \leftarrow 0$
4 $sort(\Sigma_{\mathcal{E}}^{\alpha}, s_{\mathcal{E}})$;   ▷ sort ts in $\Sigma_{\mathcal{E}}^{\alpha}$ in a decreasing order of their score $s_{\mathcal{E}}(t)$
5 **foreach** $t \in \Sigma_{\mathcal{E}}^{\alpha}$ **do**
6 | **foreach** $e \in \mathcal{E}$ **do**
7 | | **if** $sim(t,e) \geq \eta$ **then**
8 | | | $l_e.append(t)$
9 | | | $maxle \leftarrow \max(maxle, |l_e|)$
10 | | **end**
11 | **end**
12 **end**
13 $i \leftarrow 0$
14 **while** $|\tilde{\Sigma}_{\mathcal{E}}^{\alpha}| < k$ *and* $i < maxle$ **do**
15 | **if** $|\tilde{\Sigma}_{\mathcal{E}}^{\alpha}| + |\mathcal{E}| \leq k$ **then**
16 | | **foreach** $e \in \mathcal{E}$ **do**
17 | | | $\tilde{\Sigma}_{\mathcal{E}}^{\alpha}.add(l_e[i])$
18 | | **end**
19 | **end**
20 | $i \leftarrow i+1$
21 **end**
22 **return** $\tilde{\Sigma}_{\mathcal{E}}^{\alpha}$

Algorithm 1: Diversification of $\Sigma_{\mathcal{E}}^{\alpha}$.

appended to all lists l_e such that $sim(t,e) \geq \eta$. Finally, to build $\tilde{\Sigma}_{\mathcal{E}}^{k,\alpha}$, the first elements in each list are added to $\tilde{\Sigma}_{\mathcal{E}}^{k,\alpha}$, then the second ones and so forth, until $\tilde{\Sigma}_{\mathcal{E}}^{k,\alpha}$ contains k elements or $\Sigma_{\mathcal{E}}^{\alpha}$ has been fully scanned.

Note that a tuple $t = l_e[i]$ is added to the result list $\tilde{\Sigma}_{\mathcal{E}}^{k,\alpha}$ (l17 in Algorithm 1) only if t is not already present in $\tilde{\Sigma}_{\mathcal{E}}^{k,\alpha}$. It already is, then the current representative example e is considered as already covered by the result list at the same level as the other representative examples.

As in the classical case, it may happen that the final diversified result set $\tilde{\Sigma}_{\mathcal{E}}^{k,\alpha}$ does not contain the desired number of answers k for two reasons. The first obvious one is due to a not sufficient number of candidate answers, i.e. if the preliminary step does not find at least k tuples in T that sufficiently satisfy Q. The second one comes from the constraint introduced line 15 in Algorithm 1. The meaning of this constraint is to ensure that the order in which the elements from $\mathcal{E}$ are processed (l16 in Algorithm 1) has no effect on the returned diversified result set. It indeed guarantees that, for a given round of the loop line 14, all the lists representing the different expected answers (the l_es) are processed or none, hence $|\tilde{\Sigma}_{\mathcal{E}}^{k,\alpha}| = |\mathcal{E}| \times \min(k, \min_{e \in \mathcal{E}} |l_e|)$.

The use of Algorithm 1 to diversify the result set of a query defined by examples of representative examples does not add a significant computation cost to the whole querying process. Sorting the tuples from $\Sigma_{\mathcal{E}}^{\alpha}$ in a decreasing order of their score $s_{\mathcal{E}}(t)$ is done in $\mathcal{O}(|\Sigma_{\mathcal{E}}^{\alpha}|\log_2(|\Sigma_{\mathcal{E}}^{\alpha}|))$. Then, the assignment of these candidate answers into the different lists is done in linear time and bounded by the number of tuples to diversify, in other words $|\Sigma_{\mathcal{E}}^{\alpha}|$. The soundness and correctness of this algorithm are stated in the following proposition:

Proposition 1. *Algorithm 1 returns the most diversified top-k result set of a representative examples $\mathcal{E}$ according to Definition 1 of the diversity criterion.*

The sketch of the proof is as follows: at each iteration of the loop starting at line 14, the number of answers covering each representative example $e \in \mathcal{E}$ is increased by 1 and line 15 guarantees that all the representative examples of answers are covered or none of them, at the given iteration. It thus gives the guarantee that $\tilde{\Sigma}_{\mathcal{E}}^{\alpha}$ covers each $e \in \mathcal{E}$ with a same ratio. The fact that the candidate answers are processed in a decreasing order of their respective query satisfaction degree ensures that $\tilde{\Sigma}_{\mathcal{E}}^{\alpha}$ contains the tuples that best satisfy the query.

4   Illustration

This section now illustrates an implementation of the proposed approach in a complete QBE process, named *Div*-DCQ. It also describes an illustration of its relevance through experiments: the latter confirm that the diversification step allows obtaining results of interest and that it does not induce a significant overhead in terms of computation time.

4.1   *Div*-DCQ

To show how query satisfaction can be combined with a diversity criteria among the returned answers, the proposed approach is implemented on top of the QBE strategy named DCQ introduced in [7]. This choice is first motivated by the availability of an implementation of this QBE strategy on top of a commercial RDBMS, namely PostgreSQL. Then, the underlying query inference strategy, from the user-provided examples of expected answers, relies on the CHOCO-LATE approach introduced in [6] that is especially appropriate to infer a disjunctive concept underlying the user-provided representative examples. It is thus particularly relevant to build a QBE system on top of CHOCOLATE because, as compared to other QBE approaches (Sec. 2), it ensures that all the representative examples are taken into account during the computation of the satisfaction degree attached to each candidate answer.

The main principles of DCQ are briefly recalled hereafter, more details about the satisfaction degree computation may be found in [6]. They are illustrated with the 2D data shown in Fig. 1 where the diamonds represent 5 representative examples building the considered $\mathcal{E}$ set.

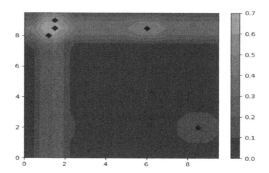

Fig. 1. Considered 2D illustration: the black diamonds show the 5 representative examples forming $\mathcal{E}$. The contour plot shows the values of the satisfaction degree computed by the CHOCOLATE method, as described in Example 1.

The first step consists in inferring a satisfaction function $s_{\mathcal{E}}$ from $\mathcal{E}$ that can be interpreted as a membership function to the fuzzy disjunctive concept exemplified by the examples in $\mathcal{E}$. Without entering into the details of the CHOCO-LATE approach [6] used to build this membership function, let us underline two properties of interest it possesses. First, it captures possible situations of generalization among the user-provided expected answers, as illustrated by the contour plot in Fig. 1 for the considered $\mathcal{E}$. The fact that three expected answers are in a same narrow subspace, around the point with coordinates $(1.5, 8.5)$, indeed gives more importance to its surrounding area. However, contrary to a mean aggregator for instance, the inferred membership function does not discard the two atypical expected answers, which constitutes the second property of interest. Still, it gives more weight to the point $(6, 8.5)$ as it shares a common y-value with other expected answers.

Technically, as shown below in Example 1, the stored procedure *infer_concept* is used to infer a satisfaction function, named here *myQBE*, that can be applied on the *testData* table, that can be a view as a result of a more complex join query.

Example 1. Use of the *infer_concept* procedure to infer a characteristic function, whose contour is depicted in Fig. 1, from few examples of expected answers. The *testData* table contains, for the purpose of this illustration, 2,000 tuples generated using normal distributions around the five representative examples (i.e. the five black diamonds).

CALL infer_concept('testData', 'myQBE', { "x"=>1.5, "y"=>8.5, "x"=>1.2, "y"=>8,
    "x"=>1.5, "y"=>9, "x"=>6, "y"=>8.5, "x"=>8.5, "y"=>2 '});

Calling the procedure *infer_concept* leads to the creation of a user function named *'myQBE'* that can then be integrated in the selection clause of a query as in Example 2: it retrieves 200 tuples ($k = 200$) from the *testData* table that satisfy $myQBE()$ with degree of at least 0.2 ($\alpha = 0.2$).

Example 2. Use of the *'myQBE'* user function in a selection clause of a query:

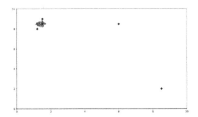 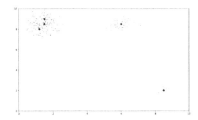

Fig. 2. Results for the query shown in Fig. 1: (left) top-200 results, (right) diversified top-200 results.

SELECT *, get_mu() as mu FROM testData WHERE myQBE() >= 0.2 LIMIT 200 ;

As shown in Fig. 1, the area around coordinates $(1.5, 8.5)$ gets the highest satisfaction scores. As a result, the top-200 answers for the above query are all located in this area only as shown in the left graph of Fig. 2. This illustrates that the result set composed of the tuples that best satisfy the selection condition may lack of diversity and representativity wrt. the different expected answers envisaged by the user.

To overcome this limitation, the proposed approach to diversify the result set may be activated by simply adding the *DIVERSIFY* keyword in the selection clause as shown in Example 3. The *DIVERSIFY* keyword indicates that an *a posteriori* diversification step has to be applied on the set of candidate answers.

Example 3. Call of the diversification process on top of the returned result set.

SELECT DIVERSIFY *, get_mu() as mu FROM testData WHERE myQBE() > 0.2 LIMIT 200 ;

The right part of Fig. 2 displays the results of this modified query: it shows that it leads to a very different result set that now covers all the representative examples of expected answers.

4.2   Experimentations

First experimentations[1] have been conducted on artificial data so as to examine the cost overhead, showing it is negligible. Second, they emphasize the compromise achieved between the overall satisfaction of the returned result wrt. the query and the diversity of the answers. The experimentation context is the following. Considering 12 randomly generated reference points in a 4-dimension space, with a shared domain $[0, 10]$, tuples are generated as mixtures of Gaussian distributions around these points, thus forming 12 elliptic clusters.

---

[1] The experimentations are available for reproducibility as a Jupyter notebook at the following url http://people.irisa.fr/Gregory.Smits/fqas2023.tgz.

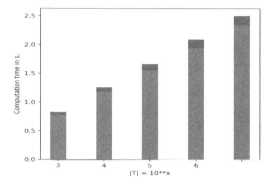

Fig. 3. Computation time wrt. the dataset size, the bottom part of each bar represents the candidate answers retrieval and the upper one the diversification

Computation Time. Figure 3 shows the evolution of the computation time wrt. different sizes of datasets (from 10^3 to 10^7 with $k = 50$); for each size of dataset, 20 queries are executed and the average of the observed computation times is used. It confirms that most of the computation time is devoted to the retrieval of the candidate answers and that the diversification uses in average $\frac{1}{11}$ of the overall time. It is however worth mentioning that in these experimentations a sequential scan of T is performed and indexes may speed up this retrieval step, but such optimizations are entrusted to the DBMS.

Compromise Satisfaction vs. Diversity. Figure 4 (left) depicts a comparison of the mean satisfaction, obtained on 20 queries, based on the $s_\mathcal{E}$ scores, of the top-k obtained without diversification and after diversification. In addition, Fig. 4 (right) shows the gain obtained in terms of diversity of the returned answers when the proposed strategy is applied. These results show that, without paying the cost of a significant loss in terms of satisfaction, the proposed diversification strategy leads to a significant improvement of the result diversity, especially for low values of k. The definition of diversity considered in this work is related to an equal coverage of the different representative examples, quantified through a coefficient of variation around the expected number of answers for each representative example. So the closer to zero, the better the diversity degree is. One may also observe that, without diversification, a low value of k will often lead to situations as the one depicted in Fig. 2 (left) where tuples around the most "important" representative example are returned only.

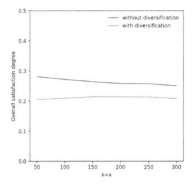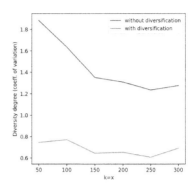

Fig. 4. Comparison of the overall satisfaction (left) and diversity (right) of the result set, for increasing k values

5   Conclusion and Perspectives

In the Query By Example context, this paper studies the issue of diversifying the set of tuples that constitute candidate answers to a query inferred from a set of representative examples. The notion of a diversified result set is redefined to fit the particularities of a QBE context. Diversity is related to a coverage of the different possible answers the user is expecting or willing to accept. An algorithm to diversify a set of candidate answers is proposed and it is shown that the cost overhead in terms of computation time is negligible compared to the execution time of the query itself. The first conducted experimentations illustrate that, without paying the cost of a significant decrease of the overall result satisfaction, the proposed diversification strategy provides a better overview of the different possible answers to a query inferred from user-provided representative examples.

Future works will perform a deeper study of the behavior of the proposed approach according to variations of the query parameters, e.g. wrt. the number of provided representative examples and the minimal satisfaction degree. A longer term perspective is to find a strategy or at least a heuristic to avoid having to identify all the candidate answers and to rank order them before starting the diversification step.

References

1. Castells, P., Hurley, N., Vargas, S.: Novelty and diversity in recommender systems. In: Ricci, F., Rokach, L., Shapira, B. (eds.) Recommender Systems Handbook, pp. 603–646. Springer, New York (2021). https://doi.org/10.1007/978-1-0716-2197-4_16

2. De Calmès, M., Dubois, D., Hullermeier, E., Prade, H., Sedes, F.: Flexibility and fuzzy case-based evaluation in querying: an illustration in an experimental setting. Internat. J. Uncertain. Fuzziness Knowl.-Based Syst. **11**(01), 43–66 (2003)

3. Lesot, M.J., Rifqi, M., Benhadda, H.: Similarity measures for binary and numerical data: a survey. Int. J. Knowl. Eng. Soft Data Paradigms **1**(1), 63–84 (2009)

4. Moreau, A., Pivert, O., Smits, G.: Fuzzy query by example. In: Proceedings of ACM Symposium on Applied Computing, SAC'18, pp. 688–695 (2018)
5. Mothilal, R.K., Sharma, A., Tan, C.: Explaining machine learning classifiers through diverse counterfactual explanations. In: Proceedings of the 2020 Conference on Fairness, Accountability, and Transparency, pp. 607–617 (2020)
6. Smits, G., Yager, R., Lesot, M.J., Pivert, O.: Concept membership modeling using a choquet integral. In: Proceedings of the International Conference on Information Processing and Management of Uncertainty in Knowledge-Based Systems (IPMU'20), pp. 359–372 (2020)
7. Smits, G., Lesot, M.-J., Pivert, O., Yager, R.R.: Flexible querying using disjunctive concepts. In: Andreasen, T., De Tré, G., Kacprzyk, J., Legind Larsen, H., Bordogna, G., Zadrożny, S. (eds.) FQAS 2021. LNCS (LNAI), vol. 12871, pp. 29–40. Springer, Cham (2021). https://doi.org/10.1007/978-3-030-86967-0_3
8. Smits, G., Pivert, O.: Linguistic and graphical explanation of a cluster-based data structure. In: Beierle, C., Dekhtyar, A. (eds.) SUM 2015. LNCS (LNAI), vol. 9310, pp. 186–200. Springer, Cham (2015). https://doi.org/10.1007/978-3-319-23540-0_13
9. Smyth, B., McClave, P.: Similarity vs. diversity. In: Aha, D.W., Watson, I. (eds.) ICCBR 2001. LNCS (LNAI), vol. 2080, pp. 347–361. Springer, Heidelberg (2001). https://doi.org/10.1007/3-540-44593-5_25
10. Thomas, J.C., Gould, J.D.: A psychological study of query by example. In: Proceedings of the May 19–22, 1975, National Computer Conference and Exposition, pp. 439–445 (1975)
11. Zadrozny, S., Kacprzyk, J., Wysocki, M.: On a novice-user-focused approach to flexible querying: the case of initially unavailable explicit user preferences. In: Proceedings of the 10th International Conference on Intelligent Systems Design and Applications, ISDA'10, pp. 696–701 (2010)
12. Zheng, K., Wang, H., Qi, Z., Li, J., Gao, H.: A survey of query result diversification. Knowl. Inf. Syst. **51**, 1–36 (2017)
13. Zloof, M.M.: Query-by-example: a data base language. IBM Syst. J. **16**(4), 324–343 https://doi.org/10.1147/sj.164.0324

Flexible Classification, Question-Answering and Retrieval with Siamese Neural Networks for Biomedical Texts

Safaa Menad$^{(\boxtimes)}$, Saïd Abdeddaïm, and Lina F. Soualmia

Univ. Rouen Normandie, LITIS UR4108, 76000 Rouen, France
{safaa.menad1,said.abdeddaim}@univ-rouen.fr, lina.soualmia@chu-rouen.fr
https://www.litislab.fr/

Abstract. Training transformers models on biomedical data has shown promising results. However, these language models require fine-tuning large models on very specific supervised data for each task. In this paper, we propose to use siamese neural models (sentence transformers) that embed texts to be compared in a vector space, and apply them to the biomedical domain on three main tasks: classification, question answering and retrieval. Training is based on articles from the MED-LINE bibliographic database associated with their MeSH (Medical Subject Headings) keywords and optimizes an objective self-supervised contrastive learning function. The representation of the texts (embeddings) obtained by our siamese models can be stored, indexed and used with transfer learning without needing the language models. The obtained results on several benchmarks show that the proposed models can solve these tasks with results comparable to biomedical cross-encoders transformers and offer a several advantages by being flexible and efficient at inference time. (Models and data available: https://github.com/arieme/BioSTransformers.git).

Keywords: Language Models · Transformers · Contrastive Learning · Siamese Neural Networks · Self-supervised Learning · Question Answering · Document Classification · Biomedical Texts

1 Introduction

The development of pre-trained transformer models, such as BERT (Bidirectional Encoder Representations from Transformers), has improved the performance of natural language processing (NLP). Moreover, the abundance of available biomedical data, such as scientific articles, has made it possible to train these models on medical and biological datasets (BioBERT [14], ClinicalBERT [1], SapBERT [16]). However, these language models require fine-tuning large models on very specific supervised data for each task, which strongly limits their use in practice.

Since most biomedical NLP tasks (named entity recognition, relation extraction, document classification, document retrieval, question-answering, etc.) can

H. L. Larsen et al. (Eds.): FQAS 2023, LNAI 14113, pp. 27–38, 2023.
https://doi.org/10.1007/978-3-031-42935-4_3

be reduced to the computation of the semantic similarity measure between two texts (e.g., category/article summary, query/results, question/answer), we propose in this paper to build a new pre-trained siamese model BioSTransformers (sentence transformer) that embeds pairs of semantically related texts (long and short) into the same vector representation space.

In addition to being applicable to various NLP tasks, a siamese model also offers the advantage of saving time during its application. For instance, in document retrieval, a siamese model can pre-compute and index the vector representations of the texts for the selected corpus, allowing for computation of only the query representations when submitted to the search engine, contrary to fine-tuned transformers that while performing better in re-ranking problems, require inputting combinations of all texts pairs to be compared, making them less suitable for efficient inference time.

With this BioSTransformers siamese model, we would like to i) avoid the costs of: data labeling, training and fine-tuning computations and ii) significantly decrease prediction costs by introducing a self-supervised reference model that can be directly applied to various biomedical tasks.

In this context, we compare several siamese transformers that we have trained on pairs of texts formed, on one side, by abstracts from the PubMed[1] biomedical articles corpus (comprising 34 million articles), and on the other side, by the associated MeSH (Medical Subject Headings) keywords[2].

We use a self-supervised contrastive learning objective function. Given a pair of texts (abstract, keywords), the model must predict which of a set of other randomly sampled text pairs is actually associated with it in PubMed. We then show experimentally on multiple standard biomedical benchmarks, that, our best pre-trained siamese model solves three NLP tasks with results comparable to biomedical or generalist cross-encoders models fine-tuned on supervised data specific to the problems addressed. We specifically focus three biomedical NLP tasks from accessible datasets: document classification, question answering, and retrieval.

In this paper, we introduce our models BioSTransformers and BioS-MiniLM designed to tackle multiple biomedical NLP tasks. Through experimental evaluation on diverse reference benchmarks, we demonstrate that our models achieve comparable performance to existing biomedical cross-encoder models, while also offering additional advantages not found in those models.

2   Related Works

Neural methods in general and pre-trained language models in particular, such as BERT, which has become a standard component for training task-specific NLP models, have shown remarkable advancements across various NLP tasks.

---

[1] https://ftp.ncbi.nlm.nih.gov/pubmed/baseline/.

[2] The MeSH (https://www.nlm.nih.gov/mesh/) is a specialized thesaurus of the biomedical domain used for indexing PubMed articles. It includes 33,000 MeSH terms.

Existing work on pre-training primarily focuses on utilizing web data. For instance, the original BERT model was trained using Wikipedia and BookCorpus [5] as training data. In specific domains such as the biomedical domain, several previous works have shown that using domain texts can provide additional gains over general domain language models. For example, pre-training with PubMed texts yields better performance in the biomedical NLP tasks [2,14,21].

The standard approach to pre-training a biomedical model involves starting with a general model and then follows by pre-training using a biomedical corpus. For this purpose, BioBERT [14] utilizes abstracts retrieved from PubMed and full-text articles from PubMed Central (PMC). BlueBERT [22] uses both PubMed text and MIMIC-III (Medical Information Mart for Intensive Care) clinical notes [12]. However, SciBERT [2] takes a different approach by conducting pre-training from scratch using scientific literature.

Transformer-based models have demonstrated success in both the retrieval and re- ranking stages. Such neural ranking models come in two flavors: dual-encoder (DE) models which learn separate (factorised) embeddings for the query and document, and cross-attention (CA) models which learn a joint embedding for the query and document. Both CA and DE models can be applied to retrieval tasks; however, empirically, CA models achieve better performance.

Several studies have explored methods to enhance DE models. In [18], the authors defend the use of dual-encoder architectures in neural ranking tasks over transformer-based models, arguing that the dual-encoders are more efficient, easier to train, and more interpretable. Dual-encoders only require encoding the query and document once, resulting in faster and more scalable models. They also have fewer hyperparameters to tune and provide a clear separation between the query and document encoding stages, facilitating model comprehension and debugging. While transformer-based models have their advantages, the authors suggest that dual-encoders should be considered as a viable and efficient alternative for neural ranking tasks.

In the survey [29], the authors focus on Dense Text Retrieval (DTR), a recent approach to information retrieval that uses dense vector representations of text to perform similarity-based retrieval. The article provides an overview of different techniques for DTR based on pre-trained language models, including cross-encoder models, bi-encoder models, and hybrid models. It discusses the advantages and limitations of each approach, as well as the tradeoffs between accuracy and computational complexity. They highlight the strengths and weaknesses of these models and provide recommendations for future benchmarking efforts.

In [15], the authors propose a method called DRAGON, which stands for Diverse Retrieval Augmented Generation Of Networks, for improving the generalization performance of dense retrieval models. DRAGON leverages diverse data augmentation techniques, including synonym replacement, word deletion, and entity masking, to increase the diversity of the training data and improve the robustness of the model to variations in the input text. The article evaluates

DRAGON on several benchmark datasets and shows that it outperforms existing methods for dense retrieval.

In [27], the authors present a new approach to pre-training text embeddings in a contrasting manner with weak supervision signals. The article shows that it achieves better performance on various downstream natural language processing tasks, such as text classification and question answering.

In [3], the authors propose to augment the training data of a language model by retrieving relevant text passages from a large corpus of unlabeled data, which significantly improves its performance on various natural language processing tasks such as question answering.

In [17] the authors introduce a generative pre-trained transformer model, BioGPT, that is specifically designed for biomedical text tasks. The article shows that BioGPT outperforms existing language models on several biomedical such as relation extraction and question answering. They adopted GPT-2 as a backbone model and pre-trained it on 15M PubMed abstracts corpus.

In [6], the authors proposed a method for training information retrieval (IR) models using natural language explanations as additional labels, which reduces the need for a large number of training examples. They demonstrate the effectiveness of ExaRanker on several benchmark datasets.

3   Transformers

Transformers are neural networks based on the multi-head self-attention mechanism that significantly improves the efficiency of training large models. They consist of an encoder that transforms the input text into a vector and a decoder that transforms this vector into output text. The attention mechanism performs better in these models by modeling the links between the input and output elements.

3.1   Pre-trained Language Models

A pre-trained language model (PLM) is a neural network trained on a large amount of unannotated data in an unsupervised way. The model is then transferred to a target NLP task (downstream task), where a smaller task-specific annotated dataset is used to fine-tune the PLM and to build the final model capable of performing the target task. The process is called fine-tuning a PLM. PLM such as BERT [5] have led to impressive gains in many NLP tasks. Existing work generally focuses on general domain data. In the biomedical domain, pre-training on PubMed texts leads to better performance in biomedical NLP tasks [2,14,21]. The standard approach to pre-training a biomedical model starts with a generalized model and then follows by pre-training using a biomedical corpus.

3.2   Siamese Models

Sentence transformers have been developed to calculate a similarity score between two sentences. They are models that use transformers for tasks related to sentence pairs: semantic similarity between sentences, information retrieval, sentence reformulation, etc. These transformers are based on two architectures: cross-encoders that process the concatenation of the pair, and bi-encoders siamese models that encode each pair element in a vector.

Sentence-BERT [23] is a BERT-based bi-encoder for generating semantically meaningful sentence embeddings that are used in textual similarity comparisons. For each input, the model produces a fixed-size vector (u and v). The objective function is chosen so that the angle between the two vectors u and v is smaller when the inputs are similar. The objective function uses the cosine of the angle: $cos(u, v) = \frac{u.v}{|u|||v||}$, if $cos(u, v) = 1$, the sentences are similar, and if $cos(u, v) = 0$, the sentences have no semantic link.

Other sentence transformers models have been developed [4,7,26], among them, MiniLM-L6-v25[3] is a bi-encoder based on a simplified version of MiniLM [28]. This fast and small model has performed well on different tasks for 56 corpora [19].

4   Proposed Models

Siamese transformer models perform well in generalist domains, but not in specialty domains, such as the biomedical domain [24]. Here we propose new siamese models pre-trained on the PubMed biomedical article corpus.

Siamese transformers were originally designed to transform sentences (of a similar size) into vectors. In our approach, we propose to transform MeSH terms, titles and abstracts of PubMed articles into the same vector space by training a siamese transformer model on this PubMed data. We want to ensure that there is a match in this vector space between the short text and the long one. For example, between the title "Effect of etafenone on total and regional myocardial blood flow" and the MeSH term "Blood Pressure".

We first adjust an initial pre-trained siamese transformer bi-encoder in the general domain to the specialized domain (biomedical in our case). Then, we create our own bi-encoder which is based on the different types of transformers PubMedBERT [8], BioBERT [14], BlueBERT [22] and BioELECTRA [13]. We used PubMed articles associated with their MeSH (Medical Subject Headings) terms. For training, we generated the following pairs of entries (title, MeSH terms) and (abstract, MeSH terms).

We have built two types of models: the first is our own BioSTransformers siamese transformer built from a pre-trained transformer and the second is a siamese transformer already pre-trained on generalist data.

Objective Function. When training a neural model, the objective is to estimate the parameters that minimize an objective function and thus determine the best neural model. Initially, a siamese transformer is assigned two sentences

---

[3] https://huggingface.co/sentence-transformers/all-MiniLM-L6-v2.

and a similarity score. As input, we have a triplet (sentence $P1$, sentence $P2$, similarity score between $P1$ and $P2$), which refers to supervised data.

However, in our case, we don't have any score for abstracts or titles and their corresponding MeSH terms, as the data from PubMed is not supervised training data as shown in Fig. 1. Therefore, we have to eliminate the similarity score and we consider that:

– An abstract, title and MeSH terms associated with the same article (identified by a PMID) are similar and the score is equal to 1;
– An abstract or title with MeSH terms that are not associated with the same article are not similar and therefore the score is 0.

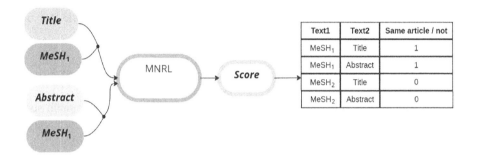

Fig. 1. Scoring method overview.

For the training, we used the Multiple Ranking Loss (MRL) objective function [10] (named MNRL in the Sentence-Transformers package[4]) which allows us to use MNRL by specifying only positive pairs (the title or abstract and a MeSH term associated with the article). The MRL objective function considers the other pairs present in the mini-batch as negative. Thus, for a positive pair (title_i or abstract_i, MeSH_i), it considers for each $i \neq j$ that (title_i or abstract_i, MeSH_j) is negative.

We made sure that MeSH terms associated with an abstract or a title are never taken as negative. Therefore, we took as training data the (abstract, MeSH) and (title, MeSH) associated with the same article in PubMed. The MRL training approach uses a siamese architecture during fine-tuning. This means that at each step of training, we embed a sentence 1 (article or abstract) into the model, followed by sentence 2 (MeSH term). This loss has played an important role in the obtained results.

---

[4] https://www.sbert.net/docs/package_reference/losses.html#
multiplenegativesrankingloss.

BioSTransformers. In this section, we describe the first type of our models. To build the BioSTransformers, we were inspired by the Sentence-BERT model by replacing BERT with another PLM. We used a transformer that was trained on biomedical data (bioTransformer), then we created the Siamese Transformer based on this bioTransformer. The second step was to train this model on the PubMed data we prepared. The training here consists of using a pre-trained neural network and adjusting its parameters by further training on target task specific data. The input sentence pairs are fed into the biomedical transformer and then into a pooling layer.

BioS-MiniLM. For the second type of model, we used an already pre-trained siamese transformer. Several general models of pre-trained siamese transformers are available. They differ in size, speed and performance. Among those which obtain the best performance, we used MiniLM-L6-v2 that was pre-trained on general text pairs (see Sect. 3.2). This model of size 80MB has been trained on 32 corpus (Reddit comments, S2ORC, WikiAnswers, PAQ etc.), however, it has not been tested on biomedical benchmarks.

5 Experiments and Results

5.1 Experiments

Model Pre-training. At first, to quickly test the different transformers and the objective function to choose, we used only the titles (and not the abstracts) and we reduced the number of MeSH terms. We selected a total of 1,402 MeSH terms and 3.79 million (title, MeSH) pairs and used 18,940 articles with their titles and MeSH terms for validation.

In a second step, once the transformers and MNRL objective function were selected, we evaluated our BioSTransformers and BioS-MiniLM models on the (title, MeSH) and (abstract, MeSH) pairs generated from all MeSH terms used in PubMed. Having found that it is not necessary to use all pairs from the 35 million PubMed articles, we randomly selected 1.5% of the pairs, that is 6.75 million pairs for fine-tuning. 18,557 articles were used for validation.

NLP Tasks The three NLP tasks and the data used are described below:

1. Document classification: The Hallmarks of Cancer (HOC) corpus consists of 1852 abstracts of PubMed publications manually annotated by experts according to a taxonomy that is composed of 37 classes. Each sentence in the corpus is assigned to zero or several classes [9].
2. Question Answering:
   (a) PubMedQA is a corpus for questions answering specific to biomedical research. It contains a set of research questions, each with a reference text from a PubMed abstract and an annotated field indicating whether the text contains the answer to the research question (yes/maybe/no) [11].

(b) BioASQ corpus contains several question answering tasks with expert annotated data, including yes/no, factoid, list and summary questions. In this work, we focus on the yes/no question type (task 7b). Each question is associated with a text containing several sentences of a PubMed abstract and a yes/no answer. We use the formal distribution of test data with 140 questions [20].

3. Information Retrieval: The TREC-COVID dataset [25] is a collection of scientific articles related to COVID-19. It was created as part of the Information Retrieval (IR) task of the Text REtrieval Conference (TREC) COVID, which aimed to support the scientific community in its response to the COVID-19 pandemic through effective IR systems. It consists of 171,000 articles and 50 queries.

We consider these tasks as a sentence similarity problem and seek to retrieve for each query the closest results. In a classification task, the query is the category and the results are the documents classified in this category. In a question answering task, the query is the question and the results are an answer. The similarity between the query and the results is measured by the cosine between the query vector and the result vectors. We consider the top-k results for each query, k being the number of results assigned to the query by the expert.

Transfer Learning. After training our models on our data and to be able to use them for classification and question answering, we added a transfer learning step. For each benchmark, we used the embeddings generated by our models for both the query and the document concatenated to train a simple feed-forward neural network that will process the specific task. Our neural network consists of two fully connected layers: the hidden layer comprises 100 neurons, while the output layer contains n neurons, where n corresponds to the number of output classes for each task.

5.2   Results

Classification and Question-Answering. We evaluated our models according to the macro F1 score used in the benchmarks Hallmarks of Cancer (HoC) [9], PubmedQA [11] and BioASQ [20] in [8]. The results obtained by our Siamese transformers models are given in Table 1.

Table 2 shows the results obtained on the same tasks by models fine-tuned specifically for these tasks by modifying inputs or adding a specific layer to the models [8]. For each benchmark, these models are fine-tuned with the supervised data available in each case (HoC, PubMedQA, BioASQ). These results show that our proposed models are able to solve these tasks in a similar way to biomedical models fine-tuned specifically for each task.

For the HoC benchmark, the results obtained by our best model S-BioBERT are much better than the results obtained by PubMedBERT+fine-tuning (0.909 vs. 0.823). On the other hand, for the PubMedQA benchmark, the results obtained by our best model are comparable to the results obtained

Table 1. Evaluation results of our models on different benchmarks according to the macro F1 score.

Data/Model	BioS-MiniLM	S-BioELECTRA	S-PubMedBERT	S-BlueBERT	S-BioBERT
HoC	0.868	0.901	**0.909**	0.900	0.898
PubMedQA	**0.590**	0.572	0.537	0.543	0.552
BioASQ	0.561	**0.621**	0.581	0.566	0.588

Table 2. Evaluation results of the models fine-tuned specifically for these tasks on different benchmarks according to the macro F1 score [8].

Data/Model	BERT +fine-tuning	RoBERTa +fine-tuning	BioBERT +fine-tuning	SciBERT +fine-tuning	ClinicalBERT +fine-tuning	BlueBERT +fine-tuning	PubMedBERT +fine-tuning
HoC	0.802	0.797	0.820	0.812	0.808	0.805	**0.823**
PubmedQA	0.516	0.528	**0.602**	0.574	0.491	0.484	0.558
BioASQ	0.744	0.752	0.841	0.789	0.685	0.687	**0.876**

by BioBERT+fine-tuning (0.590 vs. 0.602). Finally, for the BioASQ benchmark, the results obtained by our best model are below the results obtained by PubMedBERT+fine-tuning (0.621 vs. 0.876).

These results prove that our siamese models which encode the inputs (document and query) separately can achieve comparable results to cross-encoders models.

Information Retrieval. As indicated in Sect. 2, numerous studies have investigated the effectiveness of bi-encoders in information retrieval tasks. In the subsequent phase, we utilize our models for this task, specifically selecting the TREC-COVID dataset.

In order to accomplish this, we pre-calculate the documents' representations (embeddings) and we index them using Faiss[5]. During the inference phase, we simply compute the query representation.

Table 3 compare the performances of our models with the cross-attentional re-ranking model BM25+CE that gives the best results with TREC-COVID in BEIR benchmark [24]. In BM25+CE the top-100 results given by the ranking function BM25 are re-ranked using the cross-encoder model ms-marco-MiniLM-L-6-v2[6]. The time, as indicated in Table 3, represents the average query processing time in seconds. The results show that our models can surpass the performance of BM25+CE using a query processing time negligible in comparison with a re-ranking cross-encoder, demonstrating the effectiveness of our approach.

---

[5] https://github.com/facebookresearch/faiss.
[6] https://huggingface.co/cross-encoder/ms-marco-MiniLM-L-6-v2.

Table 3. Evaluation results on TREC-COVID. The scores denote nDCG@5, the average query processing is given in seconds.

Metric/Model	BM25+CE	BioS-MiniLM	S-PubMedBERT
Ranking score	0.76	0.64	**0.87**
Time	20.4	**0.04**	**0.04**

6   Conclusion

In this paper, we have proposed new siamese models BioSTransformers and BioS-MiniLM that allow to solve several NLP tasks in biomedical texts. These siamese models embed text pairs in the same representation space and allow to compute the semantic similarity between texts of different lengths.

Compared to cross-encoders, our models offer several advantages. First, they are more efficient during inference due to the use of pre-calculated document embeddings. By indexing and storing these embeddings, the models only need to encode the query once, resulting in faster inference times. Whereas cross-encoders models must encode the query for each document in the candidate set. This makes our models faster and more scalable for ranking large collections of documents.

Second, our models are easier to train and tune than cross-encoders models. Cross-encoders require extensive hyperparameter tuning, such as learning rate schedules, dropout rates, and attention masking. In contrast, bi-encoders have fewer hyperparameters to tune and can be trained with standard optimization algorithms.

Third, we can also encode the query once for some tasks and then reuse the embedding if we store the pair (text, embedding) in a cash memory.

We plan to improve our models so that they can better address the QA task. Our self-supervised models are reference models that could be directly applied to other NLP tasks.

References

1. Alsentzer, E., et al.: Publicly available clinical BERT embeddings. In: Proceedings of the 2nd Clinical Natural Language Processing Workshop, pp. 72–78. Association for Computational Linguistics, Minneapolis, Minnesota, USA (Jun 2019). https://aclanthology.org/W19-1909
2. Beltagy, I., Lo, K., Cohan, A.: SciBERT: a pretrained language model for scientific text. In: Proceedings of the 2019 Conference on Empirical Methods in Natural Language Processing and the 9th International Joint Conference on Natural Language Processing (EMNLP-IJCNLP), pp. 3615–3620 (2019)
3. Borgeaud, S., et al.: Improving language models by retrieving from trillions of tokens. In: International Conference on Machine Learning, pp. 2206–2240. PMLR (2022)

4. Cohan, A., Feldman, S., Beltagy, I., Downey, D., Weld, D.S.: Specter: document-level representation learning using citation-informed transformers. In: Proceedings of the 58th Annual Meeting of the Association for Computational Linguistics, pp. 2270–2282 (2020)
5. Devlin, J., Chang, M.W., Lee, K., Toutanova, K.: BERT: Pre-training of deep bidirectional transformers for language understanding. In: Proceedings of NAACL-HLT, pp. 4171–4186 (2019)
6. Ferraretto, F., Laitz, T., Lotufo, R., Nogueira, R.: Exaranker: Explanation-augmented neural ranker. arXiv preprint arXiv:2301.10521 (2023)
7. Gao, T., Yao, X., Chen, D.: Simcse: simple contrastive learning of sentence embeddings. In: Proceedings of the 2021 Conference on Empirical Methods in Natural Language Processing, pp. 6894–6910 (2021)
8. Gu, Y., et al.: Domain-specific language model pretraining for biomedical natural language processing. ACM Trans. Comput. Healthcare **3**(1), 1–23 (2022). https://doi.org/10.1145%2F3458754
9. Hanahan, D., Weinberg, R.A.: The hallmarks of cancer. Cell **100**(1), 57–70 (2000)
10. Henderson, M., et al.: Efficient natural language response suggestion for smart reply. arXiv preprint arXiv:1705.00652 (2017)
11. Jin, Q., Dhingra, B., Liu, Z., Cohen, W., Lu, X.: PubMedQA: a dataset for biomedical research question answering. In: Proceedings of the 2019 Conference on Empirical Methods in Natural Language Processing and the 9th International Joint Conference on Natural Language Processing (EMNLP-IJCNLP), pp. 2567–2577 (2019)
12. Johnson, A.E., et al.: MIMIC-III a freely accessible critical care database. Scientific Data **3**(1), 1–9 (2016)
13. Kanakarajan, K.r., Kundumani, B., Sankarasubbu, M.: BioELECTRA: pretrained biomedical text encoder using discriminators. In: Proceedings of the 20th Workshop on Biomedical Language Processing, pp. 143–154. Association for Computational Linguistics, Online (Jun 2021). https://aclanthology.org/2021.bionlp-1.16
14. Lee, J., et al.: BioBERT: a pre-trained biomedical language representation model for biomedical text mining. Bioinformatics **36**(4), 1234–1240 (2020)
15. Lin, S.C., et al.: How to train your dragon: Diverse augmentation towards generalizable dense retrieval. arXiv e-prints pp. arXiv-2302 (2023)
16. Liu, F., Shareghi, E., Meng, Z., Basaldella, M., Collier, N.: Self-alignment pretraining for biomedical entity representations. In: Proceedings of the 2021 Conference of the North American Chapter of the Association for Computational Linguistics: Human Language Technologies, pp. 4228–4238 (2021)
17. Luo, R., et al.: Biogpt: generative pre-trained transformer for biomedical text generation and mining. Briefings Bioinform. **23**(6) (2022)
18. Menon, A., Jayasumana, S., Rawat, A.S., Kim, S., Reddi, S., Kumar, S.: In defense of dual-encoders for neural ranking. In: International Conference on Machine Learning, pp. 15376–15400. PMLR (2022)
19. Muennighoff, N., Tazi, N., Magne, L., Reimers, N.: Mteb: massive text embedding benchmark. arXiv preprint arXiv:2210.07316 (2022)
20. Nentidis, A., Bougiatiotis, K., Krithara, A., Paliouras, G.: Results of the seventh edition of the BioASQ challenge. In: Cellier, P., Driessens, K. (eds.) ECML PKDD 2019. CCIS, vol. 1168, pp. 553–568. Springer, Cham (2020). https://doi.org/10.1007/978-3-030-43887-6_51
21. Peng, Y., Yan, S., Lu, Z.: Transfer learning in biomedical natural language processing: An evaluation of BERT and ELMo on ten benchmarking datasets. In: Proceedings of the 18th BioNLP Workshop and Shared Task, pp. 58–65 (2019)

22. Peng, Y., Yan, S., Lu, Z.: Transfer learning in biomedical natural language processing: an evaluation of BERT and ELMo on ten benchmarking datasets. In: Proceedings of the 18th BioNLP Workshop and Shared Task, pp. 58–65. Association for Computational Linguistics, Florence, Italy (Aug 2019). https://aclanthology.org/W19-5006

23. Reimers, N., Gurevych, I.: Sentence-BERT: sentence embeddings using Siamese BERT-networks. In: Proceedings of the 2019 Conference on Empirical Methods in Natural Language Processing and the 9th International Joint Conference on Natural Language Processing (EMNLP-IJCNLP), pp. 3982–3992. Association for Computational Linguistics, Hong Kong, China (Nov 2019), https://aclanthology.org/D19-1410

24. Thakur, N., Reimers, N., Rücklé, A., Srivastava, A., Gurevych, I.: BEIR: A heterogeneous benchmark for zero-shot evaluation of information retrieval models. In: Thirty-fifth Conference on Neural Information Processing Systems Datasets and Benchmarks Track (Round 2) (2021)

25. Voorhees, Eet al.: Trec-covid: Constructing a pandemic information retrieval test collection. SIGIR Forum **54**(1) (2021). https://doi.org/10.1145/3451964.3451965

26. Wang, K., Reimers, N., Gurevych, I.: Tsdae: Using transformer-based sequential denoising auto-encoderfor unsupervised sentence embedding learning. In: Findings of the Association for Computational Linguistics: EMNLP 2021, pp. 671–688 (2021)

27. Wang, L., et al.: Text embeddings by weakly-supervised contrastive pre-training. arXiv e-prints pp. arXiv-2212 (2022)

28. Wang, W., Wei, F., Dong, L., Bao, H., Yang, N., Zhou, M.: Minilm: deep self-attention distillation for task-agnostic compression of pre-trained transformers. Adv. Neural. Inf. Process. Syst. **33**, 5776–5788 (2020)

29. Zhao, W.X., Liu, J., Ren, R., Wen, J.R.: Dense text retrieval based on pretrained language models: A survey. arXiv preprint arXiv:2211.14876 (2022)

The Promise of Query Answering Systems in Sexuality Studies: Current State, Challenges and Limitations

Andrea Morales-Garzón[1]([📧]) [ID], Gracia M. Sánchez-Pérez[2] [ID],
Juan Carlos Sierra[2] [ID], and Maria J. Martin-Bautista[1] [ID]

[1] Department of Computer Science and Artificial Intelligence, University of Granada,
Granada, Spain
{amoralesg,mbautis}@decsai.ugr.es
[2] Mind, Brain, and Behavior Research Center, University of Granada,
Granada, Spain
{graciasp,jcsierra}@ugr.es

Abstract. Sexuality is a field of study that attempts to comprehend
human behaviour, improve sexual health and understand culture and
gender, among others. Recent advances and developments in artificial
intelligence, specifically in query answering and natural language processing, can help to study the social relationship between population
and sexuality. They are powerful tools to cope with crucial problems
in the field, such as subjectivity, social desirability and social opinion
biases. In this work, we review the state-of-the-art of AI-based methods
in sexuality-related studies. Focusing on the psychological perspective,
we analyse the role of query answering in this area of research. We discuss
the necessary foundations, challenges, and limitations a query answering
system must cover in this specialised and complex field.

Keywords: Query Answering · Natural Language Processing ·
Sexuality · Large Language Models · Sexual Health

1 Introduction

Sexuality is an area of expertise in health-related disciplines, such as psychology
and medicine. Sexual health refers to the state of physical, emotional, mental and
social well-being related to sexuality, not the absence of disease, dysfunction or
disability [55]. We can differentiate here between two main perspectives. First, a
medical perspective that focuses on the study of solutions applied to the healthcare sector, specifically to the hospital field and a second line that focuses on the
study of sexual functioning from a psychological perspective to enhance sexual
health and well-being [8,34,35]. The latter refers to the study of different dimensions of sexual health, such as attitudes, desire, arousal, subjective experience
of orgasm, satisfaction, assertiveness, and sexual fantasies, among many others.
Research in the sexuality area is needed to enhance sexual health and behaviour
and assess the effectiveness of prevention and treatment programs [56].

© Springer Nature Switzerland AG 2023
H. L. Larsen et al. (Eds.): FQAS 2023, LNAI 14113, pp. 39–49, 2023.
https://doi.org/10.1007/978-3-031-42935-4_4

The growing amount of data available continually enables advancements in artificial intelligence (AI) applications. The digitalisation of sexuality research laboratories and the rapid development of social networks led to large-scale datasets of sexual-related data. They offer rich knowledge about human behaviour and can help tackle many central issues of human society. AI and recent natural language processing (NLP) breakthroughs are transforming how we analyse data and interact with computational systems. Together with the advent of large language models (LLM) can boost new query answering (QA) systems for specific and expertise areas such as sexuality.

This paper summarises critical challenges and future directions for artificial intelligence in sexuality studies. We first review the related work so far in many different tasks of sexuality. Since sexuality data has a strong base of unstructured texts, we emphasise the relevance of natural language processing to address these tasks. We focus on the role of query answering, which may benefit from recent NLP models. We expose the relevance of studying QA for the sexuality area and present new research lines to pursue and current challenges and limitations. As far as we know, this is the first comprehensive work that reviews the current state-of-the-art of sexuality in artificial intelligence, offering a collection of related research studies.

Our main contributions are detailed as follows:

- A review of the state-of-the-art AI applications in sexuality for the two previously mentioned perspectives (i.e., medicine and psychology).
- An analysis of the current state, challenges, applications and needs for building query answering systems for sexuality, focusing on the psychological point of view. We emphasise their role in improving social relations of the population with sexuality and promoting research advances in the field.

2   Artificial Intelligence in Sexuality Studies

The intersection between sexuality research and AI-based systems is an emerging area, and consequently, few AI-based approximations directly apply to sexuality. Most of this work relates to specific final applications on small datasets, incorporating machine learning algorithms for supervised classification tasks. We classify the more relevant advances regarding sexual-related data in AI according to their final application. Figure 1 summarises this information.

Sexual Trauma Detection. Qualitative information about patients' habits is typically recorded in unstructured clinical notes [38]. NLP is, therefore, a key technology for extracting social health behaviours from clinical text and increasing their utility for patient care and research. It can also help to identify standard terms in sexual history data. In [40], the authors use a rule-based algorithm based on regular expressions to process unstructured text in electronic health records (EHRs). Their method identifies patients who meet inclusion criteria and supports studies and clinical decisions. [13,19] propose using NLP

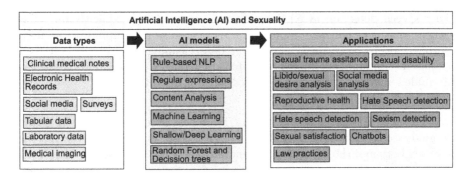

Fig. 1. State-of-the-art of artificial intelligence in sexuality: a flowchart exposing the variety of data types, models and applications.

techniques for concept extraction of sexual trauma evidence in medical notes. In [20], the authors also study the differences in the incidence and patterns regarding racial differences. However, these methods highlight the need for a standardised protocol for documenting sexual trauma histories to ensure high standards of trauma-informed care [24].

Sexual Satisfaction. Sexual satisfaction factors are a current research problem in sexuality. Machine learning approaches such as Random Forest can predict relationship variables, e.g., perception of romantic love and desire [52]. In [27], a machine learning approach uses health records data, including age, sex, physician's diagnoses, drug treatments, and the Arizona Sexual Experiences Scale (ASEX) [33] to identify sexual disability cases and potential factors involved.

Reproductive Health. Future sexual health applications will be influenced by the intersection of AI and reproductive medicine [53]. It is partly due to the capability of machine learning approaches for the feature selection of relevant variables for research advances in complex diagnosis and successful pregnancy prediction [16]. Here stand many applications for, among many others, the assessment and prediction tasks related to assisted reproductive technologies [10,12]. Shallow and deep learning, SVM, and decision tree algorithms have been used for this field of application. Also, AI can contribute to the digital transformation of healthcare systems through online applications with chatbots and video consultations for sexual health advice [36]. Obstetrics and gynaecology also benefit from AI, especially for ultrasound processing, where stands medical imaging [7] for assisting experts in diagnosis [14].

Social Media. State-of-the-art language models in this field focus on gender and sexual orientation bias detection [3]. The authors propose several deep learning models that address discrimination, focusing on feminism, misogyny and gender identity biases detection. These studies are motivated by the advances in hate speech detection in NLP [2,44]. Some are centred explicitly on counteracting sexism in language models [23,37]. These works emphasise the need for proper corpus, specialised and better data cleaning and the difficulties of unbalanced data and code-mixed or switched languages. Also noteworthy is the NLP-guided analysis of women's sexual desires in Reddit [4].

Law Practice. AI chatbots help increase awareness of sexual violence by giving legal guidance to victims of sexual violence [48]. Also, many works research the role of sex bots and the controversial, unethical and harmful uses of AI [17,47].

3   Why Sexuality Studies Require AI?

From the psychology perspective, research on sexuality includes aspects such as well-being, attitudes, satisfaction and other factors influenced by the behaviour and personality of the individual [49]. It focuses on population studies and laboratory studies [22]. Population-based studies allow for assessing sexual functioning, validated in the population and with adequate psychometric properties [33,42]. In laboratory studies, sexual stimuli are presented to record arousal levels objectively (by recording the individual's genital response) and subjectively (through questionnaires). Applying AI-based approaches to this research stage would allow to analyse patterns and study the role of feature variables to relate to and understand objective and subjective responses.

Subjective measures are mainly self-reported, which can introduce several potential biases into the results. It is challenging to ensure that the information provided by patients is valid, which could compromise the results. These include response biases (amplification or concealment) due to social desirability [6,46]. AI can help to address data reliability issues by using anomaly detection techniques and natural language processing. Language models aid for data-driven analysis of sexuality research surveys [57] and user responses [11,50], considering hate, sarcasm, deception, sexism and emotion detection among many others. Thus, it helps to understand the factors that influence social desirability and assist in preventing these situations. These techniques can also help to extract knowledge regarding sexual motivations, e.g., the reasons why humans have sexual relations. It helps to classify answers into logical, rational and scientifically meaningful categorisations.

AI also plays a leading role in predicting population behaviour [30] and counteracting disinformation [1,45]. About the latter, there have already been some initiatives with sexual experts involved[1]. Regarding the prediction of sexual behaviour we pose two open-ended questions in sexuality research where AI can bring value:

---

[1] Demystification of sexuality in media: https://www.verificat.cat/es/fact-check/que-los-hombres-reconozcan-que-se-masturban-mas-que-las-mujeres-no-significa-necesariamente-que-se-masturben-mas.

– To what extent does self-reported collected data represent people's true behaviour (it may be affected by measurement biases)?
– To what extent can we predict sexual behaviour that is difficult to observe from self-reported data, e.g., measuring satisfaction from sexual fantasies or predicting masturbation periodicity from observed pose to masturbation?

Also, it is worth mentioning the role of AI for data curating, prepossessing and alignment tasks in tabular databases and heterogeneous data [54], which also applies for sexuality studies, where tabular data is amply used in the laboratory. Also, mention the detection of potential near duplicates and data inconsistencies, where AI approaches have largely been applied.

4   The Role of Query Answering Systems in Sexuality Studies

As detailed in Sect. 2, many current applications rely on textual-related data. If we focus on sexuality from the psychology perspective, laboratory data attempts to a better categorisation from unstructured texts. Many of the current issues to be tackled rely on a better comprehension of the sexual language and automating of data cleaning and pre-processing tasks.

QA automatically processes natural language questions offering accurate answers based on a provided knowledge base [21,51]. It evaluates user queries and obtains relevant data from databases, knowledge graphs and expert data using a variety of approaches, such as natural language processing. Since most of this information is in an unstructured textual format, NLP techniques play a crucial role here due to their high dependence on the quality processing of texts. With the rise and impressive advances in conversational and generative AIs such as the GPT family of language models [5,39], there is a need to recover the extensive research in QA to ask the following question: what is their role in future expert-driven AI applications?

Large language models are deep learning language models training on extensive corpora. They are crucial for developing adaptable and general language systems that tackle the vagueness and flexibility of the language [5]. Pre-trained LLMs can push the progress of QA in specific domains [18]. Especially in sexuality studies, most data come in surveys or questionnaires. QA systems based on LLMs pose a new tool for studying sexuality, especially regarding the relation of the population with sexuality. They can help to extract relevant information and support a better understanding of sexual language.

A wide variety of QA systems depend on the kind of data and agents that intervene [29,31]. If we focus on the sexuality domain, where expert and inexpert users may interact, we detect two fundamental cases of use for QA. Firstly, as detailed in Sect. 3, expert users may use the system for specialised analysis to support their research, e.g., NLP-based analysis of surveys, social desirability detection, data mining in social media for understanding public opinion or intrinsic pattern detection, among others. Secondly, inexpert users would interact with the system for specialised and curated sexuality-related topics and questions. Thus, language models must be re-trained to the sexuality domain while considering and mitigating the potential biases and subjectivity of the field (see challenges and limitations in Subsects. 5.1 and 5.2, respectively).

5   Discussion

In this section, we discuss the current challenges and the possible limitations under which QA models for sexuality studies must operate. We also detail the more immediate social impacts of their application on sexuality.

5.1   Current Challenges

Knowledge-Based Deep Learning. The subject is very specialised and requires expert knowledge to obtain trustworthy and reliable systems. Sexual experts must guide the process in order to validate human-machine interactions.

Heterogeneous Data Handling. Sexuality-related data comes mainly from social networks, surveys, questionnaires, laboratory measurements, and specialised knowledge sources, leading to a previous intelligent fusion of the information to build systems that handle expert knowledge.

Multilingual Query Answering Systems. Develop tools and resources for languages other than English to facilitate access to the system using other languages. The long part of the research and questionnaires in the area is in English. Thus, developing tools to retrieve information in other languages is needed. Here we make mention of large multilingual language models [43] and language-independent domain-specific knowledge bases [25,28].

Data Reliability. Answer biases (amplification or concealment) due to social desirability. A need to study user behaviour and their self-reported data reliability. From the point of view of user behaviour, it is necessary to consider social pressure, prejudices, social acceptance, and other external elements that may favour incorrect or dishonest use of the system, introducing biases and inaccuracies.

5.2   Limitations

Ethical Limitations. AI has shown harmful biases in health data, and it poses a severe ethical risk to the application of machine learning in medicine [32]. Fairness solutions allow for building models that strive for non-discriminatory predictions, for example, by balancing or limiting variable expressiveness to ensure equal rates across diversity groups. These restrictions apply directly to sexuality research. AI-based applications must guarantee protected identities, including sexual orientation, pregnancy, gender identity, disabilities or genetic information (e.g., medical records), and address rare cases and generalizability [41].

Small and Imbalanced Data. Sexuality research studies are linked to laboratory data. As in other medicine-related tasks, we may have too small amounts of data for prediction tasks [26]. Data insufficiency limits the performance of AI models. Also, AI solutions must tackle difficulties regarding rare sexual attitudes, behaviour diversity and minority groups.

5.3   Social Impact

Clinical Implications. Analyzing social media data and surveys can influence the medications' impact on sexual health, the interaction of sexual desire and mental health, and guide sexual well-being research, diagnosis, and public policy.

Demystification of Sexuality. AI can help to contrast scientific evidence in sexuality research findings and bring general knowledge to the population, helping disinformation and greater awareness among the population.

Understanding of Individual Behaviour. AI approaches applied to laboratory objective and subjective studies can help to increase the understanding of sexual functioning and its relations with sexual health and well-being.

Quality of Life. Drug treatment and sexual health are related, and research in this intersection could improve patients' quality of life in many areas (e.g., psychiatry) [27]. Also, a better understanding of sexual stimulation and satisfaction contributes to psychological well-being [9].

Applications in Other Psychology Fields. The findings, the implemented AI models, and deep learning approaches applied to sexuality can be extended to other research studies in the psychology field, e.g., survey and questionnaires analysis or emotion-aware AI models.

Large Language Models in Fields of Expertise. A recent study has emphasised the role of complementary technologies to LLMs, concluding that it is necessary to integrate them into broader systems to maximise the impact of LLMs [15].

6   Conclusions

This study aimed to review the impact of AI in general and query answering in particular in sexuality studies. In this paper, we bring together the current knowledge of artificial intelligence applications to sexuality studies and present the advantages of applying QA in the area where the complexity and biases of text-related data take centre stage. With this in mind, we have exposed the main tasks to tackle, in which AI, particularly QA, can participate, and their future challenges and limitations to consider.

From a psychological perspective, sexuality biases and prejudices increase the need for modelling sexual language. They can benefit from QA systems in two main lines. Firstly, controlling and detecting sexual biases from social desirability. Secondly, helping the population with their relationship with sexuality. Among others, these models must accomplish the difficulties derived from the heterogeneity in the data sources, the need to include expert knowledge and data reliability.

Acknowledgments. This research was partially funded by the Grant PID2021-123960OB-I00 funded by MCIN/AEI/10.13039/501100011033 and by ERDF A way of making Europe. It was also funded by the Grant TED2021-129402B-C21 funded by MCIN/AEI/10.13039/501100011033 and, by the European Union NextGenerationEU/PRTR. It was also funded by "Consejería de Transformación Económica, Industria, Conocimiento y Universidades de la Junta de Andalucía" through a predoctoral fellowship program (Grant Refs. PREDOC_00289 and PREDOC_00298).

References

1. Al-Asadi, M.A., Tasdemir, S.: Using artificial intelligence against the phenomenon of fake news: a systematic literature review. In: Combating Fake News with Computational Intelligence Techniques, pp. 39–54 (2022)
2. Alkomah, F., Ma, X.: A literature review of textual hate speech detection methods and datasets. Information **13**(6), 273 (2022)
3. Arcila-Calderón, C., Amores, J.J., Sánchez-Holgado, P., Blanco-Herrero, D.: Using shallow and deep learning to automatically detect hate motivated by gender and sexual orientation on twitter in Spanish. Multimodal Technol. Interact. **5**(10), 63 (2021)
4. Belcher, R.E., et al.: A qualitative analysis of female reddit users' experiences with low libido: how do women perceive their changes in sexual desire? J. Sexual Med. (2023)
5. Brown, T., et al.: Language models are few-shot learners. Adv. Neural. Inf. Process. Syst. **33**, 1877–1901 (2020)
6. Castaño, M.E.F., Espada, A.A.: Primer estudio psicométrico de la versión española del agressive sexual behavior inventory (asbi). Revista de psicopatología y psicología clínica **13**(1), 21–31 (2008)
7. Castiglioni, I., et al.: Ai applications to medical images: from machine learning to deep learning. Physica Med. **83**, 9–24 (2021)
8. Cervilla, O., Jiménez-Antón, E., Álvarez-Muelas, A., Mangas, P., Granados, R., Sierra, J.C.: Solitary sexual desire: its relation to subjective orgasm experience and sexual arousal in the masturbation context within a Spanish population. In: Healthcare, vol. 11, p. 805. MDPI (2023)
9. Chernyavska, T., Yermakova, A., Kokorina, Y., Kolot, S., Kremenchutska, M.: Sexual satisfaction as a factor of psychological well-being. BRAIN. Broad Res. Artif. Intell. Neurosci. **13**(1), 292–307 (2022)
10. Curchoe, C.L., Bormann, C.L.: Artificial intelligence and machine learning for human reproduction and embryology presented at ASRM and ESHRE 2018. J. Assist. Reprod. Genet. **36**, 591–600 (2019)
11. Das, R., Singh, T.D.: Multimodal sentiment analysis: a survey of methods, trends and challenges. ACM Comput. Surv. (2023)
12. Dimitriadis, I., Zaninovic, N., Badiola, A.C., Bormann, C.L.: Artificial intelligence in the embryology laboratory: a review. Reprod. Biomed. Online **44**(3), 435–448 (2022)

13. Divita, G., et al.: Extracting sexual trauma mentions from electronic medical notes using natural language processing. In: MEDINFO 2017: Precision Healthcare Through Informatics: Proceedings of the 16th World Congress on Medical and Health Informatics, vol. 245, p. 351. IOS Press (2018)

14. Drukker, L., Noble, J., Papageorghiou, A.: Introduction to artificial intelligence in ultrasound imaging in obstetrics and gynecology. Ultrasound Obstetrics Gynecol. **56**(4), 498–505 (2020)

15. Eloundou, T., Manning, S., Mishkin, P., Rock, D.: GPTS are GPTS: an early look at the labor market impact potential of large language models (2023)

16. Filho, E.S., Noble, J.A., Poli, M., Griffiths, T., Emerson, G., Wells, D.: A method for semi-automatic grading of human blastocyst microscope images. Hum. Reprod. **27**(9), 2641–2648 (2012)

17. Frank, L., Nyholm, S.: Robot sex and consent: is consent to sex between a robot and a human conceivable, possible, and desirable? Artif. Intell. Law **25**, 305–323 (2017)

18. Gu, Y., et al.: Domain-specific language model pretraining for biomedical natural language processing. ACM Trans. Comput. Healthc. (HEALTH) **3**(1), 1–23 (2021)

19. Gundlapalli, A.V., et al.: Using structured and unstructured data to refine estimates of military sexual trauma status among us military veterans. Stud. Health Technol. Inform. **238**, 128 (2017)

20. Gundlapalli, A.V., et al.: Combining natural language processing of electronic medical notes with administrative data to determine racial/ethnic differences in the disclosure and documentation of military sexual trauma in veterans. Med. Care **57**, S149–S156 (2019)

21. Han, J., Huang, Y., Cercone, N., Fu, Y.: Intelligent query answering by knowledge discovery techniques. IEEE Trans. Knowl. Data Eng. **8**(3), 373–390 (1996)

22. Hyde, J.S., DeLamater, J.D.: Understanding Human Sexuality, 9th edn. McGraw-Hill, New York (2006)

23. Istaiteh, O., Al-Omoush, R., Tedmori, S.: Racist and sexist hate speech detection: literature review. In: 2020 International Conference on Intelligent Data Science Technologies and Applications (IDSTA), pp. 95–99. IEEE (2020)

24. Jones, A.L., et al.: Regional variations in documentation of sexual trauma concepts in electronic medical records in the united states veterans health administration. In: AMIA Annual Symposium Proceedings, vol. 2019, p. 514. American Medical Informatics Association (2019)

25. Khanam, S.A., Liu, F., Chen, Y.P.P.: Comprehensive structured knowledge base system construction with natural language presentation. HCIS **9**, 1–32 (2019)

26. Liu, L., et al.: Multi-task learning via adaptation to similar tasks for mortality prediction of diverse rare diseases. In: AMIA Annual Symposium Proceedings, vol. 2020, p. 763. American Medical Informatics Association (2020)

27. Liu, Y.S., Hankey, J.R., Chokka, S., Chokka, P.R., Cao, B.: Individualized identification of sexual dysfunction of psychiatric patients with machine-learning. Sci. Rep. **12**(1), 9599 (2022)

28. Lommatzsch, A., Katins, J.: An information retrieval-based approach for building intuitive chatbots for large knowledge bases. In: LWDA, pp. 343–352 (2019)

29. Magnini, B., Lavelli, A., Fabien, G., Cabrio, E., Cojan, J., Palmero Aprosio, A.: Open domain question answering: techniques, systems and evaluation. In: Tutorial of the Conference on Recent Advances in Natural Language Processing-RANLP, Borovetz, Bulgaria (2005)

30. Mariani, M.M., Perez-Vega, R., Wirtz, J.: Ai in marketing, consumer research and psychology: a systematic literature review and research agenda. Psychol. Mark. **39**(4), 755–776 (2022)
31. Martínez-Barco, P., Vicedo, J.L., Saquete Boró, E., Tomás, D., et al.: Sistemas de pregunta-respuesta (2007)
32. McCradden, M.D., Joshi, S., Mazwi, M., Anderson, J.A.: Ethical limitations of algorithmic fairness solutions in health care machine learning. Lancet Digit. Health **2**(5), e221–e223 (2020)
33. McGahuey, A., et al.: The Arizona sexual experience scale (ASEX): reliability and validity. J. Sex Marital Therapy **26**(1), 25–40 (2000)
34. Muñoz García, L.E., Gómez-Berrocal, C., Guillén-Riquelme, A., Sierra, J.C.: Measurement invariance across sexual orientation for measures of sexual attitudes. Int. J. Environ. Res. Publ. Health **20**(3), 1820 (2023)
35. Muñoz-García, L.E., Gómez-Berrocal, C., Sierra, J.C.: Evaluating the subjective orgasm experience through sexual context, gender, and sexual orientation. Arch. Sexual Behav. 1–13 (2022)
36. Nadarzynski, T., Bayley, J., Llewellyn, C., Kidsley, S., Graham, C.A.: Acceptability of artificial intelligence (AI)-enabled chatbots, video consultations and live webchats as online platforms for sexual health advice. BMJ Sexual Reprod. Health **46**(3), 210–217 (2020)
37. Parihar, A.S., Thapa, S., Mishra, S.: Hate speech detection using natural language processing: applications and challenges. In: 2021 5th International Conference on Trends in Electronics and Informatics (ICOEI), pp. 1302–1308. IEEE (2021)
38. Patra, B.G., et al.: Extracting social determinants of health from electronic health records using natural language processing: a systematic review. J. Am. Med. Inform. Assoc. **28**(12), 2716–2727 (2021)
39. Radford, A., Wu, J., Child, R., Luan, D., Amodei, D., Sutskever, I., et al.: Language models are unsupervised multitask learners. OpenAI blog **1**(8), 9 (2019)
40. Robertson, C., Mukherjee, G., Gooding, H., Kandaswamy, S., Orenstein, E.: A method to advance adolescent sexual health research: automated algorithm finds sexual history documentation. Front. Digit. Health **4** (2022)
41. Safdar, N.M., Banja, J.D., Meltzer, C.C.: Ethical considerations in artificial intelligence. Eur. J. Radiol. **122**, 108768 (2020)
42. Sánchez Fuentes, M., Moyano, N., Granados, R., Sierra Freire, J.C., et al.: Validation of the Spanish version of the Arizona sexual experience scale (ASEX) using self-reported and psychophysiological measures (2019)
43. Scao, T.L., et al.: Bloom: a 176b-parameter open-access multilingual language model. arXiv preprint arXiv:2211.05100 (2022)
44. Schmidt, A., Wiegand, M.: A survey on hate speech detection using natural language processing. In: Proceedings of the Fifth International Workshop on Natural Language Processing for Social Media, pp. 1–10 (2017)
45. Shahid, W., et al.: Detecting and mitigating the dissemination of fake news: challenges and future research opportunities. IEEE Tran. Comput. Soc. Syst. (2022)
46. Sierra, J.C., Gutiérrez-Quintanilla, R., Bermúdez, M.P., Buela-Casal, G.: Male sexual coercion: analysis of a few associated factors. Psychol. Rep. **105**(1), 69–79 (2009)
47. Sinclair, D., Dowdeswell, T., Goltz, N.: Artificially intelligent sex bots and female slavery: social science and Jewish legal and ethical perspectives. Inf. Commun. Technol. Law, 1–28 (2022)
48. Socatiyanurak, V., et al.: Law-U: legal guidance through artificial intelligence chatbot for sexual violence victims and survivors. IEEE Access **9**, 131440–131461 (2021)

49. Sprecher, S., McKinney, K.: Sexuality, vol. 6. Sage, Thousand Oaks (1993)
50. Sufi, F.K.: Ai-socialdisaster: an AI-based software for identifying and analyzing natural disasters from social media. Softw. Impacts **13**, 100319 (2022)
51. Thorne, J., Yazdani, M., Saeidi, M., Silvestri, F., Riedel, S., Halevy, A.: From natural language processing to neural databases. In: Proceedings of the VLDB Endowment, vol. 14, pp. 1033–1039. VLDB Endowment (2021)
52. Vowels, L.M., Vowels, M.J., Mark, K.P.: Identifying the strongest self-report predictors of sexual satisfaction using machine learning. J. Soc. Pers. Relat. **39**(5), 1191–1212 (2022)
53. Wang, R., et al.: Artificial intelligence in reproductive medicine. Reproduction (Cambridge, England) **158**(4), R139 (2019)
54. Wilcke, X., Bloem, P., De Boer, V.: The knowledge graph as the default data model for learning on heterogeneous knowledge. Data Sci. **1**(1–2), 39–57 (2017)
55. World Health Organization: Sexual Health. WHO Press (2006)
56. World Health Organization: Sexual and Reproductive Health and Research (SRH). WHO Press (2020)
57. Zhou, B., Yang, G., Shi, Z., Ma, S.: Natural language processing for smart healthcare. IEEE Rev. Biomed. Eng. (2022)

Some Properties of the Left Recursive Form of the Convex Combination Linguistic Aggregator

Ignacio Huitzil[1] and Fernando Bobillo[2,3]($\boxtimes$) (iD)

[1] IKR3 Laboratory, University of Milano-Bicocca, Milano, Italy
`ignacio.huitzil@unimib.it`
[2] University of Zaragoza, Zaragoza, Spain
[3] Aragon Institute of Engineering Research (I3A), Zaragoza, Spain
`fbobillo@unizar.es`

Abstract. The Left Recursive Form of the Convex Combination (CONV–LRF) is a linguistic aggregation operator which has been recently proposed in the framework of fuzzy ontology learning. The objective of this paper is to study some properties of the operator, namely commutativity, smoothness, internality, monotonicity, and orness. Our results show that, contrary to what preliminary experiments suggested, CONV–LRF has a similar orness that the Right Recursive Form (CONV–RRF).

Keywords: Fuzzy Logic · Linguistic Aggregation · Fuzzy Ontology Building

1 Introduction

Aggregation operators are crucial in many real-world applications, where different criteria must be combined to have a global value or take a decision [1,16]. Linguistic aggregation operators are an important family of functions that aggregate a list of fuzzy linguistic labels, represented using fuzzy numbers, rather than numerical values [18]. Linguistic aggregation operators have proved to be important, for example, in fuzzy ontology learning [12]. They can also be useful in flexible querying to aggregate different values (described using fuzzy numbers) to compute a global satisfaction degree.

Having a plethora of different aggregation operators satisfying different properties is important, because different applications impose different demands. Inspired by the recursive form of the OWA operator, the Left Recursive Form of the Convex Combination Linguistic Aggregator (CONV–LRF) was recently presented [12]. The objective of this paper is to study some properties of that operator, namely commutativity, smoothness, internality, monotonicity, and orness. In particular, we will show novel results about the orness that correct the intuition suggested in a previous preliminary study [12]. Moreover, we will provide a concrete algorithm to apply linguistic operators to fuzzy ontology learning, formalizing the intuitive ideas presented in [12].

H. L. Larsen et al. (Eds.): FQAS 2023, LNAI 14113, pp. 50–62, 2023.
https://doi.org/10.1007/978-3-031-42935-4_5

The remainder of this paper is structured as follows. Section 2 provides some background on aggregation operators, and Sect. 3 recalls the definition of CONV–LRF. Next, Sect. 4 studies some properties from a theoretical point of view, while Sect. 5 studies the orness empirically. Finally, Sect. 6 discusses a use case and Sect. 7 sets up some conclusions and ideas for future work.

2 Background

Aggregation operators (AO) are mathematical operations that are employed to combine different pieces of information. Given a domain $\mathbb{D}$, an AO is a mapping $@ : \mathbb{D}^K \to \mathbb{D}$, aggregating K values $x_1, \dots, x_K$ into a single one. Some typical examples are the average, the weighted mean, the maximum, or the minimum. According to the previous definition, logical operators such as t-norms and t-conorms can be thought as AOs, but it is very common to restrict to AOs verifying the internality property, i.e.,

$$\min(x_1, \dots, x_K) \leq @(x_1, \dots, x_K) \leq \max(x_1, \dots, x_K) \ . \tag{1}$$

AOs often assume a vector of weights $W = [w_1, \dots, w_K]$ with $w_i \in [0, 1]$ and $\sum_{i=1}^{K} w_i = 1$.

AOs for Numerical Values. In the literature, the most common case happens when one wants to aggregate numerical values. Without loss of generalization, we will assume $\mathbb{D} = [0, 1]$. Besides the weighted mean, another typical example is the Ordered Weighted Averaging (OWA) operator [19], defined as **OWA**$([w_1, \dots, w_K], [x_1, \dots, x_K]) = \sum_{i=1}^{K} w_i x_{\sigma(i)}$, where $\sigma(i)$ is a permutation such that $x_{\sigma(1)} \geq x_{\sigma(2)} \geq \dots \geq x_{\sigma(K)}$, i.e., $x_{\sigma(i)}$ is the i-th largest of the values $x_1, \dots, x_K$ to be aggregated.

A measure of the optimism associated to a weight vector W is orness [19]:

$$orness([w_1, \dots, w_K]) = \frac{1}{K-1} \sum_{i=1}^{K} (K - i) w_i. \tag{2}$$

Clearly, $orness([w_1, \dots, w_K]) \in [0, 1]$. The orness of the minimum t-norm is 0, i.e., $orness([0, \dots, 0, 1]) = 0$, and the orness of the maximum t-conorm is 1, i.e., $orness([1, 0, \dots, 0]) = 1$. Therefore, this measure estimates if an AO is closer to a t-norm or closer to a t-conorm.

To determine the weights of OWA operators, two popular solutions are *quantifier*-based aggregation [20] and applying *recursive OWA* [17]. The idea of recursive OWA is starting from a desired value for the orness of the OWA operator and calculate the weights in two recursive ways, a *Left Recursive Form* (LRF) or a *Right Recursive Form* (RRF).

AOs for Linguistic Values. Now, we assume a set of linguistic labels $\mathcal{L} = \{l_1, \ldots, l_L\}$ such that $l_i < l_j$ if $i < j$, so the AOs aggregate fuzzy numbers $d_1, \ldots, d_K \in \mathcal{L}$ rather than numerical values. Recall that a *fuzzy number* is a fuzzy subset of the real line $F : \mathbb{R} \to [0, 1]$ which is normal and convex [8]. Given a value $d = l_i$, we will sometimes write $d - 1$ to denote l_{i-1}.

We will consider two operators, convex combination, and linguistic OWA, but there are more methods, such as the weighted mean (WMEAN) [7] or fuzzy OWA (FOWA) [4]. Again, we will assume a vector of weights W and a permutation σ over fuzzy membership functions or numerical values such that $d_{\sigma(1)} \geq d_{\sigma(2)} \geq \cdots \geq d_{\sigma(K)}$.

1. *Convex combination* [6]. It has a recursive definition. To make it explicit that it corresponds to a Right Recursive Form, we denote it CONV–RRF. Let us start with the base case where we want to aggregate $K = 2$ fuzzy values $d_i \in \mathcal{L}$. The CONV–RRF of a vector $[d_1, d_2]$ given a vector of weights $W = [w_1, w_2]$, is defined as

$$\mathbf{CONV}^{\mathrm{RRF}}([w_1, w_2], [d_1, d_2]) = l_c \tag{3}$$

where $d_{\sigma(1)} = l_j$, $d_{\sigma(2)} = l_i$, $c = i + round(w_{\sigma(1)} \cdot (j - i))$. Note that the permutation is applied both to the weights and to the values to be aggregated, so each w_i is associated to the value d_i. Now, if $K > 2$, then:

$$\mathbf{CONV}^{\mathrm{RRF}}([w_1, \ldots, w_K], [d_1 \ldots, d_K]) =$$
$$\mathbf{CONV}^{\mathrm{RRF}}\Big([w_{\pi(1)}, 1 - w_{\pi(1)}], \Big[d_{\pi(1)}, \mathbf{CONV}^{\mathrm{RRF}}([\beta_2, \ldots, \beta_k], [d_{\pi(2)}, \ldots, d_{\pi(K)}])\Big]\Big), \tag{4}$$

where $\beta_h = w_{\pi(h)} / \sum_{j=2}^{K} w_{\pi(j)}, h = 2, \ldots, K$.

2. *Linguistic OWA* [10]. It is a variation of CONV–RRF using a ordering step as in standard OWA. As with CONV–RRF, we will call it LOWA–RRF to make it explicit that it is a Right Recursive Form. It is defined as:

$$\mathbf{LOWA}^{\mathrm{RRF}}([w_1, \ldots, w_K], [d_1 \ldots, d_K]) = \mathbf{CONV}^{\mathrm{RRF}}([w_1, \ldots, w_K], [d_{\sigma(1)}, \ldots, d_{\sigma(K)}]). \tag{5}$$

Now, as in classical OWA, each weight w_i is not associated to a value d_i.

CONV–RRF and LOWA–RRF require an ordering between fuzzy linguistic labels. There are several sorting methods, but we use the following criterion [5]:

$$d_1 \geq d_2 \text{ iff } \mathtt{transform}(d_1) \geq \mathtt{transform}(d_2), \tag{6}$$

where $\mathtt{transform}(d)$ is a transformation function from a linguistic domain (represented by trapezoidal functions) to a numerical domain defined as:

$$\mathtt{transform}(\mathtt{trapezoidal}(q_1, q_2, q_3, q_4)) = \frac{8(q_3 + q_2)H + (q_4 + q_1)H + 8(H + q_3q_4 - q_1q_2)}{24\,H},$$
$$\tag{7}$$

where $H = q_4 + q_3 - q_2 - q_1$ and $q_1 = q_2 = q_3 = q_4$ is assumed not to hold.

3   Left Recursive Form of CONV and LOWA

Inspired by the rewriting of classical OWA in two recursive forms LRF and RRF, we may view the standard definition of CONV (Eqs. 3–4) as a right recursive form. From that, we can define a left recursive form (CONV–LRF).

Definition 1 [12]. *The* Left Recursive Form *of the convex combination (CONV–LRF) of* $K \geq 2$ *linguistic labels given a weighting vector* $[w_1, \ldots, w_K]$ *is defined as:*

– *if* $K = 2$, *then*

$$\mathbf{CONV^{LRF}}([w_1, \ldots, w_K], [d_1 \ldots, d_K]) = \mathbf{CONV^{RRF}}([w_1, \ldots, w_K], [d_1 \ldots, d_K]) \quad (8)$$

– *if* $K > 2$, *then:*

$$\mathbf{CONV^{LRF}}([w_1, \ldots, w_K], [d_1 \ldots, d_K]) =$$
$$\mathbf{CONV^{LRF}}\Big([1 - w_K, w_K], \big[\mathbf{CONV^{LRF}}([\beta_1, \ldots, \beta_{k-1}], [d_1, \ldots, d_{K-1}]), d_K\big]\Big), \quad (9)$$

where $\beta_h = w_h \,/\, \sum_{j=1}^{K-1} w_j, h \in \{1, \ldots, K-1\}$.

Example 1. 4 experts provide definitions [VeryHigh, High, Low, VeryLow] and there is a weighting vector [0.45, 0.05, 0.1, 0.4]. Let us firstly aggregate using CONV–RRF:
$\mathbf{CONV^{RRF}}([0.45, 0.05, 0.1, 0.4], [\mathsf{VeryHigh, High, Low, VeryLow}]) =$
$\mathbf{CONV^{RRF}}([0.45, 0.55], [\mathsf{VeryHigh},$
    $\mathbf{CONV^{RRF}}([0.09, 0.91], [\mathsf{High}, \mathbf{CONV^{RRF}}([0.2, 0.8], [\mathsf{Low, VeryLow}])]) =$
$\mathbf{CONV^{RRF}}([0.45, 0.55], [\mathsf{VeryHigh}, \mathbf{CONV^{RRF}}([0.09, 0.91], [\mathsf{High, VeryLow}])]) =$
$\mathbf{CONV^{RRF}}([0.45, 0.55], [\mathsf{VeryHigh, VeryLow}]) = \mathsf{Low}$
    Now, let us compute CONV–LRF, obtaining a different result:
$\mathbf{CONV^{LRF}}([0.45, 0.05, 0.1, 0.4], [\mathsf{VeryHigh, High, Low, VeryLow}]) =$
$\mathbf{CONV^{LRF}}([0.6, 0.4], [\mathbf{CONV^{LRF}}([0.83, 0.17],$
    $[\mathbf{CONV^{LRF}}([0.9, 0.1], [\mathsf{VeryHigh, High}]), \mathsf{Low}]), \mathsf{VeryLow}]) =$
$\mathbf{CONV^{LRF}}([0.6, 0.4], [\mathbf{CONV^{LRF}}([0.83, 0.17], [\mathsf{VeryHigh, Low}]), \mathsf{VeryLow}]) =$
$\mathbf{CONV^{LRF}}([0.6, 0.4], [\mathsf{VeryHigh, VeryLow}]) = \mathsf{High}$ □

CONV–LRF can also be used to define a new version of the linguistic OWA, where weights are no longer associated to a specific value to be aggregated:

Definition 2 [12]. *The* Left Recursive Form *of the linguistic LOWA (LOWA–LRF) of* $K \geq 2$ *linguistic labels given a weighting vector* $[w_1, \ldots, w_K]$ *is defined as:*

$$\mathbf{LOWA^{LRF}}([w_1, \ldots, w_K], [d_1 \ldots, d_K]) = \mathbf{CONV^{LRF}}([w_1, \ldots, w_K], [d_{\sigma(1)}, \ldots, d_{\sigma(K)}]), \quad (10)$$

where σ *is a permutation such that* $d_{\sigma(1)} \geq d_{\sigma(2)} \geq \cdots \geq d_{\sigma(K)}$.

4 Some Properties of CONV–LRF and LOWA–LRF

In this section we will enumerate some properties of CONV–LRF. They also apply to LOWA–LRF, as the proofs do not depend on the particular values of the weights and LOWA–LRF is just CONV–LRF with a reordering of the weights.

- It was already known that CONV–LRF and LOWA–LRF do not care about the concrete definitions of the aggregated values (only the relative ordering matters) [12] and that they are not associative [12, Example 3].
- CONV–LRF and LOWA–LRF are not commutative, as Example 2 shows.
- CONV–LRF and LOWA–LRF are non-decreasing, as Proposition 1 shows.
- CONV–LRF and LOWA–LRF are smooth, as Proposition 2 shows.
- CONV–LRF and LOWA–LRF verify internality, as Proposition 3 shows.

Example 2. Assume that 3 experts provide definitions $[l_1, l_1, l_4]$ and we aggregate the values using CONV–LRF and a weighting vector $[0.1, 0.1, 0.8]$:

$\mathbf{CONV^{LRF}}([0.1, 0.1, 0.8], [l_1, l_1, l_4]) =$
$\mathbf{CONV^{LRF}}([0.2, 0.8], [l_4, \mathbf{CONV^{LRF}}([0.5, 0.5], [l_1, l_1])]) =$
$\mathbf{CONV^{LRF}}([0.2, 0.8], [l_1, l_4]) = l_3$

Now, let us swap the positions of the first and the third experts, i.e., let us aggregate $[l_4, l_1, l_1]$ given a weighting vector $[0.8, 0.1, 0.1]$. As we will see, the result is different:

$\mathbf{CONV^{LRF}}([0.8, 0.1, 0.1], [l_4, l_1, l_1]) =$
$\mathbf{CONV^{LRF}}([0.9, 0.1], [l_1, \mathbf{CONV^{LRF}}([0.89, 0.11], [l_4, l_1])]) =$
$\mathbf{CONV^{LRF}}([0.9, 0.1], [l_4, l_1]) = l_4$ □

Proposition 1. *CONV–LRF is non-decreasing.*

Proof. We use a proof by induction. We will firstly prove the case base, $\mathbf{CONV^{LRF}}([w_1, w_2], [d_1, d_2])$. Using Eqs. 3 and 8, we have that

$$c = i + round(w_{\sigma(1)} \cdot (j - i)) \tag{11}$$

is an integer number. Without loss of generality, assume that $d_1 = l_j$ and $d_2 = l_i$. It is trivial that the aggregation $\mathbf{CONV^{LRF}}([w_1, w_2], [d_x, d_2])$, with $d_x > d_1 = l_j$, cannot be smaller than l_c. Indeed, if we replace j with a higher value in Eq. 3, the result cannot decrease. Now, let us see what happens with a higher value than i, and let us define $l_z = \mathbf{CONV^{LRF}}([w_1, w_2], [d_1, d_2 + 1])$. Now, we have: $z = (i + 1) + round(w_1 \cdot (j - (i + 1))) = (i + 1) + round(w_1 \cdot (j - i) - w_1))$. Compared to Eq. 11, the first addend of z is $i + 1$ rather than i (so z adds 1 to c) and z has an additional subtraction of $w_1 \leq 1$. Since z adds 1 and subtracts a value which is not greater than 1, z cannot be smaller than c.

The induction hypothesis is that $l_h = \mathbf{CONV^{LRF}}([\beta_1, \ldots, \beta_{K-1}], [d_1 \ldots, d_{K-1}])$ is non-decreasing. Let us define $l_c = \mathbf{CONV^{LRF}}([w_1, \ldots, w_K], [d_1 \ldots, d_K]) = \mathbf{CONV^{LRF}}([1 - w_K, w_K], [l_h, d_K])$ and let us prove the induction step.

If we replace any of the values $d_1, \ldots, d_{K-1}$ with a higher value, by induction hypothesis, the result of the aggregation denoted $l_x \geq l_h$. Therefore, using a similar prove as in the case base, $\mathbf{CONV^{LRF}}([1 - w_K, w_K], [l_x, d_K])$ cannot be smaller than $\mathbf{CONV^{LRF}}([1 - w_K, w_K], [l_h, d_K])$, so the aggregation of K values is non-decreasing.

If we instead replace d_K with a higher value d_x, using the same proof of the case base, it is immediate to show that $\mathbf{CONV^{LRF}}([1 - w_K, w_K], [l_h, d_x])$ cannot be smaller than $\mathbf{CONV^{LRF}}([1 - w_K, w_K], [l_h, d_x])$, so the aggregation is non-decreasing. $\qquad\square$

Definition 3. *An increasing linguistic AO of arity K is smooth if the following K conditions are satisfied:*

S1 $|c - z| \leq 1$, *where* $@(d_1, d_2, \ldots, d_K) = l_c$ *and* $@(d_1 - 1, d_2, \ldots, d_K) = l_z$,
S2 $|c - z| \leq 1$, *where* $@(d_1, d_2, \ldots, d_K) = l_c$ *and* $@(d_1, d_2 - 1, \ldots, d_K) = l_z$,

...

SK $|c - z| \leq 1$, *where* $@(d_1, d_2, \ldots, d_K) = l_c$ *and* $@(d_1, d_2, \ldots, d_K - 1) = l_z$,

Definition 3 is a generalization of the condition for binary operators in [14], originally proposed in [9]. Smoothness is an important property because it is related to divisibility and can be seen as a discrete counterpart of continuity [14].

Proposition 2. *CONV–LRF is smooth.*

Proof. We use a proof by induction:

(i) we prove Property S2 for $\mathbf{CONV^{LRF}}([w_1, w_2], [d_1, d_2])$,
(ii) we prove Property S1 for $\mathbf{CONV^{LRF}}([w_1, w_2], [d_1, d_2])$, and
(iii) we use the induction step to prove it for $\mathbf{CONV^{LRF}}([w_1, \ldots, w_K], [d_1 \ldots, d_K])$.

(i) c, defined as in Eq. 11, is an integer number, so

$$c \in \left(i + w_{\sigma(1)}(j - i) - 0.5, \ i + w_{\sigma(1)}(j - i) + 0.5 \right]$$

and this interval includes exactly one integer number. Therefore, the integer number

$$c - 2 \in \left(i + w_{\sigma(1)}(j - i) - 2.5, \ i + w_{\sigma(1)}(j - i) - 1.5 \right]. \tag{12}$$

Similarly, $z = i + round(w_{\sigma(1)} \cdot (j - 1 - i))$ with

$$z \in \left(i + w_{\sigma(1)}(j - 1 - i) - 0.5, \ i + w_{\sigma(1)}(j - 1 - i) + 0.5 \right].$$

If the weight $w_{\sigma(1)} = 0$, then $c = z = i$, so both aggregations have the same value and their difference is 0, so S2 holds. If the weight $w_{\sigma(1)} = 1$, then $c = j$ and $z = j - 1$, so the difference is $j - (j - 1) = 1$, and S2 holds. Thus, it only remains to consider the case $w_{\sigma(1)} \in (0, 1)$, and we are going to show that $z > c - 2$. It suffices to show that the smallest possible value of z is greater than the highest possible value of $c-2$. The smallest possible value of z, $i+w_{\sigma(1)}(j-1-i)-0.5$, can be rewritten as $i+w_{\sigma(1)}(j-i)-w_{\sigma(1)}-0.5$ and, using the fact that $w_{\sigma(1)}<1$,

$$i+w_{\sigma(1)}(j-i)-w_{\sigma(1)}-0.5 >$$
$$i+w_{\sigma(1)}(j-i)-1-0.5 =$$
$$i+w_{\sigma(1)}(j-i)-1.5$$

which is the highest possible value of $c-2$. Because $\mathbf{CONV}^{\mathbf{LRF}}$ is non-decreasing according to Proposition 1, $z \not> c$. $z > c-2$ and $z \leq c$ imply $z \in [c-1, c]$, so the difference $c-z \leq 1$ and S2 holds.

(ii) Eq. 12 holds as in case *(i)*, but now $z = i-1+round(w_{\sigma(1)} \cdot (j-i+1))$ so

$$z \in \left(i+w_{\sigma(1)}(j-i+1)-1.5, \ i+w_{\sigma(1)}(j-i+1)-0.5\right].$$

If the weight $w_{\sigma(1)} = 0$, then $c = i$ and $z = i-1$, so the difference $c-z = i-(i-1) = 1 \leq 1$. If the weight $w_{\sigma(1)} = 1$, then $c = j$ and $z = i-1+j-i+1 = j$, so the difference $c-z = 0$. In the remaining case $w_{\sigma(1)} \in (0,1)$, we prove $z > c-2$ by showing that the smallest possible value of z is greater than the highest possible value of $c-2$:

$$i+w_{\sigma(1)}(j-i+1)-1.5 =$$
$$i+w_{\sigma(1)}(j-i)+w_{\sigma(1)}-1.5 >$$
$$i+w_{\sigma(1)}(j-i)-1.5.$$

As in case *(i)*, it turns out that $c-z \leq 1$ and S1 holds.

(iii) Now, let us assume that S1, S2, $\ldots$, and SK-1 hold for the aggregation of $K-1$ elements, i.e., for $\mathbf{CONV}^{\mathbf{LRF}}([\beta_1, \ldots, \beta_{K-1}], [d_1 \ldots, d_{K-1}])$. We will show that S1, S2, $\ldots$, SK hold for the aggregation of K elements.

To show that S1 holds, we consider $l_c = \mathbf{CONV}^{\mathbf{LRF}}([w_1, \ldots, w_K], [d_1 \ldots, d_K]) = \mathbf{CONV}^{\mathbf{LRF}}\left([1-w_K, w_K], [l_a, l_x]\right)$ and $l_z = \mathbf{CONV}^{\mathbf{LRF}}([w_1, \ldots, w_K], [d_1-1 \ldots, d_K]) = \mathbf{CONV}^{\mathbf{LRF}}\left([1-w_K, w_K], [l_b, l_x]\right)$. By induction hypothesis, $|a-b| \leq 1$, and by Proposition 1, $b \geq a-1$. Now, $c-2 \in \left(a+w_K(x-a)-2.5, \ a+w_K(x-a)-1.5\right]$, and $z \in \left(b+w_K(x-b)-0.5, \ a+w_K(x-b)+0.5\right]$. The smallest possible value of z,

$$b+w_K(x-b)-0.5 =$$
$$b+w_K x-w_K b-0.5 \geq$$
$$(a-1)+w_K x-w_K(a-1)-0.5 =$$
$$a+w_K(x-a)+w_K-1.5 \geq$$
$$a+w_K(x-a)-1.5,$$

which is the highest possible value of $c-2$. Therefore, $c-z \leq 1$ and S1 holds. Properties S2, $\ldots$, SK-1 can be proven similarly.

To show that property SK holds, we consider $l_c = \textbf{CONV}^{\textbf{LRF}}([w_1, \ldots, w_K],$ $[d_1 \ldots, d_K]) = \textbf{CONV}^{\textbf{LRF}}\Big([1 - w_K, w_K], [l_z, d_K]\Big)$ and $l_z = \textbf{CONV}^{\textbf{LRF}}$ $([w_1, \ldots, w_K], [d_1 \ldots, d_K - 1]) = \textbf{CONV}^{\textbf{LRF}}\Big([1 - w_K, w_K], [l_z, d_K - 1]\Big)$, where $l_\beta = \textbf{CONV}^{\textbf{LRF}}([\beta_1, \ldots, \beta_{k-1}], [d_1, \ldots, d_{K-1}])$, but we have again the case base, so, as proved in case *(i)*, $c - z \leq 1$ holds. □

Proposition 3. *CONV–LRF verifies internality.*

Proof. We use a proof by induction. The case base is based on the following property, proved in [6] for CONV–RRF: $c = i + round(w_{\sigma(1)} \cdot (j - i)) \in [i, j]$. Because CONV–LRF has the same case base, it also applies to it. Therefore, $l_i = \min\{d_1, d_2\} \leq \textbf{CONV}^{\textbf{LRF}}([w_1, w_2], [d_1, d_2]) \leq l_j = \max\{d_1, d_2\}$.

Now, the induction hypothesis is that $l_h = \textbf{CONV}^{\textbf{LRF}}([\beta_1, \ldots, \beta_{K-1}], [d_1 \ldots, d_{K-1}])$ verifies internality. $l_c = \textbf{CONV}^{\textbf{LRF}}([w_1, \ldots, w_K],$ $[d_1 \ldots, d_K]) = \textbf{CONV}^{\textbf{LRF}}\Big([1 - w_K, w_K], \Big[\textbf{CONV}^{\textbf{LRF}}([\beta_1, \ldots, \beta_{k-1}],$ $[d_1, \ldots, d_{K-1}]), d_K\Big]\Big)$. By induction hypothesis, this is equivalent to $\textbf{CONV}^{\textbf{LRF}}$ $\Big([1 - w_K, w_K], [l_h, d_K]\Big)$, where $l_h \in [\min\{d_1, \ldots, d_{K-1}\}, \max\{d_1, \ldots, d_{K-1}\}]$. Since we have an aggregation of two values, using the same proof of the case base, it is clear that $l_c \in [\min\{d_1, \ldots, d_{K-1}, d_K\}, \max\{d_1, \ldots, d_{K-1}, d_K\}]$, so $\textbf{CONV}^{\textbf{LRF}}([w_1, \ldots, w_K]$ verifies internality. □

5   Evaluation of the Orness

In this section we describe the evaluation of the aggregation operator CONV–LRF, comparing it with CONV–RRF. Our objective is to understand which operator returns a higher value in most cases, i.e., which operator has a higher orness.

Because these operators can be used to define LOWA–RRF and LOWA–LRF, our findings will affect these operators as well. However, because the difference between CONV and LOWA are whether weights are assigned to a specific expert or not, an evaluation of the LOWA operators does not seem necessary.

Experiment 1. We computed the results of the aggregation of four values (i.e., the opinions of four experts) with different vectors of weights using both CONV–LRF and CONV–RRF. Specifically, we aggregated the vector $[l_4, l_3, l_2, l_1]$ with each possible combination of degrees $w_i = k \cdot 0.01, \sum_{i=1}^{4} w_i = 1, k \in \{1, 2, \ldots, 100\}, i \in \{1, 2, 3, 4\}$.

Out of the 156849 possibilities, CONV–LRF and CONV–RRF give the same value in 114259 cases (72.85%). In 39538 cases (25.2%), CONV–LRF returns a higher value, whereas in 3052 cases (1.95%) CONV–RRF returns a higher value. Therefore, CONV–LRF seems to have a slightly higher orness than CONV–RRF. When the weights associated to the higher value or to the smaller value were greater than 0.83, both approaches coincided. This was also the case when the other weights were greater than 0.74.

Experiment 2. This experiment is similar but considering a different ordering of the labels to be aggregated, i.e., $[l_1, l_2, l_3, l_4]$. Now, out of the 156849 possibilities, CONV–LRF and CONV–RRF give the same value in 114210 cases (72.82%). In 39997 cases (25.50%), CONV–RRF returns a higher value, whereas in 2642 cases (1.68%) CONV–LRF returns a higher value. Therefore, it is CONV–RRF the one with a slightly higher orness. Analyzing the results of the first two experiments, when the labels are presented in a decreasing order, CONV–LRF returns higher values in general, but when the labels are presented in an increasing order, CONV–RRF returns higher values in general.

Experiment 3. This experiment generalizes Experiments 1 and 2 by considering all possible combinations of values to be aggregated, and different numbers of experts (from 2 to 5, always with non-zero weights). The number of total labels was fixed to 5 (l_1 to l_5), which is a very common option in practice.

Table 1 shows the results of the evaluation:

– the number of experts ("# Experts"),
– total number of cases ("# Cases"),
– percentage of cases where CONV–LRF gives a higher value ("% CONV–LRF"),
– percentage of cases where CONV–RRF gives a higher value ("% CONV–RRF"),
– percentage of cases where both operators coincide ("% Coincidence").

Table 1. Results of the comparison between CONV–LRF and CONV–RRF.

# Experts	# Cases	% CONV–LRF	% CONV–RRF	% Coincidence
2	2500	0	0	100
3	631250	6.62	6.67	86.71
4	107312500	10.74	10.83	78.43
5	13816484375	13.45	13.52	73.03

It is clear that for 2 experts both operators always coincide. Indeed, it is the base case and both operators have the same definition. With a higher number of experts, both operators do not always coincide, and the percentage of coincidences is inversely proportional to the number of experts. It is also interesting to remark that both operators return a higher value in more or less the same number of cases, regardless of the number of experts.

Figure 1 illustrates the difference between the two operators for two specific cases involving three experts, namely the aggregation of the vectors $[l_1, l_1, l_5]$ and $[l_5, l_1, l_1]$ for each combination of weights, with w_1 in the x-axis and w_2 in the y-axis. w_3 is not represented, as $w_3 = 1 - w_1 - w_2$. Red color means that for those weights CONV–LRF returns a higher value, while blue color means that

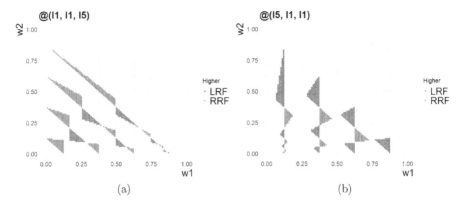

Fig. 1. Aggregation of the definitions of 3 experts: (a) case $[l_1, l_1, l_5]$ and; (b) case $[l_5, l_1, l_1]$.

CONV–RRF returns a higher value. Ties (majority of the cases) correspond to the part of the grid in white background color.

To conclude this section, note that [12] only includes Experiment 1, which suggests that CONV–LRF has a higher orness than CONV–RRF, but Experiment 3 shows that the ornesses are similar, with the orness of CONV–RRF being actually slightly higher.

6   Use Case: Fuzzy Ontology Building

Fuzzy ontologies are fundamental to represent imprecise knowledge, reason with it, and query it in many applications [15]. Therefore, fuzzy ontology learning is a fundamental problem. On the one hand, it is possible is to learn the fuzzy membership functions from numerical examples, as in the Datil [11] or the FuzzyDL-Learner [3,13] systems. On the other hand, *Fudge* (FUzzy Datatypes from a Group of Experts) is a software tool which can be used to learn fuzzy datatypes (described using fuzzy sets) by means of a linguistic aggregation of the definitions given by a group of experts [12]. Fudge has two versions for desktop computers and for Android mobile devices, uses Fuzzy OWL 2 language [2], supports 6 aggregation methods[1] and is available online[2].

Algorithm 1 computes the aggregation of fuzzy datatypes located in several fuzzy ontologies, each of them developed by a different expert. The algorithm has two inputs: a group of files (fuzzy ontologies) *SO* and an array of weights.

Firstly, we build an output fuzzy ontology as a union of the input fuzzy ontologies excluding the annotation assertion axioms that provide the individual definitions of the fuzzy datatypes (Lines 2–9). Typically, all input fuzzy ontologies will share a common schema and only the definitions of the fuzzy

---

[1] CONV–LRF, CONV–RRF, CONV–RRF, LOWA–RRF, WMEAN, and FOWA.
[2] http://webdiis.unizar.es/~ihvdis/Fudge.html.

Algorithm 1. Learning fuzzy datatypes using aggregation of definitions.

Input: A set of fuzzy ontologies SO
Input: An array of weights $\mathbf{W}$
Output: A fuzzy ontology $\mathcal{O}$

1: // Add background axioms
2: $\mathcal{O} \leftarrow \emptyset$
3: **for all** $o \in SO$ **do**
4:   **for all** axiom $a \in o$ **do**
5:     **if** a is not a fuzzy datatype definition **then**
6:       $\mathcal{O} \leftarrow \mathcal{O} \cup a$
7:     **end if**
8:   **end for**
9: **end for**
   // Retrieve fuzzy datatypes
10: $listDefs \leftarrow$ new associative array
11: **for all** $o \in SO$ **do**
12:   **for all** fuzzy datatype $fd \in o$ **do**
13:     $trapFD \leftarrow$ `trapezoidal`(fd)
14:     **if** $listDefs[fd] = \emptyset$ **then**
15:       $listDefs[fd] \leftarrow trapFD$
16:     **else**
17:       $listDefs[fd] \leftarrow listDefs[fd] \cup trapFD$
18:     **end if**
19:   **end for**
20: **end for**
   // Build consensual fuzzy datatypes
21: **for all** key fd of $listDefs$ **do**
22:   $newFD \leftarrow$ `aggregate`$(listDefs[fd], \mathbf{W})$
23:   $\mathcal{O} \leftarrow \mathcal{O} \cup newFD$
24: **end for**
25: **return** $\mathcal{O}$

---

datatypes will be different. If this is the case, the for loop in Line 2 could be restricted to just one of the input fuzzy ontologies.

Secondly, we create an associative array where the keys are fuzzy datatype names and the values are lists of the definitions given by the experts (Line 10). Next, each fuzzy datatype definition in each fuzzy ontology is represented using a trapezoidal datatype and then added to the associative array (Lines 11–20). In practice, Fudge assumes that all the definitions are given using Fuzzy OWL 2 datatypes, including trapezoidal functions but also but triangular, right-shoulder, and left-shoulder functions, which can be represented as trapezoidal fuzzy functions (provided that right-shoulder and left-shoulder functions are defined over a fixed range $[k_1, k_2]$).

Thirdly, for each fuzzy datatype, a consensual definition is built using some aggregation operator and the result is added to the output fuzzy ontology (Lines 21–24), and finally the algorithm returns the output fuzzy ontology.

Note that `aggregate` function (Line 22) can be implemented using diverse aggregation strategies: any linguistic aggregation operator aggregating trapezoidal membership functions given a vector of weights can be used.

One of the advantages of using CONV–RRF and CONV–LRF operators in such scenarios is that, contrary to other operators such as the WMEAN of FOWA, the aggregated output always correspond to one of the input values, i.e., to the definition given by one of the experts.

7   Conclusions and Future Work

In this paper we have studied a linguistic aggregation operator, the Left Recursive Form of the convex combination (CONV–LRF), which can be used to define a Left Recursive Form of the Linguistic OWA (LOWA–LRF). In particular, we have studied some properties (commutativity, smoothness, internality, and monotonicity) from a theoretical point of view, and orness from a practical point of view. Contrary to what a previous study suggested, an empirical analysis shows that the percentage of coincidences between both operators is inversely proportional to the number of experts, and that both operators have a similar orness degree. Furthermore, we have shown a use case in fuzzy ontology learning, formalizing with an algorithm the technique implemented in the Fudge tool.

We think that the properties of this operator might be useful in some real-world applications, e.g., to aggregate the partial satisfaction degrees of a flexible query in such a way that the result is always one of the aggregated values.

In future work, we would like to apply CONV–LRF and LOWA–LRF to some real-world applications and compare them with other linguistic aggregation operators.

Acknowledgments. I. Huitzil was supported by the Italian MUR under the PRIN project PINPOINT Prot. 2020FNEB27, CUP H45E21000210001. F. Bobillo was supported by the I+D+i project PID2020-113903RB-I00, funded by MCIN/AEI/10.13039/501100011033, and by DGA/FEDER. We are also grateful to Carlos Bobed and Jordi Bernad for their help to improve data visualization.

References

1. Beliakov, G., Bustince, H., Calvo, T.: A Practical Guide to Averaging Functions. Studies in Fuzziness and Soft Computing, vol. 329. Springer, Cham (2016). https://doi.org/10.1007/978-3-319-24753-3
2. Bobillo, F., Straccia, U.: Fuzzy ontology representation using OWL 2. Int. J. Approx. Reason. **52**(7), 1073–1094 (2011)
3. Cardillo, F.A., Straccia, U.: Fuzzy OWL-boost: learning fuzzy concept inclusions via real-valued boosting. Fuzzy Sets Syst. (2021)
4. Chen, S.J., Chen, S.M.: A new method for handling multicriteria fuzzy decision-making problems using FN-IOWA operators. Cybern. Syst. **34**(2), 109–137 (2003)
5. Delgado, M., Herrera, F., Herrera-Viedma, E., Martínez, L.: Combining numerical and linguistic information in group decision making. J. Inform. Sci. **107**, 177–194 (1998)

6. Delgado, M., Verdegay, J.L., Vila, M.A.: On aggregation operations of linguistic labels. Int. J. Intell. Syst. **8**(3), 351–370 (1993)
7. Dong, W.M., Wong, F.S.: Fuzzy weighted averages and implementation of the extension principle. Fuzzy Sets Syst. **21**(2), 183–199 (1987)
8. Dubois, D., Prade, H.: Operations on fuzzy numbers. Int. J. Syst. Sci. **9**, 613–626 (1978)
9. Godo, L., Sierra, C.: A new approach to connective generation in the framework of expert systems using fuzzy logic. In: Proceedings of the 18th International Symposium on Multiple-Valued Logic (ISMVL 1988), pp. 157–162 (1988)
10. Herrera, F., Herrera-Viedma, E., Verdegay, J.L.: Direct approach processes in group decision making using linguistic OWA operators. Fuzzy Sets Syst. **79**(2), 175–190 (1996)
11. Huitzil, I., Bobillo, F.: Fuzzy ontology datatype learning using Datil. Expert Syst. Appl. **228**, 120299 (2023)
12. Huitzil, I., Bobillo, F., Gómez-Romero, J., Straccia, U.: Fudge: fuzzy ontology building with consensuated fuzzy datatypes. Fuzzy Sets Syst. **401**, 91–112 (2020)
13. Lisi, F.A., Straccia, U.: A logic-based computational method for the automated induction of fuzzy ontology axioms. Fund. Inform. **124**(4), 503–519 (2013)
14. Mayor, G., Torrens, J.: Triangular norms in discrete settings. In: Klement, E., Messiar, R. (eds.) Logical, Algebraic, Analytic, and Probabilistic Aspects of Triangular Norms, pp. 189–230. Elsevier, Amsterdam (2005)
15. Straccia, U.: Foundations of Fuzzy Logic and Semantic Web Languages. CRC Studies in Informatics Series. Chapman & Hall, London (2013)
16. Torra, V., Narukawa, Y.: Modeling Decisions - Information Fusion and Aggregation Operators. Springer, Cham (2007). https://doi.org/10.1007/978-3-540-68791-7
17. Troiano, L., Yager, R.R.: Recursive and iterative OWA operators. Int. J. Uncertain. Fuzziness Knowl.-Based Syst. **13**(6), 579–600 (2005)
18. Xu, Z.: Linguistic aggregation operators: an overview. In: Bustince, H., Herrera, F., Montero, J. (eds.) Fuzzy Sets and Their Extensions: Representation, Aggregation and Models. Studies in Fuzziness and Soft Computing, vol. 220, pp. 163–181. Springer, Cham (2008). https://doi.org/10.1007/978-3-540-73723-0_9
19. Yager, R.R.: On ordered weighted averaging aggregation operators in multicriteria decision making. IEEE Trans. Syst. Man Cybern. **18**(1), 183–190 (1988)
20. Yager, R.R.: Quantifier guided aggregation using OWA operators. Int. J. Intell. Syst. **11**(1), 49–73 (1996)

Knowledge Graph Enabled Open-Domain Conversational Question Answering

Joel Oduro-Afriyie$^{(\boxtimes)}$ and Hasan Jamil

Department of Computer Science, University of Idaho, Moscow, ID 83844, USA
odur8117@vandals.uidaho.edu, jamil@uidaho.edu

Abstract. With the advent of natural language enabled applications, there has been a growing appetite for conversational question answering systems. This demand is being largely satisfied with the help of such powerful language models as Open AI's GPT models, Google's BERT, and BigScience's BLOOM. However, the astounding amount of training data and computing resources required to create such models is a huge challenge. Furthermore, for such systems, catering to multiple application domains typically requires the acquisition of even more training data. We discuss an alternative approach to the problem of open-domain conversational question answering by utilizing knowledge graphs to capture relevant information from a body of text in any domain. We achieve this by allowing the relations of the knowledge graphs to be drawn directly from the body of text being processed, rather than from a fixed ontology. By connecting this process with SPARQL queries generated from natural language questions, we demonstrate the foundations of an open-domain question answering system that requires no training and can switch domains flexibly and seamlessly.

Keywords: Natural Language Processing · Question Answering System · Knowledge Representation · Knowledge Graphs

1 Introduction

In recent years there has been a proliferation of natural language enabled applications, driven largely by the evolution of language models. With the inception of the transformer architecture [17] came such powerful language models as BERT [5], GPT-3 [2], BLOOM [13] and, very recently, GPT-4[1]. These models are powering many research efforts into natural language (NL) question answering (QA) systems like [16] and [18]. With the growing importance of conversational QA systems, the need to develop systems that can function in any NL domain, and switch those domains quickly when necessary, is becoming more pronounced. In this regard machine learning (ML) based systems face a challenge – in order to process multiple domains, ML-based systems need to be trained on very large

---

[1] https://openai.com/research/gpt-4.

© Springer Nature Switzerland AG 2023
H. L. Larsen et al. (Eds.): FQAS 2023, LNAI 14113, pp. 63–76, 2023.
https://doi.org/10.1007/978-3-031-42935-4_6

amounts of data from each of the domains in question. Additionally, accommodating a new domain typically requires retraining with data from the new domain. The data and computing requirements involved in such processes are known to be very prohibitive, and in order to get better, they need to be fed with even more data and trained with even more computing resources. As a case in point, in a quest to be better than GPT-3, the BLOOM language model [13] comprises 176 billion parameters. It was trained on 1.5 terabytes of text data containing 341.6 billion language tokens, using 384 NVIDIA GPUs with 80GB of RAM each. And even with such a huge amount of computational power, training ran for almost four months. Then comes GPT-4 – although exact figures are currently unconfirmed, it is estimated that GPT-4 contains about 100 trillion parameters, and was trained on about 10,000 Nvidia GPUs. These models are undeniably great at what they do. However, the mind-bending data and computing requirements, along with other challenges such as truthfulness of generated responses [10,15], are motivation for exploring other methods.

To circumvent the huge data and computing requirements associated with ML-based methods, we explore in this paper an alternative approach to conversational question answering. We discuss a system, which we call *Converse*, that demonstrates the foundations of an open-domain conversational QA system utilizing knowledge graphs (KGs). Our basic process is three-fold, beginning with a text-to-KG component that processes NL text from any domain to create a KG. The second component processes a natural language question into a SPARQL query representation that can be applied to the generated KG to retrieve a SPARQL response. Finally, the third component generates a natural language representation of the retrieved SPARQL response, if any, and presents that to the user as an answer. The novelty of this approach lies in the KG generation stage, which chooses relations for the KG based on the domain of the NL text being processed, rather than relying on any standard ontology, thereby allowing the system to function on any NL domain with zero training. By concatenating the above three stages, we demonstrate that an open-domain conversational QA system is feasible without the overhead of training data requirements or huge computational resources, and without the need for any additional processing when switching domains.

2 Related Research

ML-based QA systems train a model to learn from text documents and answer queries, while KG-based QA systems rely on knowledge graphs to answer queries. While ML-based QA systems have been around for many years, research into KG-based QA systems is a relatively new and rapidly growing field. In recent years, Open Information Extraction (OpenIE) approaches have garnered attention as a means to construct KGs directly from text without the need for predefined ontologies [1]. These approaches aim to automatically discover relations present in text, aligning with our goal of deriving relations directly from input text.

Bio-SODA UX [14] is a natural language KG-based question answering system over scientific data. In [14], the authors describe a generic graph-based approach for translating user questions into a ranked list of SPARQL candidate queries, a method that allows them to avoid the need for training data. This bolsters our claim that the question answering system (QAS) task can be achieved without the need for training data. However, their system is domain-limited to the field of science.

Several research efforts are focused on mitigating the effects of missing information in a KG. This is the motivation for KG enhancement, which is important for mitigating the effects of an imperfect KG generation process. The authors of [20] discuss a method of relation prediction to "fill in the blanks" using attention-based graph embeddings. A similar motive drives the work of [21], which presents a graph-based NL QA system that extracts relevant answers from a graph in the presence of missing information. The authors leverage the idea of representing the query as a semantic graph and finding answers with a subgraph matching approach. CFO (Conditional Focused approach) [4] is another KG-based approach that uses a pruning approach to improve factoid question answering. The above efforts all rely on some form of machine learning that inherently limits them to the domain of the KGs they are trained on. They are thus encumbered with the problems of domain-limitation and associated training costs in the event of domain switching. Considering the importance of KG enhancement for mitigating missing information in a KG, we describe a rudimentary enhancement process in Sect. 3.1, using hypernyms, in an attempt to avoid such domain limitations.

One interesting graph-based QAS approach that describes an open-domain system is [8]. Their work discusses the idea of using graph-matching methods to implement a natural language QA system. However, their system is unable to process queries that require reasoning over the KG. It is also unable to generalize to find an answer that exists in the KG because of a lack of semantic awareness. For example, given an input such as *"Mary wore an orange dress"*, the system of [8] is unable to answer a query such as *"what color was Mary's dress"*

3   *Converse* Architecture

We organize the *Converse* architecture according to a three-pronged model. First, a **graph generation module** processes NL text into a knowledge graph. Secondly, an a **query processing module** translates an input NL query into a SPARQL query that will be applied on the KG generated from the first step. Finally, the output from the SPARQL query is processed by an **NL generation module** to generate an NL response.

3.1   Graph Generation Module

The basic task of the graph generation module is to generate triples from natural language (NL) text, forming a knowledge graph (KG). While existing applications such as FRED [6] and Neo4j are available to support this task, we opt for a custom triple generation process to avoid the limitations imposed by their predefined ontologies and relation sets. Importantly, our approach does not rely on a predefined ontology with a specific set of relations. Instead, it allows relations to be derived directly from the input text, making it applicable to texts from any domain. As a result, our system does not require any additional processing or transition time when working with new domains, a sharp contrast to ML-based systems. This flexibility ensures domain independence and generates a more economical number of triples, enabling more efficient processing of NL text from any domain.

Consider the following short story about two friends, Bob and Alice. While this example is brief, our system, *Converse*, can process texts of any size without limitation.

> *Bob and his friend Alice went hiking. She developed knee pain, and he wanted to cheer her up, so he bought a gift for her. It was a beautiful orange dress, but she could not wear it because of her knee pain. Bob loves Alice, so he cooked a meal for her after the hike. She drank orange juice after lunch, and returned home.*

To generate a KG from this text, *Converse* employs a three-step process: text parsing, triple extraction, and KG creation. First, the system breaks down the text into individual sentences and further parses each sentence into its syntactic structure using a constituent parse tree. This tree reveals the grammatical relationships between words and phrases, providing a basis for extracting entities and relations.

In the second step, *Converse* conducts a rule-based analysis of the parse tree to identify and extract entities (generally nouns and pronouns) and relations (verbs, conjunctions, prepositions, etc.). To represent syntactic elements such as determiners, adjectives, and adverbs, the system includes within its internal process a set of standard relations distinguished by being enclosed in colons. These relations provide more context and detail to the resulting KG.

Finally, from the extracted triples, *Converse* constructs the KG, linking entities through identified relations. The system represents the generated KG visually via a graphical web interface. For instance, Fig. 1 illustrates the visualization of the triples derived from the phrase *"It was a beautiful orange dress"*, forming a mini-KG. In Fig. 1, the relations *":det:"* and *":property:"* are examples of the colon-enclosed syntactic elements described in the previous paragraph. The relation *"was"* is an example of how *Converse* derives relations directly from the text, to enable domain-independence.

Using this custom triple generation process that relies directly on the text being processed, *Converse* constructs a KG in a more domain-independent and efficient manner, eliminating the need for retraining as new domains are introduced. This approach enables the seamless processing of natural language text across diverse subject areas, remaining adaptable to different applications and use cases. Furthermore, this flexibility ensures that *Converse* remains capable and effective in KG generation as new requirements and challenges arise in the rapidly evolving field of information extraction and knowledge representation.

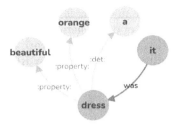

Fig. 1. Mini KG for the phrase *"It was a beautiful orange dress"* (Color figure online).

Graph Enhancements. To imbue *Converse* with the ability to answer questions whose answers are not explicitly stated in the text, we apply a number of enhancements, discussed below, to the basic generated KG.

Co-reference Resolution Coreference resolution, which attempts to connect pronouns in a text with the entities that they refer to, is usually implemented with the help of ML-based models due to the complexities involved. For the purposes of demonstrating our basic idea, we take a simpler approach by applying rule-based analyses to the syntax structure of our sentences. This involves examining the location of co-referenced entities, and the context in which they appear (e.g. number and gender), to make a best guess as to which entity is being referenced. This approach performs satisfactorily for simple sentences, and more complicated scenarios would require a more rigorous approach. Figure 2 depicts the result of this approach applied to our sample text above. It can be observed that the pronoun *"he"*, while correctly resolved to *bob*, is also incorrectly resolved to *alice*.

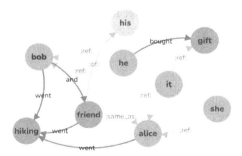

Fig. 2. *Converse* co-reference resolution.

Converse maintains a context stack that keeps track of the current entities involved in a conversation. The context stack also tracks pronouns and their references. This way, follow-up questions may be asked using pronouns without having to re-specify who or what is being referred to. The context stack is important to enable question answering in a conversational manner.

68   J. Oduro-Afriyie and H. Jamil

Hypernym Injection Hypernym injection is a process that we introduce to enhance the semantic awareness of our generated KGs. A hypernymn expresses a more general sense of another word (the hyponym). In our hypernym injection process, we attempt to describe the entities of our KG in terms of their hypernyms. Since a word or entity may have more than one hypernym, we attempt to find the hypernym that most closely represents the context in which the hyponym is used in our sentence.

Consider an entity ϵ used in a sentence sentence s_e. We implement hypernym injection according to Algorithm 1. Using this process, *Converse* is able to distinguish between the two different senses of the entity *"orange"* in our sample text, as shown in Fig. 3.

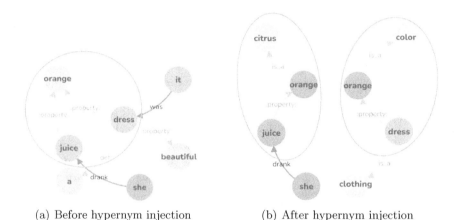

(a) Before hypernym injection   (b) After hypernym injection

Fig. 3. *Converse* hypernym injection. Before hypernym injection, the meaning of the entity *"orange"* is uncertain (Fig. 3a). After hypernym injection (Fig. 3b) the roles are clarified.

Graph Reasoning With the help of OWL reasoning, *Converse* is able to deduce information that is implied but not explicitly stated in the text. *Converse* currently supports six OWL properties (*Symmetric, Irreflexive, Reflexive, Transitive, Functional* and *Asymmetric*) that may be applied with the help of rules to selected relations. For example, if we pre-assign the *Symmetric* property to a *"love"* relation (although this is not always so in practice), then *Converse* generates the deduced triple *Alice-loves-Bob* from an existing triple *Bob-loves-Alice*. Additionally, we are able to define subclass relationships from which additional triples may be reasoned. For example, by specifying that *"gift"* is a type of *"present"*, the triple *he-bought-gift* triggers the generation of another triple *he-bought-present*.

Algorithm 1: Hypernym Identification Algorithm

Input: An entity ϵ and its context sentence s_e
Output: The most likely hypernym h for ϵ in s_e
Identify a set of hypernyms H for ϵ, with the help of WordNet[11]; **foreach**
$h \in H$ **do**

> Compile n random sentences $\{s_{hi}\}_{i=1}^{n}$ from the Web, in which h is used in an everyday sense;
> Compute and average the semantic similarity σ between s_e and each of the retrieved sentences s_{hi};

end
Take the set of sentences with the greatest average semantic similarity σ, and select its parent hypernym as h;
return h;

Semantic similarity is calculated, with the help of the NLP library spaCy, by taking the cosine similarity of the WordNet vectors after stopwords have been removed.

3.2   Query Processing Module

Our query processing module is implemented in two stages: a query-to-graph stage and a graph-to SPARQL-stage, described below.

Stage 1: Query Graph Generation. The KG generation process described in Sect. 3.1 leverages the general semantic structure of English sentences to extract entities and relations. However, questions exhibit distinct semantic characteristics, such as the presence of interrogative words (e.g., who, what, where, when, why, how) and inverted word order (e.g., is there, do you, can we), which render the KG generation process for sentences inapplicable to natural language (NL) queries. Consequently, we adopt a distinct methodology to process and generate query graphs from NL queries in *Converse*.

Pradel et al. [12] assert that everyday NL queries can be classified into a limited set of general categories. Based on this observation, we devise a series of pattern-based rules within *Converse* that dictate the construction of query triples according to the syntax patterns present in the query. For instance, a syntax pattern of *who-auxiliary-subject-verb* is mapped to a triple pattern of *subject-verb-who*. In *Converse*, query words such as *"who"*, *"what"*, and *"where"* are substituted with *"?"* within the final query graph. Zou et al. [21] propose a similar pattern-based approach for query creation.

We adopt this relatively straightforward technique for two primary reasons. First, NL queries in conversations are usually simple and unambiguous, as supported by research conducted by Brożek et al. [3] and Hirschman et al. [7]. Second, complex queries that could potentially arise in discourse are often segmented into a series of simpler queries within the context of a conversation, further contributing to the advantage of employing a pattern-based approach [3]. To accommodate queries with slightly increased complexity, *Converse* implements query decomposition, effectively handling a broader range of questions while maintaining its technical robustness and adaptability to various query types. This approach ensures a seamless NL query processing experience within the *Converse* system, making it proficient in generating query graphs across diverse conversational contexts and scenarios.

More complex queries may require decomposition in order to be processed successfully. To carry out query decomposition, the basic pattern-based process described above may be extended to accommodate slightly more complicated query patterns. We may wish to reduce a query such as *"Who sold the dress that Alice got?"* into a main query supported by a series of facts. In the query above, the supporting fact is that Alice got a dress, based on which the main query seeks the identity of the entity that sold the dress. Thus the above query may be decomposed into *"Alice got a dress"* (supporting fact) and *"Who sold the dress?"* (main query). By defining pattern rules as already described, we can map more complex syntax structures to sets of simpler syntax structures, from which the query graphs can be constructed. Figure 4a shows the query graph obtained from decomposing the above query.

Stage 2: SPARQL Query Construction. Once the query graph is obtained, we proceed to the construction of a corresponding SPARQL query, a crucial step that enables the retrieval of information from the knowledge graph. Our approach leverages the query decomposition process mentioned earlier, whereby the resulting query graph consists of a series of straightforward triples, simplifying the traversal and construction of a SPARQL query template.

To build the SPARQL query, we employ the following scheme: the unknown element, represented by a question mark (*?*), determines the contents of the *SELECT* clause, which specifies the variables to be extracted. Subsequently, the remaining elements of the query graph are iteratively visited following their directional relationships, systematically constructing the body of the SPARQL query. During this process, any relevant filter clauses are also incorporated into the query structure, ensuring that the results meet the desired conditions and constraints.

This efficient and systematic approach enables the conversion of various query graph structures into accurate and coherent SPARQL queries, facilitating the retrieval of pertinent information from the knowledge graph. As an example, Fig. 4b displays the SPARQL query generated by applying this process to the query graph depicted in Fig. 4a. This method enables a seamless transition from natural language queries to SPARQL queries.

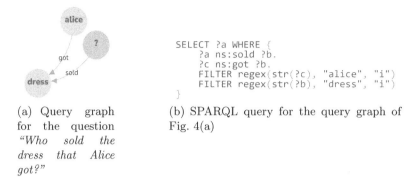

(a) Query graph for the question *"Who sold the dress that Alice got?"*

(b) SPARQL query for the query graph of Fig. 4(a)

Fig. 4. *Converse* query processing: (a) NL query to query graph, followed by (b) query graph to SPARQL.

3.3   Natural Language Generation (NLG) Module

The Natural Language Generation (NLG) module constitutes the third component of our system, which is responsible for transforming the results of the SPARQL query from the previous stage into a coherent natural language output that can be presented to the user as an answer. Given that the triples in our KG are generated from natural language sentences, we hypothesize that the SPARQL result (which is a triple), along with its surrounding triples, inherently represent natural language phrases. Consequently, we can arrange entities and associated relations in the answer triple according to English grammar rules to generate a comprehensible natural language output.

To implement this approach, we draw inspiration from programming language compilers, which parse a sequence of tokens to determine if it conforms with a specified syntax. Our system essentially reverses this process: we provide a random sequence of tokens and employ the parser to generate a syntactically correct sequence. The random input sequence is derived by collecting the entities and relations present in the answer triple and those directly connected to it. Since this may include irrelevant relations and entities, we selectively include neighboring entities that match the relations in the query graph. Additionally, we incorporate nodes connected by the helper relations discussed in Sect. 3.1.

For example, consider the query *"Who went hiking?"* based on our sample paragraph. The SPARQL result returned from our KG contains three entities: *bob, alice, friend*. Figure 5b illustrates the answer graph along with its surrounding entities. These surrounding entities are those connected to the main answer graph (*bob, friend, alice*) by the relation *went* from the query graph (Fig. 5a), as well as helper relations (identified by their surrounding colons).

From the graph in Fig. 5, we extract the entities and relations (excluding helper relations) to form the input for the parser-based NLG module. Provided with the input *"bob hiking friend his and went alice"*, the parser reorganizes the tokens according to the defined syntax rules, generating the output *"bob and his friend (alice) went hiking"*. The inclusion of parentheses around *"alice"*

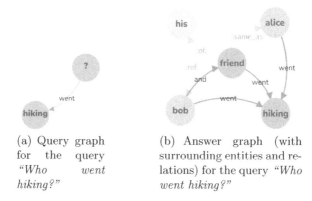

(a) Query graph for the query *"Who went hiking?"*

(b) Answer graph (with surrounding entities and relations) for the query *"Who went hiking?"*

Fig. 5. *Converse* answer graph for NL generation.

represents a cosmetic adjustment implemented in the NLG module to cater for cases involving the *:same_as:* helper relation.

4   Evaluation

In Table 1 we evaluate *Converse*'s ability to answer conversational-style questions based on our sample paragraph from Sect. 1, with and without KG enhancements.

We observe from Table 1 that the ability of the system to find answers is improved when the KG is enhanced. Questions regarding implied information (such as whether Alice or Bob took a walk, or the color of the dress) are unanswerable using the unenhanced KG. The addition of semantic information improves the system's ability to find answers. We also observe that the use of coreference resolution enables the system to answer more intelligently, as shown by the answers to the questions *"Who bought a gift?"* and *"What was it?"*. We do observe an effect of wrong coreference resolution, leading the system to return both Bob and Alice as answers for the buyer of the gift. Improved coreference resolution is an important component of future work. We also note how the KG enhanced with triples from the reasoning process allows the system to answer questions whose answers are not explicitly stated in the text, but are implied by the general relationships described by the OWL rules.

To evaluate how closely the generated answers match the expected answers, we computed the semantic similarity of each generated answer with the expected answer. We excluded yes/no answers since they only specify the extremes of presence or absence of information, and are unable to quantify anything in-between. Semantic similarity was calculated by excluding stopwords and taking the cosine similarity of the WordNet [11] vectors of the remaining terms. With this process we find that, in Table 1, answers from the unenhanced graph were on average 46% semantically similar to the expected answers, compared to an

Table 1. KG Enhancement Test.

Question	Unenhanced KG	Enhanced KG	Enhancement at Play	Expected Answer
Who went hiking?	Bob and his friend (Alice) went hiking	Bob and his friend (Alice) went hiking	–	Bob and Alice
Did Alice go on a walk?	No	Yes	Hypernym Injection	Yes
Who bought a gift?	He bought a gift	Bob and Alice* bought a gift	Co-reference Resolution	Bob bought a gift
Did he buy a present?	No	Yes	Co-reference Resolution	Yes
Did he buy clothing?	No	Yes	Hypernym Injection, Co-reference Resolution	Yes
What color was the gift?	(no answer)	Orange	Hypernym Injection, Co-reference Resolution	Orange
What was it?	(no answer)	It was a dress	Co-reference Resolution	A dress
Does Bob love Alice?	Yes	Yes	–	Yes
Does Alice love Bob?	No	Yes	Reasoning	Yes

*This error is propagated from the co-reference mis-assignment of *he* to *Alice*, depicted in Fig. 2

average of 98% for answers from the enhanced graph. Hence, KG enhancements are an important component of our approach.

5   Future Research

The current graph generation module, which relies on rule-based syntax analysis, remains limited in its ability to encapsulate information from long and convoluted text structures. This also impacts the accuracy of co-reference resolution. In future work we would like to explore the possibility of incorporating ML-based triple extraction methods [9,19]. To maintain domain independence and avoid the need to retrain when switching domains, any incorporation of ML-based methods will have to be in domain-insensitive areas such as general rules of natural language syntax.

In order to move the system from proof-of-concept, the ability to generalize in query processing is an important feature that we intend to pursue by means of semantic querying. Future work will explore subgraph matching algorithms, together with word vector embeddings, to implement semantic querying. Finally, in the NLG module, we intend to explore the possibility of priming a language model to generate creative expressions given an input statement and context. This would enable the system to express an answer in a creative, NL fashion.

6   Conclusion

We have presented in this paper the outline of an open-domain question answering system based on knowledge graph generation from natural language text. With a basic and limited system, we have demonstrated the ability to answer simple, conversational-style questions. We have also demonstrated that enhancing the generated knowledge graphs improves the ability to answer questions, and highlighted some challenges to be addressed in order to move the system to a more competitive standard compared to existing ML-based systems.

We believe that there is significant potential for open-domain conversational question answering using knowledge graphs as an alternative to ML-based approaches, because the growing demand for more data and computing power to train better ML solutions is unsustainable. Many research efforts already exist in the three basic modules described in this paper (NL to graph, NL query to SPARQL and graph to NL). We believe that as the research community turns its attention to the potential of unifying these areas, a new of generation powerful open-domain conversational QA systems can be realized without the daunting costs of data, time and computing resources that currently plague ML-based approaches.

Acknowledgement. This publication was partially made possible by an Institutional Development Award (IDeA) from the National Institute of General Medical Sciences of the National Institutes of Health under Grant #P20GM103408.

References

1. Angeli, G., Johnson, M., Manning, C.D.: Leveraging linguistic structure for open domain information extraction. In: Annual Meeting of the Association for Computational Linguistics (2015)
2. Brown, T.B., et al.: Language models are few-shot learners. arXiv abs/2005.14165 (2020)
3. Brożek, A.: The Structure of Natural Language Questions, pp. 129–169. Brill, Leiden, The Netherlands (2011)
4. Dai, Z., Li, L., Xu, W.: CFO: conditional focused neural question answering with large-scale knowledge bases. ArXiv abs/1606.01994 (2016)
5. Devlin, J., Chang, M., Lee, K., Toutanova, K.: BERT: pre-training of deep bidirectional transformers for language understanding. In: Burstein, J., Doran, C., Solorio, T. (eds.) Proceedings of the 2019 Conference of the North American Chapter of the Association for Computational Linguistics: Human Language Technologies, NAACL-HLT 2019, Minneapolis, MN, USA, June 2–7, 2019, Volume 1 (Long and Short Papers), pp. 4171–4186 (2019)
6. Gangemi, A., Presutti, V., Recupero, D.R., Nuzzolese, A.G., Draicchio, F., Mongiovì, M.: Semantic web machine reading with FRED. Semant. Web **8**(6), 873–893 (2017)
7. Hirschman, L., Gaizauskas, R.J.: Natural language question answering: the view from here. Nat. Lang. Eng. **7**(4), 275–300 (2001)
8. Jamil, H., Oduro-Afriyie, J.: Semantic understanding of natural language stories for near human question answering. In: FQAS (2019)
9. Kim, K., Hur, Y., Kim, G., Lim, H.: GREG: a global level relation extraction with knowledge graph embedding. Appl. Sci. **10**, 1181 (2020)
10. Lin, S.C., Hilton, J., Evans, O.: TruthfulQA: measuring how models mimic human falsehoods. In: Annual Meeting of the Association for Computational Linguistics (2021)
11. Miller, G.A.: WordNet: a lexical database for English. Commun. ACM **38**, 39–41 (1992)
12. Pradel, C., Haemmerlé, O., Hernandez, N.: Natural language query interpretation into SPARQL using patterns. In: Fourth International Workshop on Consuming Linked Data - COLD (2013)
13. Scao, T.L., et al.: BLOOM: A 176b-parameter open-access multilingual language model. CoRR abs/2211.05100 (2022)
14. Sima, A.C., et al.: Bio-SODA: enabling natural language question answering over knowledge graphs without training data. In: Zhu, Q., Zhu, X., Tu, Y., Xu, Z., Kumar, A. (eds.) SSDBM 2021: 33rd International Conference on Scientific and Statistical Database Management, Tampa, FL, USA, July 6–7, 2021, pp. 61–72. ACM (2021)
15. Sobieszek, A., Price, T.: Playing games with Ais: The limits of GPT-3 and similar large language models. Minds Mach. **32**, 341–364 (2022)
16. Vakulenko, S., Longpre, S., Tu, Z., Anantha, R.: Question rewriting for conversational question answering. In: Proceedings of the 14th ACM International Conference on Web Search and Data Mining (2021)
17. Vaswani, A., et al.: Attention is all you need. In: NIPS (2017)
18. You, C., Chen, N., Zou, Y.: Contextualized attention-based knowledge transfer for spoken conversational question answering. In: Interspeech (2021)

19. Zeng, D., Liu, K., Chen, Y., Zhao, J.: Distant supervision for relation extraction via piecewise convolutional neural networks. In: EMNLP (2015)
20. Zhao, F., Hou, J., Li, Y., Bai, L.: Relation prediction for answering natural language questions over knowledge graphs. In: International Joint Conference on Neural Networks, IJCNN 2021, Shenzhen, China, July 18–22, 2021, pp. 1–8. IEEE (2021)
21. Zou, L., Huang, R., Wang, H., Yu, J.X., He, W., Zhao, D.: Natural language question answering over RDF: a graph data driven approach. In: Proceedings of the 2014 ACM SIGMOD International Conference on Management of Data (2014)

Advanced Methods and Applications in Natural Language Processing (NLP)

Automatic Generation of Coherent Natural Language Texts

Oleksandr Marchenko[1,2] and Mariam Isoieva[1(✉)]

[1] Taras Shevchenko National University of Kyiv,
60 Volodymyrska Street, Kyiv 01033, Ukraine
omarchenko@univ.kiev.ua, isoyevamaryam@gmail.com
[2] International Research and Training Center for Information Technologies
and Systems, Kyiv, Ukraine

Abstract. Text generation models are widespread nowadays, there are more and more use cases for them. The majority of the most prominent and efficient, in terms of output quality, ones require vast computational resources for training and inference, which becomes an obstacle for their practical usage. However, even for big and powerful architectures, the texts they generate often lack coherence, logical links can be broken, which makes texts less readable and less useful. This paper presents a method for increasing coherence of text generated by neural network models and we emphasize the importance of languages' nature analysis prior to building new generation methods. We have analysed the existing decoding methods and have built the mechanism for maximizing coherence of the output sequences into some of them.

Keywords: Natural Language Texts Generation · Text Coherence · Natural Language Texts Processing · Decoding Methods in Generative Neural Networks · Semantic Analysis

1 Introduction

1.1 The Multifaceted Nature of Natural Language Texts Generation

Today, the attention of scientists around the world is focused on artificial intelligence technologies. Back in the last century, with the advent of more and more powerful computing devices, researchers were making attempts to model the intellectual activity of a human, to automate it in a certain way. But at that time, the level of computing power did not allow for conducting large-scale research and achieving significant results. Powerful processors are now available, which opens up new opportunities for the study of human intellectual creativity, its automation.

One of the main tasks, related to artificial intelligence, is natural language text generation. Text is a complex concept. For creating it, humans use their memory, imagination, fantasy, knowledge of formal language rules, vocabulary, etc. A person first forms an idea by choosing a set of concepts, forms a text

H. L. Larsen et al. (Eds.): FQAS 2023, LNAI 14113, pp. 79–92, 2023.
https://doi.org/10.1007/978-3-031-42935-4_7

based on their ideas and knowledge about the world, uses various syntactic constructions. This process is so complicated that even the most powerful models still cannot reproduce it and achieve the high quality of the generated text with a 100% guarantee.

At the same time, the demand for text generation systems is growing, and the need for automatic text creation for solving tasks in various spheres of human activity is increasing. Such a generated text should be easy to understand and logically and syntactically correct. Achieving such properties of the resulting text is an open problem that requires new solutions. In addition, algorithms that do not require the use of significant amounts of computing resources are important, because they are still quite expensive and not always available. Automatic generation of coherent and correct text that fully conveys the main idea and has practical value for the end user is still an unsolved task that requires the invention of effective approaches to its solution.

Modern GPT models, namely GPT-3,5 [27] and GPT-4 [16] show impressive results, but it is important to take into account the amounts of computational resources needed for their training and inference. Apart from that, training of such models requires enormous sizes of the training corpora, which are not publicly available and the process of getting them raises various legal and ethical issues.

Approach of having large model and big datasets can help achieve good results of text generation. But it has various practical limitations, requires access to data and lots of processors. We believe that relatively good results can be also obtained by building systems based on the analysis of the language itself, its nature, syntax peculiarities and we see potential in researching and developing such methods. It is possible to use analysis of subtle connection in texts, links and interconnections between different parts of texts in order to create advanced language generation models.

Most modern models of natural language text generation are based on the process of statistical learning. Algorithms and mechanisms of their work are built in such a way that the main criterion for generation is the similarity of the computed distribution of probabilities for a given dictionary to the distribution that was observed in the training sample, i.e., in the text corpus that was used for training the model.

But unfortunately, this approach is not always efficient and needs significant modifications because it does not take into account many aspects that make the text suitable for meeting the needs of the end user, easy to understand and perceive. Even a high probability of the generated text does not guarantee the high quality of the resulting text. Furthermore, some studies show that it is the deviations from the "learned" distributions that can make the text interesting to read [8].

The approach outlined above does not take into account the most important characteristics that make the text readable. In particular, coherence, logical unity, meeting the needs of the user. The way how the main idea of the text is described and whether the lexical content corresponds to the topic, the linguistic style of the text are also crucial. It does not take into account ease of perception by the end user, grammatical correctness.

Researchers are trying to improve the performance of such autoregressive models in various ways. Most often, such approaches require significant complications of models, their architectures, increasing number of parameters. And this, in turn, requires significant computing resources, which are not always available and are currently quite expensive. This fact makes many powerful and effective models unsuitable for use in solving real problems.

That is why resource-efficient methods of text generation, which would take into account the semantic and syntactic features of the text's coherence, would ensure the logical structure and unity of all concepts, and would guarantee a certain level of the text's coherence, are necessary.

The coherence metric [14] allows for qualitative analysis of the generated texts, it allows to analyse both syntactic and semantic aspects of coherence. This metric was used in this work to modify modern decoding methods.

We propose a modification of decoding methods, which does not depend on the peculiarities of the generative model itself, therefore, it is possible to apply it to various autoregressive models of natural language text generation. Apart from that, it is possible to apply this algorithm to the generation of texts in various languages, since its basis is the metric [14], which only requires an existing lexical-semantic base and a syntax parser, and similar systems are available today for many languages.

1.2   Existing Decoding Methods Used for Generation

For the autoregressive neural network models, in particular, Transformer-based ones, which we consider further, one of the key parts is decoding. Autoregressive models generate text word by word based on the input text and the pre-generated text. The decoding task is to select each subsequent word according to the formed probability distribution to maximize the probability of the entire chain.

It is difficult to overestimate the importance of the decoding process and its impact on the quality of the text that will be obtained as a result of the generation process. After all, even for the powerful models themselves, it is at the decoding stage that the syntactic and semantic structure of the text, its conceptual and lexical content is determined, and logical integrity and coherence are ensured.

The quality of the future text depends on the quality of the decoding, so it is worth paying special attention to the choice of the decoding algorithm when creating natural language text generation systems. Some of modern decoding methods and their advantages and disadvantages are the following.

Greedy Search. The greedy search algorithm is the basic decoding algorithm. It consists in choosing at each step the next word that has the highest probability according to the obtained distribution.

The disadvantage of this algorithm is that it ignores the chain with a higher resulting probability and instead chooses the one that had a higher probability of initial words at each step.

But when working with generative models, it is important to take into account not only the probabilities obtained as a result of training on the training corpus but also the syntactic and semantic structure of the generated text, and the relationship between different parts of the text.

Apart from that, some studies show that often using greedy search during decoding can lead to the model having self-repetitions, when the same piece of text is repeated several times, or there is a loop in general, and the network endlessly generates text by repeating one piece of text. It is obvious that in order to use such a network to satisfy the information needs of users, this algorithm must be improved.

To enhance the performance of this algorithm, the following decoding methods are used.

Beam Search. The beam search algorithm is more complex than the previous one but gives better results for finding the sequence with the highest probability, and not just the next word. Before starting the algorithm execution, the number of "rays" N, which will be considered, is set, that is, chains that will be evaluated. Next, at each step, N variants of words with the highest probability are considered. And all the possible variants of those words are generated. Next, the one with the highest probability is selected from the generated chains. This way, a sequence with a higher probability than that obtained by greedy decoding can be obtained. But it is worth noting that the complexity of this algorithm is higher than the complexity of the greedy search. There is also no guarantee that the sequence formed in this way will have the highest probability possible because only a part of the options is considered. But in practice, it is necessary to maintain a balance between the speed, the amount of resources needed and the quality of the text. It is not advisable to consider all possible options. Therefore, a certain sufficient value of the parameter N is usually set. The operation of this algorithm can be illustrated by an example. Let $N = 2$, then the algorithm works in the a way shown in Fig. 1a.

It should be noted that when using beam search, it is important to specify the maximum length of the resulting sequence because there is no guarantee that the end of the sequence token will be generated. Even with this modification of the decoding algorithm, self-repetitions of neural networks may occur. To overcome such a phenomenon, a check is applied to see if a certain sequence of fixed length has already been generated. This approach can reduce the quality of the text and is not applicable to many tasks, but with the open-end generation, this method is quite effective, which is emphasized, for example, in the study [20]. There is also a stochastic variant of beam search [10] and various sampling variants, which are described below.

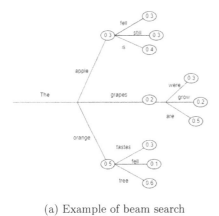

(a) Example of beam search

(b) Comparison of token probabilities given input sequence for human-written text and automatically generated text using beam search, source [8]

Fig. 1. Beam search algorithm.

Sampling Methods for Decoding. Sampling consists in modifying the decoding algorithm by randomly selecting the next word, according to the computed probability distribution, during generation.

According to work [8], human-written texts are more unpredictable, word probabilities follow different distributions. A human can change the topic, outline the connections between different parts of the text describing different events or phenomena, but at the same time preserve the coherence and structure of the text, which is still hard to achieve even for powerful modern methods of generating natural language texts today. It is because of this unpredictability, but while maintaining the coherence and logical correctness, that the text written by a person is usually much more interesting and easier to understand than the automatically generated one. Therefore, random sampling methods can be used to improve the existing generation systems.

The same study [8] presents the method of nucleus sampling, which we also consider. This algorithm is based on discarding from consideration the tails of the distributions during generation and on each step choosing a set of words for which their cumulative probability mass exceeds some threshold. Further, sampling is done only from the dynamically allocated "nucleus". The probabilities are normalized according to the selected threshold, such a new distribution is used further. The size of the new sample can change dynamically at each stage of the algorithm [8].

The algorithm of top-k sampling [10], which authors of [8] also use for comparison, is similar. With this algorithm, k tokens with the highest probability are chosen. Next, the probabilities are proportionally "projected", redistributed among the most probable words [10]. This method is used in some of today's most powerful natural language text generation models.

1.3   Coherence Aspect of the Text Quality

Coherence is one of the main quality indicators of a natural language text. However, the concept of coherence is difficult to formalize, this phenomenon is multifaceted.

There are different definitions of coherent text but most of them have it being logical, consistent, characterized by the unity of its elements in common. Linguists study text coherence as a phenomenon that finds its manifestation through the use of certain linguistic means: ellipses, synonyms, conjunctions, coreferences and other connections.

It can be considered on the syntactic and semantic levels. Text coherence is ensured by the semantic connections of the main concepts and described phenomena, the syntactic consistency of the components of individual sentences and their unity within a group of sentences.

A distinction is made between local and global text coherence. Local coherence "works" at the level of individual sentences and connections between parts of neighbouring sentences, it deals with the semantic transitions between consecutive sentences. This property is important for building high-quality natural language text. Local coherence is necessary for global coherence, which consists in the logical unity and integrity of the entire text.

To date, very few studies focus on controlling the level of coherence in the process of text generation using artificial neural networks because this task is quite complex and requires extensive approaches to its solution.

Many works related to practical automatic analysis of coherence have roots in the centering theory, developed by Grosz et al. [7]. The name "centering" originated from the main statement of this theory. According to Grosz et al., some entities mentioned in texts are central. The author's choice of syntactic constructions and coreferences is influenced by the central entities and their features. Therefore, the coherence of the discourse depends on how compatible the properties of the central entity and those related to it are [7]. Examples of coherence analysis methodologies based directly on the centering theory include work by Lapata and Barzilay [11].

The technique proposed by Iida and Tokunaga [9] is also related to the centering theory. When constructing their metric of text coherence, researchers also analyse coreferences. The authors propose to use the metric as one of the features for building a model based on the matrix of entities and demonstrate an improvement of the basic model [9].

Since many methods of estimating and modelling text coherence require some training data, the question of how to make these methods independent of a specific subject and ensure the quality of the systems built on their basis arises. Apart from that, the methods discussed above focus on only certain aspects of coherence. There is a need to improve these algorithms by integrating the paradigms that they are based on. Researchers Li and Jurafsky [12] considered the ways for such improvement and proposed a method for assessing coherence and generating coherent text. The proposed discriminative model is based on deep learning methods, namely, they used LSTM for forming sentence embeddings and another neural network as a coherence classifier. They also use hidden Markov model and latent Dirichlet allocation for the related experiments. Basile et al. defined a metric of coherence between individual frames [4]. Some results of this study were used in the development of the method [14], which was used for this paper.

Thematic homogeneity and coherence are also distinguished. There are studies of thematic homogeneity, which are based on the use of latent Dirichlet allocation [6].

Coherence consists in the semantic unity of components, therefore its modelling involves semantic analysis of the text, which is related to the tasks of natural language understanding. An example can be the Story Cloze Test [15]. We have used the dataset, developed for this test, for our experiments at the pre-computing stage needed for the coherence metric [14]. This dataset consists of texts, each 5 sentences long, which describe ordinary daily life situations using general vocabulary.

In this work, the decoding methods used for the generation of natural language texts are modified by applying the coherence metric [14] when choosing the optimal generated chain.

2 Modified Generation Method Based on the Coherence Metric

2.1 Coherence Metric Used

Most of the popular neural network architectures are not constructed with explicit coherence control mechanisms built into the generation process by design. Defining the numerical definition of coherence is itself a complex task, which requires taking into account the multidimensionality of this phenomenon.

We use metric [14], which allows to comprehensively assess the generated texts and numerically determine the level of logical integrity and semantic unity. This metric combines measuring how well different aspects of coherence are materialized in the generated text. Apart from that, this metric is easy to use in practice. What makes it a good choice is also that it does not require lots of computational resources for inference after the pre-processing is done.

The metric is calculated in the following way [14].

$$Coherence(T) = \frac{\sum_{i=1}^{n-1} FRel(s_i, s_{i+1})}{n-1},$$

where T is the text, s_i is the ith sentence of the text.

The metric used to calculate the coherence value is:

$$FRel(S_1, S_2) = \alpha * FRelPred(S_1, S_2) + (1 - \alpha) * FRelArgs(S_1, S_2),$$

where α is the balancing coefficient between the two components (according to research [4], the optimal value is 0.5).

The relatedness between the predicates is calculated as follows:

$$FRelPred(S_1, S_2) = \log_2 \frac{|c_{p_1 p_2}|}{|c_{p_1}||c_{p_2}|},$$

where c_{p_1} and c_{p_2} are subsets of sentences from the corpus, which have common predicate p_1 with sentence S_1 and predicate p_2 with sentence S_2 correspondingly; $c_{p_1 p_2}$ is a subset of ordered pairs of sentences that can be found in the texts together, and p_1 and p_2 are the predicates of the first and second sentences correspondingly [14].

This quasi-metric (it does not satisfy the symmetry condition) is calculated dynamically given that the parts of speech for each word are tagged on the pre-computation stage and that the verbs that correspond to predicates of each sentence are marked [14].

For the elements of a sentence dependent on the predicate, the relatedness is calculated as:

$$FRelArgs(S_1, S_2) = \frac{1}{2} \left(\frac{1}{|args_1|} \sum_{N_i \in args_1} \max_{N_j \in args_2} wpsim(N_i, N_j) + \right.$$

$$\left. \frac{1}{|args_2|} \sum_{N_i \in args_2} \max_{N_j \in args_1} wpsim(N_i, N_j) \right)$$

Wu-Palmer metric is also used:

$$wpsem(s_1, s_2) = \frac{2 * depth(lcs)}{depth(s_1) + depth(s_2)}$$

where $depth(lcs)$ is the depth of the nearest common ancestor for synsets s_1 and s_2. Wu-Palmer similarity belongs to the methods of measuring the semantic similarity of certain word meanings based on the length of paths in the WordNet ontology (in the original article, Wu and Palmer consider not WordNet but an arbitrary hierarchical structure of concepts when choosing the correct word meanings for solving the problem of machine learning translation for English and Chinese) [24]. WordNet is one of the most widely used ontologies and we also use it for this work.

WordNet is publicly available, which makes this lexical-semantic database applicable to many studies in the field of natural language processing. There are also versions for other languages, e.g., a Ukrainian WordNet [2].

2.2 Generic Modification of Decoding Methods Based on Coherence Metric

The generation problem, which we will consider further, can be formulated as follows.

Let S_0 be the input sentence (assuming inputs are only in English). Given this sentence, the task is to generate the next sentence S_1, which would form a coherent text with the initial one.

The decoding method for selecting the next word in the generation process to be considered can be applied to arbitrary natural language text generation models that generate text word by word.

We consider the GPT2 [23] as the main model for the experiments. It shows relatively high quality results on generation tasks but is less resource-intensive than the newer models of natural language text generation.

This modification of the decoding methods is an attempt to build a coherence assessment mechanism into the architecture of natural language text generation models based on neural networks.

We also take the beam search algorithm described in the previous section as a base method for modification. The main idea is to apply the coherence metric [14] described above at the decoding stage when choosing the optimal generated chain. This way, we rely not only on the one having maximum probability.

The main steps of the proposed algorithm are as follows:

1. The sentence S_0, written in English, is taken as input to the algorithm
2. The parameter values of the number of beams considered, N, and the number of generated chains with the highest probability, from which the optimal one will be chosen, *ReturnSequences*, are set as constants
3. The token of the end of the sequence, the maximum and minimum length of the sequence to be generated are set, and the text generation process starts
4. Next, the beam search process itself takes place, chains are generated, and *ReturnSequences* chains with the highest probability are selected
5. For each such chain, the value of the coherence metric is calculated
6. From all sequences, the one with the highest coherence value is selected, it is the result of the algorithm

This algorithm is applicable to an arbitrary autoregressive model of natural language text generation and a decoding algorithm, for which several variants of the generated chains are obtained as a result.

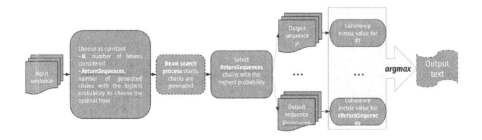

Fig. 2. Visual representation of the proposed algorithm.

The main goal of this algorithm is to embed a coherence assessment mechanism into modern neural network architectures designed for generating natural language texts.

It is possible to expand this algorithm and further integrate the coherence metric into neural network models at earlier stages of generation.

We have used Python 3.6 programming language, the freely distributed library Stanza (formerly known as Stanford NLP) [22], NLTK (Natural Language Toolkit) [5], and the WordNet lexical-semantic database [21] to implement the proposed algorithm. Apart from that, we have used Google Colaboratory resources to conduct the experiments. Apart from that, the Gradio framework [1] has been used. It is useful for creating applications for demonstrating the results of machine learning systems' work. This framework is publicly available and is designed specifically for experiments with machine learning models.

2.3   Examples of the Generated Texts

Absence of a commonly used metric for comprehensive assessment of text quality and subjectivity of this task make it hard to compare results of text generation models. Thus, we show some examples of the texts generated using the beam search modification based on the coherence metric, which we described in the article. Here, we list only short texts due to the article size limits. We put the input part in bold.

- **Today is Tuesday, October 5th**, and we're going to be back with a new episode of the podcast. This week, we'll be talking about the new season of The Walking Dead, as well as some of our favorite moments from the show. We'll also be discussing the upcoming season finale of AMC's The Vampire Diaries, which is set to air on Sunday, September 30th at 10:00pm ET/PT on AMC.com.
- **Tom had a very short temper.** "I don't know what you're talking about," he said. "I mean, I'm not going to lie to you, but I think he's a good guy. He's got a lot of respect for me, and I've got to respect him. I mean it's just a matter of time before he gets hurt."
- **Marcus needed clothing for a business casual event.** "I'm not going to go out and buy clothes," he said. "I don't want to be in a situation where I have to buy a pair of jeans. I'm just going out there and doing what I love doing."
- **Andy was invited to a Halloween party.** "I was like, 'Oh my God, I'm going to have to do this,' " he said. "And then I got to the party and I was just like: 'I don't want to go to this party.' I didn't know what to expect. I had no idea what was going on. It was really weird."
- **Lance was going to make a bet.** "I'm not sure if it's a good bet," he said. "I don't know. I'm just trying to figure it out."
- **The candidates were running a tight campaign.** "I think it's important for us to get out there and say, 'We're not going to let this happen to you,'" he said. "And I think that's what we're doing. We're trying to do the right thing for our community."

- **Bob was feeling very tired everyday.** "It's not like I'm going to be able to go to the gym every day," he said. "I've been working out a lot, but I don't have the energy to do it. It's just a matter of getting used to it."
- **I always hated jam on bread.** It was so bad. I had to go to the grocery store and buy a bunch of jam. "I was like, 'Oh my God, I'm going to have to eat this.' And then I went back to my house and bought some jam and it was good. But I was really, really hungry. And I didn't know what to do with it. So I just ate it and went to bed."

We also analyse the quality of the generated texts of different length. For this, we have invited 20 subject matter experts to evaluate the quality of the generated texts, 10 texts per length category. The score for a text is the weighted sum of scores for coherence and readability (40%), semantic correctness and whether the main idea is transparent (40%), syntax correctness (20%), with each of the aspects having 10 as maximum and 0 as minimum scores. The average of scores given by the experts are presented in Table 1.

Table 1. Evaluation of the generated texts by experts.

Text length	Average score
up to 30 tokens	8,3
up to 50 tokens	8,56
up to 100 tokens	7,88
up to 1000 tokens	6,91
up to 3000 tokens	5,97

3 Discussion

3.1 Need for Text Quality Estimation Methodologies

Here, we do not compare our results to the ones of the existing methods quantitatively as currently there are no comprehensive and widely used metrics for estimating text quality broadly automatically, which would take into account coherence, semantic and syntactic correctness, readability, and consistency of logical links inside the text at the same time. Those features are crucial when choosing a metric for comparison. And the absence of a standardly used metric makes it hard to compare new results to the previous ones.

Thus the question of creating such a metric arises. Text generation technologies are developing fast, existing models are being modified, and conceptually new ones appear. Having a common metric for comparison, which would assess the quality of the text itself, can speed up the process even more and make the results more understandable from a usability viewpoint. It would also allow improvement of the existing models and make the development process for the new ones easier and more manageable.

It is important to note that there are widespread quality metrics for some tasks, such as summarisation and machine translation, e.g., ROUGE [13], BLEU [18], METEOR [3], but not for the text as it is. There is some research on this topic, but none has become a standard, which makes it hard to compare the results.

Examples of more broad metrics, which incorporate evaluation on both syntactic and semantic levels and take into account coherence and semantic correctness, include GRUEN [26]. Some works that analyse the issue of text quality estimation include [17, 19, 25].

3.2 Points for Improvement, Possible Applications, and Further Development of the Method

Since the proposed modification of the decoding method does not depend on the features of the generative model itself, it is possible to extend the application of this modification to other autoregressive models of natural language text generation.

The versatility of the coherence metric [14] also makes it possible to generalize this method to languages other than English, which would be significant for improving generation quality for low-resource languages. For this, only a lexical-semantic base and a syntactic parser are required. Such systems are available for many languages, for example, Ukrainian [2], and are constantly being improved.

It is also possible to embed coherence metrics [14] into generation models based on generative adversarial networks (GANs). Thus, the coherence metric can be the main objective function of the discriminative part of the neural network, and accordingly, the generative part will be "adjusted" to the discriminative one in the process of training.

Regarding the improvement of the developed modification, it is worth noting that the ability to "embed" the metric into the generation models themselves, even before the decoding process, in such a way that the model determines the very distribution of probabilities for the next word, already taking into account coherence, can potentially be useful for improving the existing models and making them more efficient. Currently, only the distribution that is formed based on weight matrices obtained in advance, as a result of training, is used. As the studies mentioned in this paper show, this is often not enough, it is necessary to change the classical architectures in such a way as to take into account the features and characteristics of the text itself during generation, to determine how coherent and meaningful it is.

Integration of metric [14] into generative architectures would have a number of important applications. In addition to improving the generation results, such a mechanism would allow a better understanding of how the text generation systems work. Today, the problems of interpretability and explainability of neural networks are separate, quite important fields of research on artificial intelligence systems. The application of such modern methods as the coherence metric [14] and their usage in the context of generating natural language texts would make it possible to achieve significant progress in this field.

References

1. Abid, A., Abdalla, A., Abid, A., Khan, D., Alfozan, A., Zou, J.: Gradio: hassle-free sharing and testing of ML models in the wild. ArXiv abs/1906.02569 (2019)
2. Anisimov, A., Marchenko, O., Nikonenko, A., Porkhun, E., Taranukha, V.: Ukrainian WordNet: creation and filling. In: Larsen, H.L., Martin-Bautista, M.J., Vila, M.A., Andreasen, T., Christiansen, H. (eds.) Flexible Query Answering Systems, pp. 649–660. Springer, Berlin Heidelberg, Berlin, Heidelberg (2013)
3. Banerjee, S., Lavie, A.: METEOR: an automatic metric for MT evaluation with improved correlation with human judgments. In: Proceedings of the ACL Workshop on Intrinsic and Extrinsic Evaluation Measures for Machine Translation and/or Summarization, pp. 65–72. Association for Computational Linguistics, Ann Arbor, Michigan (2005)
4. Basile, V., Lopez Condori, R., Cabrio, E.: Measuring frame instance relatedness. In: Proceedings of the Seventh Joint Conference on Lexical and Computational Semantics, pp. 245–254. Association for Computational Linguistics, New Orleans, Louisiana (Jun 2018). https://doi.org/10.18653/v1/S18-2029 https://doi.org/10.18653/v1/S18-2029
5. Bird, S., Loper, E., Klein, E.: Natural Language Processing with Python. O'Reilly Media Inc. (2009)
6. Blei, D., Ng, A., Jordan, M.: Latent dirichlet allocation. J. Mach. Learn. Res. **3**, 601–608 (2001)
7. Grosz, B.J., Joshi, A.K., Weinstein, S.: Centering: a framework for modeling the local coherence of discourse. Comput. Linguist. **21**(2), 203–225 (1995)
8. Holtzman, A., Buys, J., Du, L., Forbes, M., Choi, Y.: The curious case of neural text degeneration. In: International Conference on Learning Representations ICLR 2020 (2020)
9. Iida, R., Tokunaga, T.: A metric for evaluating discourse coherence based on coreference resolution. In: Proceedings of COLING 2012: Posters, pp. 483–494. The COLING 2012 Organizing Committee, Mumbai, India (2012)
10. Kool, W., van Hoof, H., Welling, M.: Stochastic beams and where to find them: the Gumbel-Top-k trick for sampling sequences without replacement. ArXiv abs/1903.06059 (2019)
11. Lapata, M., Barzilay, R.: Automatic evaluation of text coherence: models and representations. In: Proceedings of the 19th International Joint Conference on Artificial Intelligence, pp. 1085–1090 (01 2005)
12. Li, J., Jurafsky, D.: Neural net models of open-domain discourse coherence. In: Proceedings of the 2017 Conference on Empirical Methods in Natural Language Processing, pp. 198–209. Association for Computational Linguistics, Copenhagen, Denmark (2017). https://doi.org/10.18653/v1/D17-1019
13. Lin, C.Y.: ROUGE: a package for automatic evaluation of summaries. In: Text Summarization Branches Out, pp. 74–81. Association for Computational Linguistics, Barcelona, Spain (2004)
14. Marchenko, O., Radyvonenko, O., Ignatova, T., Tytarchuk, P., Zhelezniakov, D.: Improving text generation through introducing coherence metrics. Cybernet. Syst. Anal. **56**, 13–21 (2020). https://doi.org/10.1007/s10559-020-00216-x

15. Mostafazadeh, N., Roth, M., Louis, A., Chambers, N., Allen, J.: LSDSem 2017 shared task: the story cloze test. In: Proceedings of the 2nd Workshop on Linking Models of Lexical, Sentential and Discourse-level Semantics, pp. 46–51. Association for Computational Linguistics, Valencia, Spain (Apr 2017). https://doi.org/10.18653/v1/W17-0906 https://doi.org/10.18653/v1/W17-0906

16. Open AI: GPT-4 Technical Report. ArXiv abs/2303.08774 (2023)

17. Opitz, J., Frank, A.: Towards a decomposable metric for explainable evaluation of text generation from AMR. ArXiv abs/2008.08896 (2020)

18. Papineni, K., Roukos, S., Ward, T., Zhu, W.J.: BLEU: a method for automatic evaluation of machine translation. In: Proceedings of the 40th Annual Meeting of the Association for Computational Linguistics, pp. 311–318. Association for Computational Linguistics, Philadelphia, Pennsylvania, USA (Jul 2002). https://doi.org/10.3115/1073083.1073135

19. Parcalabescu, L., Cafagna, M., Muradjan, L., Frank, A., Calixto, I., Gatt, A.: VALSE: a task-independent benchmark for vision and language models centered on linguistic phenomena. In: Annual Meeting of the Association for Computational Linguistics (2021)

20. Paulus, R., Xiong, C., Socher, R.: A deep reinforced model for abstractive summarization. ArXiv abs/1705.04304 (2017)

21. Princeton University: about WordNet. https://wordnet.princeton.edu/

22. Qi, P., Zhang, Y., Zhang, Y., Bolton, J., Manning, C.D.: Stanza: A Python natural language processing toolkit for many human languages. In: Proceedings of the 58th Annual Meeting of the Association for Computational Linguistics: System Demonstrations (2020)

23. Radford, A., Wu, J., Child, R., Luan, D., Amodei, D., Sutskever, I.: Language models are unsupervised multitask learners (2019)

24. Wu, Z., Palmer, M.: Verb semantics and lexical selection. In: 32nd Annual Meeting of the Association for Computational Linguistics, pp. 133–138. Association for Computational Linguistics, Las Cruces, New Mexico, USA (Jun 1994). https://doi.org/10.3115/981732.981751

25. Zhao, W., Strube, M., Eger, S.: Discoscore: evaluating text generation with BERT and discourse coherence. ArXiv abs/2201.11176 (2022)

26. Zhu, W., Bhat, S.: GRUEN for evaluating linguistic quality of generated text. In: Findings of the Association for Computational Linguistics: EMNLP 2020, pp. 94–108. Association for Computational Linguistics, Online (Nov 2020). https://doi.org/10.18653/v1/2020.findings-emnlp.9

27. New GPT-3 capabilities: edit & insert https://openai.com/blog/gpt-3-edit-insert

Interlingual Semantic Validation

Carolina Gallardo[1]([✉])[ID], Jesús Cardeñosa[1][ID], and Samantha Baragaño[2]

[1] Universidad Politécnica de Madrid, Madrid, Spain
{carolina.gallardop,jesus.cardenosa}@upm.es
[2] Dail Software, S.L., Madrid, Spain
samanta@dail-software.com

Abstract. The validation of machine translation systems has depended on metrics that compare both form and content of the translated text, where direct human participation was almost indispensable. Within the paradigm of "language pairs" and direct translation, whether rule or statistics-based, the process of evaluating MT systems rely on assessing grammatical correctness and similarity to reference translations. As a counterpart, interlingua-based systems pivot on an intermediate representation of the contents to be translated. In this article, we propose a model for validating the output of automatically translated text in a interlingua-based system, based on the automatization of the semantic validation of source, target and interlingual representation.

Keywords: Semantic equivalence · Interlingua · Graph-based knowledge representation · Machine Translation evaluation

1 Introduction

Machine translation is one of the oldest applications and research areas of NLP, dating back to 1950. For several decades (1950–1980), the approach to the problem was rule-based MT, with two main -still active- paradigms: transfer and interlingual systems. The decade of the 1980 and 1990 knew the explosion of example-based MT; which derive in statistical MT in the next two decades, and current neural MT approaches (see [23] for a current review of the evolution of MT field). Rule-based MT established the foundation of the field, illustrated by systems like Logos, Systran, ETAP, KANT or UNL. Soon, data-driven approaches clearly dominate the research community and efforts, until the irruption and predominance of neural MT, a sophisticated evolution of statistical MT, both in the academia and in commercial and industrial applications (DeepL, Google Translation or MS Bing).

Be it rule-based or empirical-based, the predominant approaches deals with the translation problem as a transfer approach: performing the translation process within a pair a languages. On the other hand, the interlingual approach,

---

Supported by DAIL Software, https://www.dail.es.

H. L. Larsen et al. (Eds.): FQAS 2023, LNAI 14113, pp. 93–106, 2023.
https://doi.org/10.1007/978-3-031-42935-4_8

that is, translating from a natural language text into an intermediate representation and from this representation towards another natural language, has been in minority, and usually ascribed to predominantly rule-based approaches. Systems like KANT [14], PIVOT [15] or UNITRAN [10] exemplify this. Apart from showing up as a viable solution for highly multilingual environments [4], the interlingua may serve as an adequate bridge between distant languages in a MT system, as suggested in [17] and more recently in [25].

Wherever the approach, the output of an MT system requires evaluation and there is a sense in the field of translation, human also, that there exists no perfect translation and thus an unavoidable loss of meaning. Acknowledging the impossibility of perfect translations, we may think of a continuum of translation options. So, what is quality in (Machine) Translation? In [11] it is provided a broad definition for quality in MT systems: "A quality translation demonstrates accuracy and fluency required for the audience and purpose and complies with all other specifications negotiated between the requester and provider, taking into account end-user needs."

Assuming this definition, there are two main factors when assessing MT quality: one is *fluency*, which comprises style, grammaticality, and formal issues of the text; the other is *adequacy* when conveying the semantics and pragmatics of the text, which is the target of this paper, especially in denotational aspects. Although, translation is more than conferring meaning (it is also conferring intention, context, and style), there are contexts where grammaticality and the confidence that there is no loss in meaning is crucial. In this paper, we are going to describe a model for evaluation of translated texts within an interlingua-based framework in terms of semantic equivalence and loss of meaning. Thus, the informational items of source, intermediate representation and target text are compared and measured to assess the degree of semantic equivalence between the different representations and thus establish a confidence degree on the outputted text.

2 Related Work. Assessing Quality in Machine Translation

There are two main paradigms in Machine Translation Evaluation: human-based and automated evaluation [7]. Most research efforts are directed towards automated evaluation and embedded in transfer systems.

2.1 Human-Based Evaluation

Human based evaluation follows two paradigms: Directly-Expressed-Judgement (DEJ) evaluation and non-DEJ approaches. When performing human-based evaluation, two main issues of the text are evaluated: fluency, target language correctness; and accuracy, degree of semantic equivalence. The source text acts as the reference translation, thus bilingual experts are required to perform such type of evaluation. The dependence on human experts is the main burden of such type of evaluation, together with subjectivity.

In DEJ evaluation, human experts must score a translated text using usually a five-point scale for fluency and for adequacy. In terms of accuracy, it is judged how much of the content in the reference translation or in the source text is transmitted, for example everything (5), most of (4), a big part of (3), a small part of (2) or none (1) [6]. Fluency is evaluated in the similar terms. It has been referenced in the literature the degree of overwhelming subjectivity of the process, taking into account even the lack of guidelines or checklists provided to the experts.

Human non-DEJ assessment tries to overcome some of the weaknesses of DEJ evaluation: ambiguity and broadness of the evaluation scales, correlation among both, and alleviate the degree of subjectivity. For example, *Multidimensional Quality Metrics* (MQM) [26] is a framework for analytic Translation Quality Evaluation, that can be applied to both human translation and machine translation. It poses a typology consisting of seven categories (accuracy, fluency, terminology, style, locale convention, design and verity). Other approaches are task oriented, like the degree of post-edition effort as an assessment evaluation.

2.2   Automatic Metrics-Based Evaluation

Automatic metrics prevail over other approaches when evaluating MT systems. There are two main families of automatic metrics: those that rely on a reference-gold standard translation (usually human-produced one) and those used to predict the quality of a system's output without any reference about the expected output [19]. They are not metrics for assessing MT quality per se but are considered as discriminators to rank different MT systems [20].

For the first type, a reference translation-based metric assigns a score to the MT output based on the degree of similarity to a reference translation [16]. To calculate the score, several techniques are used like calculating the edit distance or the precision and recall of n grams. Although they need a human reference translation, they are cheap and quick metrics, fully reproducible and repeatable. These metrics merely operate on the superficial of the text -even at the character level- and do not attempt to assess the semantic adequacy of the text. The BLEU metric [16] fall under this category and have become a de-facto standard in MT evaluation.

BLEU is based on n-gram precision between translated text and a reference translation. It aggressively penalizes lexical differences, even when desirable, like synonymy or paraphrasing. The main criticism of ngram-based metrics like BLEU is that, although they may punctuate accurately fluency, they do not reflect the degree of semantic preservation of the translated text with regard with the reference translation. It merely counts whether the lexical choices of the MT system coincide with those of the reference translation.

METEOR [9] is an MT evaluation metric which tries to consider both grammatical and semantic knowledge by taking into account synonymy and paraphrase corpus. However, the reliability of such evaluation metrics has been questioned. In [5,6], authors present evidence that BLEU tend to underestimate the translation quality of rule-base systems and even in high quality human translations [2]. These papers unveil the inappropriateness of assessing MT quality with metrics that merely measure surface text similarity based on lexical identity. In [1] it is reported the application of traditional evaluation metrics like BLEU, F1 or Fmean to an English-Arabic interlingual MT system, the three of them modified in order to support peculiarities of Arabic language.

It seems there is a sort of parallelism between data-driven MT and rule-based MT and their respective evaluation paradigm, to the extent that rule-based systems and even human translation usually show poor performance when confronted with automated metrics like BLUE [6,12]. In this sense, SYSTRAN (a rule-based system), that obtains one of the best human evaluation score, is strongly punished by the BLEU metric. Each approach defines its own methodology for evaluation and results and techniques cannot be crossed.

Closer to our interest are quality estimation metrics. Quality metrics assess the quality of a translated text according to several parameters: fluency, complexity or adequacy of the text. One important bulk of metrics are those aiming at measuring the semantic similarity of translated texts. Features to compute structure and meaning preservation rely on the ratio of the number of tokens, percentages, numbers, named entities, content and non-content words in the source and target text, the pro-portion of dependency relations between aligned constituents in the source and target text, etc [20].

In order to account for the variability of MT output and human reference, different levels of linguistic analysis are incorporated into the metrics. Thus, Wordnet is used to measure the matching of synonyms and to device word similarity measures: they look for semantic similarity of words with respect to a reference translation.

When trying to assess semantic adequacy, the metric MEANT [13] propose to assess semantic adequacy of output texts by measuring the degree of parallelism of verb frames and semantic roles between hypothesis and reference translation. The metric TINE [18] favors the preservation of named entities and the similarity of semantic frames by aligning verb predicates, assuming a one-to-one correspondence between semantic roles, and considering ontologies for inexact alignment [22].

Within the field of Neural Machine Translation, sentence and document embeddings have been used for evaluating semantic similarity of source and translated texts [21,24], just to mention two works from the overwhelming production in NMT. In order to assume that these models assess semantic adequacy depends on the relationship between similarity and adequacy, in the sense that similar semantic texts (assuming the algebraic definition of semantics underlying word, sentence or document embeddings models) are texts equivalent in meaning. Certainly, the inclusion of named entities, lexical variation, argument frames are relevant items to discern semantic adequacy would help in this purpose.

3   A Model for Semantic Validation

We frame this work under an interlingua-based MT system. The module for semantic validation is inserted within the MultiMail Project, a multilingual e-mail manager that allows the user to write an e-mail in one language and reaching the recipient in the desired language, in a transparent manner to the user. The Semantic Validation Module checks that both emails (sent and received) have the same meaning (checks for semantic adequacy) so that no information is lost during the conversion process.

3.1   Description of Graph-Based Representation

U3+ is an extension of the interlingua UNL [3]. It is a general purpose interlingua for MT purposes, it constitutes the pivotal element of the multilingual MT system [4] as well as a language for knowledge representation [8] since it conforms the basis for the semantic validation of the translation process.

A U3+ sentence represents written content as an acyclic directed graph. Formally, a U3+ expression can be viewed as a semantic net: the nodes of this semantic net are the **universal words** (UWs), which are linked by arcs labelled with **relations**. Universal words are modified by **attributes**. UWs constitute the vocabulary of the language, postulating a relational representation of the lexicon. Relations form a closed set defined in the specifications of the interlingua that characterize a set of semantic roles applicable to most existing natural languages (causal, temporal, locative, logical, numerical, argumentative, circumstantial relation, ontological relations). Finally, attributes convey contextual information. They express a heterogeneous type of information, like speaker-dependent information, contextual information affecting the predicate, pragmatic notions and typographical conventions.

For example, a simple sentence in English like "I go to the office tomorrow" is represented graphically in U3+ form Fig. 1.

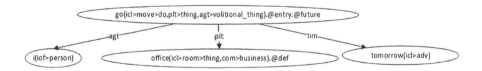

Fig. 1. Graphical representation of sample sentence.

It is graph composed of four nodes, containing the following UWS:

- `go(icl>move>do,plt>thing,agt>volitional_thing).@entry.@future`
- `i(iof>person)`
- `office(icl>room>thing,com>business).@def`
- `tomorrow(icl>adv)`

Three of these UWs are adorned with contextual attributes (in bold, and preceded by symbol .@), attributes express contextual information like time of the action, deontic and epistemological modality, number and determination of nouns. Binary relations of this sample sentence are: **agt** stands for agent, **plt** for place-to, and **tim** for time of action.

3.2   Semantic Validation

As it is an interligua-based system, the proposed semantic validation model works with three different representations:

1. Source text (ST): User's input in source language. Although it is not the scope of this article, this input is automatically processed and corrected (orthographic corrections, division of sentences if possible, and validated by the user).
2. U3+ Graph (UG): interlingual representation in form of U3+ graph of the source text.
3. Generated Text (GT): translated text into the target language. It is the result of the generation process from the U3+ graph into the target language, the text that will receive the recipient of the email.

The comparison between the three representations is done sentence by sentence, assuming that the information is in the same order. Therefore, the semantic adequacy of two texts will be determined by two consecutive processes pivoting on the U3+ graph:

– **Quantitative Analysis**: which determines whether the number of "informative items" is the same in the different texts (ST and GT) and the U3+ graph. In case any informative item is missing, we can assure that there are not semantically equivalent.
– **Qualitative Analysis** which determines if the information items have the same meaning and the relations between them hold in the different texts. In this case, we may state that there is semantic equivalence between texts.

Quantitative Analysis. This analysis relies on the concept of *fundamental data*. We understand by *fundamental data* the elements in a sentence that provide meaning, essentially, content words. Thus, quantitative analysis aims at determining whether the number of fundamental data remain consistent in the two natural language texts (source and generated) and that there are no missing or extra items. For example, in the sentence "I am going to the office tomorrow", data would be: "I", "go", "office", "tomorrow". This means fundamental data can be any term of one or more words, excluding particles like articles, conjunctions, prepositions, auxiliary verbs and modal verbs or discourse markers. Data can also be classified in nouns, adjectives, pronouns, verbs and adverbs. So there are two process in quantitative analysis: identifying fundamental data in natural language texts (source text and generated text) and identifying data in the U3+ graph representation.

In order to identify fundamental data of a sentence in natural language, it is necessary to carry out an analysis of all the words it contains, discarding those mentioned above. In addition, fundamental data can be also multiword terms like "base de datos", "Comunidad de Madrid" or proper nouns. To obtain the fundamental data in Spanish, once the sentence has been tokenized, multiword data (like proper nouns, adverbial locutions, fixed expressions, or compound verb forms) must be identified. Finally, stop words are removed from the list of candidate data. The result is the data of the sentence.

When identifying data in natural language texts, it has to be taken into account syntactical aspects that interfere with the identification of fundamental data in the sentence. For instance, in Spanish, pronoun subjects can be omitted, as in sentence "Mañana voy a la oficina", where the subject "yo" is not explicitly included in the sentence.

Another issue to take into account is morphological variation of lexical items. This is the case, for example, with the personal pronoun "yo", which can appear as "me" when it is fulfilling the function of direct or indirect object. In the sentence "Dime qué es y [yo] lo busco" we would have that the words "me" and "I" represent the same concept which, due to the form of language, present a different form. It would therefore be necessary, in these cases, to keep only the form of the personal pronoun. Therefore, the process of identifying fundamental data cannot rely on just the explicitly written data, but it is required a shallow morphosyntactic analysis.

In order to facilitate their subsequent comparison in the qualitative analysis, and to provide more accuracy to quantitative analysis, data obtained from the sentence are classified into several classes, namely:

- Word: this is the classification of most data, it also includes compound verbs and verbal periphrases.
- Term: multi-word data, classified in a different category from Words because they include proper nouns that are could not be translated.
- Number: this category includes, exclusively, those numbers written with digits or Roman numerals. For example: "12", "5", "25%" or "IX" would be classified as a number, while "five" would not.
- Date: dates in numerical format are classified as dates.
- Time: data representing a time in numerical format ($[0–24]$: $[0–59]$) are classified in this way. E.g.: "22:05", "10:15".
- Web page address (URL): data that corresponds to a valid URL is classified as a URL.
- E-mail address: data that corresponds to a valid email address is classified as an email address.

In addition to its data class, morphological information is also stored for each identified datum, which will be used in the subsequent qualitative comparison between data to ensure that there is semantic equivalence between them. This stored information depends on the grammatical category of data and can be:

- Adjectives: type, subtype, degree, gender, number, possessor, person.

– Verbs: type, mood, tense, person, number, gender, genre, form
– Nouns: type, gender, number
– Pronouns: type, person, gender, number, case, case holder
– Adverb: type

The process of identifying pieces of data in U3+ graph representations is rather straightforward. U3+ graphs are graph-based semantic representations of texts based on binary relations. Thus, in U3+ graphs, each node of the graph will correspond to an informative item. Thus, sentence of Fig. 1 counts for 4 fundamental data.

The process of identifying and extracting fundamental data, together with the necessary grammatical information, is performed by the linguistic modules within the MultiMail system, in particular, by the Extraction Module. This module requires the existence of a Spanish dictionary, with rich morphological information, and English dictionary (morphsyntactic), and lists of stopwords in Spanish and English. At this moment, the Spanish dictionary has coverage for more than 430000 inflected forms in Spanish and about 10000 different lemmas. Due to inherent features of emails texts (mixture of oral and written language), the so-called Module for Controlled Language cleans up spelling and punctuation of input texts to facilitate the subsequent task of dictionary lookup.

Once fundamental data have been obtained from the three representations, a quantitative comparison is made between them. In other words, it is checked whether the number of data coincides in the Spanish sentence, the U3+ representation and the English sentence. Therefore, the quantitative analysis is considered correct only and exclusively when this number of data is the same. If any of the three parts has a different number of data, the existence of the semantic paraphrase is automatically ruled out. Otherwise, we proceed to the qualitative analysis.

Qualitative Analysis. This analysis is meant to determine is there's semantic equivalence between texts by verifying two aspects:

– Data/Informative items from the original and generated texts and the U3+ graphs have the same meaning, namely semantic equivalence.
– Relations among such data in the different texts are the same or equivalent.

This analysis is meant to determine is there's semantic equivalence between texts by verifying two aspects: first, data from the three texts are meaning-equivalent; second, relations among such data in the different texts are the same or equivalent. In this article, we are going to focus on the first aspect.

In Sect. 3.2, it was stated that for each fundamental datum, relevant morphological information was stored. For example, the informative item "estuve" (conjugation of the verb "estar") is the UW $be(icl>be, aoj>thing, plc>uw)$ and the datum "was" in English. As we can see, it's not enough to check the equivalent in the dictionary because we then lost the morphological aspects of the data, which can also change the meaning of the sentence (cf. *I'm here* vs. *I was here*). This means we also need to evaluate the attributes of the U3+ data and check them against the morphological aspects of the natural language data obtained from the text. Thus, we need to analyze the attributes present in the U3+ graph representation since they are used to represent contextual information that shapes the sentence meaning.

For the purpose of semantic validation, a set of attributes is selected, so that they must necessarily coincide with the morphological features of data present in the source and generated texts. These are:

– Determination (@def, @undef, @generic): semantic equivalence requires that nominal concepts in both texts have the same level of determination.
– Number (@pl): this attribute expresses cardinality of the nominal concept. For semantic equivalence to hold, the number of concepts must coincide in the three representations. There is a note of caution at this point with words that expresses sets (such as tress and wood). This fall out from the scope of this work since it is closer to paraphrase and ontological semantics.
– Tense attributes: two sentences expressed in different tense or modality do not mean the same, thus it is necessary that the time and modal attributes.

The second element of the qualitative analysis connects to the application of U3+ as a knowledge representation language and the notion of semantic patterns, as depicted in [8]. Once data equivalence has been checked, we need to check the relations that indicate how these data interact at the semantic level. Since the comparison is done using sentences in natural language (original and generated text) and the U3+ graph, we need to define semantic patterns that match one representation (natural language) into the other (U3+). A linguistic pattern is formally defined as [8]:

Linguistic pattern is the conjunction of semantic relations (in our case, those from the UNL model) and nodes, representing the terms of a domain and linked by the semantic relations, that allows for the expression of events and situations in a semantically coherent way.

We assume that semantic patterns are finite, which means that all graphs could be made up from subgraphs that match such patterns, which also match a natural language phrase. Thus, to evaluate the semantic equivalence of two texts, we ultimately need to identify their phrases and then matching them against a repository of subgraphs. However, this approach has not been properly evaluated yet, and we do not have concluding results due to the combinatorial explosion derived from the potential combination of linguistic patterns, still object of experimentation.

4 Quantitative Evaluation

We can show the process of quantitative analysis will be illustrated together with its preliminary results. A sample of 25 sentences belonging to different mails written in Spanish. Next, a sample mail in Spanish is shown (source text), together with its representation in U3+ (for space reasons, only the first sentence is represented), and the generated text in English (target text).

Email 1 in Spanish: *Por otro lado, estoy revisando el contrato de MAX. He hablado con ellos e inicialmente pagarán 432.000€. Los pagos se efectuarán en la cuenta del BBVA. También solicitan información sobre proveedores de servicios de software.*

Email 1 in U3+ representation

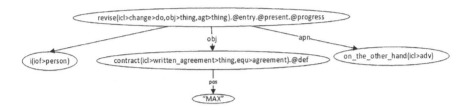

Fig. 2. Graphical representation of sentence 1.

Email 1 in English (generated): *On the other hand, I am revising MAX's contract. I have spoken with them. They will pay 432.000€ initially. The payments will be effected in BBVA's account. Also, they ask information about providers of software facilities.*

Let's have a look over sentence 1. Extracted data in Spanish text, u3+ representation and English text are:

- #Data in source text (Spanish): **5** [yo] [por otro lado] [estoy_revisando] [contrato] [Max]
- #Data in U3+ graph: **5** (number of nodes).
- #Data in translated text (English) **5**: [I] [on the other hand] [revising] [MAX] [contract]

The three representations have the same number of informative data (pronoun subject "yo" is not in the sentence but is recovered from the verb morphology).

Starting from a set of several hundred mails, we have outlined the initial steps to validate our approach. For each mail, its original representation in Spanish is compared to the interlingual and English outputs. Results are shown in Table 1, where columns *ESP*, *U3+*, and *ENG* indicate the number of fundamental data extracted in the Spanish text, the interlingual representation and the generated English text respectively; the value in column *Autom Eval* stands for the result of the automatic evaluation (TRUE when the three representations are equivalent,

Table 1. Evaluation results.

Id.	ESP	U3+	ENG	Autom Eval	Expert Eval	Coincide
1	5	5	5	TRUE	TRUE	OK
2	5	5	5	TRUE	TRUE	OK
3	3	3	3	TRUE	TRUE	OK
4	4	4	4	TRUE	TRUE	OK
5	4	4	4	TRUE	TRUE	OK
6	8	8	8	TRUE	TRUE	OK
7	10	10	10	TRUE	TRUE	OK
8	12	12	12	TRUE	TRUE	OK
9	8	8	7	FALSE	FALSE	OK
10	5	5	5	TRUE	TRUE	OK
11	13	12	12	FALSE	FALSE	OK
12	3	3	3	TRUE	TRUE	OK
13	8	8	8	TRUE	TRUE	OK
14	7	7	7	TRUE	TRUE	OK
15	5	5	5	TRUE	TRUE	OK
16	3	3	3	TRUE	TRUE	OK
17	8	6	6	FALSE	TRUE	NOK
18	5	5	5	TRUE	TRUE	OK
19	3	3	3	TRUE	TRUE	OK
20	3	3	3	TRUE	TRUE	OK
21	3	3	3	TRUE	TRUE	OK
22	6	6	6	TRUE	TRUE	OK
23	2	2	2	TRUE	TRUE	OK
24	4	4	4	TRUE	TRUE	OK
25	6	6	6	TRUE	TRUE	OK

FALSE otherwise) and *Expert Eval* gathers the evaluation performed by a human expert. Finally, column *Coincide* simply states the coincidence of automatic and human evaluations. The results of 25 mails sample is regarded as sufficiently representative to consider whether the model yields reasonable correct results.

The coincidence of the evaluation of machine and expert overcomes a minimum threshold of precision (90%), which can be considered as sufficient to establish the viability of our approach. As can be seen, in 96%, both human evaluation and automatic evaluation coincide; just in one case, the judgment of the human expert and the result of the semantic module reached different results. Table 2 summarizes the precision of the quantitative analysis.

Table 2. Evaluation results.

	Number	Percentage
Automatic & Human coincide True	22	0,88
Automatic & Human coincide False	2	0,08
Automatic & Hum do not coincide	1	0,04

5   Conclusions

We have presented a model for semantic validation of texts in an interlingua-based MT system where accuracy and fidelity of meaning is crucial. This approach based on an interlingual representation is language independent (from source and target language) and easy to deploy in a particular language. The statement of this problem is still an active research line: how to determine when a document written in one language means the same as another document written in a different language.

Evaluation from the quantitative analysis yields satisfactory results to assume reliability of the outputs of the translation system, however its development should be expanded with the inclusion of richer lexical and semantic phenomena. The quantitative metric is a preliminary step, not without difficulty however. We are still working, as future line, in the incorporation of the qualitative approach into the model for semantic validation of emails, with the aim of establishing a metric that yields a trustworthy level of confidence for semantic adequacy of texts. To do that, the combination and frequency of already identified linguistic patterns must be studied and experimented in order to open up a promising way for determining the semantic equivalence of utterances in highly sensible contexts like the one intended in the MultiMail.

References

1. Adly, N., Al Ansary, S.: Evaluation of Arabic machine translation system based on the universal networking language. In: Horacek, H., Métais, E., Muñoz, R., Wolska, M. (eds.) NLDB 2009. LNCS, vol. 5723, pp. 243–257. Springer, Heidelberg (2010). https://doi.org/10.1007/978-3-642-12550-8_20
2. Babych, B., Hartley, A.: Sensitivity of automated MT evaluation metrics on higher quality MT output: BLEU vs task-based evaluation methods. In: Proceedings of the Sixth International Conference on Language Resources and Evaluation (LREC'08) (2008)
3. Boguslavsky, I., Cardeñosa, J., Gallardo, C., Iraola, L.: The UNL initiative: an overview. In: Gelbukh, A. (ed.) CICLing 2005. LNCS, vol. 3406, pp. 377–387. Springer, Heidelberg (2005). https://doi.org/10.1007/978-3-540-30586-6_41
4. Boguslavsky, I.., Cardeñosa, J.., Gallardo, C.., Iraola, L..: The UNL initiative: an overview. In: Gelbukh, Alexander (ed.) CICLing 2005. LNCS, vol. 3406, pp. 377–387. Springer, Heidelberg (2005). https://doi.org/10.1007/978-3-540-30586-6_41

5. Callison-Burch, C., Osborne, M., Koehn, P.: Re-evaluating the Role of Bleu in Machine Translation Research. In: 11th Conference of the European Chapter of the Association for Computational Linguistics, pp. 249–256, Association for Computational Linguistics (2006)
6. Callison-Burch, C., Fordyce, C., Koehn, P., Monz, C., Schroeder, J.: (Meta-) Evaluation of Machine Translation. In: Proceedings of the Second Workshop on Statistical Machine Translation, pp. 136–158, Prague, Czech Republic. Association for Computational Linguistics (2007)
7. Chatzikoumi, E.: How to evaluate machine translation: a review of automated and human metrics. Nat. Lang. Eng. **26**(2), 137–161 (2020)
8. Cardeñosa, J., de la Villa, M.Á., Gallardo, C.: Linguistic patterns for encyclopaedic information extraction. In: Larsen, H.L., Martin-Bautista, M.J., Vila, M.A., Andreasen, T., Christiansen, H. (eds.) FQAS 2013. LNCS (LNAI), vol. 8132, pp. 661–670. Springer, Heidelberg (2013). https://doi.org/10.1007/978-3-642-40769-7_57
9. Denkowski, M., Lavie, A.: Meteor Universal: language specific translation evaluation for any target language. In: Proceedings of the Ninth Workshop on Statistical Machine Translation (2014)
10. Dorr, B.J.: Interlingual machine translation a parameterized approach. Artif. Intell. **63**(1–2), 429–492 (1993)
11. Koby, G., Fields, P., Hague, D., Lommel, A., Melby, A.: Defining translation quality. Tradumàtica: tecnologies de la traducció. 413 (2014). https://doi.org/10.5565/rev/tradumatica.76
12. Koehn, P., Monz, C.: Manual and automatic evaluation of machine translation between european languages. In: Proceedings on the Workshop on Statistical Machine Translation, pp. 102–121, New York City. Association for Computational Linguistics (2006)
13. Lo, C., Wu, D.: MEANT at WMT 2013: A tunable, accurate yet inexpensive semantic frame based MT evaluation metric. In: Proceedings of the Eighth Workshop on Statistical Machine Translation (2013)
14. Mitamura, T., Nyberg, E.H., Carbonell, J.G.: An efficient interlingua translation system for multi-lingual document production. In: Proceedings of Machine Translation Summit III: Papers (1991)
15. Muraki, K.: PIVOT: Two-Phase machine translation system. In: Proceedings of Machine Translation Summit I (1987)
16. Papineni, K., Roukos, S., Ward, T., Zhu, W.-J.: BLEU: a method for automatic evaluation of machine translation. In: Proceedings of the 40th Annual Meeting on Association for Computational Linguistics, Philadelphia, Pennsylvania (2002)
17. Reeder, F., et al.: Interlingual annotation for MT development. In: Frederking, R.E., Taylor, K.B. (eds.) AMTA 2004. LNCS (LNAI), vol. 3265, pp. 236–245. Springer, Heidelberg (2004). https://doi.org/10.1007/978-3-540-30194-3_26
18. Rios, M., Aziz, W., Specia, L.: TINE: a metric to assess MT adequacy. In: Proceedings of the Sixth Workshop on Statistical Machine Translation (2011)
19. Specia, L., Turchi, M., Cancedda, N., Cristianini, N., Dymetman, M.: Estimating the sentence-level quality of machine translation systems. In: Proceedings of the 13th Annual Conference of the European Association for Machine Translation (2009)
20. Specia, L., Shah, K., de Souza, J.G.C., Cohn, T.: QuEst - a translation quality estimation framework. In: Proceedings of the 51st Annual Meeting of the Association for Computational Linguistics: System Demonstrations (2013)

21. Sultan, M.A., Bethard, S., Sumner, T.: DLS@CU: sentence similarity from word alignment and semantic vector composition. In: Proceedings of the 9th International Workshop on Semantic Evaluation (2015)
22. Vela, M., Tan, L.: Predicting machine translation adequacy with document embeddings. In: Proceedings of the Tenth Workshop on Statistical Machine Translation, pp. 402–410, Lisboa, Portugal. Association for Computational Linguistics (2015)
23. Wang, H., Wu, H., He, Z., Huang, L., Church, K.W.: Progress in machine translation. Engineering **18**, 143–153 (2022)
24. Wieting, J., Berg-Kirkpatrick, T., Gimpel, K., and Neubig, G.: Beyond BLEU: training neural machine translation with semantic similarity. In: Proceedings of the 57th Annual Meeting of the Association for Computational Linguistics, pp. 4344–4355, Florence, Italy, Association for Computational Linguistics (2019)
25. Xue, N., Bojar, O. Vrej, Jan, H., Palmer, M., Zdenka, U., Zhang, X.: Not an interlingua, but close: comparison of English AMRs to Chinese and Czech. In: Proceedings of the Ninth International Conference on Language Resources and Evaluation, pp. 1765–1772. European Language Resources Association (2014)
26. https://themqm.info/typology/. Accessed 07 Mar 2023

How Tasty Is This Dish? Studying User-Recipe Interactions with a Rating Prediction Algorithm and Graph Neural Networks

Andrea Morales-Garzón[✉][ID], Roberto Morcillo-Jimenez[ID], Karel Gutiérrez-Batista[ID], and Maria J. Martin-Bautista[ID]

Department of Computer Science and Artificial Intelligence, University of Granada, Granada, Spain
{amoralesg,robermorji,karel,mbautis}@decsai.ugr.es

Abstract. Food computing has gained significant attention in recent years due to its direct relation to our health, habits, and cultural traditions. Food-related data have been extensively studied, and graph-based solutions have emerged to combine user-recipe data for various purposes, such as recipe recommendation and food-data alignment tasks. In this study, we propose a graph-based approach to predict the rating a specific user would give a recipe, harnessing the structured form of user-recipe interaction data. The approach incorporates two additional features into the user-recipe interactions graph: 1) user-recipe review embeddings generated by a sentence-based transformer model and 2) a selection of healthy recipe features inferred from nutritional content and international nutrition standards. Results obtained from experiments on a publicly available dataset demonstrate that the proposed method achieves competitive performance compared to recent advancements.

Keywords: Food computing · Recipe rating · Heterogeneous graph · Natural Language Processing

1 Introduction

Food and culinary activities are daily tasks directly related to our health, habits, and traditions. For this reason, it has been a focus of attraction for the design of computational systems in recent years. Food computing emerges as the area that gathers all those computational approaches involving food data [17].

Recipe data have been extensively studied in food computing. Given its structured information, graph-based solutions have emerged as a way of combining the data included in the recipes for several final purposes, such as recipe recommendation or food-data alignment tasks. One of the most studied tasks has been the analysis of recipes from two main perspectives: (1) from the point of view of nutritional content for analysis and studies based on the implications and

© Springer Nature Switzerland AG 2023
H. L. Larsen et al. (Eds.): FQAS 2023, LNAI 14113, pp. 107 117, 2023.
https://doi.org/10.1007/978-3-031-42935-4_9

benefits of diets; (2) from the perspective of users. The latter includes preferences, user interactions with food combinations, flavours, and regional influence on dishes.

In the literature, several works analyse user-recipe interactions along with user preferences. These works rely on collaborative-filtering approaches based on historical user data to predict user taste in new recipes [3,5,20]. Recent studies have used graph-based solutions for encoding recipe data, including user interactions and preferences. These approaches leverage the structural information inherent to user-recipe interactions to improve the rating prediction task [23,25]. However, predicting if a user would like a recipe is a highly complex task because of the subjectivity of user preferences [18].

In this work, we focus on studying the preferences and interactions of users with recipe data. We propose to take advantage of the graph-structured form of user-recipe interactions to design a graph-based model to predict the rating that a specific user would give to a recipe. In contrast to previous works in the literature, we incorporate two additional features to the user-recipe interactions graph: (1) the user-recipe review embeddings generated by a sentence-based transformer model and (2) a selection of healthy recipe features inferred from nutritional content and international nutrition standards.

The main contributions of the work are detailed as follows:

- We create a heterogeneous user-recipe graph that models user-recipe interactions, considering user text reviews and nutritional features.
- A GNN-based encoder is devised to learn the user and recipe embeddings.
- We propose a novel rating prediction algorithm to predict recipe ratings from user interactions history data with recipes.

The rest of the paper is organized as follows: Sect. 2 details the previous work regarding studying user preferences in recipe data. Section 3 contains a detailed description of our method and Sect. 4 the experimentation designed for the evaluation. Finally, Sect. 5 encloses the main conclusions of our work and the future lines of research.

2   Related Work

Recipe ratings are a fundamental task of study in food computing due to their relevance in food-based recommendation systems. In [11], the authors remark on the relevance of considering user preferences. Thus, rating studies have awakened a significant level of interest. They implemented several recipe recommendation models to understand users' likes and dislikes better. Also, there is an effort to improve user suggestions parting from user history data [8]. The authors decompose recipes in their ingredients and create user profiles with ingredients that users may like based on ratings for recipes including these ingredients.

In [21], the authors propose a regression-based neural network that maps an ingredient list to a recipe rating. They iterate over ingredients to alter recipe ingredients to improve existing recipes. Other recent works incorporate rating data and healthy nutritional features in food recommendation systems [13,20]. In [27], the authors propose a framework that automatically detects a recipe's main ingredient. They propose food alternatives to change that ingredient based on nutrition properties and user data. In [10], the authors propose to use recurrent neural networks and a variational auto-encoder to predict new recipes based on calorie content and user preferences, among others.

Text reviews gathered from recipe social networks contains rich knowledge about culinary culture, user preferences, and their relation with specific ingredients [24]. They can aid to predict the popularity of specific dishes [16]. Recipe social networks like Food.com (url: https://www.food.com), AllRecipes (url: https://www.allrecipes.com), or Yummly (url: https://www.yummly.com) are crucial for rating-related tasks due to their registers regarding user ratings, reviews, and interactions [17].

Graph-based approaches have been proposed for food computing tasks to their capability to represent recipe objects as structured data [2,9]. Heterogeneous graph neural networks [30] allow for building deep networks to process heterogeneous data. Recipe recommendation systems use this feature to build sophisticated recipe representations [26] and propose recipe recommendation algorithms [7,23,25]. Also, they allow for food ingredients-based rating prediction. [20] proposes to use a collaborative filtering-based algorithm based on user previous preferences. They combine it with a food clustering for non-rated foods in the dataset. They assign food scores to represent users' interest in a specific food item and distinguish between general food scores and user scores. Rating prediction also takes part in explainable food recommendation systems [29]. They use the historical data to interpret the top-k recommendations for the user. The authors employ user interactions and recipes from Food.com to build a recipe recommendation system.

Link prediction refers to inferring new relationships in graph networks [12]. It deduces the behaviour of the network, thus exploring how networks will change. Link prediction has been applied in food computing for predicting new regional recipes [31]. In [26], the authors propose to use link prediction to optimize a recipe recommendation model.

3   Method

3.1   Overview

The proposed approach for rating prediction is outlined in Fig. 1. The used dataset consists of recipe features and user-recipe interactions. Using this dataset, we construct a heterogeneous graph that captures the relationships between users and recipes. This graph also includes information about the nutrient content of the recipes, such as the amount of macro and micronutrients.

The heterogeneous graph, comprising interactions between recipes and users, is fed into a GNN-based encoder [22]. The encoder is trained to learn the embedding representation of both users and recipes, taking into account the recipe features, user-recipe interactions, and user reviews. These embeddings capture the complex relationships in the data and provide an efficient way to process and analyse it.

Finally, a neural network-based classifier uses the embeddings for rating prediction. This rating information can be used for recipe recommendations based on previous users' preferences.

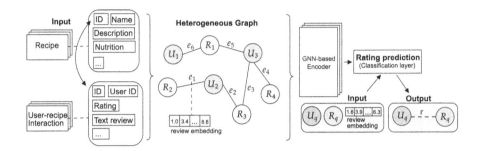

Fig. 1. Overview of the proposed method for rating prediction.

3.2   Graph Neural Network Model

The approach suggested depends on using a graph-based encoder to acquire user and recipe embedding representations. Graph neural networks (GNNs) are neural networks explicitly designed for graph data and offer a practical solution for node-level, edge-level, and graph-level prediction tasks. GNNs are based on the notion that a node in a graph is characterized by its connections and interactions with its neighbours. Thus, the information about a node in a graph is influenced by the data from its neighbouring nodes and their relationships.

GNNs are a type of neural network that operate on graph-structured data. Over the years, several variations of GNNs have been proposed in the literature, such as **Spectral-based methods** [6], **Spatial-based methods** (including all variants of Graph Convolutional Networks (GCN) [14]) and **Attention-based methods (GAT)** [28].

The proposed GNN-based encoder's structure includes two embedding layers, one for each node type and a linear layer that incorporates recipe features and is concatenated with the recipe embedding layer. Additionally, two GATConv convolution layers are used. The reason for selecting GATConv over other GCNs is the requirement to utilise user-provided reviews for each tasted recipe while learning the embeddings (Eq. 1). It calculates the node embeddings by the sum of attention coefficients multiplied by a shared weight matrix (Θ) [28]. The user reviews are transformed beforehand in sentence embeddings using a sentence-based transformer model (SBERT [19]) and are used as edge features.

$$x_i^{'} = \alpha_{i,j}\Theta x_i + \sum_{j \in N(i)} \alpha_{i,j}\Theta x_j \qquad (1)$$

where the attention coefficients $\alpha_{i,j}$ for multi-dimensional edge features $e_{i,j}$ are computed as

$$\alpha_{i,j} = \frac{exp(LeakyReLU(a^\top [\Theta x_i \| \Theta x_j \| \Theta_e e_{i,j}]))}{\sum_{k \in N(i) \cup (i)} exp(LeakyReLU(a^\top [\Theta x_i \| \Theta x_k \| \Theta_e e_{i,k}]))} \qquad (2)$$

As loss function, the Categorical Cross-Entropy loss (CE) has been selected for training the model. It is a loss function commonly known as Softmax Loss, which involves combining a Softmax activation with a Cross-Entropy loss. This function allows training the model in order to generate a probability distribution over C classes for each edge. Softmax Loss is typically utilised for multi-class classification tasks, as is the use case presented in this paper (Eq. 3), where C represents the number of classes, s_i the score given to the i class and $t_i = 1$ if i-th is the label for the input, otherwise equal to 0. This loss is computed for each data point and then averaged.

$$CE = -\sum_i^C t_i \log \left(\frac{\exp(s_i)}{\sum_j^C \exp(s_j)} \right) \qquad (3)$$

3.3   Rating Prediction Layer

The rating prediction layer leverages user and recipe embeddings to predict ratings between users and recipes. The GNN-based model learns these embeddings by considering a range of inputs, including recipe features, user-recipe ratings, and user reviews.

As discussed in Sect. 2, there are several embedding-based approaches to rating prediction. One popular approach is to train a classifier that takes user and recipe embeddings as input and combines them using operations like concatenation or mean. Other approaches involve computing measures, such as cosine similarity, dot product, and others, between the user and recipe embeddings to predict ratings based on reviews.

These previous methods harness the learned embeddings to capture the relationships between users and recipes and provide a way to predict how users might rate new recipes based on their past behaviour. However, the effectiveness of each approach can vary depending on the specific dataset and task and may require careful tuning of various hyper-parameters.

In the approach proposed in this paper, the prediction layer concatenates user-recipe embeddings pairs and uses a neural network-based classifier to predict ratings. The classifier comprises two feed-forward layers, with a *RELU* activation function and *Dropout* layer between them. By using the learned embeddings and leveraging the classifier mentioned above, the model can accurately predict how users rate different recipes.

4   Experiments and Discussion

This section describes the process of obtaining and pre-processing the data to build a heterogeneous graph and also outlines the objectives and experimental setup of our study. We then proceed to analyse and discuss the results that we obtained. By presenting our experimental design and results in a clear and concise manner, we aim to provide a comprehensive understanding proposed approach.

4.1   Data

Data Acquisition. The publicly available *Food.com Recipes and Interactions dataset*[1] was used for our experiments, a comprehensive collection of recipe data from the Food.com website spanning over 18 years of user interactions [15]. The dataset comprises several files containing user, recipe, and user-recipe interaction data. Recipe and user interaction items are related by the recipe ID.

For our experimentation, we used two raw files containing recipe and user interaction data. The recipe file contains information on more than 180,000 recipes, such as recipe names, descriptions, ingredients, and preparation steps. It also contained a recipe identifier linked to the user-recipe interaction data, including recipe reviews from Food.com users. The interaction data comprised text reviews, user IDs, and preferences from more than 700,000 interactions in the form of recipe ratings.

Due to computing restrictions, 200,000 interactions (reviews) have been selected for training and testing the model. These interactions comprise 63,354 users and 40,792 recipes.

Data Preprocessing. The recipe data contains a field with nutrition quantities of total fat, sugar, sodium, protein, saturated fat, and carbohydrates. They are measured in Percent Daily Feature (PDV), i.e., how much a nutrient contributes to a daily diet [1]. We split these values into independent columns to better understand and process the recipe.

The user interactions file contains a numeric rating and a text review that a user gives to a specific recipe. We use one-hot encoding to encode the rating. We use SBERT [19], a sentence-based transformers model, for obtaining a sentence-level encoding of the user reviews. It allows to generate numeric quality representations of the user's opinions regarding recipes.

4.2   Setup

The objective of the experiments carried out in this paper is to analyse and discuss the outcomes of the GNN-based rating prediction method. In order to

---

[1] Link to the Food.com Recipes and Interactions dataset: https://www.kaggle.com/datasets/shuyangli94/food-com-recipes-and-user-interactions?select=RAW_recipes.csv.

showcase the feasibility of the proposal, the model has been evaluated considering two scenarios: 1) training the model without considering the users' reviews, and 2) considering the users' reviews. The following outlines the action plan.

1. First, the chosen dataset mentioned in the previous section is partitioned into training and validation sets, comprising 80% and 20% of the data, respectively.
2. Subsequently, the model is trained to obtain the embeddings of users and recipes and to learn the weight matrix for rating prediction. The model is trained for 50 epochs, employing GATConv as the convolutional layer, categorical cross-entropy as the loss function, and stochastic gradient descent as the optimizer. As stated before, the model is trained using two scenarios.
3. Finally, the model performance is evaluated on the validation set in terms of accuracy.

4.3   Results and Discussion

In this section, we present and discuss the results obtained in the experiments to evaluate the proposed graph-based rating prediction approach. The first experiment evaluates the accuracy of the model in predicting ratings using recipe and user features without considering the users' reviews. Next, we evaluated the accuracy of the model when considering the users' reviews in addition to the recipe and user features.

The loss and accuracy during the training phase for both scenarios are shown in Figs. 2 and 3, respectively. The figures reveal that the loss behaves similarly for both cases. However, the accuracy of the model that considers the users' reviews (light blue line) yields better results than the model that does not take the reviews into account (dark blue line).

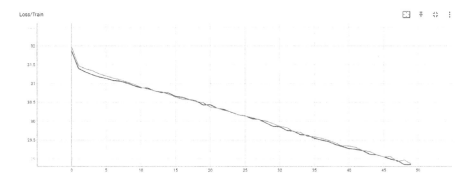

Fig. 2. Loss for training phase considering both scenarios (the dark blue line stands for the model that does not consider the reviews and the light blue line for the model that takes user reviews into account). (Color figure online)

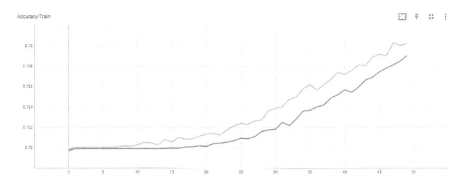

Fig. 3. Accuracy for training phase considering both scenarios (the dark blue line stands for the model that does not consider the reviews and the light blue line for the model that takes user reviews into account). (Color figure online)

Table 1 presents the validation results for both scenarios regarding accuracy. The table indicates that the proposed approach effectively predicts ratings with an accuracy of 72.95 on the validation set without considering the users' reviews and an accuracy of 73.2 when users' reviews are considered. It is observed that incorporating users' reviews into the model results in a slight improvement in accuracy, suggesting that such inclusion can lead to more accurate rating predictions.

Table 1. Validation results in terms of accuracy for both scenarios.

Approach	Accuracy
Without reviews	72.95
Considering users' reviews	73.2

The experiments demonstrate that the proposed graph-based rating prediction approach effectively predicts user-recipes ratings. Incorporating user reviews jointly with healthy recipe features can further improve the model's accuracy. The proposed approach can be useful in various food-related applications, such as recipe recommendations and personalised diet planning.

We want to remark on the added difficulty in modelling user preferences since user opinions are subjective and hard to predict. The graph structure considers the recipe network and user relations with recipes, not just user-recipe user interactions. This structure enables to train of recipes encoded more inherently. Table 1 shows that text reviews improve the model's performance. It is because text opinions contain more detailed information about user preferences. User reviews also usually contain positive (e.g., love, excellent) or negative (e.g., hate, disgusting) words. It helps the model with more expressiveness when predicting ratings.

5   Conclusions and Future Work

This work illustrates the need for food computing algorithms focused on dealing with data heterogeneity. GNNs are a suitable option, especially in food computing, where user-recipe interaction can be easily structured as a heterogeneous graph. Studying recipe-interaction networks is necessary for food computing. It is important to note that rating prediction is a challenging task since there is a high presence of subjectivity. It is compelling to model user preferences since they are varied, and personal habits, culture, and regional aspects could strongly influence them. Studying recipe ratings and reviews allows for a better comprehension of the relationship between population and food habits. They not only favour recommending highly customized recipes to users. It also helps combine preferences with nutritional guidelines to favour better adherence to healthy diets, one of the leading research topics in Nutrition [4].

We plan to incorporate the proposed rating prediction algorithm in a multimodal recommendation system to assist final recipe suggestions to specific users considering their preferences. We believe that encoding the information of the recipe images will allow for a better understanding of rating decisions. It also remains as future work applying explainability approaches to illustrate which review tokens influence the final rating the most.

Acknowledgments. This research was partially funded by the Grant PID2021-123960OB-I00 funded by MCIN/AEI/10.13039/501100011033 and by ERDF A way of making Europe. It was also funded by the Grant TED2021-129402B-C21 funded by MCIN/AEI/10.13039/501100011033 and, by the European Union NextGenerationEU/PRTR. It was also funded by "Consejería de Transformación Económica, Industria, Conocimiento y Universidades de la Junta de Andalucía" through a predoctoral fellowship program (Grant Ref. PREDOC_00298). In addition, this research has been partially supported by the European Social Fund and the "Consejería de Transformación Económica, Industria, Conocimiento y Universidades de la Junta de Andalucía" through the PAIDI postdoctoral fellowships (Grant Ref. DOC_01451).

References

1. The new nutrition facts label (2022). https://www.fda.gov/food/nutrition-education-resources-materials/new-nutrition-facts-label, [homepage on the internet]
2. Adaji, I., Sharmaine, C., Debrowney, S., Oyibo, K., Vassileva, J.: Personality based recipe recommendation using recipe network graphs. In: Meiselwitz, G. (ed.) SCSM 2018. LNCS, vol. 10914, pp. 161–170. Springer, Cham (2018). https://doi.org/10.1007/978-3-319-91485-5_12
3. Chavan, P., Thoms, B., Isaacs, J.: A recommender system for healthy food choices: building a hybrid model for recipe recommendations using big data sets (2021)
4. Critselis, E., Panagiotakos, D.: Adherence to the mediterranean diet and healthy ageing: Current evidence, biological pathways, and future directions. Crit. Rev. Food Sci. Nutr. **60**(13), 2148–2157 (2020)

5. Cueto, P.F., Roet, M., Słowik, A.: Completing partial recipes using item-based collaborative filtering to recommend ingredients. arXiv preprint arXiv:1907.12380 (2019)
6. Defferrard, M., Bresson, X., Vandergheynst, P.: Convolutional neural networks on graphs with fast localized spectral filtering. In: Advances in Neural Information Processing Systems, vol. 29 (2016)
7. Forouzandeh, S., Rostami, M., Berahmand, K., Sheikhpour, R.: Hfrs-Han: health-aware food recommendation system based on the heterogeneous attention network, Razieh, Hfrs-Han (2023)
8. Freyne, J., Berkovsky, S.: Intelligent food planning: personalized recipe recommendation. In: Proceedings of the 15th International Conference on Intelligent User Interfaces, pp. 321–324 (2010)
9. Gharibi, M., Zachariah, A., Rao, P.: Foodkg: a tool to enrich knowledge graphs using machine learning techniques. Front. Big Data 3, 12 (2020)
10. Gona, S.N.R., Marellapudi, H.: Suggestion and invention of recipes using bi-directional LSTMs-based frameworks. SN Appl. Sci. 3, 1–17 (2021)
11. Harvey, M., Ludwig, B., Elsweiler, D.: You are what you eat: learning user tastes for rating prediction. In: Kurland, O., Lewenstein, M., Porat, E. (eds.) SPIRE 2013. LNCS, vol. 8214, pp. 153–164. Springer, Cham (2013). https://doi.org/10.1007/978-3-319-02432-5_19
12. Hasan, M.A., Zaki, M.J.: A survey of link prediction in social networks. In: Social Network Data Analytics, pp. 243–275 (2011)
13. Khan, M.A., Rushe, E., Smyth, B., Coyle, D.: Personalized, health-aware recipe recommendation: an ensemble topic modeling based approach. arXiv preprint arXiv:1908.00148 (2019)
14. Kipf, T.N., Welling, M.: Semi-supervised classification with graph convolutional networks. arXiv preprint arXiv:1609.02907 (2016)
15. Majumder, B.P., Li, S., Ni, J., McAuley, J.: Generating personalized recipes from historical user preferences. arXiv preprint arXiv:1909.00105 (2019)
16. Mao, X., Rao, Y., Li, Q.: Recipe popularity prediction based on the analysis of social reviews. In: 2013 International Joint Conference on Awareness Science and Technology & Ubi-Media Computing (iCAST 2013 & UMEDIA 2013), pp. 568–573. IEEE (2013)
17. Min, W., Jiang, S., Liu, L., Rui, Y., Jain, R.: A survey on food computing. ACM Comput. Surv. (CSUR) 52(5), 1–36 (2019)
18. Morales-Garzón, A., Gómez-Romero, J., Martin-Bautista, M.J.: A word embedding-based method for unsupervised adaptation of cooking recipes. IEEE Access 9, 27389–27404 (2021)
19. Reimers, N., Gurevych, I.: Sentence-BERT: sentence embeddings using Siamese BERT-networks. In: Proceedings of the 2019 Conference on Empirical Methods in Natural Language Processing. Association for Computational Linguistics (2019). https://arxiv.org/abs/1908.10084
20. Rostami, M., Farrahi, V., Ahmadian, S., Jalali, S.M.J., Oussalah, M.: A novel healthy and time-aware food recommender system using attributed community detection. In: Expert Systems with Applications, p. 119719 (2023)
21. Russo, A., Hurst, B., Weber, T.: TastifyNet: leveraging adversarial examples for generating improved recipes (2021)
22. Scarselli, F., Gori, M., Tsoi, A.C., Hagenbuchner, M., Monfardini, G.: The graph neural network model. IEEE Trans. Neural Netw. 20(1), 61–80 (2008)

23. Song, Y., Yang, X., Xu, C.: Self-supervised calorie-aware heterogeneous graph networks for food recommendation. ACM Trans. Multimedia Comput. Commun. Appl. **19**(1s), 1–23 (2023)
24. Teng, C.Y., Lin, Y.R., Adamic, L.A.: Recipe recommendation using ingredient networks. In: Proceedings of the 4th Annual ACM Web Science Conference, pp. 298–307 (2012)
25. Tian, Y., Zhang, C., Guo, Z., Huang, C., Metoyer, R., Chawla, N.V.: RecipeRec: a heterogeneous graph learning model for recipe recommendation. arXiv preprint arXiv:2205.14005 (2022)
26. Tian, Y., Zhang, C., Metoyer, R., Chawla, N.V.: Recipe representation learning with networks. In: Proceedings of the 30th ACM International Conference on Information & Knowledge Management, pp. 1824–1833 (2021)
27. Vani, K., Maheswari, K.L.: Novel nutritional recipe recommendation. J. Inf. Technol. **5**(1), 1–12 (2023)
28. Veličković, P., Cucurull, G., Casanova, A., Romero, A., Lio, P., Bengio, Y.: Graph attention networks. arXiv preprint arXiv:1710.10903 (2017)
29. Yera, R., Alzahrani, A.A., Martinez, L.: Exploring post-hoc agnostic models for explainable cooking recipe recommendations. Knowl.-Based Syst. **251**, 109216 (2022)
30. Zhang, C., Song, D., Huang, C., Swami, A., Chawla, N.V.: Heterogeneous graph neural network. In: Proceedings of the 25th ACM SIGKDD International Conference on Knowledge Discovery & Data Mining, pp. 793–803 (2019)
31. Zhang, M., Cui, Z., Jiang, S., Chen, Y.: Beyond link prediction: predicting hyperlinks in adjacency space. In: Proceedings of the AAAI Conference on Artificial Intelligence, vol. 32 (2018)

"Let It BEE": Natural Language Classification of Arthropod Specimens Based on Their Spanish Description

Bartolome Ortiz-Viso[1,2]([✉]) [iD] and Maria J. Martin-Bautista[2] [iD]

[1] Research Centre for Information and Communications Technologies (CITIC-UGR),
University of Granada, 18014 Granada, Spain
bortiz@ugr.es
[2] Department of Computer Science and Artificial Intelligence,
University of Granada, 18071 Granada, Spain
mbautis@decsai.ugr.es

Abstract. Currently, image recognition and classification systems based on artificial intelligence are a well-established technology. In particular, numerous applications and systems have been developed for animal recognition in photographs, yielding excellent results. However, the identification of arthropods remains a challenge for these technologies due to the great variety and complexity of arthropods, and the difficulties that arise from visual identification. In such cases, a textual description based on observers' memory may be the only starting point available. To address this problem, this article presents a NLP-based system for classifying arthropods at different taxonomic levels, as well as an associated corpus of arthropod descriptions in Spanish.

Keywords: Text classification · Entomology · Taxonomy · Natural Language Processing

1 Introduction

Nowadays, a multitude of tools are used for the visual identification of animals. One of the most representative is iNaturalist [11]. These tools have proven useful for people with less knowledge to easily identify different animals, from large mammals to small insects. This process of identification tries to identify the scpeimen moving from a general category (in the worst cases) to a more specific one (that would be being able to identify the species correctly). However to better understand what are those categories or clases, it is necessary to talk about taxonomy.

Taxonomy [10] refers to the science of classifying organisms based on their characteristics and relationships. As mentioned, Taxonomy is organized into a hierarchy of taxonomic levels from more general to more specific (see Fig. 1). These levels help to categorize organisms into groups based on their similarities and differences. The core of this idea is to use the organisms' characteristics to reflect the evolutionary relationships among organism (phylogeny), both living and extinct.

© Springer Nature Switzerland AG 2023
H. L. Larsen et al. (Eds.): FQAS 2023, LNAI 14113, pp. 118–128, 2023.
https://doi.org/10.1007/978-3-031-42935-4_10

There is a vast array of measurable characteristics that can be used for this task, but as an example they could be Morphological characters as external morphology, genitalia or anatomy, as well as ecological or behavioural ones.

These characters as you can see, can vary from very obvious in broad categories (different morphology to distinguish between families) to very obscure ones (genitalia differences in insects to distinguish species). But all of them let us identify organism in a very precise and deep way, see Fig. 2 for an example.

More general   More specific

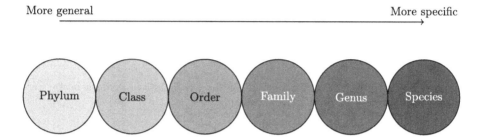

Fig. 1. Taxonomic levels name from more general to more specific.

From the perspective of the average citizen, we intuitively use this procedure to identify organisms, particularly animals. Thus, the visual differences between a ladybug (Coccinella septempunctata) and an ant (Formica rufa) allow us to identify them as individuals of different species, even though both are recognized as insects (belonging to the class Insecta). However, the average entomological knowledge usually covers only the most common species, leaving the average user without resources to correctly identify even the Order (Himenoptera vs Coleoptera) when encountering different specimens. That is where modern computational techniques can help us.

Motivated by this need, there is a well-established branch of visual identification with a multitude of proposals for the classification and identification of insects from images. These works have multiple areas of application. Such identification capabilities can be useful if we are interested, for example, in predicting the behavior of these insects or if we are concerned about their impact on our health, our livestock [9] or crops [4].

Along with this approach there is another interesting one, where a set of questions are asked to the user to assign a probability of a certain species [8].

The notable problem arises when for some reason we cannot take a proper photo of the organism we want to visualize. This often happens with small-sized arthropods, as macro cameras are not yet advanced enough, encounters can be very fast, and many people become scared when encountering insects. That is why, in this case, we believe that a natural language-based support that allows us to reduce the search to several taxonomic orders through the description of the organism and/or its behavior can be very interesting. However, the textual

More general   More specific

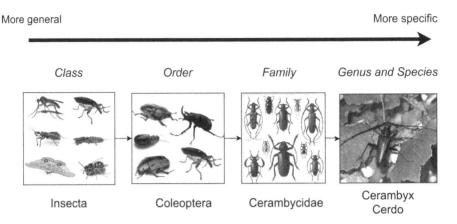

| Class | Order | Family | Genus and Species |

Insecta   Coleoptera   Cerambycidae   Cerambyx Cerdo

Fig. 2. A example of the taxonomic levels for the widely known Spanish beetle Cerambyx cerdo.

description of animals may varies a lot and it is unclear whether this can be a source of useful data for classification or not.

Our work aims to answer that question. We present a novel system (see Fig. 3) that allows exploring textual description as a source of information to identify arthropod specimens. Our system uses a text classification pipeline, comparing classical and fine-tuning transformers techniques. Moreover, this system is only one that exist with this approach (based on GoogleScholar and Scopus searches and the authors' knowledge) and the only one (to the authors' knowledge) that uses Spanish language for classification.

After the Introduction, we will present the working methodology in Methods (Sect. 2), where we will explain the nature of the dataset used and the algorithms employed. We will present the results of these methods in Results (Sect. 3). Finally, we will discuss in Sect. 4 the conclusions of the work, as well as the next research questions to be explored.

2 Methods

2.1 Text Cleaning and Preparation

The corpus of the text were obtained thanks to the Animalandia website [1]. On this website, there is a specific record for each animal species stored, with a total of 4740 different species. The record includes a taxonomic description that allows us to classify the species at all taxonomic levels (from Subkingdom to Species). In addition, each record has a brief textual description about the species. The information varies and is not homogeneous, as some records have more precise descriptions, location data, or behavioral data in varying degrees of detail. This data varies in terms of user expertise, so a wide range of descriptions are found. Most of them use a common word as a descriptor of the specimen (i.e. 'bee',

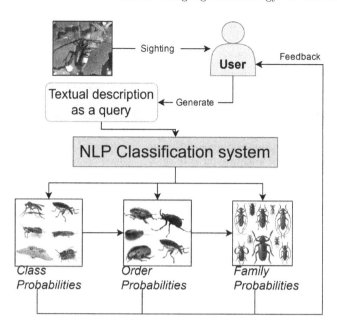

Fig. 3. Final diagram of the system proposed.

'wasp', 'beetle') but it also common to use some specific vocabulary to describe parts of the specimens in a more deailed and scientific way (i.e. 'elytra', 'torax'). This obviously produces a bias towards those descriptions and words uncommon for the non-expert user. A detailed description with translation can be found in Table 1.

The data was imbalanced, which is normal considering that certain arthropod species are more common, recognizable, and attractive (for example beetles has the highest number of species in Spain). We select Classes, Orders and Families based on their number of species to be diverse but at the same time having a representative amount of representative members (Top 3 in Classes, Top 8 in Orders and Top 15 in Families, see Table 2). The information we can share between the different taxonomy levels is limited. It could be useful specially in insects, as it is the one that has deeper associated levels. In regards of Arachnida or Malacostraca Class, we can only go one step further (in the case of Arachnidda, to Araneae) or none extra step (Malacostraca). A remark in this regard is made in Sect. 4.

Furthermore, to alleviate the "popularity effect", we first divided the dataset into training and test sets to reduce possible biases in the test subset and ensure that it is representative of the queries it will receive. We then performed data augmentation using WordNet synonyms to replace some words in the text [5]. However, as some words were uncommon, we expect this process to have a similar effect to just oversampling.

Table 1. Examples of descriptions in database

Specimen	Description	Translation
(Curculionidae) Ips typographus	se trata de un escarabajo de aspecto completamente cilindrico ya que la cabeza se encuentra oculta bajo el escudo toracico que se continua con unos elitros de igual anchura que este se alimentan de madera muy joven de piceas pinos y alerces normalmente los danos que producen son escasos pero en caso de multiplication masiva los danos pueden ser muy importantes en estos arboles	is a beetle that has a completely cylindrical appearance, as the head is hidden beneath the thoracic shield, which is continued by elytra of the same width. They feed on very young wood of spruces, pines, and larches. Normally, the damage they cause is minimal, but in case of massive multiplication, the damage can be significant to these trees.
(Cerambycidae) Phosphorus jansoni	este escarabajo bellamente coloreado y de larguisimas antenas constituye una plaga de los arboles de la cola africanos sus larvas arrancan un aro de corteza en la base de una rama esta se muere y asi consiguen la madera muerta que necesitan como alimento	This beautifully colored beetle with elongated antennae is a pest of African tail trees. Its larvae strip a ring of bark at the base of a branch, causing it to die. This allows them to access the dead wood they need as food

In Sect. 3 some of the methods that do not use augmentation are preserved to be able to compare them with the ones that uses it.

2.2   Classical Machine Learning Classifier Approaches

After the text is cleaned and standardized (stop-words were also removed). We proceed to use a TF-IDF approach to vectorize the sentences. TF-IDF is a method for text classification where the features are the TF-IDF values of the words in the document. In this approach, each animal description is represented as a vector of TF-IDF values for each word in the vocabulary. Once the TF-IDF values have been obtained, we consider the following machine learning methods:

1. Naive Bayes Text Classifier using TF-IDF: Naive Bayes is a probabilistic classifier that works on the principle of Bayes' theorem. The probability of a document belonging to a particular class is computed using Bayes' theorem, which involves calculating the conditional probability of each word given the class and multiplying them together. The naive assumption made in this approach is that the features (words) are independent of each other given the class label.

2. Linear Support Vector Machine Text Classifier using TF-IDF: Linear SVM is a popular machine learning algorithm used for text classification. The SVM algorithm finds the hyperplane that maximally separates the documents of different classes based on the TF-IDF values.
3. Logistic Regression Text Classifier using TF-IDF: Logistic Regression learns a linear function that maps these TF-IDF values to a probability score. As we are dealing with a multiclass classification, the training algorithm uses the one-vs-rest (OvR) scheme. The logistic regression algorithm minimizes the logistic loss function to learn the optimal weights for the linear function.

2.3   Modern Transformer-Based Approaches

RoBERTa is a pre-trained language model that was introduced by Facebook AI Research in 2019. It is a variant of the BERT (Bidirectional Encoder Representations from Transformers) model, which is another pre-trained language model. In our specific case we used the The *roberta-base-bne model* [3] that have been pre-trained using the largest Spanish corpus known to date, compiled from the web crawlings performed by the National Library of Spain (BNE). The model can be found online [2].

To obtain a classifier based on this model, we conduct a fine tuning training, focus on text classification. The learning rate was set to 2e-5, batch size = 8 and epochs = 6. The training was conducted using the trainer method of Transformers Library [12]. We allowed Spanish stop-words to stay in the descriptions.

Table 2. Classes, Orders and Families selected with their number of appearances

Class	Orders	Families
Insecta 1306	Lepidoptera 439	Nymphalidae 134
Arachnida 159	Coleoptera 332	Cerambycidae 62
Malacostraca 114	Hemiptera 131	Scarabaeidae 49
	Diptera 129	Papilionidae 46
	Araneae 122	Chrysomelidae 36
	Decapoda 97	Noctuidae 34
	Hymenoptera 92	Lycaenidae 31
	Orthoptera 59	Pieridae 30
		Syrphidae 30
		Pentatomidae 26
		Acrididae 24
		Curculionidae 23
		Carabidae 23
		Apidae 22
		Coccinellidae 22

3   Results

In this section we describe the results obtained comparing all the approaches stated in the methods section. A full description of these results can be found in Table 2.

Table 3. Results table with all the metric of the experiments of methods section. In bold the model with the best performance. Recall, F1 and Precision are averaged using a weighting strategy across all classes.

Class classification: Insecta, Arachnida, Malacostraca				
Model	Accuracy	Recall	F1	Precision
Naives Bayes Classfifier (Augmented)	0.86	0.86	0.81	0.88
Linear Support Vector Machine (Augmented)	0.97	0.97	0.97	0.97
Logistic Regression(Augmented)	0.97	0.97	0.97	**0.98**
RoBERTa-Based model (Augmented)	0.97	0.97	0.97	0.97
Naives Bayes Classfifier (No augmentation)	0.85	0.85	0.78	0.72
Linear Support Vector Machine (No augmentation	0.97	0.97	0.96	0.97
Logistic Regression (No augmentation)	0.97	0.97	0.97	0.97
RoBERTa-Based model(No augmentation)	**0.98**	**0.98**	**0.98**	**0.98**
Order Classification: Lepidoptera, Coleoptera, Hemiptera, Diptera, Areneae, Decapoda, Hymenoptera, Orthoptera				
Model	Accuracy	Recall	F1	Precision
Naives Bayes Classifier (Augmented)	0.78	0.78	0.77	0.85
Linear Support Vector Machine (Augmented)	**0.96**	**0.96**	**0.96**	**0.97**
Logistic Regression (Augmented)	0.95	0.95	0.95	0.96
RoBERTa-Based model (Augmented)	0.93	0.93	0.93	0.93
Naives Bayes Classifier (No Augmentation)	0.55	0.55	0.41	0.40
Linear Support Vector Machine (No Augmentation)	0.95	0.95	0.95	0.95
Logistic Regression (No Augmentation)	0.95	0.95	0.95	0.95
RoBERTa-Based model (No Augmentation)	0.95	0.95	0.95	0.95
Family Classification: 15 most popular Families				
Model	Accuracy	Recall	F1	Precision
Naives Bayes Classifier(Augmented)	0.65	0.66	0.67	0.77
Linear Support Vector Machine (Augmented)	0.73	0.74	0.74	0.79
Logistic Regression (Augmented)	0.73	0.74	0.73	0.79
RoBERTa-Based model(Augmented)	0.70	0.70	0.69	0.72
Naives Bayes Classifier (No Augmentation)	0.32	0.33	0.17	0.12
Linear Support Vector Machine (No Augmentation)	**0.76**	**0.76**	**0.75**	**0.80**
Logistic Regression (No Augmentation)	0.74	0.74	0.73	0.81
RoBERTa-Based model(No Augmentation)	0.55	0.55	0.48	0.60

As can be seen in the table, there is a notable worsening as we demand more granularity from the model. Even so, both in the augmented and non-augmented case, the model is able to capture the differences between the proposed categories, offering a remarkable accuracy (Table 3).

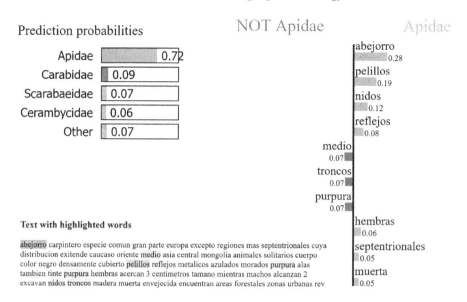

Fig. 4. A bumblebee (Apidae) output made with Naive Bayes (Augmented case) where "bumblebee", "setae" (hair-like structures), "nests", "females", "northern" are key to identify the family.

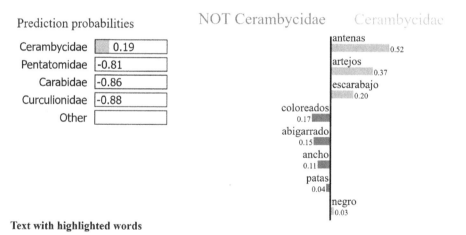

Fig. 5. A beetle (Cerambydae) output made with LSVM (Augmented case). "Antennae", "beetle", "Legs" and "black" support the decision.

The descriptions vary from one another in terms of terminology and content, so there are no significant differences between classical models to differentiate between taxonomy Classes. These could be because of the keywords the appears

Legend: ■ Negative □ Neutral ■ Positive

n/a	Prediction Score	Attribution Label	Attribution Score	Word Importance
Cerambycidae	(0.48)	Acrididae	1.27	#s se trata de una especie de mari quita de color negro con grandes manchas rojo intenso o naranja tanto en la parte anterior de la cabeza y del pron oto como sobre la parte posterior de los eli tros que estan trun cados en el extremo de forma ol b ic ua tiene forma oval ada un tanto alar gada y con ve xa se trata de un en dem ismo ib er ico presente en toda la penins ula rev junio 17 #/s
Cerambycidae	(0.38)	Apidae	-1.15	#s se trata de una especie de mari quita de color negro con grandes manchas rojo intenso o naranja tanto en la parte anterior de la cabeza y del pron oto como sobre la parte posterior de los eli tros que estan trun cados en el extremo de forma ol b ic ua tiene forma oval ada un tanto alar gada y con ve xa se trata de un en dem ismo ib er ico presente en toda la penins ula rev junio 17 #/s
Cerambycidae	(0.36)	Carabidae	0.52	#s se trata de una especie de mari quita de color negro con grandes manchas rojo intenso o naranja tanto en la parte anterior de la cabeza y del pron oto como sobre la parte posterior de los eli tros que estan trun cados en el extremo de forma ol b ic ua tiene forma oval ada un tanto alar gada y con ve xa se trata de un en dem ismo ib er ico presente en toda la penins ula rev junio 17 #/s
Cerambycidae	(0.30)	Cerambycidae	-2.79	#s se trata de una especie de mari quita de color negro con grandes manchas rojo intenso o naranja tanto en la parte anterior de la cabeza y del pron oto como sobre la parte posterior de los eli tros que estan trun cados en el extremo de forma ol b ic ua tiene forma oval ada un tanto alar gada y con ve xa se trata de un en dem ismo ib er ico presente en toda la penins ula rev junio 17 #/s
Cerambycidae	(0.54)	Chrysomelidae	0.56	#s se trata de una especie de mari quita de color negro con grandes manchas rojo intenso o naranja tanto en la parte anterior de la cabeza y del pron oto como sobre la parte posterior de los eli tros que estan trun cados en el extremo de forma ol b ic ua tiene forma oval ada un tanto alar gada y con ve xa se trata de un en dem ismo ib er ico presente en toda la penins ula rev junio 17 #/s
Cerambycidae	(1.00)	Coccinellidae	3.62	#s se trata de una especie de mari quita de color negro con grandes manchas rojo intenso o naranja tanto en la parte anterior de la cabeza y del pron oto como sobre la parte posterior de los eli tros que estan trun cados en el extremo de forma ol b ic ua tiene forma oval ada un tanto alar gada y con ve xa se trata de un en dem ismo ib er ico presente en toda la penins ula rev junio 17 #/s
Cerambycidae	(0.34)	Curculionidae	-2.43	#s se trata de una especie de mari quita de color negro con grandes manchas rojo intenso o naranja tanto en la parte anterior de la cabeza y del pron oto como sobre la parte posterior de los eli tros que estan trun cados en el extremo de forma ol b ic ua tiene forma oval ada un tanto alar gada y con ve xa se trata de un en dem ismo ib er ico presente en toda la penins ula rev junio 17 #/s

Fig. 6. A ladybug (Coccinellidae) output made with Roberta (Augmented case). "Ladybug", "black", "color" and "spots" support the decision. Other insects from Chrysomelidae. They can be mistaken for ladybugs, hence why the word appears in the description.

in them, such as common names ("beetle" implies the order "coleoptera") to refer to specimens.

Other terms such as "spider", "wasp" or "butterfly" allow us to easily assign an order category. However, it is worth noting how we are able to maintain a reasonable high performance when dealing with more complex classification, where thanks to the physical descriptions of the specimens. We analyzed some of the outputs through LIME software [7] and transformer-interpret [6] to gain more insight on how the classifier is working (a detailed output of two examples is shown in Figs. 4 and 5). As stated, in the family task, word as antennae, wings or shape, with the common descriptor, allow the classifier to perform reasonably well. This remark fits better models that account the presence of certain terms, while transformers are not able to reach the performance even with the data augmentation (Fig. 6).

4   Conclusions and Future Work

The presented work represents a first breakthrough in the ability of text classifiers to be used as support in the identification of animals (specifically insects and arachnids) when there is an absence of visual material, or when it is of poor quality for some reason. The results reveal an additional difficulty: most descriptions are produced for the most common insects, relegating those with a bad reputation or those that are less probable. This results in tremendously imbalanced datasets. Nonetheless, this is the first known dataset that contains textual descriptions that can be used to train natural language processing systems. Most of the descriptions were made by volunteers but the had biological knowledge which make the system unable to provide useful insight to those that are not able to describe an insect with some of the standard scientific vocabulary. The next steps that we want to take are:

– Complete and add new descriptions to the dataset, trying to balance it using more precise augmented data techniques.
– Improve and classify the descriptions with common words. Translate in an additional dataset full description but with their "common" synonims. Use this approach to decrease the entry-level knowledge of the user.
– With more representative species, use the taxonomy levels relationships to increase the taxonomic precision of the classifier (pre-filtering by Class, Order or even Family once we have categories in all of them).
– Merge the textual classification with the image recognition systems to improve accuracy.

Acknowledgements. We would like to acknowledge support for this work from the Grant TED2021-129402B-C21 funded by MCIN/AEI/ 10.13039/501100011033 and, by the European Union NextGenerationEU/PRTR and Grant PID2021-123960OB-I00 funded by MCIN/AEI/10.13039/501100011033 and by ERDF A way of making Europe.
– We would like to acknowledge Fernando Lisón Martín
(*fernando.lison@educa.madrid.org*) creator and maintainer of Animalandia (as well as the other Animalandia collaborators) for their work and for letting us use the database.
– We would like to acknowledge authors Bugboy52.40, Lidewijde and Georgiy Jacobson as the authors of the images in Fig. 2, extracted from Wikipedia.

References

1. Animalandia website. https://animalandia.educa.madrid.org/. Accessed 23 Mar 2023
2. Plantl-gob-es/roberta-base-bne.   https://huggingface.co/PlanTL-GOB-ES/roberta-base-bne. Accessed 23 Mar 2023
3. Fandiño, A.G., et al.: Maria: Spanish language models. Procesamiento del Lenguaje Natural **68** (2022). https://doi.org/10.26342/2022-68-3. https://upcommons.upc.edu/handle/2117/367156#.YyMTB4X9A-0.mendeley
4. Kasinathan, T., Singaraju, D., Uyyala, S.R.: Insect classification and detection in field crops using modern machine learning techniques. Inf. Process. Agric. **8**(3), 446–457 (2021)
5. Ma, E.: Nlp augmentation (2019). https://github.com/makcedward/nlpaug
6. Pierse, C.: Transformers Interpret, February 2021. https://github.com/cdpierse/transformers-interpret
7. Ribeiro, M.T., Singh, S., Guestrin, C.: "Why should I trust you?": explaining the predictions of any classifier. In: Proceedings of the 22nd ACM SIGKDD International Conference on Knowledge Discovery and Data Mining, San Francisco, CA, USA, 13–17 August, 2016, pp. 1135–1144 (2016)

8. Rodríguez García, A., Bartumeus, F., Gavaldà Mestre, R.: Machine learning assists the classification of reports by citizens on disease-carrying mosquitoes. In: SoGood 2016: Data Science for Social Good: Proceedings of the First Workshop on Data Science for Social Good co-located with European Conference on Machine Learning and Principles and Practice of Knowledge Dicovery in Databases (ECML-PKDD 2016): Riva del Garda, Italy, September 19, 2016, pp. 1–11. CEUR-WS. org (2016)
9. Schurischuster, S., Kampel, M.: Image-based classification of honeybees. In: 2020 Tenth International Conference on Image Processing Theory, Tools and Applications (IPTA), pp. 1–6. IEEE (2020)
10. Simpson, G.G.: Principles of animal taxonomy. In: Principles of Animal Taxonomy. Columbia University Press (1961)
11. Van Horn, G., et al.: The inaturalist species classification and detection dataset. In: Proceedings of the IEEE Conference on Computer Vision and Pattern Recognition, pp. 8769–8778 (2018)
12. Wolf, T., et al.: Transformers: state-of-the-art natural language processing. In: Proceedings of the 2020 Conference on Empirical Methods in Natural Language Processing: System Demonstrations, pp. 38–45. Association for Computational Linguistics, Online, October 2020. https://www.aclweb.org/anthology/2020.emnlp-demos.6

New Advances in Disinformation Detection

Bot Detection in Twitter: An Overview

Salvador Lopez-Joya[✉], J. Angel Diaz-Garcia, M. Dolores Ruiz, and Maria J. Martin-Bautista

Department of Computer Science and A.I., University of Granada, Granada, Spain
{slopezjoya,joseangeldiazg}@ugr.es, {mdruiz,mbautis}@decsai.ugr.es

Abstract. Bot detection in social media, particularly on Twitter, has become a crucial issue in recent years due to the increasing use of bots for malicious uses such as the spreading of false information in order to manipulate public opinion. In this paper, we review the most widely available tools for bot detection and the categorization models that exist in the literature. This paper put focus on providing a concise and informative overview of state-of-the-art bot detection on Twitter. This overview can be useful for developing more effective detection methods. Overall, our paper provides valuable insights into the current state of bot detection in social media, suggesting new challenges and possible future trends and research.

Keywords: bot detection · Twitter · social media · botnet · misinformation spread

1 Introduction

With the rise of social networks, part of people's lives takes place on online platforms where they interact with each other. These ecosystems are more than enough incentive to develop automated programs that interact and try to emulate human behavior. These programs can be beneficial tools in some cases for society, for example: helping journalists to automatize their uploads or providing customer service with chatbots instead of humans [2]; but the most worrying side is that they can be equally harmful or even more. Mass distribution of political messages, fake news, or malicious links is a very efficient and effective way to influence or deceive many people without the need to be an influential person. Many studies reveal that in various political events in recent years, social bots have had a remarkable impact. Some examples are: the 2016 US elections where Donald Trump won, the armed conflict between Ukraine and Russia prior to the current open war where it was revealed that there were online discussions involving these bots or the Catalan referendum (2017) in Spain where the 23.6% of the posts of that day where made by bots [9].

All these events have made the community realizes the importance and impact that bots can generate on the population. For this reason, the development of

© Springer Nature Switzerland AG 2023
H. L. Larsen et al. (Eds.): FQAS 2023, LNAI 14113, pp. 131–144, 2023.
https://doi.org/10.1007/978-3-031-42935-4_11

new techniques for the detection of these has become a necessity. In this paper, an overview of the state of the art of bot detection is presented. The main aim of the paper is to be a starting point for bot detection techniques enabling the study and development of new techniques based on what has been developed up to now.

In the literature, several reviews can be found on the topic [11,13]. These reviews were published in 2020, and with the rapid pace of technological advancements, such as the development of BERT (Bidirectional Encoder Representations from Transformers) [7] in the last two years, has led to the emergence of new and improved research findings in the field of bot detection. Another interesting and actual review was published in 2023 [2]. It may provide a more recent analysis, but our review offers a unique perspective by including an analysis of the available public tools for bot detection. This is an important contribution as it provides practical insights for researchers and practitioners who may be looking for tools to aid their work. This approach is likely to be more helpful for readers who are looking for a comprehensive and cohesive overview of the field. The main contributions to the state of the art are:

– A comprehensive and concise analysis of the state-of-the-art and theoretical background in the field of bot detection.
– A brief and concise compilation of the different ways of categorizing bots that exist in the literature.
– The review of the most widespread public and available tools for bot detection.

The rest of the paper is structured as follows: Next section describes the methodology used to elaborate the review. Section 3 introduces some basic concepts related to bots that are necessary for a better understanding of the next sections of the paper. Section 4 reviews the latest work in the field of bot detection. Section 4.2, provides a practical overview of the most widespread tools for bot detection. Finally, in Sect. 5 discussion on the topic and conclusions are provided.

2   Methodology

To conduct our review of bot detection on Twitter, we employed a comprehensive search strategy that involved the use of two different databases, Web of Science and Google Scholar. Our focus was on Twitter as it is currently the most popular social network for bots.

To ensure that our review was up-to-date and included the latest research findings, we set a cut-off point of 2019, which was a year of significant contributions to the state-of-the-art in bot detection, including the development of BERT. To identify relevant studies, we used a range of search terms and queries, including *"bot detection in Twitter"*, *"Twitter bot detection"*, and *"identifying bots in Twitter"*. To narrow down the search, we also used a combination of keywords related to the most widespread data science technologies for bot detection, such as *"machine learning"*, or *"natural language processing"*.

After an initial search using these terms, we screened the titles and abstracts of the resulting articles to identify those that met our inclusion criteria. Our inclusion criteria focused on studies that specifically addressed bot detection on Twitter and were published between 2019 and the present.

Following this initial screening, we read the full text of the selected articles and extracted relevant information about the research findings including any tools or frameworks that were proposed or employed in the studies.

3   Bots in Twitter

Before addressing the subject, we must be clear about some definitions and concepts that can be used for a better understanding of the paper.

3.1   Bot Definition

In the literature, there is no clear consensus on a bot definition. Many authors give their own definitions trying to cover most of their field of study. Computer scientists and engineers usually focus their definition on the technical details, however, social scientists focus their attention on social implications [11].

In [1] a bot is defined as an agent working automatically on an online platform, adding that they can work independently of human intervention. In [2] the authors argue that one of the main features of a bot is that works faster than humans at automated and recurring tasks. A similar thought is given in [3] emphasizing that the goal of a bot is to perform tasks regularly, in fact, they are created for that purpose. As this review is focused on Twitter, the concept of a bot can be refined using this context, so we will define what a SMB (social media bot) is. Definitions of SMB vary in the literature, this is understandable because of the speed at which this technology is advancing, the different objectives and behaviors that bots can have, and the many scientific communities that are studying them.

Some researchers consider an SMB to be a program that acts in the same way as a person would act in a social space [27]. Others are less restrictive and consider any account in a social media controlled by software as an SMB [26]. Some papers share the above definition with a slight but important change. They say that the account can be controlled only in part by software [32,33].

One of the most restrictive definitions in the literature is given in [4] which considers a SMB as a program that interacts with humans in a social environment and produces content automatically, adding that their intention is to mimic and perhaps alter human behavior.

We agree more with the general definitions. There are bots that do not necessarily produce content, bots that do not necessarily try to mimic human behavior, and accounts that are not entirely controlled by software. So for our review, a SMB is an account that is automated enough to produce content and/or interact with other accounts within a social media context.

In the next section, we make a review of the different classifications of SMBs given by researchers, associating the mentioned characteristics with some of them but not necessarily with others.

3.2 Categorization

SMBs categorization is a complex task. There is an enormous diversity of bots and they can have mixed features. It is difficult to establish clear boundaries between one type of bot and another, and the categorization of these bots can be approached in different ways. Different topologies have been given by various authors.

In [5] they classify bots taking into account two dimensions: the intention of the bot and the similarity with human behavior. In the first dimension, they split the intention into benign, neutral, and malicious; on the other, they make a binary distinction according to their similarity to human behavior. Although benign bots have a beneficial function for society (for example, in Japan there are bots that automatically warn of a possible earthquake [14]), for some researchers it is much more interesting to try to detect bots with malicious intent.

Another possible bot categorization is the one given in [1]. The authors have relied on three categories to give a classification: structure, function, and use of the bot. Based on this classification we can split bots into [1,5,8]:

- **Crawlers and Scrapers.** Crawlers and scrapers are programs designed to perform crawling, indexing, and scraping functions. The authors do not consider this kind of bot as an automated social media account because they do not interact directly with the user, but they can still have a real impact on them.
- **Chatbots.** A chatbot is a human-computer dialogue system that enables communication via text or speech, simulating human conversation with natural language and interacting directly with users through an interface.
- **Spam bots.** A spam bot is a type of bot whose goal is to spread unwanted content. Among that content, we can find things like ads, malicious links, or pornography. Spam bots are usually more active than other types of bots.
- **Social bots.** Social bots are those that try to imitate human behavior, acting in such a way that social interaction with them seems possible.
- **Sockpuppets and Trolls.** A "sockpuppet" can be defined as a fake identity created to engage with regular users on social networks, and includes both manually operated accounts and automated bot accounts. When these sockpuppets are politically motivated, they are often referred to as "trolls".
- **Cyborgs.** A cyborg is an account partially controlled by an automatic program. It is not clear in the literature how much automation an account must have to be considered a cyborg.

In [15] they propose a totally different and more general approach to those seen previously. Their topology is based on how the information flows between the user, the bot, and the content and the type of the latter. One of them is spam bots, which we are already familiar with, and the others are two new categories:

– **Broadcast bot.** In this type of bot, the information flows from the user to the content, passing through the bot. The users of this type of bot are usually organizations or groups of people who want to disseminate information.
– **Consumption bot.** In this case, the direction of the information flow goes from the content to the user, passing through the bot, which is responsible for collecting information from multiple sources for personal consumption.

Another different way of classifying bots is proposed in [16], with some concepts included in [22,30,45]. They rely on the complexity, their activities, and the way bots are organized to classify them:

– **Simple bots.** Simple bots are bots that post only one type of content automatically, making them easy to identify.
– **Sophisticated bots.** Sophisticated bots are bots that use sophisticated techniques such as copying profile information of real users but making small changes, using machine learning techniques to generate content, mimicking the temporal patterns of real users, or engaging in realistic conversations with other users.
– **Influence expansion bots.** Influence expansion bots are bots that are dedicated to expanding their social connections to amass influence.
– **Fake followers.** Fake followers are accounts managed by entities that are paid to follow users, usually with the aim of increasing perceived popularity and credibility, often forming networks of mutual following to avoid detection.

There is also a category called "botnets" that is a particularly interesting one that is related to the trend of the evolution of bot detectors and will be discussed in more detail in the next section.

3.3   Botnet

In the last classification proposed by [16], "botnet" was indicated as a category. It is interesting to explore what this concept consists of because of its relevance and its possible influence on the work of developing new methods of bot detection.

In most cases the repercussion of a single bot is not enough to make an impact, that is the reason why botnets exist. A botnet is a set of bots that are programmed to interact with others with a common goal [3]. Botnets are normally associated with malware and some of their goals could be: to spread spam, create and spread fake news or manipulate elections and online ratings [9]. Behind these botnets there is usually at least one bot master.

There are also some researchers who develop botnets in a benign way to anticipate possible improvements that can be implemented in malicious ones. For example, in [17] they say that one of the ways in which some botnets could be detected is the information they share between nodes. Therefore, these authors explore the idea of using ways to hide this information, specifically focusing on the use of stenography techniques.

As we said, having a network of bots working synchronously for a common goal is, by far, more effective, but could be an opportunity for the detection methods. Some authors use the behavior of these nets to detect if the accounts are bots or not. Their purpose is based on the assumption that groups of bots will have automation traces because they have a common goal. Analyzing individual accounts could be a harder task as the bots become more sophisticated [11].

4   Bot Detection

The history of bots and bots detectors is a cyclical struggle made up of waves. When a new way of detecting bots is born, a new generation of more complex bots is also born with the aim of avoiding that new method [12]. The first approaches to the problem were aimed at creating a general-purpose classifier using supervised learning techniques and focusing on individual accounts. Assuming that legitimate individual accounts could be distinguished from bot accounts based on their features [11]. But, with the advent of more sophisticated bots researchers had to rethink that assumption.

Trying to detect simple bots is a relatively overdone task for the most popular types of bots and there are many detectors in the literature that do it very well. The problem comes when these bots behave in a more sophisticated way. In [18] we can see that sophisticated bots can mimic human behavior so well that even humans have trouble telling a legitimate account from a bot account. They do an experiment with volunteers classifying by hand 4428 accounts between the classes: spam bot, genuine, and unable to classify. The results show that the human reviewers obtained less than 0.24 accuracy.

In recent years this problem is more present than ever. With large language generation models like GPT, different imaging tools generation, and deep fakes, bot accounts can be even more like legitimate ones. Making the line between what is real and what is fake blur more than ever. This is one of the reasons why there is a growing trend in recent years to focus bot detectors on studying groups of bots instead of individual accounts [11].

There is also another path that is being explored in recent years. And that is the inclusion of BERT (Bidirectional Encoder Representations from Transformers) [7] to bot detectors. BERT gives contextualized embeddings of the whole text of the tweet that has proven to be valuable in improving text-based models [41]. When Google paper came out, it broke with state-of-the-art of natural language processing. Examples of its use can be seen in [41], where this language representation model is used to directly extract features from tweet content for later input into a deep neural network, or in [29], where it is used for sentiment analysis of tweets for later classification.

4.1   Techniques

Most of the techniques used in the state of the art by researchers can be included in the following categories. Within those categories we will give some notable examples of bot detectors that are focused on or can be applied to Twitter.

Graph-Based. Since we are working with social networks, it is logical to think of using graph-based techniques to detect bots. These techniques try to interpret the user and his interactions as a graph in order to study his characteristics. Being the nodes of these graphs the entities in the networks (e.g. a user account) and the edges the connection between the nodes (e.g. the interactions between users) researchers use different features to find bots. Bot detection techniques using graph-based approaches are varied and can use centrality measures, community detection techniques, or GNNs (Graph Neural Networks). In the use of these techniques, we can highlight some of the works of recent years.

In [21] they propose a combination between the use of BERT and convolutional graph networks thus realizing a model that has large-scale pre-training and transductive learning.

Another interesting study is the one proposed by [23]. They use community detection techniques and machine learning combined with feature engineering, claiming the state-of-the-art in their field.

As the last work to be highlighted in this section, we will mention the one carried out in [24]. They propose a bot detection system based on anomaly detection. They make use of centrality measures such as: In-Degree (ID) and Out-Degree (OD), In-Degree Weight (IDW) and Out-Degree Weight (ODW), Betweenness Centrality (BC), Local Clustering Coefficient (LCC) and Alpha Centrality (AC); using a two-phase machine learning process with supervised and unsupervised learning to predict whether an account is a bot or not.

Feature-Based. Feature-based methods are the most widespread in the literature. These methods try to use the information that we can find both in the metadata of the account as well as in the content of the text written by the user. In this category we will include most of the methods based on machine learning and deep learning techniques. These methods fall into three categories:

- **Account-based.** They use the user's account information as features or to infer new ones, e.g., account age, username length, number of retweets, number of followers, or follower growth rate.
- **Content-based.** Use the information in the content of tweets as features, e.g., number of URLs, number of hashtags, sentiment, or tweet length.
- **Hybrid.** Use a combination of features from the user's account and their content.

In [25] and in [11] it was discussed the need to anticipate new adaptations of malicious bots and, for this purpose, the use of GANs (Generative Adversarial Networks) is proposed. A GAN is a deep learning framework consisting of two neural networks, a generator and a discriminator, engaged in a competitive process to generate realistic data. Genetic algorithms are used to synthetically produce new sophisticated bots in the first network, boosting detection performance, and, in addition, to generate robustness against possible new real sophisticated bots [25]. In the following we give some examples of the work done in recent years on feature-based bot detectors.

An interesting method is proposed in [10]. This study falls into the category of content-based methods. It is based on the temporal activity of retweets between accounts on Twitter. They use an LSTM variational autoencoder (i.e. a specialized neural network architecture that merges the ability to model sequential data of LSTM networks with variational autoencoders, which introduce probabilistic distributions to the neural network framework for generative modeling purposes) to extract latent features from the retweet time series of each account. To determine whether an account is a bot or not, they use a clustering algorithm. One of the interesting things about this paper is that, in addition to providing good results, they rely on graphs to visually analyze the time patterns of each account, making it stand out in explainability compared to other papers.

In [34] they propose a method to detect bots based on GANs. This study falls into the category of hybrid methods as they use both features of tweets, such as temporal patterns or sentiment, and also include features of the user's account. The authors use two GAN models to create realistic synthetic bots of multiple types that are added to the dataset. This provides robustness to the model and the ability to proactively detect multi-type evolving bots. Finally, they use a random forest to give a final classification, justifying their choice by saying that it is one of the most widely used classifiers in the literature for bot detection.

As a last example of a bot detector we will talk about the one given in [28]. Their work involves the development of a bot detector that relies on the use of word embeddings of tweet text. The authors use GLOVE (Global Vectors) [43] and ELMO (Embeddings from Language Models) [31] for a contextualized semantic representation of tweet text. In the next stage of the detector eight neural networks are trained based on four features: age, personality, gender, and education. Due to the combination of the use of word embeddings of tweet text and these features, we can classify this study as a hybrid method. The authors claim that training the networks to classify between humans and bots by splitting the dataset according to similar profiles increases the classification accuracy. In the last phase of the detector, a final model is implemented that has as input the values resulting from the different networks of the previous step. The authors experiment with different architectures for the final model to see which one gives the best results, with Feedforward neural network (FNN) being the winner.

Crowdsourcing. Crowdsourcing techniques are deprecated and are based on human involvement when detecting bots on social networks. Some works have been proposed such as online platforms [20] for its detection, but it was more effective in the early days of social networks. Now it is a technique that is very time-consuming, expensive, and not scalable.

To this, we must add one of the most problematic types of bots that we have mentioned in the classification: cyborgs. Accounts that, some of the time, are actually legitimate, making detection of these bots by humans a really difficult task.

4.2   Available Tools

Throughout the past sections, it has been shown how social bots can be used for nefarious purposes, including spreading misinformation, spamming, and manipulating public opinion. To combat this issue, several bot detection tools have been developed. In this section, we will analyze some of the most common bot detection tools, precisely Debot [46], Tweetbotornot [40], SocialBotHunter [44], BotSentinel [50], and Botmeter [32].

One of the first tools on the topic dates back to 2016 and is Debot, which uses warped correlation to analyze the temporal patterns of activity in Twitter accounts and detect deviations from normal human behavior, the final version of the algorithm can be used by means of an API and a web application. At the moment of testing the websites, Debot has not yielded any results so its interface could not be tested.

In 2018, Tweetbotornot and SocialBotHunter can be found. The former is an R package and the latter is an algorithm for which we have found no abstraction layer for use beyond its code based on a semi-supervised algorithm that takes the network topology as input. Tweetbotornot is based on several machine learning algorithms and takes into account features such as the frequency and timing of tweets, the use of hashtags and URLs, and the content of the tweets. More recently, there are the BotSentinel and Botometer tools, both of which offer API access, but provide the non-technical user with a web application interface. Figure 1 and Fig. 2 show the output interface of a real account. Both offer similar colour coding ranging from blue for real accounts to red for bots depending on the strength of the ranking. We can see how Botmeter also provides information about the content of the tweets and features analyzed.

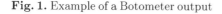
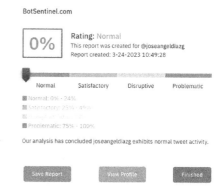

Fig. 1. Example of a Botometer output

Fig. 2. Example of a BotSentinel output

We believe that Botometer should be highlighted and we agree with the reasons given in [42]: it is well maintained and regularly updated to remain accurate, it has a free use API and website, it is referenced in the literature and many of the bot detector papers compare their results with it. For now, Botometer is focused on Twitter, uses feature-based methods, and works with features from different categories. Its distinctive idea is the use of an ensemble of classification models specialized in different classes of bots: simple bots, spammers, fake followers, self-declared, political bots, and others. They use supervised learning, specifically random forests with default values for each classifier [35]. Each model gives a score between 0 and 1 for each type of bot (as can be seen in Fig. 1) and, from these, a vote is produced that returns a final score between 0 and 5. The higher the value, the more likely it is that the analysed account is a bot. According to the authors, their approach generalizes better and is more robust than a monolithic model [35]. Additionally, it is worth noting that Botometer also provides a language-independent score, leaving language-based features out of the voting [42].

As for limitations, we found that many of the strategies presented in this section require some base knowledge about data science or machine learning models also, knowledge of R or Python, as well as connection and configuration of APIs. Botometer, DeBot, and BotSentinel provide a final website that can be used by people without technical knowledge. Also, Botometer proposes several papers with use cases and technical guides [42] for different audiences based on their technical skills.

There are other kinds of tools more democratized for a user without technical knowledge and focused on the topic of detecting fake followers. We must bear in mind, that in the vast majority of cases, a fake follower is created or even manipulated by a bot, and due to that, it is worth mentioning some of the most common tools in the topic. It must be noted that many of these tools are APIs or independent or private developments that do not have a scientific development behind them, but we consider that given their usefulness and relation to the topic they should be mentioned. Some of them are the tools developed by Conbin [48] or HypeAuditor [47] for Instagram and FollowerAudit [49] for Twitter. Finally, it is important to note that no bot detection algorithm is perfect, and the ones presented in this section are not an exception. Users should always interpret the results of the analysis with caution and consider other factors when evaluating the authenticity of a Twitter account.

5   Conclusions and Future Challenges

In this paper we have given an overview of the state-of-the-art of bot detection on Twitter, we have analyzed the different categorizations that researchers propose in the literature and we have done a review of the most widespread tools available for detecting these bots.

Despite the increase in the number of articles on the subject in recent years, there is still a lot of work to be done. A point to take into consideration would be trying to find a consensus on terminology between authors. This would help when comparing methods, to avoid confusion in the literature and improve the speed at which the field advances.

Although the work on bot detectors is diverse, there is clearly less work in unsupervised and semi-supervised methods when compared in number with supervised methods. This is also seen in the number of real-time detection works that exist. The inclusion of BERT in future work, the use of GANs models, as well as the use of specific model ensembles instead of a general-purpose model, seems promising avenues to explore.

This review has focused on the social network Twitter as it is currently the most important and where most bots have been developed, but there are other social networks such as Instagram, Reddit or LinkedIn where less research has been done and may also be useful.

Acknowledgment. The research reported in this paper was supported by the DesinfoScan project: Grant TED2021-129402B-C21 funded by MCIN/AEI/10.13039/501100011033 and, by the European Union NextGenerationEU/PRTR, and FederaMed project: Grant PID2021-123960OB-I00 funded by MCIN/AEI/10.13039/501100011033 and by ERDF A way of making Europe. Finally the project is also partially supported by the Spanish Ministry of Education, Culture and Sport (FPU18/00150).

References

1. Gorwa, R., Guilbeault, D.: Unpacking the social media bot: a typology to guide research and policy. Policy Internet **12**(2), 225–248 (2020)
2. Aljabri, M., Zagrouba, R., Shaahid, A., Alnasser, F., Saleh, A., Alomari, D.M.: Machine learning-based social media bot detection: a comprehensive literature review. Soc. Netw. Anal. Min. **13**(1), 20 (2023)
3. Loyola-González, O., Monroy, R., Rodríguez, J., López-Cuevas, A., Mata-Sánchez, J.I.: Contrast pattern-based classification for bot detection on twitter. IEEE Access **7**, 45800–45817 (2019)
4. Ferrara, E., Varol, O., Davis, C., Menczer, F., Flammini, A.: The rise of social bots. Commun. ACM **59**(7), 96–104 (2016)
5. Stieglitz, S., Brachten, F., Ross, B., Jung, A.K.: Do social bots dream of electric sheep? a categorisation of social media bot accounts. arXiv preprint arXiv:1710.04044 (2017)
6. Davis, C.A., Varol, O., Ferrara, E., Flammini, A., Menczer, F.: Botornot: a system to evaluate social bots. In Proceedings of the 25th International Conference Companion on World Wide Web, pp. 273–274, April 2016
7. Devlin, J., Chang, M.W., Lee, K., Toutanova, K.: Bert: pre-training of deep bidirectional transformers for language understanding. arXiv preprint arXiv:1810.04805 (2018)
8. Zhao, C., Xin, Y., Li, X., Zhu, H., Yang, Y., Chen, Y.: An attention-based graph neural network for spam bot detection in social networks. Appl. Sci. **10**(22), 8160 (2020)
9. Shahid, W., Li, Y., Staples, D., Amin, G., Hakak, S., Ghorbani, A.: Are you a cyborg, bot or human?-a survey on detecting fake news spreaders. IEEE Access **10**, 27069–27083 (2022)
10. Mazza, M., Cresci, S., Avvenuti, M., Quattrociocchi, W., Tesconi, M.: Rtbust: exploiting temporal patterns for botnet detection on twitter. In: Proceedings of the 10th ACM Conference on Web Science, pp. 183–192, June 2019

11. Cresci, S.: A decade of social bot detection. Commun. ACM **63**(10), 72–83 (2020)
12. Cresci, S., Petrocchi, M., Spognardi, A., Tognazzi, S.: Better safe than sorry: an adversarial approach to improve social bot detection. In: Proceedings of the 10th ACM Conference on Web Science, pp. 47–56, June 2019
13. Orabi, M., Mouheb, D., Al Aghbari, Z., Kamel, I.: Detection of bots in social media: a systematic review. Inf. Process. Manage. **57**(4), 102250 (2020)
14. Haustein, S., Bowman, T.D., Holmberg, K., Tsou, A., Sugimoto, C.R., Larivière, V.: Tweets as impact indicators: examining the implications of automated "bot" accounts on Twitter. J. Am. Soc. Inf. Sci. **67**(1), 232–238 (2016)
15. Oentaryo, R.J., Murdopo, A., Prasetyo, P.K., Lim, E.-P.: On profiling bots in social media. In: Spiro, E., Ahn, Y.-Y. (eds.) SocInfo 2016. LNCS, vol. 10046, pp. 92–109. Springer, Cham (2016). https://doi.org/10.1007/978-3-319-47880-7_6
16. Yang, K.C., Varol, O., Davis, C.A., Ferrara, E., Flammini, A., Menczer, F.: Arming the public with artificial intelligence to counter social bots. Hum. Behav. Emerg. Technol. **1**(1), 48–61 (2019)
17. Nagaraja, S., Houmansadr, A., Piyawongwisal, P., Singh, V., Agarwal, P., Borisov, N.: Stegobot: a covert social network botnet. In: Filler, T., Pevný, T., Craver, S., Ker, A. (eds.) IH 2011. LNCS, vol. 6958, pp. 299–313. Springer, Heidelberg (2011). https://doi.org/10.1007/978-3-642-24178-9_21
18. Cresci, S., Di Pietro, R., Petrocchi, M., Spognardi, A., Tesconi, M.: The paradigm-shift of social spambots: evidence, theories, and tools for the arms race. In: Proceedings of the 26th International Conference on World Wide Web Companion, pp. 963–972, April 2017
19. Heidari, M., et al.: Bert model for fake news detection based on social bot activities in the covid-19 pandemic. In: 2021 IEEE 12th Annual Ubiquitous Computing, Electronics & Mobile Communication Conference (UEMCON), pp. 0103–0109. IEEE, December 2021
20. Wang, G., et al.: Social turing tests: crowdsourcing sybil detection. arXiv preprint arXiv:1205.3856 (2012)
21. Guo, Q., Xie, H., Li, Y., Ma, W., Zhang, C.: Social bots detection via fusing bert and graph convolutional networks. Symmetry **14**(1), 30 (2021). https://www.overleaf.com/project/64072d4f13e3abf8ca3ff145
22. Freitas, C., Benevenuto, F., Ghosh, S., Veloso, A.: Reverse engineering socialbot infiltration strategies in twitter. In: Proceedings of the 2015 IEEE/ACM International Conference on Advances in Social Networks Analysis and Mining 2015, pp. 25–32, August 2015
23. Li, S., Zhao, C., Li, Q., Huang, J., Zhao, D., Zhu, P.: BotFinder: a novel framework for social bots detection in online social networks based on graph embedding and community detection. In: World Wide Web, pp. 1–17 (2022)
24. Abou Daya, A., Salahuddin, M.A., Limam, N., Boutaba, R.: BotChase: graph-based bot detection using machine learning. IEEE Trans. Netw. Serv. Manage. **17**(1), 15–29 (2020)
25. Cresci, S., Petrocchi, M., Spognardi, A., Tognazzi, S.: The coming age of adversarial social bot detection. First Monday (2021)
26. Morstatter, F., Wu, L., Nazer, T.H., Carley, K.M., Liu, H.: A new approach to bot detection: striking the balance between precision and recall. In: 2016 IEEE/ACM International Conference on Advances in Social Networks Analysis and Mining (ASONAM), pp. 533–540. IEEE, August 2016

27. Abokhodair, N., Yoo, D., McDonald, D.W.: Dissecting a social botnet: Growth, content and influence in Twitter. In: Proceedings of the 18th ACM conference on Computer Supported Cooperative Work & Social Computing, pp. 839–851, February 2015

28. Heidari, M., Jones, J.H., Uzuner, O.: Deep contextualized word embedding for text-based online user profiling to detect social bots on twitter. In: 2020 International Conference on Data Mining Workshops (ICDMW), pp. 480–487. IEEE, November 2020

29. Heidari, M., Jones, J.H.: Using bert to extract topic-independent sentiment features for social media bot detection. In: 2020 11th IEEE Annual Ubiquitous Computing, Electronics & Mobile Communication Conference (UEMCON), pp. 0542–0547. IEEE, October 2020

30. Cresci, S., Di Pietro, R., Petrocchi, M., Spognardi, A., Tesconi, M.: Fame for sale: efficient detection of fake Twitter followers. Decis. Support Syst. **80**, 56–71 (2015)

31. Sarzynska-Wawer, J., et al.: Detecting formal thought disorder by deep contextualized word representations. Psychiatry Res. **304**, 114135 (2021)

32. Yang, K.C., Varol, O., Hui, P.M., Menczer, F.: Scalable and generalizable social bot detection through data selection. In: Proceedings of the AAAI Conference on Artificial Intelligence, vol. 34, No. 01, pp. 1096–1103, April 2020

33. Assenmacher, D., Clever, L., Frischlich, L., Quandt, T., Trautmann, H., Grimme, C.: Demystifying social bots: On the intelligence of automated social media actors. Social Media+ Society **6**(3), 2056305120939264 (2020)

34. Dialektakis, G., Dimitriadis, I., Vakali, A.: CALEB: a conditional adversarial learning framework to enhance bot detection. arXiv preprint arXiv:2205.15707 (2022)

35. Sayyadiharikandeh, M., Varol, O., Yang, K.C., Flammini, A., Menczer, F.: Detection of novel social bots by ensembles of specialized classifiers. In: Proceedings of the 29th ACM International Conference on Information & Knowledge Management, pp. 2725–2732, October 2020

36. Cresci, S., Lillo, F., Regoli, D., Tardelli, S., Tesconi, M.: Cashtag piggybacking: uncovering spam and bot activity in stock microblogs on Twitter. ACM Trans. Web (TWEB) **13**(2), 1–27 (2019)

37. Ratkiewicz, J., Conover, M., Meiss, M., Gonçalves, B., Flammini, A., Menczer, F.: Detecting and tracking political abuse in social media. In Proceedings of the International AAAI Conference on Web and Social Media, vol. 5, No. 1, pp. 297–304 (2011)

38. Subrahmanian, V.S., et al.: The DARPA Twitter bot challenge. Computer **49**(6), 38–46 (2016)

39. Elyashar, A., Fire, M., Kagan, D., Elovici, Y.: Guided socialbots: infiltrating the social networks of specific organizations' employees. AI Commun. **29**(1), 87–106 (2016)

40. Kearney, M.W.: tweetbotornot: R package for detecting Twitter bots via machine learning. Version 0.1. 0) [R package]. CRAN (2018). Accessed 24 Mar 2023

41. Dukić, D., Keča, D., Stipić, D.: Are you human? Detecting bots on Twitter Using BERT. In: 2020 IEEE 7th International Conference on Data Science and Advanced Analytics (DSAA), pp. 631–636. IEEE, October 2020

42. Yang, K.C., Ferrara, E., Menczer, F.: Botometer 101: Social bot practicum for computational social scientists. J. Comput. Soc. Sci., 1–18 (2022)

43. Pennington, J., Socher, R., Manning, C.D.: Glove: global vectors for word representation. In: Proceedings of the 2014 Conference on Empirical Methods in Natural Language Processing (EMNLP), pp. 1532–1543, October 2014

44. Dorri, A., Abadi, M., Dadfarnia, M.: Socialbothunter: Botnet detection in twitter-like social networking services using semi-supervised collective classification. In: 2018 IEEE 16th Intl Conf on Dependable, Autonomic and Secure Computing, August 2018
45. Hwang, T., Pearce, I., Nanis, M.: Socialbots: voices from the fronts. Interactions **19**(2), 38–45 (2012)
46. Chavoshi, N., Hamooni, H., Mueen, A.: Debot: Twitter bot detection via warped correlation. In: Icdm, vol. 18, pp. 28–65, December 2016
47. HypeAuditor. (n.d.). HypeAuditor. https://hypeauditor.com/. Accessed 24 Mar 2023
48. Combin. (n.d.). Combin. https://combim.com/. Accessed 24 Mar 2023
49. FollowerAudit. (n.d.). FollowerAudit. https://www.followeraudit.com/. Accessed 24 Mar 2023
50. BotSentinel. (n.d.). BotSentinel. https://botsentinel.com/info/about. Accessed 24 Mar 2023

A Fuzzy Approach to Detecting Suspected Disinformation in Videos

Jared D. T. Guerrero-Sosa[1]([⊠]) [iD], Francisco P. Romero[1] [iD],
Andres Montoro-Montarroso[2] [iD], Victor H. Menendez[3] [iD],
Jesus Serrano-Guerrero[1] [iD], and Jose A. Olivas[1] [iD]

[1] Department of Information Systems and Technologies, University of Castilla La
Mancha, Paseo de la Universidad, 4, Ciudad Real, Spain
`jareddavidtadeo.guerrero@alu.uclm.es`
`{FranciscoP.Romero,Jesus.Serrano,JoseAngel.Olivas}@uclm.es`
[2] Department of Computer Science and Artificial Intelligence, University of Granada,
Granada, Spain
`andres.montoro@ugr.es`
[3] Mathematics School, Autonomous University of Yucatan, Merida, Yucatan, Mexico
`mdoming@correo.uady.mx`

Abstract. Disinformation has become an increasingly significant problem in today's digital world, spreading rapidly across various multimedia platforms. To combat this issue, we propose a novel hybrid intelligence framework that combines the power of deep learning and fuzzy logic-based methods to detect multimodal disinformation content. The framework comprises two main components: the multimodal feature analyzer and the multimodal disinformation content detector. In the multimodal feature measurement step, we extract features from different modalities of a multimedia piece and then use deep learning methods to obtain a set of different measures. Finally, in the multimodal disinformation content detection step, we use a fuzzy logic-based method to detect disinformation content based on previously obtained multimodal features. To validate the effectiveness of our proposed framework, we conducted experiments using a dataset of TikTok videos containing various forms of disinformation. Our experiments demonstrated the viability of our approach and its potential to be applied to other social media platforms.

Keywords: Knowledge Engineering · Behaviour detection ·
Multimodal disinformation detection

The Spanish Government has partially supported this work under the grant SAFER:
PID2019-104735RB-C42 (ERA/ERDF, EU).

H. L. Larsen et al. (Eds.): FQAS 2023, LNAI 14113, pp. 145–158, 2023.
https://doi.org/10.1007/978-3-031-42935-4_12

1 Introduction

Knowing whether someone is producing a piece of misleading video is a complex task. Techniques that assess fake speeches are mainly based on two primary sources: the nonverbal behaviour of the speaker and verbal language or explicit verbal content of the speech. There are many ways to detect fake content using video analysis. Some standard methods include observing body language and facial expressions, analysing movement patterns and monitoring changes in behaviour over time. Different methods may be more or less effective depending on the behaviour to detect. For example, some psychological studies have stated that specific facial actions are more difficult to inhibit if the associated facial expressions are genuine. Similarly, facial expressions are equally difficult to fake; then, there is an opportunity to detect if someone is introducing fake information into their speech [15]. Many machine learning techniques are best suited for detecting fake behaviours using video analysis. However, the poor performance of many machine learning (ML) systems in the social context have been well documented due to these methods can perpetuate human prejudices such as sexism and racism when trained on biased datasets.

A range of different methodologies have been proposed to tackle the issue of multimodal disinformation, each with unique approaches and characteristics. In the work of Singh et al. [12] they handle the issue of fake news detection via a multimodal methodology that fuses textual and visual analysis. In this study, the authors pinpoint a variety of textual and visual traits linked to either fake or reliable news articles. They conduct predictive analytics to discern the traits most closely tied to fake news. The gathered traits are then combined into predictive models with the aid of several machine learning techniques. Their experiments demonstrate that a multimodal approach is superior to unimodal approaches, enabling more accurate fake news detection. In a distinct approach, a study conducted by Giachanou et al. [3] presents a multimodal system grounded on a neural network that amalgamates textual, visual, and semantic information to distinguish between fake and authentic news. This system extracts textual information from the post's content, visual data from the associated image, and semantic data from the similarity between the image and text. The experiments conducted on the MediaEval, PolitiFact, and GossipCon collections underline the significance of these features in fake news detection.

Our proposal consists of a novel hybrid intelligence framework that combines the power of deep learning and fuzzy logic-based methods to detect multimodal disinformation content. The framework comprises two main components: the multimodal feature analyzer and the multimodal disinformation content detector. The former extracts features from different modalities of a multimedia piece, such as text, image, and audio, using advanced deep learning techniques to obtain a set of accurate measurements. These measurements are then used as input for the multimodal disinformation content detector, which employs a fuzzy logic-based approach to identify disinformation content.

The structure of this paper is as follows: In Sect. 2, we provide a detailed overview of the theoretical foundations of our proposal, including the integration of fuzzy artefacts and the Computer Theory of Perceptions. Section 3 presents the two-phase methodology for multimodal analysis that we utilize in this study. Section 4 shows a comprehensive case study that evaluates specific disinformation behaviours in the TikTok social network. Finally, in Sect. 5, we present our conclusions and highlight areas for future research.

2   Granular Linguistic Model of Phenomena

The problem of describing a behaviour could be dealt with a multi-level approach. Granulation groups the input data into information units called granules and depends on the phenomenon and its context. A granule is a collection of physical or abstract objects clustered by similarity, proximity, or functionality criteria [17].

Granular Linguistic Model of Phenomena (GLMP) [2] is a general-purpose model that describes phenomena at different granularity levels. GLMP is built on two main concepts: Computational Perception (CP) and Perception Mappings (PM).

In general, CPs cover specific aspects with a certain degree of detail or granularity of the information produced by the analyzed part of the system. As we mentioned above, to create a computer model of disinformation behaviour, the evaluator analyzes the video with the aim of identifying different aspects (units of information or granules) based on his/her subjective perceptions.

A CP is a tuple (A, W, R) where:

- A: $(a_1, a_2, \ldots, a_n)$ is a vector of linguistic expressions (words or sentences in natural language) that represents the whole linguistic domain of CP. Each component a_i is the most suitable linguistic value of CP in each behaviour with a specific granularity degree. For example, "the perception level of extroversion of the person who sent the message" is modelled with $A = (low, medium, high)$
- W: $(w_1, w_2, \ldots, w_n)$ is a vector of validity degrees $w_i \in [0, 1]$. The validity value w_i represents the degree of each linguistic expression a_i to describe the specific input data. The sum of all validity degrees must be $\sum w_i = 1$
- R: $(r_1, r_2, \ldots, r_n)$ $r_i \in [0, 1]$ assigned to each a_i in the specific context, e.g., the relevance of the linguistic expressions $A = (Low, Medium, High)$ is $R = (0.5, 0.5, 1)$ means the perception of high is considered more relevant than the other two choices. By default, all the relevance degrees take the maximum value ($r_i = 1$).

Perception Mappings (PM) are used to create and aggregate CPs. Each PM takes a set of input CPs and aggregates them into a single CP. A PM is a tuple (U, y, g, T) where:

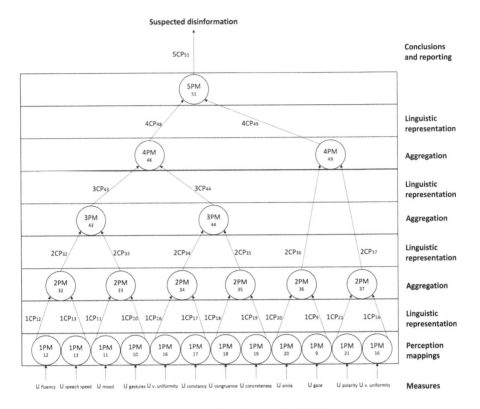

Fig. 1. Example of a simple GLMP.

- $U := (u_1, u_2, \ldots, u_n)$ is a vector of n input CPs $u_i = (A_{ui}, W_{ui}, R_{ui})$. In the special case of first-level Perception Mappings $(1PM)$, the inputs are values $z in R$ being provided either by measurement procedures.
- y: (A_y, W_y, R_y) is the output CP.
- g is the aggregation function. In Fuzzy Logic, many different types of aggregation functions have been developed. Indeed these aggregation functions are computational models that allow the designer to use different types of linguistic expressions. In the case of 1PMs, we built g by using a set of membership functions.
- T: is a text generation algorithm which allows generating all the possible sentences associated with the linguistic expressions in A_y. T is defined as a linguistic template representing a set of possible linguistic expressions.

A GLMP shows the information in a granular through a PM network, depending on the detail required. An input (CP) at one level is the output of an earlier level and can have many levels as necessary. The PM network is a map of input and output nodes and CPs represented by edges. An example is shown in Fig. 1, which is a fragment of a GLMP of 51 PMs and CPs to detect disinformation content. A CP is a perception generated by the system. The input data are introduced into the model through 1 PMs, which interpret these data and generate 1CPs. Then, 2 PMs take several 1CPs as input and generate 2CPs, in the second level of the hierarchy. Of course, additional upper levels can be added. In such levels, 2 PMs take several 2CPs as input and generate new 2CPs as output. Each PM has a membership function that maps the inputs to output CP.

3   Methodological Proposal

We split the process into four components to face the complexity of the whole system (see Fig. 2).

3.1   Conceptualization Framework

A conceptualization framework is a methodological approach designed to study and analyze multimedia data in order to identify the most relevant characteristics of behaviour to be detected in video footage. The framework is constructed through collaborative work, where a panel of experts provides the dimensions and attributes of each behaviour, and an engineering team defines the tools to measure each attribute and the aggregation procedures. The framework aims to establish a structured and systematic process for identifying and characterizing behaviours of interest in multimedia data, which can then be used to develop more accurate and reliable automated systems for behaviour detection and analysis. By providing a standardized and consistent methodology for conceptualizing behaviours, the framework helps ensure that all relevant dimensions and attributes are considered and that the resulting system is valid and effective.

Each concept represents a CP, and then a membership function is associated with it and an aggregation process, such as a set of rules. From the evaluation of the aggregation process, we obtain conclusions in form of PMs. Measures are $1PM$ and attribute and dimensions are aggregations of CPs.

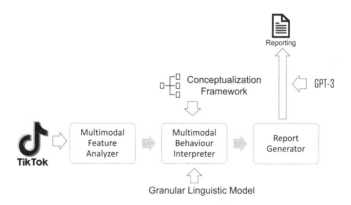

Fig. 2. Overview of the proposed approach

3.2 Multimodal Feature Analyzer

The data from the videos will be cleaned and standardized. The audio and video will be split into smaller segments and converted to WAV and MP4 formats using the FFmpeg library. The following procedures have been applied to analyze the audio and video separately.

Audio Transcription. Whisper [11], an open-source speech recognition system trained on 680,000 h of multilingual data, was used to transcribe and translate a video from multiple languages to English using an encoder-decoder architecture. The audio is divided into 30-second chunks, processed by a CNN, and fed into a transformer for language identification, transcription, and time stamping.

Audio Analysis. MyProsody [18] is used to analyse the audio that can be extracted from the video. Then, we can measure acoustic characteristics of speech, such as simultaneous speech and high entropy, compared with those of native speakers. The acoustic features of native speech patterns have been observed and established by employing machine learning algorithms (Classification and Regression Trees - CART -, Multiple Regression, etc.). An acoustic model divides the recorded utterances and detects syllable boundaries, contours of fundamental frequencies, etc. Its built-in functions recognize and measure many factors that, when aggregated, can yield relevant indicators for the solution of the problem.

Text Analysis. The Natural Language Processing (NLP) tasks were mainly performed using the Spacy [16] library. This library offers pre-trained models for various languages and enables the creation of new models or the retraining of existing models with custom data for specific fields. In our task, the text from the video is analyzed, information is extracted from the text, and the model's predictions about its meaning are based on the context. The techniques used for this analysis are Part of Speech Tagging (POS Tagging) and identification of discursive markers. In addition, we use the Word2Vec (Word to Vector) [8] and GloVe (Global Vectors for Word Representation) [10] techniques for word representation employing vectors.

Text Classification. The thematic categories of the text were obtained by using an API that automatically classifies text based on a hierarchical classification or taxonomy to extract topics and calculate other metrics [5]. Texts are classified using specific keywords related to the text's topic found in one of the vocabularies, for example, EUROVOC, which covers a wide range of topics related to the European Union. This classification process is useful for quantifying the relevance of the speech extracted from the video to the questions asked by evaluating the text's depth, coherence, and key elements related to the topic. This process has been previously applied in other works in which the objective is the analysis of the text to detect specific behaviours [7].

Video Analysis. OpenCV, a set of software tools for image and video processing and analysis [6], has been used for video analysis to measure specific aspects of the video using advanced computer vision algorithms. Video analytics capabilities have been used for recognizing and tracking people and facial features such as faces, eyes, and lips. One of the most widely used models for the detection of landmarks that define the human face is 68-point facial landmark detector [19]. Results from the literature [4] indicate that non-voluntary and semi-voluntary facial cues are used to objectively estimate emotions. These measures include eye-related events (gaze and blink), mouth activity, and head movement parameters and have been found to achieve good accuracy and are suitable as indicators of stress and anxiety. The Haar Cascades models, based on machine learning for visual object detection, can process images quickly and accurately.

3.3   Multimodal Behaviour Interpreter

The proposed GLMP aims to produce linguistic reports of the analyzed behaviour. Each level validates and generates sentences that describe the current condition according to a specific level of granularity. The first part indicates the status based on the results of the multimodal feature analyzer. Then, these values are aggregated using fuzzy procedures to represent different attributes or dimensions of the behaviour, and the last part analyses the level of disinformation of the video.

3.4   Report Generation

The purpose of this module is to take the output from the previous module and use it to create a detailed linguistic report. This report is generated using predefined templates. After the linguistic report is produced, a Generative Pretrained model is utilized [1] to further improve the report by providing more nuanced and descriptive information about the involved behaviours. The final report generated by this module includes essential observations and statements highlighting essential aspects of the observed behaviour.

4   Case of Study

The proposed case of study examines the feasibility of multimodal video analysis in assessing whether a TikTok user is suspected of spreading false information. The experiment involves capturing and analyzing video footage of people delivering a speech about the Invasion of Ukraine throughout the year 2022. For this purpose, we used the dataset generated by the Network Dynamics Lab at McGill University [14] which defined keywords and hashtags to collect related videos. From the dataset, user names and video IDs were extracted and we subsequently identified some videos that include close-up shots of the presenter. A detailed description of the proposed approach is given below.

4.1 Conceptualization Framework

Through the analysis of video footage, we focused on identifying psychosociological traits that can accurately predict suspicion of spreading disinformation. We used the classification known as *Big-5* which describes individual differences in behaviour and thinking [9]. Then, the conceptualization framework of this specific behaviour is divided into different dimensions/attributes (provided by a panel of experts) and measures (equivalent to $1PM$) (see Table 1).

Using the GLMP we can represent the values of the metrics with linguistic labels to obtain the defined attributes, dimensions, and behaviours that correspond to the Perceptual Mappings and Conceptual Perceptions.

4.2 Multimodal Feature Analyzer

This component assumes responsibility for computing the first-order perceptions ($1PM$) involved in the procedure. It comprises a multitude of components based on machine learning techniques. Some of these elements consist of approaches such as speech transcription from videos, audio retrieval, or video segmentation into frames. Others constitute sophisticated tools founded on Convolutional Neural Networks capable of detecting emotions from audio or identifying blink/gaze patterns, as well as transformers and autoencoders to extract textual topics (through MeaningCloud's trained models).

The audio is analyzed to obtain the values of the measures *reaction time* (duration in seconds it takes to start the speech), *mood* (reading, normal or passionate), *fluency* (number of pauses and interruptions) and measures of the fundamental frequency of the voice (voice uniformity). Moreover, the textual content of the speech is transcribed from the audio in WAV format using the speech recognition system Whisper.

The analysis of the transcription of the audio allows computing measures like concreteness, organization, crutches, vagueness in language, and order in speech structure. On the other hand, originality (use of specific and uncommon vocabulary) and redundancy in the discourse (number of times the most repeated words have been repeated) were evaluated by using specific dictionaries. The occurrence of adjectives and the verb tense are computed from the Part of Speech Tagging process. To calculate the coherence of the text with a topic, we use text classification through MeaningCloud's trained models. The taxonomy classification depends on the text's language (EuroVoc classification for Spanish texts, IPTC classification for other languages). This measure is computed according to the similarity between the text categories and the topic. Finally, measuring the polarity of a speech is done by using MeaningCloud's sentiment analysis API, classifying the speech delivered in the video as positive, negative, or neutral.

The analysis of the video allows for obtaining detailed information about the person's actions, movements, and emotions throughout the video, making a more complete and accurate analysis. Regarding metrics, Haar-Cascade models were used to detect the regions of interest of faces, eyes, and smiles and how frequently

Table 1. Dimensions, attributes and measures to detect suspected disinformation.

Dimension	Attribute	Measure	Source
Openness			
Quality of the text	Vocabulary	Redundancy, Originality, Examples, Crutches, Verb tense	Text
	Ideas	Quantity, Appropriateness to the subject	Text
		Reaction time	Audio
Non Verbal Comm.	Non Verbal Comm	Gaze, Gestures	Video
		Mood	Audio
Conscientiousness			
Accuracy	Speed	Reaction time, Fluency, Speech speed	Audio
	Firmness	Organization	Text
		Mood	Audio
Clearness	Ideas	Vagueness, Examples, Crutches	Text
Extroversion			
Energy	Speech Fluency	Fluency, Speech Speed	Audio
	Expressiveness	Mood	Audio
		Gestures	Video
Assertiveness	Confidence	Voice uniformity, Constancy	Audio
	Conviction	Congruence, Concreteness	Text
Agreeableness			
Empathy	Empathy	Smile, Gaze	Video
Interaction tone	Interaction tone	Polarity	Text
		Voice uniformity	Audio
Neuroticism			
Nervousness	Non-Verbal Comm	Blinking, Gestures, Gaze, Posture changes	Video
	Communication	Crutches	Text
		Constancy, Noise	Audio
Expression	Expression	Concreteness, Polarity	Text
		Mood	Audio

they are detectable throughout the video. For pose changes, the area of the rectangle that makes up the face region of interest was identified and assessed whether it changes drastically in size and position in the video, i.e., whether it moves left, centre, right, up, or down. Gaze focus and blink detection was performed through dlib's 68-point facial landmark predictor pre-trained neural network to detect and recognize the 68 key points or "landmarks" that define the features of a human face in an image. With this pre-trained model, it is possible to detect whether the person is looking to the left, to the right, to the centre, or if there is a blink. Gestures have been detected through the DeepFace library based on its pre-trained model for facial emotion detection, and thus the dominant expression is obtained, which belongs to one of the following classes: angry, sad, neutral, disgust, surprise, fear and happiness.

4.3 Multimodal Behaviour Interpreter

After obtaining the result of each metric or $1PM$ through the multimodal feature analyzer, we represent each behaviour's attributes and dimensions employing fuzzy aggregations. According to GLMP theory, each attribute, dimension, and behaviour is considered a PM obtained by an aggregation function of its CPs. When the number of CPs to aggregate is low the aggregation function is implemented using the sets of Mamdani-type fuzzy rules; on the other hand, we apply the fuzzy weighted average.

Once the fuzzy values corresponding to each of the behaviours - openness, conscientiousness, extroversion, agreeableness, and neuroticism - have been calculated using fuzzy aggregation techniques, we proceed to combine these values to obtain a single output indicating the suspicion of disinformation in a video which can be interpreted more intuitively than the individual values of the behaviours. However, each behaviour's influence on disinformation differs depending on the domain to which the message belongs. Since the invasion of Ukraine is a political event, it is required to know the behaviours shared by people who spread disinformation in this domain, and from what was mentioned in [13], the spreaders of disinformation in the political domain are neurotic by nature. In this case, the behaviours are not independent of each other but are interrelated and can influence each other. Once the criteria and the general fuzzy measure have been defined, we proceed to aggregate by means of the formula presented in Eq. 1

$$C_v(x) = \sum_{i=1}^{n}[x_i - x_{i-1}]v(H_i) \tag{1}$$

where:

- $\{x_1, x_2, x_3, ..., x_n\}$ is a set of criteria ordered in ascending order
- $x_0 = 0$
- v is a fuzzy measure
- $H_i = \{i, ..., n\}$ is the subset of indices of the $n - i + 1$ largest components of x

$C_v(x)$ is a value in the $[0, 1]$ interval that indicates that the higher it is, the higher the suspicion of disinformation in the video evaluated.

4.4 Report Generation

The use of GLMP allows us to analyze the problem to be solved by dividing the factors that compose it into smaller units and to describe how they are related considering different levels of granularity.

A detailed example of the use of GLMP for the evaluation of a 52-second video where the study subject is an adult male is described below.

In our model, we use 51 PMs of which 25 are first level (measures, from $1PM_1$ to $1PM_{25}$), 15 are second level (attributes, from $2PM_{26}$ to $2PM_{40}$), 5 are third level (dimensions, from $3PM41$ to $3PM_{45}$), 5 are fourth level (behaviors, from $4PM_{46}$ to $4PM_{50}$) and 1 is fifth level (end result, $5PM_{51}$).

4.5 Example

- **First-level Perception Mappings.** Each first-order PM accepts a single input, U, reflecting a specific measure related to our study. Inputs can be normalized values between 0 and 10 or direct data source values. Based on these, each PM outputs a CP y, using a set of linguistic expressions A. We generally define membership functions g for the labels *Low*, *Medium* and *High* as $(0, 0, 2.5, 5)$, $(2.5, 5, 7.5)$ and $(5, 7.5, 10, 10)$, respectively. For instance, in the case of $1PM_{16}$, which models voice uniformity, a uniformity level of 5.97, $U = 5.97$, results in an output of $1CP_{16}$ with $A = (Low, Medium, High)$ and $W = (0, 0.62, 0.38)$. This informs us that the voice uniformity is *Medium*.
- **Second-level Perception Mappings.** Second-order PMs receive multiple inputs from first-order PMs' outputs, generating an output CP based on these inputs and predefined linguistic expressions, namely:
  - $A = (Bad, Normal, Good)$ for vocabulary, ideas, non verbal communication, interaction tone and communication.
  - $A = (Low, Medium, High)$ for speed, firmness, speech fluency, expressiveness, confidence, conviction, empathy and expression.
  Membership degrees are consistent across all inputs. For up to three inputs, the aggregation function g uses fuzzy rules. For more than three, it uses a fuzzy weighted average. For instance, $2PM_{34}$, modeling Confidence, takes two inputs: voice uniformity and constancy, from $1CP_{16}$ and $1CP_{17}$ respectively. With the relevant validity vectors, it applies fuzzy rules to output *The confidence is low.*
- **Third and fourth-level Perception Mappings.** In both cases, each PM takes two CPs as inputs and outputs are defined with the same set of linguistic labels, $A = (Low, Medium, High)$, and the corresponding membership degrees as $(0, 0, 2.5, 5)$, $(2.5, 5, 7.5)$ and $(5, 7.5, 10, 10)$, respectively, and the corresponding outputs are calculated using a set of fuzzy rules for aggregation function g. For the third-order PMs, they receive the inputs from the output CPs of the second-order PMs, but the fourth-order PMs, depending on the specific behavior being modeled, these inputs can be from third-order PMs, second-order PMs, or a combination of both.

– **Fifth-level Perception Mapping.** In our model, the final stage involves a
fifth-order perception mapping ($5PM_{51}$) that provides an overall evaluation
of the suspicion of disinformation in a video. This mapping integrates the outputs of the five preceding fourth-order PMs, which represent behaviors. The
aggregation function for this stage is the Choquet Integral, which considers
not only the individual contribution of each behaviour but also their interde-
pendencies. This is achieved through a fuzzy measure that assigns weights to
each behaviour and their combinations. In this case, we have conscientiousness at 2.08, agreeableness at 2.19, neuroticism at 4.07, openness at 7.12,
and extroversion at 7.5. The application of the Choquet Integral yields an
aggregated value of 0.62, which, following our membership functions, corresponds to a *Medium* level of disinformation suspicion. The output of this
fifth-order PM, $5CP_{51}$, is, therefore, a holistic and nuanced measure of the
potential disinformation content in the video, taking into account both individual behaviours and their synergistic effects. Thus, a hierarchical structure
report template has been developed that begins with the lowest level of detail
(the degree of suspected disinformation) and progresses to the highest level of
detail (the representation of metrics). The level of detail of the explanations
generated with the template is improved by using OpenAI's Generative Pre-
trained model (GPT-3). Table 2 shows the provided report for this example.

Table 2. Example of Results

Video	Natural Language Report
1	The person who sent the message has a *medium* probability of spreading disinformation, because he is *very* **open**, *not very* **conscious**, *very* **extroverted**, *not very* **agreeable** and **emotionally stable** *on average*. The person is *very* **open** because the **quality of the text** is *high* and the **nonverbal language** is *normal*. The person is *not very* **conscious** because the **accuracy** and **clearness of the message** is *low*. The person is *very* **extroverted** because he has *high* **energy** and an **assertive attitude**, although he is *not very* confident. The person is *not very* agreeable because he has *low* **empathy** and the **tone of interaction** is *not good*. *On average*, the person has *normal* **emotional stability**, although there are some signs of inconsistency in **communication**

5 Conclusions

The described approach to represent the evaluation of disinformation behaviours
using video analysis is a novel and promising methodology that delivers insightful
descriptions of the input data. The model is developed through the integration of

several components related to computer vision, audio and text analysis, psychology, and fuzzy logic. The utilization of this interdisciplinary approach enables the capture of various aspects of the behaviour, resulting in a more comprehensive and accurate representation of the behaviour under investigation.

In future work, it is essential to carry out a tuning process of the measures scales to ensure that the results are consistent and reliable. This tuning process can refine and optimise the methodology to provide more accurate and precise detection of disinformation behaviours.

References

1. Brown, T.B., Mann, B., Ryder, N., Subbiah, M., et al.: Language models are few-shot learners (2020). https://doi.org/10.48550/ARXIV.2005.14165. https://arxiv.org/abs/2005.14165
2. Conde-Clemente, P., Alonso, J.M., Trivino, G.: Toward automatic generation of linguistic advice for saving energy at home. Soft. Comput. **22**(2), 345–359 (2018)
3. Giachanou, A., Zhang, G., Rosso, P.: Multimodal fake news detection with textual, visual and semantic information. In: Sojka, P., Kopeček, I., Pala, K., Horák, A. (eds.) TSD 2020. LNCS (LNAI), vol. 12284, pp. 30–38. Springer, Cham (2020). https://doi.org/10.1007/978-3-030-58323-1_3
4. Giannakakis, G., et al.: Stress and anxiety detection using facial cues from videos. Biomed. Signal Process. Control **31**, 89–101 (2017). https://doi.org/10.1016/j.bspc.2016.06.020
5. Herrera-Planells, J., Villena-Román, J.: MeaningCloud at TASS 2018: news headlines categorization for brand safety assessment. In: Estevez-Velarde, S., et al. (eds.) CEUR Workshop Proceedings, p. 139622. CEUR-WS, Sevilla (2018)
6. Kaehler, A., Bradski, G.: Learning OpenCV 3 - Computer Vision in C++ with the OpenCV Library. O'Reilly Media, Inc. (2016)
7. Losada, D.E., Gamallo, P.: Evaluating and improving lexical resources for detecting signs of depression in text. Lang. Resour. Eval. **54**(1), 1–24 (2018). https://doi.org/10.1007/s10579-018-9423-1
8. Mikolov, T., Chen, K., Corrado, G., Dean, J.: Efficient estimation of word representations in vector space (2013). https://doi.org/10.48550/ARXIV.1301.3781. https://arxiv.org/abs/1301.3781
9. Novikova, I.A., Vorobyeva, A.A.: The five-factor model: Contemporary personality theory. Cross-Cultural Psychology: Contemporary Themes and Perspectives, pp. 685–706 (2019)
10. Pennington, J., Socher, R., Manning, C.D.: GloVe: global Vectors for Word Representation. In: Proceedings of the 2014 Conference on Empirical Methods in Natural Language Processing (EMNLP), pp. 1532–1543. Association for Computational Linguistics, Doha (2014)
11. Radford, A., et al.: Introducing Whisper (2022). https://openai.com/blog/whisper/
12. Singh, V.K., Ghosh, I., Sonagara, D.: Detecting fake news stories via multimodal analysis. J. Am. Soc. Inf. Sci. **72**(1), 3–17 (2021). https://doi.org/10.1002/asi.24359
13. Srinivas, P., Das, A., Pulabaigari, V.: Fake spreader is a narcissist; real spreader is machiavellian prediction of fake news diffusion using psycho-sociological facets. Expert Syst. Appl. **207**, 117952 (2022). https://doi.org/10.1016/j.eswa.2022.117952

14. Steel, B., Parker, S., Ruths, D.: Invasion of Ukraine discourse on TikTok dataset (2023). https://doi.org/10.5281/zenodo.7534952
15. Su, L., Levine, M.: Does "lie to me" lie to you? an evaluation of facial clues to high-stakes deception. Comput. Vis. Image Understanding **147**, 52–68 (2016). https://doi.org/10.1016/j.cviu.2016.01.009
16. Vasiliev, Y.: Natural Language Processing with Python and SpaCy: A Practical Introduction. No Starch Press (2020)
17. Zadeh, L.A.: Granular computing as a basis for a computational theory of percep-tions. In: 2002 IEEE World Congress on Computational Intelligence. 2002 IEEE International Conference on Fuzzy Systems. FUZZ-IEEE'02. Proceedings (Cat. No. 02CH37291), vol. 1, pp. 564–565. IEEE (2002)
18. Zechner, K., Higgins, D., Xi, X., Williamson, D.M.: Automatic scoring of non-native spontaneous speech in tests of spoken English. Speech Commun. **51**(10), 883–895 (2009). https://doi.org/10.1016/j.specom.2009.04.009
19. Zheng, Y., Wang, B., Zheng, Y.: 68 face feature points detection based on cascading convolutional neural network with small filter. Highlights in Science, Engineering and Technology 9, 135–142, September 2022. https://doi.org/10.54097/hset.v9i.1731

All Trolls Have One Mission: An Entropy Analysis of Political Misinformation Spreaders

J. Angel Diaz-Garcia[1]([⊠])(iD) and Julio Amador Díaz López[2]

[1] Department of Computer Science and A.I., University of Granada, Granada, Spain
jagarcia@decsai.ugr.es
[2] Imperial College London, London, UK
j.amador@imperial.ac.uk

Abstract. Social media heavily influence the world. Its leverage has propitiated the rise of nefarious uses of social media platforms, such as spreading misinformation. This paper investigates whether entropy can be used to differentiate non-organic from organic political content. Two datasets related to political issues in the United States have been used. One of the datasets comprises the content generated by left and right-wing Russian trolls in coordinated information operations. Another is organic and contrasts with original Republican or Democrat-oriented tweets. Our results show that the entropy in the case of the organic dataset has different entropy between right-wing and left-wing, while in the information operations dataset, we have the same value between both language wings. The homogeneity of the messages allows us to distinguish organic content from inorganic, coordinated information operations. Our findings suggest that entropy could be a helpful feature in identifying and combating fake news and could be incorporated into automated systems for content moderation and fact-checking.

Keywords: credibility · misinformation · social media mining · entropy

1 Introduction

Social networks significantly influence the world in which we live. Every day, we consume or generate social network data. Unfortunately, the success of social media platforms has led to the rise of bad uses of the social media platforms, such as the dissemination of misinformation to interfere in electoral processes [2]. Addressing this problem requires a multidisciplinary approach that draws on insights from fields such as psychology [17] or computer science. Regarding computer science and artificial intelligence, the current trend in misinformation detection lies in deep-learning approaches [7,13,16]. These approaches, employing pre-trained language models such as BERT [3], can obtain a high accuracy facing classification tasks but needs more interpretability and high amounts of

© Springer Nature Switzerland AG 2023
H. L. Larsen et al. (Eds.): FQAS 2023, LNAI 14113, pp. 159–167, 2023.
https://doi.org/10.1007/978-3-031-42935-4_13

tagged data to work correctly and tend not to generalise. Due to this, other approaches based on traditional data science techniques remain necessary. Zhang et al. [21] proposed a probabilistic method that has demonstrated promising results in combating fake news. In a comprehensive study by Galli et al. [5], the authors compare various approaches based on deep learning, traditional statistical methods, and machine learning (ML). They found that traditional ML models achieve fast, interpretable, and robust results. These papers highlight the value of traditional ML and statistical methods in the field of misinformation detection and analysis.

We propose using the information entropy to measure the differences in word distribution between real and content generated by information operations. Entropy has already been used in other areas, such as malware detection [12] to capture differences in distribution between malicious and non-malicious software. Thus, the potential of the metric to discern differences between two samples is demonstrated. In our paper, we use that potential to capture the differences between two samples of text content, demonstrating that information operations using non-generic content can be differentiated from generic content.

In this paper, the information entropy metric introduced by Shannon [19] has been used. Information entropy can be defined mathematically by the Eq. 1, where $H(X)$ is the entropy of the random variable X, n is the number of possible values that X can take on, $p(x_i)$ is the probability that X takes on the value x_i, and b is the base of the logarithm used.

$$H(X) = -\sum_{i=1}^{n} p(x_i) \log_b p(x_i) \tag{1}$$

Regarding interpretation, if two texts have the same entropy, their word frequency distributions are equally unpredictable or uncertain. In other words, the two texts have similar word usage patterns, even if the words themselves may differ. However, it is essential to note that having the same entropy does not necessarily mean that the two texts are similar in content or meaning. For example, two texts could have the same entropy even if one is a novel and the other is a technical manual, as long as their word frequency distributions are similar. Nevertheless, entropy has been used in many application areas such as text classification using max-entropy algorithm [14], clustering [15] or text preprocessing, employing feature selection techniques based on entropy values [9].

To sum up, the main objective of this research lies in using entropy to analyse non-generic content on Twitter about different ideological sides, trying to obtain knowledge about the disinformation strategies carried out by the Russian Internet Research Agency (IRA) trolls during the United States presidential election campaigns. The main contributions to the state-of-the-art are:

- A comprehensive analysis of the IRA's content on political and ideological areas within the United States.
- The provision of robust evidence that there is a large-scale, orchestrated disinformation strategy in certain electoral processes.

The rest of the paper is organised as follows: Next section focuses on the study of related work. In Sect. 3, we motivated the problem under analysis and the datasets used. We provide the results in Sect. 4. Finally, in Sect. 5, we examine the conclusions, discussion and future work.

2   Related Works

Entropy-based methods have been widely used in Natural Language Processing (NLP). One of the earliest papers to propose using entropy in this area was [14]. In this paper, the authors enhance the validity of max-entropy for classification tasks. With the democratisation of the internet and the success of online social networks, research on the topic has increased significantly. In [4] Erşahin et al. proposed using entropy as a cut-off point for discretising continuous variables. With this approach, they improved the results in a classification task of fake and real accounts using Naive Bayes. Also, in the Twitter domain, in [8], authors explore the influence of entropy over n-grams aiming to predict stock prices. More related to our approach, in [18], authors explore the entropy of time intervals to detect spam bots.

In the area of malware detection, entropy is one of its most outstanding areas of application [12,20]. In these papers, entropy is used as a value that can capture the differences in usage patterns between web attacks and regular web access. Moving to misinformation, one of the first studies that relate the concept of fake content with entropy is [10], where authors propose two models that can detect fake content or non-human generated content.

One of the most recent papers on the topic, and also one of the most related to ours, is the one proposed by Lokesh in [6]. The paper focused on using entropy for rumour control in social networks. The systems proposed to apply different data mining techniques, such as polarity analysis and social networks analysis, in conjunction to build a system that gets a 91% value in terms of accuracy for rumour detection in three different datasets, coming from Twitter, Instagram and Reddit. One of the components of the system uses entropy as a value to discerning the tweet's authenticity, creating a threshold over reliable content.

Our proposal uses, as the studies reviewed in this section, the power of entropy as a measure for the distribution and usage of a different kind of content, being able to set cut points and thresholds to contrast that content. This is the first paper that addresses the problem of spreading political misinformation using entropy to measure the information differences between organic and troll or fake content.

3   Data

The dataset that has motivated our research is the one proposed by Linvill et al. [11]. The original dataset comprises 9 million tweets generated by accounts determined by the FBI as malicious and belonging to the Internet Research Agency (IRA). Specifically, we have focused on the subsection of the dataset categorised as left-trolls and right-trolls. To enhance comprehension, it is important to include the following definitions. In this context, a troll refers to accounts that systematically generate content aimed at targeting a specific sector of society. Specifically, right-trolls are trolls who support the right-wing of the political spectrum, while left-trolls are associated with the opposing left-wing ideology. In total, after preprocessing the data, by eliminating links, numbers, retweets, empty words, and tweets that remain empty, the total number of tweets taken into account in the case of left-troll is 72378, and in the case of right-troll is 397183.

In these datasets, an anomaly (red frame in the figures) can be observed in terms of the volume of content generation. Paying attention to the volume of tweets generated from July 2017 to January 2018 shows a decreasing volume of left-wing tweets when right-wing tweets peaked in Fig. 1 and 2 the distribution in terms of tweets generated according to different emotions can be seen. In the case on the left, the generation of tweets has been constant from 2015 to the end of the sample in 2018. On the right, we have, in contrast, a prominent peak at the end of the period covered by the dataset.

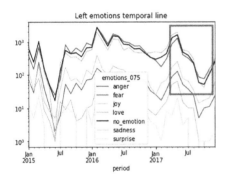 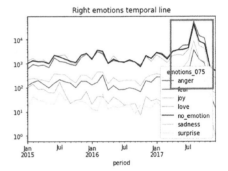

Fig. 1. Left trolls tweets temporal distribution

Fig. 2. Right trolls tweets temporal distribution

Figure 3 and 4 show the temporal distribution according to a random sample of 36189 tweets in both datasets, showing how the distribution of content is unrelated to the difference in terms of the data volume of the datasets.

When the tweets on the right are activated, the tweets on the left are deactivated, which may clash with the ordinary course of conversations on Twitter. This anomaly leads us to hypothesise that the same people act as managers of the accounts of both ideological wings, thus demonstrating a defined and planned strategy of disinformation. To contrast our hypothesis, an original dataset [1] of tweets related to the right-wing and left-wing discussion in the United States has been used. We tag this type of content as organic content because it is generated by real users in genuine Twitter conversations. In contrast, the troll-related content is considered non-organic content since it is produced by fake accounts following a guided strategy.

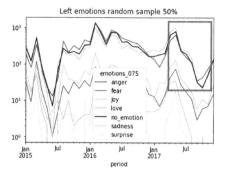
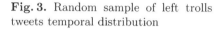
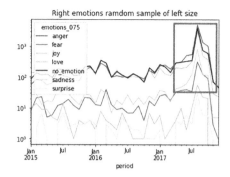

Fig. 3. Random sample of left trolls tweets temporal distribution

Fig. 4. Random sample of right trolls tweets temporal distribution

The organic dataset comprises 86460 tweets, 49% corresponding to the democratic party and 51% to the republican party. These data subsets will be considered as a left-wing test and a right-wing test. It would have been interesting to create the same plots for organic content as it was done with the non-organic content, but it has been impossible because the dataset [1] needs the creation date, only the content. It is worth mentioning that although it is impossible to get the exact date of tweet publication, the last tweets are from 2018, so the vast majority of the tweets are related to the exact dates, both in organic and non-organic content.

4   Experimentation

This section details the results and experimentation regarding information entropy at the character and word levels. The results in this section correspond with the average of 5 executions over different random sub-samples of each dataset.

4.1   Character-Level Entropy

A set of experiments at the character level have been carried out. The character level experimentation has been used to demonstrate that the entropy gets the same value over different datasets because the letters used and their conjugation are distributed with equal probability as all the content is in the same language, English. Looking at Table 1, we can see how the average value between the different n-gram configurations and the different datasets are very similar. That is because the character usage between different datasets is similar, i.e. the probability of using the character l followed by a vowel, e.g. o is the same in the different datasets since it is dealing with the same language. A statistical test of contrast has been performed, for a significance alpha value of 0.05, obtaining an upper p-value which leads us to conclude that there is not enough evidence to say that there are significant changes between the samples. That experiment has been used as a base to demonstrate that entropy can capture a language's different usages.

Table 1. Entropy results at character-level for different datasets and n-gram configuration

Dataset	Configuration	Entropy
Organic right	1-gram	4.228
Organic left	1-gram	4.220
Left-Troll	1-gram	4.257
Right-Troll	1-gram	4.230
Organic right	2-gram	3.623
Organic left	2-gram	3.626
Left-Troll	2-gram	3.594
Right-Troll	2-gram	3.644

4.2 Word-Level Entropy

Table 2. Entropy results at word-level for different datasets and n-gram configuration

Dataset	Configuration	Entropy
Organic right	1-gram	11.8722
Organic left	1-gram	12.1166
Left-Troll	1-gram	12.0418
Right-Troll	1-gram	12.040
Organic right	2-gram	16.687
Organic left	2-gram	16.890
Left-Troll	2-gram	16.345
Right-Troll	2-gram	16.319

It has been proven that the entropy of the English language remains the same between different datasets at the character level. So, at this point, it will be tried to show that at the word level, there are significant differences between the left-wing and right-wing American political discourse regarding real datasets. However, the case of troll-generated content will remain the same. So, our hypothesis test is:

- H_0: The entropy values of the left and right wings are equal.
- H_1: The entropy values of the left and right wings differ.

We used a two-sample t-test as our statistical contrast method to test this hypothesis. This method allowed us to compare the means of the two samples and determine whether any observed difference was statistically significant or likely due to chance. Using this method, we could test our hypothesis and conclude the potential differences between the entropy values of the left and right-wing datasets, both for troll-generated and genuine content. In Table 2, the average results in terms of word usage entropy can be seen. The two-sample t-test has been applied over the five different executions of the entropy for each dataset. With an alpha significance value set at 0.05, we can conclude that among the troll-generated datasets, we do not have sufficient evidence to reject the null hypothesis, i.e. there is no significant difference between the entropy.

On the contrary, in the case of the real datasets, we have in both cases (1-gram and 2-gram) a p-value that forces us to reject the null hypothesis, showing significant differences between both ideological poles. In Table 3, the complete and precise p-values obtained for each experiment can be found. In the case of the 2-gram analysis for the non-organic content coming from trolls, the p-value is very close to 0.05; although it does not allow us to reject the null hypothesis, it is close. Even in this case, the values of the statistics are far from those of the organic content, where we could reject the hypothesis even with a significance value of 0.01, which leads us to support and maintain our hypotheses and results.

Table 3. t-statistics and p-values for each experiment

Comparison	Configuration	t-statistics	p-value
Organic right & organic left	1-gram	54.924	1.339e-11
Right-Troll & Left-Troll	1-gram	**0.196**	**0.849**
Organic right & organic left	2-gram	54.167	1.496e-11
Right-Troll & Left-Troll	2-gram	**2.10**	**0.068**

These results led us to derive a new clue that supports the motivation introduced in Sect. 3, where a clear shift in the content volume generated by right-wing and left-wing trolls was presented. These entropy results, being different among the real datasets and the same among those generated by trolls, as well as the deactivation of some accounts at the same time as others were activated, lead us to conclude that these trolls were following a perfectly orchestrated disinformation strategy and that it was most likely the same people or bots that were managing the accounts on both sides of the US political discourse.

5   Conclusions and Future Work

In this paper, an entropy analysis of the political misinformation spread has been conducted. Entropy can be used to model the probability distribution in language models. Using this potential, have been demonstrated that the distribution of words in both political sides of the Russian trolls are precisely the same, having the base experiments with organic data signified differences. That led us to argue that the same people could manage all the Russian troll accounts located by the FBI in a structured information operation. The results presented by this paper are promising, but they need to be further explored. In future works, we explore other possible strategies trolls, bots, and misinformation spreaders use.

Acknowledgment. The research reported in this paper was supported by the project DesinfoScan:
Grant TED2021-129402B-C21 funded by MCIN/AEI/10.13039/501100011033 and, by the European Union NextGenerationEU/PRTR, and by the project FederaMed: Grant PID2021-123960OB-I00 funded by MCIN/AEI/10.13039/501100011033 and by ERDF A way of making Europe. Finally, the project is also partially supported by the Spanish Ministry of Education, Culture and Sport (FPU18/00150).

References

1. Democrat vs. republican tweets. https://www.kaggle.com/kapastor/democratvsrepublicantweets (2017). Accessed 8 Mar 2023
2. Bovet, A., Makse, H.A.: Influence of fake news in twitter during the 2016 us presidential election. Nat. Commun. **10**(1), 7 (2019)
3. Devlin, J., Chang, M.W., Lee, K., Toutanova, K.: Bert: Pre-training of deep bidirectional transformers for language underst4anding. In: Proceedings of the 2019 Conference of the North American Chapter of the Association for Computational Linguistics: Human Language Technologies, pp. 4171–4186. Association for Computational Linguistics, Minneapolis, Minnesota (2019). https://doi.org/10.18653/v1/N19-1423. https://www.aclweb.org/anthology/N19-1423/
4. Erşahin, B., Aktaş, D., Kılınç, D., Akyol, C.: Twitter fake account detection. In: 2017 International Conference on Computer Science and Engineering (UBMK), pp. 388–392 (2017). https://doi.org/10.1109/UBMK.2017.8093420
5. Galli, A., Masciari, E., Moscato, V., Sperlí, G.: A comprehensive benchmark for fake news detection. J. Intell. Inf. Syst. **59**(1), 237–261 (2022)
6. Jain, L.: An entropy-based method to control covid-19 rumors in online social networks using opinion leaders. Technol. Soc. **70**, 102048 (2022)
7. Kaliyar, R.K., Goswami, A., Narang, P.: Fakebert: fake news detection in social media with a bert-based deep learning approach. Multimed. Tools Appl. **80**(8), 11765–11788 (2021)
8. Kanavos, A., Vonitsanos, G., Mohasseb, A., Mylonas, P.: An entropy-based evaluation for sentiment analysis of stock market prices using twitter data. In: 2020 15th International Workshop on Semantic and Social Media Adaptation and Personalization (SMA), pp. 1–7. IEEE (2020)
9. Largeron, C., Moulin, C., Géry, M.: Entropy based feature selection for text categorization. In: Proceedings of the 2011 ACM Symposium on Applied Computing, pp. 924–928 (2011)
10. Lavergne, T., Urvoy, T., Yvon, F.: Detecting fake content with relative entropy scoring. PAN **8**, 27–31 (2008)
11. Linvill, D.L., Warren, P.L.: Troll factories: manufacturing specialized disinformation on twitter. Polit. Commun. **37**(4), 447–467 (2020)

12. Lyda, R., Hamrock, J.: Using entropy analysis to find encrypted and packed malware. IEEE Secur. Privacy **5**(2), 40–45 (2007)
13. Mridha, M.F., Keya, A.J., Hamid, M.A., Monowar, M.M., Rahman, M.S.: A comprehensive review on fake news detection with deep learning. IEEE Access **9**, 156151–156170 (2021)
14. Nigam, K., Lafferty, J., McCallum, A.: Using maximum entropy for text classification. In: IJCAI-99 Workshop on Machine Learning for Information Filtering, vol. 1, pp. 61–67. Stockholom, Sweden (1999)
15. Osamy, W., Salim, A., Khedr, A.M.: An information entropy based-clustering algorithm for heterogeneous wireless sensor networks. Wireless Netw. **26**, 1869–1886 (2020)
16. Palani, B., Elango, S., Viswanathan, K.V.: Cb-fake: A multimodal deep learning framework for automatic fake news detection using capsule neural network and bert. Multimed. Tools Appl. **81**(4), 5587–5620 (2022)
17. Pennycook, G., Rand, D.G.: The psychology of fake news. Trends Cogn. Sci. **22**(4), 335–336 (2018). https://doi.org/10.1016/j.tics.2018.02.001
18. Perdana, R.S., Muliawati, T.H., Alexandro, R.: Bot spammer detection in twitter using tweet similarity and time interval entropy. Jurnal Ilmu Komputer dan Informasi **8**(1), 19–25 (2015)
19. Shannon, C.E.: Prediction and entropy of printed English. Bell Syst. Tech. J. **30**(1), 50–64 (1951)
20. Threepak, .T., Watcharapupong, A.: Web attack detection using entropy-based analysis. In: The International Conference on Information Networking 2014 (ICOIN2014), pp. 244–247. IEEE (2014)
21. Zhang, D., Xu, J., Zadorozhny, V., Grant, J.: Fake news detection based on statement conflict. J. Intell. Inf. Syst. **59**(1), 173–192 (2022)

Data and Text Mining

A First Evolutionary Fuzzy Approach for Change Mining with Smart Bands

David Padilla[1], M. Asunción Padilla-Rascón[1], Rubén Cámara[1],
and Cristóbal J. Carmona[2,3(✉)]

[1] Department of Computer Science, University of Jaen, Campus Las Lagunillas,
23071 Jaén, Spain
{dpm00040,rcr00061}@red.ujaen.es, mprascon@ujaen.es
[2] Andalusian Research Institute on Data Science and Computational Intelligence,
University of Jaen, Campus Las Lagunillas, 23071 Jaén, Spain
ccarmona@ujaen.es
[3] Leicester School of Pharmacy, De Montfort University, Leicester 9BH, UK

Abstract. Data Science is one of the most prominent interdisciplinary
fields of Artificial Intelligence at the moment. It aims to analyze large
volumes of data (big data) in complex environments in order to extract
knowledge from them. In this contribution a first approach to change
mining is presented. The algorithm employs an evolutionary fuzzy system and it is developed within an Android application which will allow
us the incorporation and comparison of new algorithms in the future.
The accompanying study is based on the analysis of data generated by
wearables, more specifically smart bands, in order to discover knowledge
in sleep and activity data generated by the user in different time periods.

Keywords: Change mining · eHealth · data stream mining ·
evolutionary fuzzy systems

1 Introduction

Traditionally in data mining there are two possible approaches: supervised learning and unsupervised learning. However, there is a group of techniques halfway
between the prediction of supervised algorithms and the description of unsupervised algorithms, the supervised descriptive rule discovery [2] where techniques
like Subgroup Discovery [3] or Emerging Pattern Mining [13] are grouped. The
latter includes a concept where the target variable is defined by the time, and
this is defined as Change Mining [22]. It is described as the search for frequent
descriptive rules in a given set of information and the discovery of the changes
or anomalies that appear over time. The use of data in time is encompassed
within the data stream concept which is of special interest because the data
comes from different devices and sources, or with different formats [11], i.e., a
complex environment in Big Data [20] is defined.

In this contribution, we present a preliminary approach to extracting changing patterns through a multiobjective fuzzy system with data received from

© Springer Nature Switzerland AG 2023
H. L. Larsen et al. (Eds.): FQAS 2023, LNAI 14113, pp. 171–181, 2023.
https://doi.org/10.1007/978-3-031-42935-4_14

different smart bands. The proposal is based on soft computing techniques, in particular an evolutionary fuzzy system (EFS) [15]. The EFS is an hybridization of fuzzy logic [23–25] and evolutionary algorithms [14]. The former allows us to obtain of fuzzy emerging patterns which facilitate the analysis and understanding by the experts; the latter is an evolutionary algorithm based on FEPDS [12], a proposal for the extraction of fuzzy emerging patterns in data streams. Specifically, this algorithm establishes a high level of exploitation and exploration of the data during the search process.

The paper is organized as follows: Sect. 2 presents the main concepts and properties of change mining and EFSs. In Sect. 3 the main characteristics of the SDATEP algorithm are shown. Sections 4 and 5 present the experimental study and analysis in order to show all the properties of the study, the results and their analysis. Finally, the conclusions extracted from this paper are depicted in Sect. 6.

2 Background

2.1 Change Mining

Change mining is defined within emerging pattern mining as the search for patterns whose support increase significantly from one dataset (D_1) to another (D_2) [13]. Specifically, D_1 contains examples for one class and D_2 examples for the remaining classes where both classes are defined by time: D_1 contains data for one period and D_2 for another. In this way, a pattern is emerging/changing if the growth rate (GR) is greater than a threshold $\rho > 1$ and it is defined as [13]:

$$GR(x) = \begin{cases} 0, & IF\ Supp_{D_1}(x) = Supp_{D_2}(x) = 0, \\ \infty, & IF\ Supp_{D_1}(x) \neq 0 \wedge Supp_{D_2}(x) = 0, \\ \frac{Supp_{D_1}(x)}{Supp_{D_2}(x)}, & another\ case \end{cases} \tag{1}$$

These patterns are usually represented by means of conjunctions of attribute-value pairs which represents the discriminative characteristics they wish to describe; and the analysis of patterns is calculated through different quality measures based on the number of examples covered or not covered by the patterns which belong or do not belong to the class of the pattern. A complete description of these quality measures (Weighted Relative Accuracy, Growth Rate, True Positive Rate, False Positive Rate and Confidence) can be found in [13].

2.2 Evolutionary Fuzzy Sytems

Fuzzy systems [23–25] augmented with a learning process based on evolutionary algorithms [10] are defined as evolutionary fuzzy systems (EFSs) as can be observed in [15]. In this definition two concepts are presented: fuzzy systems and evolutionary algorithms. The former are usually considered in the form of fuzzy-rule based systems (FRBSs), which are composed of "IF-THEN" rules. One of their advantages is the use with continuous variables as linguistic ones, where values are represented through fuzzy linguistic labels (LLs) in fuzzy sets [17]. These fuzzy sets facilitate their application to real-world problems because the representation of continuous variables is very close to human reasoning, e.g. a variable such as *Age* could be represented with three linguistic labels such as *Low/Small*, *Normal* and *High/Tall* making it possible to achieve better analysis. On the other hand, evolutionary algorithms are stochastic algorithms for optimizing and searching. These algorithms were introduced by Holland [16]. The evolutionary algorithms imitate the principles of natural evolution in order to address optimization and learning problems.

The EFSs have demonstrated an interesting behaviour in real-world applications for supervised descriptive rule discovery [18]. For example, in [1,4,9] with problems related to bioinformatics and medicine, e-learning problems [5,6], industry [7,8], and other interdisciplinary areas such as natural language processing [19].

3   SDATEP: Smart Bands Drift Analysis Through Emerging Patterns

3.1   Android App

The algorithm is included in an Android App development within of the project "Aplicación Android para análisis de datos generados por bandas inteligentes" [21] (Android application of the analysis of data generated by smart bands). One of the main topics of the project is the collection and compilation of data for the analysis. The information will be divided into what it is and how the information is treated, how it is collected and it is subsequent processing.

Data Request. The data request is managed through two APIs (Huawei and Google/Xiaomi) on their different health applications, respective to the smart bands used. We assign the dates when the APIs must make the request/measurement. The chosen granularity was every day, since when performing data collection tests have shown empirically that this is the longest period that could be taken without affecting the quality or quantity of information being obtained. After sending the request asynchronosly a response will arrive, it will be stored in memory and subsequently saved in a database.

Preprocessing. Once data have been collected, they must be preprocessed by trying to fill null value with interpolations between the two closest data, or in the case of a constant value, such as the number of steps, by replicating the last valid value obtained. Preprocessing is executed when new data are included in the database.

Block Search. Finally, this process is executed at the time of generating training/test files that are going to be introduced into the algorithm. Since not all time data are useful, it will be necessary to search for blocks of time where relevant data actually exist. This generates the search for useful time blocks. Therefore, two dedicated functions have been developed, one for activity and the other for sleep.

– Activity: it is in charge of searching for the selected day for all those periods of time in which the sensors have captured movement, i.e., steps or displacement. It returns a grouping of all of these periods where there is significant activity.
– Sleep: it searches for the periods where the sensors have detected sleep. It is not limited to one day, since it would not make sense if someone goes to bed one day and wakes up the next, so the complete block of sleep is studied. The start and end of these sleep periods are searched, since it is not known when the user wearing the smart band slept (generated sleep data) or how long the sleep lasted.

3.2 SDATEP

It is based on the FEPDS algorithm for extracting emerging patterns for data streams [12] where different modifications are implemented in order to adapt it to Change Mining in spaces with a reduced number of samples. The SDATEP algorithm is an EFS fully implemented in Java. The algorithm was taken and compiled externally with all the libraries in an executable java file. This file can be included directly in the application to be developed or imported as an external library.

SDATEP employs a DNF (disjunctive normal form) representation because DNF is a compact and flexible form of knowledge that allows the generation and extraction of the rules generated. A representation of a binary string of set length where each bit corresponds to each of the possible values, with a value of 0 indicating that the value will not be used and 1 indicating that it will be used. A DNF rule for the SDATEP algorithm can be observed in Fig. 1. On the other hand, in the initialization the current rule model of the system is considered and new rules can evolve with the random generation of the remaining individuals.

$$\textit{Genotype}$$
$$\left| \begin{array}{c} X_1 \\ 1 \ \emptyset \ 1 \end{array} \right\| \begin{array}{c} X_2 \\ 1 \ 1 \ 1 \end{array} \right\| \begin{array}{c} X_3 \\ 1 \ \emptyset \ \emptyset \ \emptyset \end{array} \right\| \begin{array}{c} X_4 \\ \emptyset \ \emptyset \ \emptyset \end{array} \right|$$

$$\Downarrow$$

$$\textit{Phenotype}$$
$$IF(X_1 = (Low \lor High)) \land (X_3 = Museum) \ THEN \ (Class = 0)$$

Fig. 1. Representation of a fuzzy DNF rule with continuous and categorical variables in SDATP algorithm

One of the most important aspects of SDATEP is the restart mechanism. It is used to avoid falling into a local maximum, and with that objective the restart method will be launched when one of these two cases occurs: when it has not evolved or when it has not been able to cover new examples during twenty-five percent of the total of the evaluations performed. In addition, during the final processes the model is also performed. Those individuals that have passed the non-dominance criteria and the token competition will be incorporated, the remaining ones may be of interest when it comes to exploring uncovered areas so they will be used for a new population that will be in charge of exploring previously uncovered search areas.

The operational scheme is shown in Algorithm 1 where it is important to remark that the objectives of the evaluation are weighted relative accuracy, confidence and true positive rate. The already evaluated population will be joint with the initial population of the loop and a non-dominated sorting, obtaining the F population. If the pareto front does not evolve, a new population with a token competition will be obtained. Finally, after the generational loop a last token competition is performed and the rules or patterns are obtained, which will be stored in memory and these will be the rules obtained from this study batch.

Algorithm 1. SDATEP operational scheme

```
input: M - data instance
output: fPS - pattern model
if batch not full then
    Save to batch(M)
else
    initializeDatabase(batch)
    generation ⟸ 0
    Pg ⟸ initialize(data)
    Evaluate(Pg)
    while generation < maxGen do
        Offg ← GeneticOperators(Pg)
        Evaluate(Offg)
        Rg ← Union(Pg,Offg)
        F ← SortDominance(Rg)
        if F does not evolve then
            Pg+1 ← reset()
        end if
        g ← g+1
    end while
end if
```

---

4   Experimental Framewok

The quality of the proposed algorithm is analyzed through an experimental study. The Android application has been previously tested and analyzed because the algorithm and collection data process are executed within an Android device. This section presents the main properties of the study.

4.1   Data Collected

The algorithm SDATEP is executed with data obtained from different smart bands (Huawei band 4 pro and Smart Band 5 Xiaomi). Both smart bands have been worn by the same user during a determined time period. The objective is to collect data related to *heartRate*, *steps*, *accumulatedSteps*, *distance*, *accumulatedDistance* and *sleep* in order to analyze two states: *activity* and *sleep*. The former includes those that are taken as most relevant when performing a period of activity, whereas sleep includes only *heartRate* and *sleep*. Data collected in the same instant by different devices are combined in order to avoid repeated values. In addition, data are considered with two groups: A and B. The data labelled with A is the data group on the new package to be tested. However, the group B stores data for the remaining days and in the experimental study different days are used for this group.

The smart bands have taken data continuously during a month from one person. The only downtime has been shower and recharge time of the smart bands. The person has been sleeping around seven hours per day with a few exceptions, with a normal to low level of steps and exercise. Data were collected and saved in a data base, processed and used during the experimentation.

4.2   Parameters of the Algorithm and Characteristics of the Device

The parameters of the evolutionary algorithms are: number of generations of 70, population length of 50, crossover and mutation probabilities 0.8 and 0.1, respectively. These values are employed without changes for the complete study. Moreover, we employ different linguistic labels with the values 3, 5 and 7 where a triangular uniform shape is employed. The days for the data collection in group B were set as 1, 7, 14 and 21 making in combination with the linguistic labels a total of twelve experiments for each activity.

The experimental study was performed on an android Xiaomi Redmi Note 8 Pro with SO Android 11. The requirements of the experiments need to be proportional to the performance of the device, making the time and space use important to take in consideration. The different executions were performed in 3234 ms. This time is acceptable because the device can still work normally without interruption. With respect to the disk space, the study uses around 100 MB space, making that space value negligible.

4.3   Quality Measures and Results

The measures for the quality shown in the tables of the experimental study are related to the main characteristic of emerging patterns in order to estimate the reliability and conciseness of the SDATEP. Those measures of quality are the number of patterns (NR), number of variables (NV), normalized weighted relative accuracy (WRAcc), true positive rate (TPR), false positive rate (FPR), growth rate percentage (GR) and confidence (CONF). In addition, execution (Exec) time (in milliseconds) and memory (Mem) consumption (in megabytes) can be analyzed. These results allow us to check the different experiments and to determinate the capacity of SDATEP to discover drift changes.

The results shown are the execution of twenty-four different experiments, each one with the same static parameters but changing the quantity of data and the number of LLs they need to use during the execution. They were separated into two groups of studies, one of them with sleep data taken from the sleep time with heart rate and sleep values (deep sleep, REM, awake), while the other group is the activity study, with heart rate, steps, distance and accumulated steps and distance.

5   Results and Analysis of the Study

5.1   Sleep

Table 1. Results obatined in the Sleep Data experiment

LLs	Days	NR	NV	WRAcc	TPR	FPR	GR	CONF	Exec	Mem
3	1	3	1.33	0.65	0.68	0.38	1.00	0.76	1810	64
	7	2	1.00	0.56	0.87	0.75	1.00	0.15	1894	83
	14	2	1.50	0.50	1.00	1.00	1.00	0.07	2085	71
	21	3	1.33	0.50	1.00	1.00	1.00	0.05	2225	59
5	1	3	1.33	0.65	0.07	0.38	1.00	0.76	2111	66
	7	2	1.50	0.82	0.99	0.95	1.00	0.13	1928	27
	14	1	1.00	0.51	1.00	0.99	1.00	0.07	2206	29
	21	2	1.50	0.50	1.00	0.99	1.00	0.05	2360	32
7	1	3	1.67	0.51	0.35	0.33	0.67	0.83	2030	39
	7	3	1.33	0.57	0.68	0.54	1.00	0.16	2115	20
	14	1	1.00	0.55	0.99	0.89	1.00	0.07	2363	42
	21	1	1.00	0.60	0.89	0.69	1.00	0.06	2239	32

The results of the sleep experiments are represented in Table 1. It can be seen how better results are obtained in terms of the number of rules and variables in a greater number of days even with an experiment with a larger amount of data. Only one rule and a single variable for this experiment. In general, the number of rules varies between one up to three, which is not an excessive amount knowing that the amount of data being handled is not very large, which is desirable in order to improve the interpretability of the model.

On the other hand, the values of WRAcc reflect an evolution with respect to the number of days, in a few days (few data) a smaller number of labels work better while in more days (from fourteen) the maximum number of labels works better and allows us to obtain better values for this result. In TPR it can be seen that in the experiments with the lowest number of days this number was low. Increasing the number of days and therefore the data increases the TPR values, indicating that the accuracy of the rules that have been obtained is also improved. In the experiments with fourteen or more days a TPR is close to 1, indicating that the rule covers almost the largest percentage of the data. This fact is actually positive.

5.2   Activity

Table 2. Results obatined in the Activity Data experiment

LLs	Days	NR	NV	WRAcc	TPR	FPR	GR	CONF	Exec	Mem
3	1	5	3.40	0.77	1.00	0.45	1.00	0.45	2647	51
	7	1	4.00	0.64	1.00	0.73	1.00	0.11	2239	35
	14	2	3.50	0.62	0.99	0.76	1.00	0.07	1970	37
	21	2	3.50	0.62	0.99	0.74	1.00	0.06	2401	53
5	1	1	2.00	0.51	0.02	0	1.00	1.00	2176	37
	7	2	5.00	0.54	0.13	0.05	1.00	0.21	2651	31
	14	5	2.80	0.65	0.77	0.48	1.00	0.27	2477	36
	21	1	5.00	0.71	1.00	0.59	1.00	0.08	2780	41
7	1	5	2.40	0.80	0.72	0.28	1.00	0.55	2922	51
	7	6	3.00	0.73	0.96	0.5	1.00	0.15	3217	28
	14	4	5.00	0.68	0.65	0.29	1.00	0.16	3234	26
	21	1	4.00	0.58	0.20	0.04	1.00	0.19	2853	32

This subsection is focused on Table 2, where the results of the sleep experiments are represented. It is of interest to analyze the number of rules and variables which unlike sleep are much more diverse. These results present between 1 and 6 rules with between 2 and 5 variables. As in the sleep study one batch at a time is studied, so as the number of data increases it is desirable that these rules do not increase. For example, in the 21-day experiments the number of rules is one and the number of variables is between 3.5 and 5, as in the previous experiment. It is the objective of the algorithm to obtain the minimum number of rules with the largest possible coverage.

It can be seen that the WRAcc measure in the study of activity has better results than sleep results. This may be due to the fact that there is a greater amount of data or that there is a greater variation between them, because the sleep data are more homogeneous. But in WRAcc is possible to see several cases that have lower results: five labels and one day, five labels and three days, and the last one in Table 2. In all these cases the TPR drops greatly, which affects the WRAcc, especially in the first one mentioned where the FPR is 0.5.

Earlier in the sleep study the TPR increases as the number of days increases, because the data are very homogeneous. This favors the creation of simple rules that accurately cover as many of them as possible. But in case of activity they are not so homogeneous; the activity time between different days is not the same, neither the intensity of the activity.

6   Conclusions

This contribution presents a first approach based on evolutionary fuzzy systems with smart bands and an android application for change mining. The use of an evolutionary fuzzy system in this data mining task allows us the achievement of an interpretable analysis of trends and possible drifts detection in data generated during activities and sleep for the user who uses this type of wearable. In this way, rules are represented through fuzzy logic and are considered explainable knowledge.

The experimental study was performed with different combinations of days in order to search for drift detection in 1, 7, 14 and 21 days. The results show the abilities of this type of algorithm for obtaining results in a space with a small number of samples. It is also important to highlight the design of an android application where this and future algorithms could be incorporated in order to improve this type of study.

Acknowledgments. This work is financed by the Ministry of Science, Innovation and Universities with code PID2019-107793GB-I00/AEI/10.13039/501100011033.

References

1. Carmona, C.J., Chrysostomou, C., Seker, H., del Jesus, M.J.: Fuzzy rules for describing subgroups from influenza a virus using a multi-objective evolutionary algorithm. Appl. Soft Comput. **13**(8), 3439–3448 (2013)
2. Carmona, C.J., del Jesus, M.J., Herrera, F.: A unifying analysis for the supervised descriptive rule discovery via the weighted relative accuracy. Knowl.-Based Syst. **139**, 89–100 (2018)
3. Carmona, C.J., González, P., del Jesus, M.J., Herrera, F.: Analysis of the impact of using different diversity functions for the subgroup discovery algorithm NMEEF-SD. In: Proceedings of the IEEE International Workshop on Genetic and Evolutionary Fuzzy Systems, pp. 17–23 (2011)
4. Carmona, C.J., González, P., del Jesus, M.J., Navío, M., Jiménez, L.: Evolutionary fuzzy rule extraction for subgroup discovery in a psychiatric emergency department. Soft Comput. **15**(12), 2435–2448 (2011)

5. Carmona, C.J., González, P., del Jesus, M.J., Romero, C., Ventura, S.: Evolutionary algorithms for subgroup discovery applied to e-learning data. In: Proceedings of the IEEE International Education Engineering, pp. 983–990 (2010)
6. Carmona, C.J., González, P., del Jesus, M.J., Ventura, S.: Subgroup discovery in an e-learning usage study based on Moodle. In: Proceedings of the International Conference of European Transnational Education, pp. 446–451 (2011)
7. Carmona, C.J., González, P., García-Domingo, B., del Jesus, M.J., Aguilera, J.: MEFES: an evolutionary proposal for the detection of exceptions in subgroup discovery: an application to Concentrating Photovoltaic Technology. Knowl.-Based Syst. **54**, 73–85 (2013)
8. Carmona, C.J., Ramírez-Gallego, S., Torres, F., Bernal, E., del Jesus, M.J., García, S.: Web usage mining to improve the design of an e-commerce website: OrOliveSur.com. Expert Syst. Appl. **39**, 11243–11249 (2012)
9. Carmona, C.J., et al.: A fuzzy genetic programming-based algorithm for subgroup discovery and the application to one problem of pathogenesis of acute sore throat conditions in humans. Inf. Sci. **298**, 180–197 (2015)
10. Eiben, A.E., Smith, J.E.: Introduction to Evolutionary Computing. NCS, Springer, Heidelberg (2015). https://doi.org/10.1007/978-3-662-44874-8
11. Gama, J.: Knowledge Discovery from Data Streams. CRC Press, Boca Raton (2010)
12. García-Vico, A.M., Carmona, C.J., González, P., del Jesus, M.J., Seker, H.: Fepds: a proposal for the extraction of fuzzy emerging patterns in data streams. IEEE Trans. Fuzzy Syst. **28**(12), 3193–3203 (2020)
13. García-Vico, A.M., Carmona, C.J., Martín, D., García-Borroto, M., del Jesus, M.J.: An overview of emerging pattern mining in supervised descriptive rule discovery: taxonomy, empirical study, trends and prospects. WIREs: Data Mining Knowl. Disc. **8**(1), e1231 (2018)
14. Goldberg, D.E.: Genetic Algorithms in Search, Optimization and Machine Learning. Addison-Wesley Longman Publishing Co., Inc., Boston (1989)
15. Herrera, F.: Genetic fuzzy systems: taxomony, current research trends and prospects. Evol. Intell. **1**, 27–46 (2008)
16. Holland, J.H.: Adaptation in Natural and Artificial Systems. University of Michigan Press, Ann Arbor (1975)
17. Hüllermeier, E.: Fuzzy sets in machine learning and data mining. Appl. Soft Comput. **11**(2), 1493–1505 (2011)
18. Kralj-Novak, P., Lavrac, N., Webb, G.I.: Supervised descriptive rule discovery: a unifying survey of constrast set, emerging pateern and subgroup mining. J. Mach. Learn. Res. **10**, 377–403 (2009)
19. López, M., Martínez-Camara, E., Luzón, M.V., Herrera, F.: ADOPS: aspect discovery opinion summarisation methodology based on deep learning and subgroup discovery for generating explainable opinion summaries. Knowl.-Based Syst. **231**, 511–520 (2021)
20. Mayer-Schonberger, V., Cukier, K.: Big data: the essential guide to work, life and learning in the age of insight. Hachette UK (2013)
21. Padilla, D.: Trabajo fin de grado: Aplicación android para análisis de datos generados por bandas inteligentes. Technical report, Universidad de Jaen (2021)
22. Song, H.S., Kim, J.K., Kim, S.H.: Mining the change of costumer behavior in an internet shopping mal. Expert Syst. Appl. **21**, 157–168 (2001)
23. Zadeh, L.A.: The concept of a linguistic variable and its applications to approximate reasoning. Parts I. Inf. Sci. **8**, 199–249 (1975)

24. Zadeh, L.A.: The concept of a linguistic variable and its applications to approximate reasoning. Parts II. Inf. Sci. **8**, 301–357 (1975)
25. Zadeh, L.A.: The concept of a linguistic variable and its applications to approximate reasoning. Parts III. Inf. Sci. **9**, 43–80 (1975)

Federated Learning in Healthcare with Unsupervised and Semi-Supervised Methods

Juan Paños-Basterra$^{(\boxtimes)}$, M. Dolores Ruiz, and Maria J. Martin-Bautista

Department of Computer Science and A.I., Research Centre for Information and
Communication Technologies (CITIC -UGR), University of Granada, Granada, Spain
panosjuan@ugr.es, {mbautis,mdruiz}@decsai.ugr.es

Abstract. The federated paradigm has made possible the development of techniques capable of solving advanced problems in the healthcare field through the protection of data privacy. However, most existing research is centered around supervised methods and real world data tends to be unevenly distributed and scarcely labelled. This paper aims to provide an overview of existing unsupervised and semi-supervised methods implemented in a federated healthcare setting in order to identify state of the art methods and detect current challenges and future lines of research.

Keywords: federated learning · unsupervised · semi-supervised · healthcare

1 Introduction

Over the last years, the privacy and protection of data have become great concerns in the healthcare setting, thus traditional machine learning techniques which depend on vast quantities of centralized data are not always applicable without compromising data confidentiality. An alternative paradigm called Federated Learning (FL) has emerged to solve these challenges, and its applications in the healthcare setting look specially promising. However, most existing research is centered around supervised learning [3,4], where it is assumed that most data is labelled and labels can be trusted. In reality, medical datasets are prone to having vast amounts of unlabeled or unreliably labelled data. It is interesting to study the current methods and challenges associated when dealing with this kind of data, both in semi-supervised and unsupervised federated learning. Therefore we propose as the main contributions of this work:

- A comprehensive review of the state of the art methods and current trends in federated unsupervised and semi-supervised learning.
- An identification of remaining challenges in these lines of research.

The paper is structured as follows. Next Section provides the methodology which has been utilized in the research for this paper. Section 3 introduces the concepts

© Springer Nature Switzerland AG 2023
H. L. Larsen et al. (Eds.): FQAS 2023, LNAI 14113, pp. 182–193, 2023.
https://doi.org/10.1007/978-3-031-42935-4_15

of federated learning, with several categories relevant to this study. In Sect. 4, data characteristics and existing supervised and unsupervised methods relevant in the medical domain are presented and finally in Sect. 5, conclusions and current challenges are presented and future research lines are proposed.

2   Methodology

To conduct our review of federated unsupervised and semi-supervised methods we implemented a research methodology involving two different databases, Web of Science and Google Scholar. Furthermore, we have set a special focus on federated techniques and algorithms which have been implemented in the healthcare setting. Due to the recent development of these techniques, most reviewed research has occurred in the last years and therefore there has been no need for a cut-off point. To identify relevant research, we have used a wide array of search key terms, including but not limited to: *"federated unsupervised learning"*, *"federated semi-supervised learning"*, and for each sub-category, relevant searches have been established, such as: *"federated clustering"*, *"federated anomaly detection"*... Whenever possible, we have sought to select only research from the medical domain, therefore the keywords *"... in healthcare"*, *"medical federated..."* have been utilized wherever possible. After identifying the potential studies with which to construct our review, we have declared our inclusion criteria, that is, methods which implement novel federated variants of previously existing methods or federated techniques which improve the existing state of the art. Again, whenever possible, studies relating to the healthcare domain have been selected. When not possible more general studies have been examined.

3   The Federated Paradigm

In traditional Artificial Intelligence (AI) approaches, data is usually collected from many different sources and centralized in one server. Machine learning (ML) or data mining (DM) algorithms are then applied to extract knowledge or obtain models capable of performing intended tasks. Data privacy and security might be infringed with traditional methodologies because data needs to be sent to a third party/device and its confidentiality and security cannot be guaranteed. Furthermore, certain regulations, such as the European Union's General Data Protection Regulation (GDPR) protect user's data from being shared due to these concerns. Federated learning, first proposed by McMahan et al. [1] and more extensively defined by Yang et al. [2] is an emerging paradigm for exploiting distributed data through AI techniques with a focus on data privacy and security. In summary, FL provides a decentralized framework where different nodes which own the data (also called clients) participate in a process to train machine learning models or apply data mining techniques. Several different categories of FL architectures can be differentiated.

3.1 Data Partitions

Federated systems can be categorised based on the data partitioning they implement:

Horizontal Split: In some settings, different nodes can share a feature space, but differ on the sample space. In a network of hospitals, the generated data will be relatively similar and standardized, for example by using an Electronic Health Record (EHR), which can contain data such as medical history, diagnoses, radiology images... However, the individuals attended by each hospital (sample space) will be mostly different. In similar settings we can apply horizontal federated learning, because a feature space is shared, though in Sect. 4.1 we explain how data distribution within the nodes can pose a challenge to solving the desired federated task.

Vertical Split: While most implementations have been carried out in horizontally split data, in other settings, nodes participating in the federated process share the sample space but have distinct feature spaces, with overlapping samples being found using entity alignment techniques [26] which can prove quite challenging. Vertically split data is much less explored compared to horizontally split data and is limited by the number of samples, features and collaborating parties, though a more in depth review can be found in [51]

3.2 Scale of the Federation

Another category federated systems fall into depends on the number of nodes that participate in the federated process, which tends to be correlated to the amount of data and processing power of each node. The main categories are:

Cross-Device: Jin et al. [4] define the cross-device setting as one in which the number of participants is massive (up to 10^{10} clients), local dataset size is small and inconsistent, and devices have reduced computing capabilities. Typically, nodes in this context are smartphones, IoT devices or other similar systems.

Cross-Silo: Another category of the scale of a federation is cross-silo, where client nodes are usually bigger entities, such as a network of hospitals and banks, typically the number of clients does not exceed 10^2. These nodes have much bigger computing power and dataset sizes, with data usually being more consistent than in cross-device settings.

In healthcare settings, both architectures are found, with networks of hospitals falling into a cross-silo category while other architectures, such as an Internet of Health Things (IoHT) monitoring system belong more to a cross-device setting.

3.3   Governance

Another category in which we can divide federated architectures is along the governance system that controls the federated process. Most existing studies implement some form of **centralized architecture**, where a hierarchical system is established since one (or more) nodes control the process, usually by updating a global model and handling communication and updates from the client nodes. In **decentralized architecture**, however, there is no central authority or node guiding the federated process and nodes need to collaborate with each other to carry out the desired task, therefore complexity is greatly augmented. Some of the most common implementations of decentralized federated architectures include Peer to Peer (P2P) [27], graph [28] and blockchain [29].

Other Categories: Other categories of federated paradigms can be identified from existing literature [2,7], along the lines of privacy measures implemented to protect underlying data or the level of trust in federated networks. However, these are out of the scope of this paper and will not be discussed.

4   Federated Learning in Medical Environments

This section will discuss the application of the federated paradigm to the healthcare domain, the existing issues with medical data and some state of the art techniques in semi-supervised and unsupervised learning that have a medical application, or that could be helpful in related challenges.

4.1   Data Characteristics in Medical Environments

In [3], Pfitzner et al. provide a thorough review of different characteristics that medical data tends to exhibit, as well as challenges that arise from them:

- **Massively distributed:** A large number of devices participate in the FL process, the number of participating agents or nodes can greatly vary depending on the setting, take for example an Internet of Medical Things (IoMT) system where thousands of devices are generating data, in contrast to another architecture where the main hospitals of a region are collaborating to train a ML model, this system might have comparatively few nodes.
- **Non Independently and Identically Distributed (IID):** Data in medical settings originates from different distributions, whether it be patient demographics, varying medical procedures or other underlying reasons, it cannot be assumed that data in every node follows a similar distribution.
- **Unbalanced:** Data is not evenly distributed between the participating nodes, whether it be in quantity, in data labels and in the feature space. We can imagine a big hospital in a metropolitan city will have data from many more patient cohorts and diseases than a smaller healthcare center. FL models may also be trained on hospital data and data extracted from patient's IoT devices, where only data from that specific patient is available.

In [5], several non-IID mitigation methods are proposed, with different non-IID characteristics requiring diverse mitigation applications, some of the most interesting are:

- **Dataset balancing**, utilizing techniques such as Generative Adversarial Networks (GAN) [7], Synthetic Minority Oversampling Technique (SMOTE) [8] or geometric transformations [9]. These techniques can be applied locally or with server data sharing, which provides a greater performance boost [10] but exposes some node data to the server.
- **Adaptive Hyperparameters method**, which tries to find the optimal FL hyperparameters values for each node, such as learning rate, loss score and weighting coefficient. The weighting coefficient [11] is a variable that controls the relative influence of each node in the aggregation process. Several formulae for calculating it have been proposed in [12,13]. The other published method is the adaptive loss function, which has the ability to change conditions based on the loss score function. Huang et al. [15] proposed the LoAdaBoost method to boost the training process adaptively from the weak learner nodes.
- **Domain Adaptation method** (DA) is utilized to minimize discrepancies in data distributions in order to increase the overall performance of nodes with non-IID data [16]. To achieve this, a model trained in one or more source domains is applied to a new target domain in which the feature space is shared but data representation and distribution are not.

4.2 Unsupervised Methods

Unsupervised methods are used when no information is given about data, that is, data has no labels. These methods allow for the discovery of hidden patterns, data grouping and other insights. We will now cover some of the most widely utilized unsupervised methods, as well as some implementations in the federated healthcare setting.

Anomaly Detection. Chandola et al. [40] define anomaly detection as the problem of finding patterns in data that do not conform to expected behaviour. A wide variety of applications can be found for the field of anomaly detection, such as bank fraud detection, cyber-security intrusion detection, critical system failures and in the healthcare setting, specially when combined with IoHT devices [41] in order to implement measures such as cardiac disease prevention. When dealing with sensitive medical data, it is paramount to implement a data privacy and security approach. To this aim several federated methods have been proposed for anomaly detection, both supervised and unsupervised methods. For the supervised case we can highlight the use of Generative Adversarial Networks (GANs) to detect patient data and network traffic anomalies [42]. Some federated unsupervised anomaly detection proposals exist, such as the adaptation of Isolation Forests (IF) [43] to a federated architecture by Cavallin et al. [44] to solve several anomaly detection problems such as credit card fraud detection and ann-thyroid anomaly detection. However, the proposed methods obtain poor performance and authors conclude that adaptability of federated versions of algorithms needs to improve and more anomaly detection algorithms should be considered in the federated settings. Another more successful approach has been implemented by Bercea et al. [45] for detecting abnormalities such as tumors, inflammation, multiple sclerosis or acute infarcts in brain magnetic resonance imaging (MRI). This is achieved by merging the federated paradigm with well established unsupervised techniques such as convolutional auto-encoders (AE) [46], the main contributions are model parameter disentanglement to leverage global anatomical structure while mitigating domain shifts. Another anomaly detection technique which is not very explored in the federated setting is time series analysis. In [54], authors propose a federated time series analysis framework for the IoMT paradigm which shows promising results in Electroencefalograph, Electrocardiogram, Photomicrography for disease detection.

Association Rule Mining. The mining of association rules in medical data can prove extremely useful, since it can serve to identify co-morbidities, predict disease progression and identify risk factors, among other benefits. The original proposal by Kantarcioglu et al. [56] utilized Secure Multiparty Computation (SMC) and cryptography techniques such as Commutative Encryption to guarantee privacy of the mining process, the developed techniques were improved by Tassa et al. [57] reducing the complexity and improving performance. More recently, Molina et al. [53] propose a federated data mining method to discover association rules and interesting itemsets in horizontally partitioned Electronic Health Records (EHRs). In [55], Domadiya et al. propose a privacy-preserving vertical federated association rule mining for different healthcare metrics, mainly correlation between disease detection and abnormal test results.

Dimensionality Reduction. Data generated in the healthcare industry is prone to be highly dimensional, which affects the performance and efficiency of most methods which utilize the data and increases complexity of other. Therefore it is essential to reduce the dimensionality of the data utilizing unsupervised methods, however, traditional approaches such as the linear Principal Component Analysis (PCA), the non-linear t-Distributed Stochastic Neighbor Embedding (t-SNE) and the variable selection Random Forests methods need to be adapted to the federated paradigm. In [47], Grammenos et al. implement a federal, asynchronous and differentially private PCA algorithm in the memorylimited setting, which unlike previous methods, proves itself robust against straggler or failed nodes and is horizontally scalable. Chai et al. [49] propose a masking-based federated singular vector decomposition method (FedSVD), which achieves lossless accuracy and high efficiency over billion-scale data. A novel technique is proposed in [48] by Cui et al. which consists of a federated sparse sliced inverse regression algorithm that can simultaneously estimate the central dimension reduction subspace and perform variable selection in a federated setting. Lastly, Islam et al. [50] propose a feature selection mechanism based on correlation value of the features to reduce dimensionality in genomic data in order to maximize the utility of ML models.

Clustering. One of the most useful techniques when dealing with unlabelled data is clustering, the centralized and distributed approaches have been studied extensively and can be greatly summarized as:

- **Centralized clustering:** In traditional centralized clustering, all data is unified, and through a variety of methods (usually variants of Lloyd's heuristic [30]) a set of clusters are obtained. This approach allows for greater control over the clustering process and increased simplicity. However data privacy concerns are not addressed.
- **Paralellized or distributed clustering:** Other works have studied parallel or distributed methods for clustering techniques [31,32]. These algorithms are usually distributed implementations of methods derived from Lloyd's heuristic or DBSCAN [33], and perform several communication rounds. Other proposals are centered around communication efficient clustering methods which require few communication rounds [34–36]. These methods fail to explore the federated setting, with its special emphasis on security and privacy of data and with the heterogeneity challenge.

Federated Clustering. In federated clustering, the objective is to group together local data that are globally similar to data located in another node with global data remaining private. Node heterogeneity is also an important concept in federated clustering, and is defined as:

Definition 1 (Heterogeneity in Clustering). *In the context of clustering, we state that a federated network with sufficient data is heterogeneous if $k' \leq \sqrt{k}$. The lower the ratio between k' and $\sqrt{k}$, the more heterogeneity exists in the network. Where k' is the maximum number of clusters present in a local node and k is the total number of clusters in a network.*

The main challenges in federated clustering are dealing with high heterogeneity, minimizing communication rounds and approaching the results obtained through centralized approaches without compromising data privacy. Though not many concrete applications of federated clustering in healthcare settings exist in the literature, here we present more general techniques that could be applied in this domain. In [37], authors propose a new federated fuzzy c-means (FFCM) algorithm which obtains promising results with client data remaining local, however it performs poorly in settings where clusters are overlapping and locally absent and the computational cost is high. A one-shot clustering approached is proposed by Dennis et al. [14] based on the k-means clustering approach (k-FED). The proposed method benefits from cluster heterogeneity and requires only one round of communication for each device, which do not require network-wide synchronization, making it resistant to device failure. In [52], non-IID heart rate variability is addressed using Personalized Federated Cluster Models, a hierarchical clustering-based FL process.

Clustered Federation: In contrast to federated clustering, clustered federation tackles the task of identifying distinct clusters which can represent for example groups of users with varying interests to train models for every cluster of users, which has proven to be effective when working with non-IID data among clients [38,39]. Huang et al. [12] leverage this technique to cluster patients in order to improve ML model efficiency and efficacy.

4.3   Semi-Supervised Methods

In many highly specialised cross-silo environments, such as a network of hospitals, it is common to encounter highly heterogeneous, label-scarce datasets due to the complexity and cost of correctly labeling the data. Furthermore, in each client (in this case, any given hospital), the class distribution of labelled and unlabelled data may differ, we can imagine data from a rare disease will not be labelled easily while data from more common diseases will be mostly labelled. We can identify two main settings in which data is not fully labeled, the first is that all client nodes have partially labelled data and partially unlabelled data, as opposed to a setting in which some nodes have fully labelled data, and some nodes have fully unlabelled data. In this challenging context, several Federated Semi Supervised Learning (FSSL) techniques have been proposed to solve these issues, stemming from the original proposals of Semi-Supervised Learning (SSL) [17], which leverage unlabelled data to improve performance and prevent overfitting caused by small labelled datasets. Some widely utilized SSL methods include generative models [18], adversarial training [19], regularization [20], pseudo-labeling [21], connections between samples [22] and multi-view ensemble training [23], a more in depth review of recent trends in semi supervised techniques for medical image classification can be vound in [24]. The previously described methods perform well in a FSSL setting when the clients have IID data, however in a more realistic setting where this is not the case, performance tends to suffer. To address this challenge, several new FSSL methods have been proposed, in [25], authors propose a Random Sampling Consensus Federated Learning (RSCFed) which mitigates the uneven reliability of non-IID local clients via aggregation of multiple sub-consensus models, as opposed to more traditional aggregation of all local models which can introduce noisy client data into the central model. In [6], authors propose FedSSL, a federated semi supervised learning framework which is based on support agents (clients which have only labelled data) and query agents (clients which have only unlabelled data), and aims to improve the collective capacity of both types of agents through FSSL, it has achieved better results than other state of the art methods, specially in extreme data-scarce conditions.

5   Conclusions and Remaining Challenges

Over the last years, federated systems have emerged as a promising solution that addresses data protection and privacy concerns, with special interest in the healthcare setting due to the extreme sensitivity of this data. However most existing research has been dedicated to supervised methods, which rely on fully and truthfully labelled data, which is difficult to come across in many real world healthcare settings. Therefore, this paper has provided an overview of different federated unsupervised and semi-supervised methods which have been proposed over the last years, with special interest in the healthcare field. This will enable future researchers to understand the current trends in these fields, and obtain a comprehensive understanding of existing state of the art techniques.

The most pressing challenge in this field is the correct adaptation of traditional techniques to complex, massive and privacy-constrained medical data without sacrificing the quality of obtained results in diverse settings. Future lines include further research into federated techniques which utilize the widespread unlabelled data, and provide interpretability and advance solutions in many remaining medical challenges.

Acknowledgements. We would like to acknowledge support for this work from the Grant PID2021-123960OB-I00 funded by MCIN/AEI/10.13039/501100011033 and by ERDF A way of making Europe.

References

1. McMahan, H.B., Moore, E., Ramage, D., Hampson, S., Arcas, B.A.: Communication-Efficient learning of deep networks from decentralized data (2016). arXiv. 1602.05629
2. Yang, Q., Liu, Y., Chen, T., Tong, Y.: Federated machine learning: concept and applications. ACM Trans. Intell. Syst. Technol. (TIST) **10**(2), 12 (2019)
3. Pfitzner, B., Steckhan, N., Bert Arnrich, B.: Federated learning in a medical context: a systematic literature review. ACM Trans. Internet Technol. **21**(2), 31 (2021)
4. Jin, Y., Wei, X., Liu, Y.: Qiang Yang. Towards utilizing unlabeled data in federated learning, A survey and prospective (2020)
5. Prayitno.: A systematic review of federated learning in the healthcare area: from the perspective of data properties and applications. Appl. Sci. **11**, 11191 (2021). https://doi.org/10.3390/app112311191
6. Fan, C., Hue, J., Huang, J.: Private semi-supervised federated learning. In: Proceedings of the Thirty-First International Joint Conference on Artificial Intelligence (IJCAI-22) (2022)
7. Zhang, L., Shen, B., Barnawi, A., Xi, S., Kumar, N., Wu, Y.: FedDPGAN: Federated differentially private generative adversarial networks framework for the detection of COVID-19 pneumonia. Inf. Syst, Front (2021)
8. Wu, Q., Chen, X., Zhou, Z., Zhang, J.: FedHome: cloud-edge based personalized federated learning for in-home health monitoring. IEEE Trans. Mobile Comput. **21**, 2818–2832 (2020)

9. Yang, D., Xu, Z., Li, W., Myronenko, A., Roth, H.R., Harmon, S., Xu, S., Turk-bey, B., Turkbey, E., Wang, X., et al.: Federated semi-supervised learning for COVID region segmentation in chest CT using multi-national data from China, Italy. Japan. Med. Image Anal. **70**, 101992 (2021)

10. Zhao, Y., Li, M., Lai, L., Suda, N., Civin, D., Chandra, V.: Federated learning with non-IID data (2018), arXiv:1806.00582

11. McMahan, H.B., Moore, E., Ramage, D., Hampson, S., y Arcas, B.A.: Communication-efficient learning of deep networks from decentralized data. In: Proceedings of the Artificial Intelligence and Statistics Conference, Fort Lauderdale, FL, USA, pp. 1273–1282 (2017)

12. Huang, L., Shea, A.L., Qian, H., Masurkar, A., Deng, H., Liu, D.: Patient clustering improves efficiency of federated machine learning to predict mortality and hospital stay time using distributed electronic medical records. J. Biomed. Inform. **99**, 103291 (2019)

13. Chen, Y., Qin, X., Wang, J., Yu, C., Gao, W.: FedHealth: A federated transfer learning framework for wearable healthcare. IEEE Intell. Syst. **35**, 83–93 (2020)

14. Dennis, D.K., Li, T., Smith, V.: Heterogeneity for the Win: one-shot federated clustering. In: Proceedings of the 38th International Conference on Machine Learning, PMLR 139 (2021)

15. Huang, L., Yin, Y., Fu, Z., Zhang, S., Deng, H., Liu, D.: LoAdaBoost: Loss-based AdaBoost federated machine learning with reduced computational complexity on IID and non-IID intensive care data. PLoS ONE **15**, e0230706 (2020)

16. Tran, K.; Bøtker, J.P., Aframian, A., Memarzadeh, K.: Artificial intelligence for medical imaging. In: Artificial Intelligence in Healthcare; Elsevier: Amsterdam, The Netherlands, pp. 143–162 (2020)

17. Cohen, I., Cozman, F.G., Sebe, N., Cirelo, M.C., Huang, T.S.: Semisupervised learning of classifiers: theory, algorithms, and their application to human-computer interaction. IEEE Trans. Pattern Anal. Mach. Intell. **26**(12), 1553–1566 (2004)

18. Kingma, D.P., Mohamed, S., Rezende, D.J., Welling, M.: Semisupervised learning with deep generative models. Adv. Neural Inf. Process. Syst. **27**, 3581–3589 (2014)

19. Miyato, T., Maeda, S., Koyama, M., Ishii, S.: Virtual adversarial training: a regularization method for supervised and semi-supervised learning. IEEE Trans. Pattern Anal. Mach. Intell. **41**(8), 1979–1993 (2018)

20. Tarvainen, A., Valpola, H.: Mean teachers are better role models: weightaveraged consistency targets improve semi-supervised deep learning results. Adv. Neural Inf. Process. Syst. **30**, 1195–1204 (2017)

21. Berthelot, D., et al.: A holistic approach to semi-supervised learning. In H. Wallach, H. Larochelle, A. Beygelzimer, F. d Alche-Buc, E. Fox, and R. Garnett, editors, Adv. Neural Inf. Process. Syst.**32**, 5049–5059. Curran Associates Inc (2019)

22. Kipf, T.N., Welling, M.: Semi-supervised classification with graph convolutional networks. arXiv preprint arXiv:1609.02907 (2016)

23. Chen, D.-D.,Wang, W., Gao, W., Zhi-Hua Zhou, Z.-H.: Tri-net for semi-supervised deep learning. In: Proceedings of the 27th International Joint Conference on Artificial Intelligence, pp. 2014–2020. AAAI Press (2018)

24. Solatidehkordi, Z., Zualkernan, I.: Survey on Recent Trends in Medical Image Classification Using Semi-Supervised Learning. Appl. Sci. **12**, 12094 (2022). https://doi.org/10.3390/app122312094

25. Liang, X., Lin, Y., Fu, H., Zhu, L., Li, X.: Proceedings of the IEEE/CVF Conference on Computer Vision and Pattern Recognition (CVPR), pp. 10154–10163 (2022)

26. Yan, Z., Guoliang, L., Jianhua, F.: A survey on entity alignment of knowledge base. J. Comput. Res. Dev. **53**(1), 165–192 (2016). https://doi.org/10.7544/issn1000-1239.2016.20150661

27. Roy, A.G., Siddiqui, S., Pölsterl, S., Navab, N., Wachinger, C.: BrainTorrent: a Peer-to-Peer Environment for Decentralized Federated Learning (2019). https://doi.org/10.48550/arXiv.1905.06731

28. Singh, S., Rathore, S., Alfarraj, O., Tolba, A., Yoon, B.: A framework for privacy-preservation of IoT healthcare data using Federated Learning and blockchain technology. Futur. Gener. Comput. Syst. **129**, 380–388 (2022)

29. Rizk, E., Sayed, A.H.: A graph federated architecture with privacy preserving learning. In: 2021 IEEE 22nd International Workshop on Signal Processing Advances in Wireless Communications (SPAWC)

30. Lloyd, S.: Least squares quantization in PCM. IEEE Transactions on Information Theory (1982)

31. Dhillon, I.S., Modha, D.S.: A data-clustering algorithm on distributed memory multiprocessors. In: Large-Scale Parallel Data Mining (2002)

32. Tasoulis, D.K. Vrahatis, M.N.: Unsupervised distributed clustering. In: Parallel and Distributed Computing and Networks (2004)

33. Ester, M., Kriegel, H.-P., Sander, J., Xu, X., et al.: A densitybased algorithm for discovering clusters in large spatial databases with noise. In: International Conference on Knowledge Discovery & Data Mining (1996)

34. Kargupta, H., Huang, W., Sivakumar, K., Johnson, E.: Distributed clustering using collective principal component analysis. Knowl. Inf. Syst. **32**, 422–448 (2001) https://doi.org/10.1007/PL00011677

35. Feldman, D., Sugaya, A., Rus, D.: An effective coreset compression algorithm for large scale sensor networks. In: International Conference on Information Processing in Sensor Networks (2012)

36. Bachem, O., Lucic, M., Krause, A.: Scalable k-means clustering via lightweight coresets. In: International Conference on Knowledge Discovery & Data Mining (2018)

37. Stallmann, M., Wilbik, A.: Towards Federated Clustering: A Federated Fuzzy c-Means Algorithm (FFCM) (2022). arXiv:2201.07316v1

38. Ghosh, A., Chung, J., Yin, D., Ramchandran, K.: An Efficient Framework for Clustered Federated Learning. In: Larochelle, H., Ranzato, M., Hadsell, R., Balcan, M.F., Lin, H. (eds.) Advances in Neural Information Processing Systems, vol. 33, pp. 19586–19597. Curran Associates Inc (2020)

39. Sattler, F., Muller, K.-R., Samek, W.: Clustered federated learning: model-agnostic distributed multitask optimization under privacy constraints. IEEE Trans. Neural Netw. Learn. Syst. **32**, 3710–3722 (2020)

40. Chandola, V., Banerjee, A., Kumar, V.: Anomaly detection: a survey. ACM Comput. Surv. **41**(3), Article 15 (2009). https://doi.org/10.1145/1541880.1541882

41. Ukil, A., Bandyoapdhyay, S., Puri, C., A. Pal, A.: IoT Healthcare Analytics: The Importance of Anomaly Detection. In: 2016 IEEE 30th International Conference on Advanced Information Networking and Applications (AINA), Crans-Montana, Switzerland, pp. 994–997 (2016), https://doi.org/10.1109/AINA.2016.158

42. Siniosoglou, I., et al.: Federated intrusion detection in NG-IoT healthcare systems: an adversarial approach. In: ICC 2021 - IEEE International Conference on Communications (2021)

43. Liu, F.T., Ting, K.M., Zhou, Z.-H.: Isolation forest. In: 2008 8th IEEE International Conference on Data Mining, Pisa, Italy. IEEE (2008)

44. Cavallin, F., Mayer, R.: Anomaly Detection from Distributed Data Sources via Federated Learning. In: Barolli, L., Hussain, F., Enokido, T. (eds.) AINA 2022. LNNS, vol. 450, pp. 317–328. Springer, Cham (2022). https://doi.org/10.1007/978-3-030-99587-4_27

45. Bercea, C.I., Wiestler, B., Rueckert, D., et al.: Federated disentangled representation learning for unsupervised brain anomaly detection. Nat. Mach. Intell. **4**, 685–695 (2022). https://doi.org/10.1038/s42256-022-00515-2

46. Baur, C., Denner, S., Wiestler, B., Navab, N., Albarqouni, S.: Autoencoders for unsupervised anomaly segmentation in brain MR images: a comparative study. Med. Image Anal. **69**, 101952 (2021)

47. Grammenos, A., Mendoza Smith, R., Crowcroft, J., Mascolo, C.: Federated principal component analysis. Adv. Neural. Inf. Process. Syst. **33**, 6453–6464 (2020)

48. Cui, W., Zhao, Y., Xu, J., Cheng, H.: Federated sufficient dimension reduction through high-dimensional sparse sliced inverse regression (2023). arXiv preprint arXiv:2301.09500

49. Chai, D., Wang, L., Fu, L., Zhang, J., Chen, K., Yang, Q.: . Federated singular vector decomposition. arXiv e-prints, https://arxiv.org/abs/2105.08925 (2021)

50. Islam, T. U., Ghasemi, R., Mohammed, N.: Privacy-preserving federated learning model for healthcare data. In: 2022 IEEE 12th Annual Computing and Communication Workshop and Conference (CCWC) (pp. 0281–0287). IEEE (2022)

51. Wei, K., et al.: Vertical federated learning: Challenges, methodologies and experiments. arXiv preprint arXiv:2202.04309 (2022)

52. Yoo, J. H., et .: Personalized federated learning with clustering: non-IID heart rate variability data application. In: 2021 International Conference on Information and Communication Technology Convergence (ICTC), pp. 1046–1051. IEEE (2021)

53. Molina, C., Prados-Suarez, B., Martinez-Sanchez, B.: Federated Mining of Interesting Association Rules Over EHRs. In: Applying the FAIR Principles to Accelerate Health Research in Europe in the Post COVID-19 Era, pp. 3–7. IOS Press (2021)

54. Sun, L., Wu, J.: A scalable and transferable federated learning system for classifying healthcare sensor data. IEEE J. Biomed. Health Inf. **27**, 866–877 (2022)

55. Domadiya, N., Rao, U.P.: Privacy preserving distributed association rule mining approach on vertically partitioned healthcare data. Procedia Comput. Sci. **148**, 303–312 (2019)

56. Kantarcioglu, M., Clifton, C.: Privacy-preserving distributed mining of association rules on horizontally partitioned data. IEEE Trans. Knowl. Data Eng. **16**(9), 1026–1037 (2004)

57. Tassa, T.: Secure mining of association rules in horizontally distributed databases. IEEE Trans. Knowl. Data Eng. **26**(4), 970–983 (2013)

Exploring Hidden Anomalies in UGR'16 Network Dataset with Kitsune

Joaquín Gaspar Medina-Arco$^{(\boxtimes)}$, Roberto Magán-Carrión,
and Rafael A. Rodríguez-Gómez

Universidad de Granada - Network Engineering & Security Group (NESG), Granada,
Spain
jgasparmedina@correo.ugr.es, {rmagan,rodgom}@ugr.es

Abstract. Given the significant increase in cyberattacks and attempts
to gain unauthorized access to systems and information, Network Intrusion Detection Systems (NIDS) have become essential tools for their
detection. Anomaly-based systems apply machine learning techniques
with the goal of being able to distinguish between normal and abnormal
traffic. To this end, they use training datasets that have been previously
labeled, which allow them to learn how to detect anomalies in future
data. This work tests Kitsune, one of the state-of-the-art NIDS based on
an ensemble of *Autoencoders*. To do so, four experimental scenarios have
been implemented using the UGR'16 dataset. The results obtained not
only validate Kitsune as a reliable reference anomaly detector although
is very sensitive to poisoned data, but also reveal new and potential
anomalous behaviors that have not been identified until to date.

Keywords: anomaly detection · NIDS · deep learning · neuronal
networks · autoencoders · UGR'16

1 Introduction

Network Intrusion Detection Systems (NIDS) are a type of security mechanism
for computer networks. Their purpose is to detect malicious traffic within the
network by learning from previous detections [1].

The typology of NIDS is diverse as they can be classified according to different criteria, such as architecture (whether they are based on a single device,
a network, or are collaborative), the protocol or physical layer they supervise
(specific to Wi-Fi or wired networks), etc. [2]. They can also be classified based
on the techniques used for attack detection: signature-based, anomaly-based, or
stateful protocol analysis [3].

Anomaly-based NIDSs use Machine Learning (ML) techniques to identify
anomalies in the network according to the data observed during monitoring.
Specifically, they look for patterns that represent anomalous behavior in the
network: (i) those that occur infrequently or (ii) those that are completely misaligned with the rest. This process is known as Anomaly Detection and requires
a sufficiently large dataset to learn what is considered normal and what is not.

© Springer Nature Switzerland AG 2023
H. L. Larsen et al. (Eds.): FQAS 2023, LNAI 14113, pp. 194–205, 2023.
https://doi.org/10.1007/978-3-031-42935-4_16

There are several datasets containing real traffic collected from large net-works. These datasets are broken down into multiple variables (e.g., port, pro-tocol, source, and destination IPs, etc.), and with sufficient historical depth, thus they can be used as a basis for training for various purposes. For instance, anomaly detection or classification. Some of the most commonly and widely used datasets are

NSL-KDD, created by UNB, UNSW-NB15, created by UNSW Canberra, and UGR'16, created by the University of Granada, among others.

These datasets are usually labeled so that for each registered traffic flow, it is indicated whether it is normal or not, allowing for supervised learning models training and for validating and testing ML-based NDIS as well. However, this implies trusting that the training dataset is correctly labeled since incorrect labeling may compromise the inferences drawn from it for future predictions. In the case of UGR'16, it has been detected that the training set contains unlabeled anomalies (botnet related attacks) in one of the registered months, so the results obtained using this dataset may be compromised.

This article will test a state-of-the-art anomaly-based NIDS, called Kitsune, with the UGR'16 dataset, carrying out several experiments that will measure the goodness of the NIDS itself and the quality of UGR'16. The main contribu-tions are therefore: 1) the first application of Kitsune to the UGR'16 dataset; 2) confirmation of the presence of anomalies in UGR'16 in June that have not been detected during the construction of the dataset; and 3) identification of possible anomalies in the UGR'16 training dataset, specifically in May, that have not been detected or labeled so far.

The article is structured as follows. Section 2 presents a study of related works regarding different NIDS and the use of UGR'16. Section 3 presents the methods and materials used for the development of this contribution. Section 4 describes and details the experiment performed on which the results obtained will be presented and discussed in Sect. 5. Finally, Sect. 6 will provide a summary of the conclusions and propose potential future work.

2 Related Work

There are multiple techniques available for anomaly detection that have been developed over the years. Additionally, there are several bibliographic references that perform a comparative and survey of all these techniques, such as the works of Thottan et al. [4], Patcha et al. [5], Fernandes et al. [6], or Ahmed et al. [7]. These works show that the most common anomaly detection techniques in the field of networks rely on the use of statistical and classification models or algo-rithms.

Regarding statistical techniques, there are works such as Shyu et al. [8], where they define a methodology based on Principal Component Analysis (PCA) for anomaly detection in networks and apply it to the KDD'99 dataset.

Related to classification techniques, there are references based on Bayesian classification trees such as that of Swarnkar and Hubballi [9], in which they use

Naïve Bayes as a classification technique to identify suspicious network traffic loads focused on examining the HTTP protocol. It can be found models based on Support Vector Machines (SVM), such as the work of Wang et al. [10], where they propose an intrusion detection system based on SVM but manipulating the input data to increase the features they have before introducing them into the learning process.

Neural networks are widely applied for this purpose too. Kwon et al. [11] review the literature on different solutions that implement techniques of deep neural networks, recurrent neural networks, or conventional neural networks. On the other hand, Naseer et al. [12] conduct a study on how to apply complex neural networks and deep learning as a tool for anomaly detection in network traffic.

In this context, autoencoders are a particular case of neural networks that are gaining greater relevance as detectors of anomalies in network traffic. Evidence of this is the work of Aygun and Yavuz [13], where a model based on autoencoders is described that allows identifying anomalies in network traffic in real-time (zero-days). Or the work of Mirsky, Y. et al. [14], in which they design a low-computational-requirements NIDS called Kitsune that shows great results in known and real attacks. Kitsune has become a state-of-the-art solution, as indicated by its more than 700 citations since 2018. In light of this, new avenues of research on how to carry out adversary attacks against NIDS use Kitsune as a target.

Regarding UGR'16, since it is a relatively new dataset that includes both real and synthetic traffic, its use is also widely extending [15–17].

Regarding the detection of unlabeled anomalies in network traffic datasets, the authors have not been able to find any literature on the subject.

3   Methods and Materials

3.1   UGR'16 Network Dataset

UGR'16 is a dataset presented and analyzed by Maciá-Fernández et al. in [18]. It is divided into the following sub-sets:

- **Training set** (*calibration*): Real traffic data observed in an Internet Service Provider (ISP) during the four months from March to June 2016.
- **Test set**: Real traffic data observed in the same ISP and synthetic attack traffic during the two months of July and August 2016.

Since the data source is the gathered traffic from the ISP facilities, the heterogeneity of the captured records is high, with data associated with a wide variety of communication protocols (HTTP, FTP, DNS, etc.), communications generated by a wide range of user types, and not limited to a delimited set of actors belonging to a single company, university, or laboratory.

For the synthetic attack data, simulated Denial of Service (DoS) attacks, port scanning, and attacks caused by malware (specifically, botnet attacks) are included. These attacks are concentrated to run on specific days between July and August, using two strategies: with fixed execution dates and times, and with random attack time (see [18] for more information).

As an additional feature of UGR'16, anomalies were detected in the dataset related to SPAM campaigns, SSH port scanning, and UDP port scanning. Both synthetically generated attacks and detected anomalies were properly labeled in the dataset using state-of-the-art techniques. Additionally, traffic belonging to IP addresses on blacklists was also labeled.

An inherent problem to the capture of real traffic is that it is possible that real attack traffic flows may already be present in the training data but have gone unnoticed and have been erroneously labeled as normal or background traffic. This can generate noise in the dataset and its quality will be reduced as it may be computing as normal traffic flows those that actually are not, thereby hindering the detection methods that are built. In fact, García Fuentes, M., in his doctoral thesis "Multivariate Statistical Network Monitoring for Network Security based on Principal Component Analysis" [19], identifies in the UGR'16 dataset, specifically in the calibration part of June, an undetected botnet related attack. This makes anomalous traffic considered as normal traffic. In Sect. 5, its impact on the performance of NIDS systems based on autoencoders will be studied in deep.

3.2 Feature as a Counter

Captured network traffic generally consists of a large number of binary format files with diverse information that cannot be directly used in machine learning algorithms [20]. Therefore, an aggregation process is necessary to obtain a universe of data that can be handled as a dataset.

Camacho, J. et al. propose in [21] a technique called *Feature as a Counter* (*FaaC*) whose mission is to transform a set of data associated with network traffic (network flows) into a single observation matrix that can be used in multivariate analysis or as input for machine learning algorithms in a customized way. With this tool, captured network traffic flows from different sources can be flexibly combined and aggregated such that new observations are formed from new counting variables of certain values present in the original variables. For example, it may be interesting to know the total number of connections per minute directed to ports 80 and 443 of a web server, so that if a very high number is recorded in a certain time window (one minute by default), it could be a symptom of a *Denial of Service* (DoS) attack. To do this, FaaC allows converting the raw data of all captured network flows (timestamp, source and destination IP address, source and destination ports, packet size, flags, etc.) into a dataset in which, for each minute, the number of packets using port 80, 443, 22, etc., is counted.

A specific implementation of FaaC can be found in a library called FCParser [22], which has been applied to calculate minute-aggregated counters for all available observations in UGR'16. In this aggregation, a total of 134 new counting variables or features are determined for each minute, including the different most common ports of both origin and destination (*FTP*, *SSH*, *SMTP*, *HTTP*, etc.), the different protocols involved (*TCP*, *UDP*, *ICMP*, etc.), the different flags of *TCP* packets (*ACK*, *RST*, etc.), the priority and size of packets, and the total flows of each type of anomaly.

3.3   Kitsune

Kitsune [14] is a particular case of autoencoder applied to network intrusion detection. According to its authors, it is an NIDS designed to efficiently detect anomalous network traffic, computationally simple, and feasible to be deployed on any router for real-time detection. It is composed of a **Packet Capturer** that captures network packets, a **Packet Parser** that extracts metadata from those packets, a **Feature Extractor** that extracts numeric features from the previous metadata, a **Feature Mapper** that makes a dimensionality reduction, and, finally, an **Anomaly Detector**.

The Anomaly Detector, referred to by its authors as **KitNET**[1] (*Kitsune NETwork*), can be used independently as an anomaly detector if data is available in the form of continuous feature vectors.

KitNET is an unsupervised learning neural network designed for real-time anomaly detection. To carry out this task, its architecture is divided into two clearly differentiated elements:

1. **Ensemble of Autoencoders**: It is a set of k identical autoencoders, formed by three layers, of which the input has m neurons corresponding to the m characteristics chosen by the feature mapper. The objective of this ensemble is to measure the degree of anomaly that each observation has independently. To do this, the root-mean-squared error or RMSE (Eq. 1) of the observation is calculated at the output of each autoencoder. All observations go through all autoencoders, although only a subset of m characteristics of the observation is used in each one of them.

$$RMSE = \sqrt{\frac{\sum_{i=1}^{n}(predicted_i - actual_i)^2}{n}} \tag{1}$$

2. **Output Layer**: It is also a three-layer autoencoder that receives as input the output of the entire previous ensemble (the RMSE generated by each autoencoder), and whose output is also an RMSE that is transformed into probability by applying a logarithmic distribution. This probability indicates the degree to which the observation is considered anomalous traffic.

From the perspective of KitNET operation, the execution sequence is divided into four phases:

1. **Initialization:** based on a set of observations, the model calculates the number of autoencoders that will form the ensemble and the features that will be used in each of them.

---

[1] KitNET link: https://github.com/ymirsky/KitNET-py

2. **Training:** using a new set of observations, the internal parameters of each autoencoder are adjusted to reduce the RMSE generated in their output layers. This phase is subdivided into:

   (a) **Calibration:** the weights and internal parameters of the neural networks of the autoencoders are adjusted using a subset of the provided training data.

   (b) **Testing:** after the previous process, the remaining data in the training set is used to create a probability distribution based on which to choose the threshold that will distinguish a normal observation from an anomalous one.

3. **Detection:** once the internal parameters of the autoencoders are fixed, each new observation that passes through the architecture generates an RMSE in each autoencoder of the ensemble. All these values serve as input to the output layer of the model.

4. **Labeling:** the final result that KitNET produces is the calculation of the probability that the observation is anomalous. Using the threshold obtained during training, it is determined whether that probability makes the observation considered anomalous or not.

Finally, it is important to highlight that KitNET (and therefore Kitsune) assumes that the data used for the initialization and training phases are observations of normal traffic, that is, free of anomalies.

4 Experimental Setup and Scenarios

4.1 Preconditions

Given the size of the UGR'16 dataset, the complete application of Kitsune has been discarded in this experiment for several reasons:

- The dataset is in NetFlow format, which is incompatible with Kitsune since it only supports traffic in *pcap* format.
- Therefore, it is necessary to apply a preprocessing step that transforms the data into a valid dataset to feed into Kitsune. To do this, the authors of UGR'16 have already performed a feature representation of the entire dataset using `FCParser` (described in Sect. 3.2). This reduces the total universe of flows to 134 counters that summarize all observed traffic per minute.
- In addition, this feature extraction, concerning the training or calibration data of UGR'16, has eliminated flows detected and identified as anomalous in the dataset generation and labeling process. This meets Kitsune's premise that requires training data to be normal traffic.

Thus, the use of this feature representation directly in KitNET, Kitsune's engine, is proposed, avoiding the previous modules of the architecture.

On the other hand, regarding the hyperparameters of the KitNET model, some criteria are established that are maintained in all proposed experimental scenarios:

- The maximum size of each autoencoder in the ensemble is set at 10 neurons in the hidden layer. This value is set empirically.
- The number of instances of the training dataset used for the initialization phase of KitNET is set at 2,000. Like the previous one, this parameter is also set empirically.
- The percentage of instances of the training dataset used for the training subphase of KitNET will be 70%.
- The percentage of instances of the training dataset used for the validation subphase of KitNET will be 30%.
- In the choice of the threshold or tolerance level for anomaly detection, the same value has been applied in all cases: standard deviation plus the mean of the probabilities detected in the training phase. Values that exceed this threshold will be considered anomalous.

4.2 Experimental Scenarios

To carry out the experimentation with KitNET on the UGR'16 dataset, the following incremental scenarios of the training set are established before evaluating its effectiveness with the UGR'16 test set that comprises the months of July and August:

1. **Scenario 1:** The model will be trained with data corresponding to the month of March.
2. **Scenario 2:** The model will be trained with data corresponding to the months of March and April.
3. **Scenario 3:** The model will be trained with data corresponding to the months of March, April, and May.
4. **Additional scenario:** The model will be trained with data corresponding to the months of March, April, and May, and tested, unlike the previous scenarios, with the month of June that contains anomalies not considered during the construction of the dataset.

An additional scenario is proposed to evaluate whether this technique is capable of detecting hidden anomalies, not detected during the dataset generation and therefore not labeled, thus corroborating the work done by García Fuentes, M. [19].

4.3 Metrics

To measure the performance and effectiveness of each proposed scenario, classic metrics as **Precision**, **Recall**, **Accuracy**, and **F-measure** will be used. [23].

   In addition to these metrics, the **ROC** curve (from the acronym Receiver Operating Characteristics) of each scenario will also be computed, allowing to compare the two most relevant ratios in classification problems (true positives and false positives), facilitating the selection of the optimal model or algorithm. Moreover, it is also usual to compute the AUC (Area Under the ROC Curve), which offers a quantitative measure of the detector's performance based on its ROC curve [20].

Table 1. Results.

(a) Results applying KitNET over UGR'16.

Scenario	Class	Precision	Recall	F1-Measure	Accuracy
Scenario 1	Normal	0.99	1	0.99	0.97
	Anomalous	0.75	0.17	0.27	
Scenario 2	Normal	0.98	1	0.99	0.99
	Anomalous	0.9	0.66	0.76	
Scenario 3	Normal	0.98	1	0.99	0.98
	Anomalous	0.87	0.23	0.36	

(b) Detection ratios by attack type.

Attack	Scenario 1	Scenario 2	Scenario 3
DOS	34%	64%	56%
SCAN11	1%	1%	1%
SCAN44	51%	72%	57%
BOTNET	4%	74%	1%
UDPSCAN	0%	0%	0%
Total	16%	65%	22%

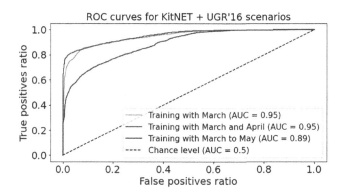

Fig. 1. ROC curves corresponding to the experimental scenarios.

5   Results and Discussion

5.1   Results

The performance results obtained for each scenario according to the metrics mentioned above are presented in Table 1a. The degree of detection for each type of attack for each scenario is shown in Table 1b.

For each scenario, the metrics associated with the possible prediction classes are collected: normal or anomalous traffic. Only accuracy is a global metric because it measures the total of correct predictions for both classes against the total observations of the dataset. The ROC curves and AUC values for each scenario are shown in Fig. 1.

According to Table 1a, in the case of the first scenario, where only data from March is used for training, the precision in detecting normal traffic is absolute, while the precision associated with anomaly detection drops to 75%. However, the really relevant metric is recall, which measures the rate of actual anomaly detection, with a very low value of only 17%. This means that only 17% of the anomalies identified by the model are real (according to the UGR'16 labeling used as a reference). In terms of the ROC curve (see Fig. 1), a very positive result is achieved, with a final AUC of 95%. Finally, according to Table 1b regarding the type of attacks, the results are poor as it barely detects half of the *SCAN44* attacks, a third of the *DoS* attacks, and only 4% of the *botnet* attacks.

When observing these same metrics in the second scenario, where training is done with March and April data, a significant improvement in anomaly detection is appreciated, with a precision that rises to 90%. Additionally, the recall also presents a qualitative increment, raising its result to 66%. Therefore, the reliability in this model means that 2 out of every 3 detected anomalies are real. In total, the accuracy rate rises to 99%. The ROC curve (see Fig. 1), on the other hand, reflects the best behavior obtained in the experimentation although it does not improve the AUC with respect to the previous scenario (95%). The detection ratio by type of attack skyrockets compared to the previous scenario, with a high detection capability (74%) of *botnet* attacks.

Regarding the third scenario, where the training set is expanded until May, the behavior suffers a setback in terms of model quality. The precision on detecting anomalies drops to 87%, while the recall falls back to 36%, it being much lower than the previous scenario and similar to that obtained in the first one. Finally, the ROC curve presents worse behavior, with its AUC falling to 89%. With regard to the detection ratio by type, the drastic drop in *botnet* attacks is particularly striking, where it can barely detect 1%.

To further analyze this behavior, KitNET is applied using March and April as training data and May as test data. Because of the inherent problem of any real data in general and network data in particular which is the lack of a reliable ground truth, the analysis must be based on the probabilities of normality each observation has.

As shown in Fig. 2a, where the probability of an anomaly occurrence is shown if the RMSE value is exceeding the threshold (the continuous red line in the figure), a different behavior appears in May compared to previous months. This fact increases the probability that the traffic would be anomalous. In addition, at the end of the period (exactly at 2016-05-30 17:49:00), an observation marked in red (and bigger than the rest of the points) with an excessively high probability of being anomalous appears. If this observation is taken into account as training data, the chosen threshold for determining whether a flow is normal could be raised enough to let anomalous traffic pass as normal traffic.

Regarding the additional scenario where KitNET is applied to June as test data and March to May as training data, observing Fig. 2b, a stepped pattern of probabilities marked with a purple rectangle appears in June. However, this pattern is not detected as an anomaly since the threshold is slightly above these measurements, as previously anticipated.

Figure 3a shows a stepped increase in IRC traffic during June, similar to that detected by KitNET, which persists over time, fulfilling the pattern of botnet-type attacks as shown in the figure between red dashes vertical lines. This attack was first identified by García Fuentes, M. [18], having gone unnoticed in the calibration dataset labeling and was therefore considered normal traffic.

Given that, according to the results obtained, the quality of the May data could be questioned, KitNET is applied again using March and April as training to apply it to June. The result obtained can be seen in Fig. 3b, where the pattern associated with the botnet attack in Fig. 3a is perfectly replicated with greater

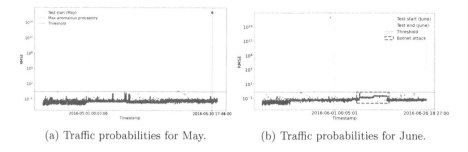

(a) Traffic probabilities for May.   (b) Traffic probabilities for June.

Fig. 2. Anomalous traffic probabilities over time.

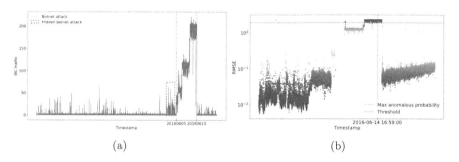

(a)   (b)

Fig. 3. IRC traffic registered in UGR'16 calibration set (a) and Anomalous traffic probabilities for June without considering May (b).

clarity and distance from normal traffic. The maximum anomalous value that coincides with the actual period of the attack is marked with a dashed red line.

This could confirm, therefore, that there would be a distortion element in the May data that would require detailed analysis, and which is in connection with the drastic deterioration of botnet-type attack detection capability when this month is included as part of the training. In Fig. 3a, marked with a dotted green line, it can be observed how the IRC activity in the last days of May is unusual, which could indicate that the botnet attack actually started earlier, going unnoticed until now.

6   Conclusion and Future Work

This work addresses the problem of anomaly detection in computer network traffic by applying Kitsune, one of the state-of-the-art machine learning-based NIDS, to the UGR'16 dataset for the first time. UGR'16 consists of real traffic that includes both real and synthetic attacks, as well as mislabeled anomalous traffic. The approach taken is an incremental experimental one, aimed at measuring both the efficacy of Kitsune and the level of contamination in UGR'16.

To carry out the experiment, different scenarios are proposed where the training dataset used is gradually expanded. Additionally, a scenario is added where the traffic from the month of June is reviewed to evaluate the possible detection of previously unlabeled attacks. The results obtained in each scenario are analyzed and discussed, concluding with the applicability and efficacy of Kitsune as an NIDS, as it is capable of detecting the botnet attack collected in June that other anomaly detection techniques did not show. Similarly, the possible contamination of UGR'16 dataset in May is also questioned, given the significant impact on anomaly detection performance when this month is considered during training. Those results also reveal that Kitsune is very sensitive to poisoned data.

Future analysis and research work will include: (i) delving into the behavior recorded in May in UGR'16 to identify the goodness of that traffic and its labeling; (ii) analyzing the feasibility of applying Kitsune to the complete set of UGR'16 flows to also evaluate the capacity and efficacy of the Feature Extractor; and (iii) evaluating the robustness of the model defined in Kitsune against adversarial attacks to determine the extent to which the model is resistant to poisoning or evasion attacks that modify or condition the functioning of the NIDS.

Acknowledgments. This work has been partially funded by the SICRAC (PID2020-114495RB-I00) and ANIMaLICoS (PID2020-113462RB-I00) projects of the Spanish Ministry of Science, Innovation and Universities and the PPJIA2022-51 and PPJIA2022-52 projects from the University of Granada's own funding plan.

References

1. De la Hoz, E., De la Hoz, E.M., Ortiz, A., Ortega, J.: Modelo de detección de intrusiones en sistemas de red, realizando selección de características con FDR y entrenamiento y clasificación con SOM. Revista INGE CUC **8**, 85–116 (2012)
2. Othman, S.M., Alsohybe, N.T., Ba-Alwi, F.M., Zahary, A.T.: Survey on intrusion detection system types. Int. J. Cyber-Secur. Digital Forensics **7**(4), 444–463 (2018)
3. Liao, H.-J., Richard Lin, C.-H., Lin, Y.-C., Tung, K.-Y.: Intrusion detection system: a comprehensive review. J. Network Comput. Appl. **36**(1), 16–24 (2013)
4. Thottan, M., Liu, G., Ji, C.: Anomaly detection approaches for communication networks. Algorithms for Next Generation Networks, pp. 239–261 (2010)
5. Patcha, A., Park, J.-M.: An overview of anomaly detection techniques: existing solutions and latest technological trends. Comput. Netw. **51**(12), 3448–3470 (2007)
6. Fernandes, G., Rodrigues, J.J.P.C., Carvalho, L.F., Al-Muhtadi, J.F., Proença, M.L.: A comprehensive survey on network anomaly detection. Telecommun. Syst. **70**(3), 447–489 (2019)
7. Ahmed, M., Naser Mahmood, A., Hu, J.: A survey of network anomaly detection techniques. J. Network Comput. Appl. **60**, 19–31 (2016)
8. Shyu, M.-L., Chen, S.-C., Sarinnapakorn, K., Chang, L.: A novel anomaly detection scheme based on principal component classifier. In: Proceedings of International Conference on Data Mining (2003)
9. Swarnkar, M., Hubballi, N.: OCPAD: One class Naive Bayes classifier for payload based anomaly detection. Expert Syst. Appl. **64**, 330–339 (2016)
10. Wang, H., Gu, J., Wang, S.: An effective intrusion detection framework based on SVM with feature augmentation. Knowl.-Based Syst. **136**, 130–139 (2017)

11. Kwon, D., Kim, H., Kim, J., Suh, S.C., Kim, I., Kim, K.J.: A survey of deep learning-based network anomaly detection. Clust. Comput. **22**(1), 949–961 (2019)
12. Naseer, S., Saleem, Y., Khalid, S., Bashir, M.K., Han, J., Iqbal, M.M., Han, K.: Enhanced network anomaly detection based on deep neural networks. IEEE Access **6**, 48 231–248 (2018). 246, 2018, conference Name: IEEE Access
13. Aygun, R.C., Yavuz, A.G.: Network anomaly detection with stochastically improved autoencoder based models. In: 2017 IEEE 4th International Conference on Cyber Security and Cloud Computing (CSCloud), pp. 193–198, June 2017
14. Mirsky, Y., Doitshman, T., Elovici, Y., Shabtai, A.: Kitsune: an ensemble of autoencoders for online network intrusion detection. In: Network and Distributed System Security Symposium (2018)
15. Yilmaz, I., Masum, R.: Expansion of cyber attack data from unbalanced datasets using generative techniques. arXiv preprint arXiv:1912.04549 (2019)
16. Yasin, S.M.A.: Anomaly-based network intrusion detection system using deep neural networks (anids-dnn), Ph.D. dissertation, Al-Quds University (2023)
17. Yilmaz, I., Masum, R., Siraj, A.: Addressing imbalanced data problem with generative adversarial network for intrusion detection. In: 2020 IEEE 21st International Conference on Information Reuse and Integration for Data Science (IRI), pp. 25–30. IEEE (2020)
18. Maciá-Fernández, G., Camacho, J., Magán-Carrión, R., García-Teodoro, P., Therón, R.: Ugr '16: a new dataset for the evaluation of cyclostationarity-based network idss. Comput. Secur. **73**, 411–424 (2018)
19. García Fuentes, M.N.: Multivariate Statistical Network Monitoring for Network Security based on Principal Component Analysis. Universidad de Granada, 2021, accepted: 2021–04-14T08:40:39Z. [Online]. https://digibug.ugr.es/handle/10481/67941
20. Magán-Carrión, R., Urda, D., Díaz-Cano, I., Dorronsoro, B.: Towards a reliable comparison and evaluation of network intrusion detection systems based on machine learning approaches. Appl. Sci. **10**(5), 1775 (2020)
21. Camacho, J., Maciá-Fernández, G., Díaz-Verdejo, J., García-Teodoro: Tackling the big data 4 vs for anomaly detection. In: 2014 IEEE Conference on Computer Communications Workshops (INFOCOM WKSHPS), pp. 500–505 (2014)
22. Camacho, J.: "FCParser." https://github.com/josecamachop/FCParser (2017)
23. Powers, D.M.: Evaluation: from precision, recall and f-measure to roc, informedness, markedness and correlation (2020). arXiv preprint arXiv:2010.16061

An Orthographic Similarity Measure for Graph-Based Text Representations

Maxime Deforche[1]([envelope]) [ID], Ilse De Vos[2] [ID], Antoon Bronselaer[1] [ID], and Guy De Tré[1] [ID]

[1] Department of Telecommunications and Information Processing, Ghent University, St.-Pietersnieuwstraat 41, 9000 Ghent, Belgium
{Maxime.Deforche,Antoon.Bronselaer,Guy.DeTre}@UGent.be
[2] Department of Linguistics, Ghent University, Blandijnberg 2, 9000 Ghent, Belgium
I.DeVos@UGent.be

Abstract. Computing the orthographic similarity between words, sentences, paragraphs and texts has become a basic functionality of many text mining and flexible querying systems and the resulting similarity scores are often used to discover similar text documents. However, when dealing with a corpus that is inherently known for its orthographic inconsistencies and intricate interconnected nature on multiple levels (words, verses and full texts), as is the case with Byzantine book epigrams, this task becomes complex. In this paper, we propose a technique that tackles these two challenges by representing text in a graph and by computing a similarity score between multiple levels of the text, modelled as subgraphs, in a hierarchical manner. The similarity between all words is computed first, followed by the calculation of the similarity between all verses (resp. full texts) by using the formerly determined similarity scores between the words (resp. verses). The resulting similarities, on each level, allow for a deeper insight into the interconnected nature in (parts of) text collections, indicating how and to what degree the texts are related to each other.

Keywords: Text Analysis · Orthographic Similarity · Graph Databases · Fuzzy Graphs

1 Introduction

Similarity measurements between data objects play a crucial role in applications and research related to information management and data mining. In case of textual data, computing relevant similarities between texts helps in tasks like, among other things, flexible query answering, retrieval of information based on partial specification, and determining whether two text documents are duplicate or modified versions of the same document or display any general kind of interconnection between them.

The Database of Byzantine Book Epigrams (DBBE)[1] [6] deals with a collection of orthographically inconsistent texts with a complex history of (partial)

---

[1] https://dbbe.ugent.be.

© Springer Nature Switzerland AG 2023
H. L. Larsen et al. (Eds.): FQAS 2023, LNAI 14113, pp. 206–218, 2023.
https://doi.org/10.1007/978-3-031-42935-4_17

reuse, resulting in many intricate interconnections [17]. Byzantine Book Epigrams are Greek poems which can be found in the margins of manuscripts and tell the reader more about the manuscripts they are part of. Traditional orthographic (or string-based) similarity measures, computed over the entire texts, are not able to deal with the inconsistencies nor handle the interconnections on multiple levels of the text. Therefore, similar epigrams or verses are presently identified and grouped manually by experts. These groups are defined in a crisp way, implicating that the content is either similar or not without any specification on the degree of similarity between the verses or epigrams in the group.

In this paper, we propose an algorithm for determining an orthographic similarity score between such Byzantine epigrams, which are hierarchically represented by means of a graph database. A hierarchical approach is used, in order to identify the interconnections on different parts of the texts, alongside a graph database in order to represent and handle the large amount of interconnections between them. As relevant parts we consider words, verses and epigrams, the latter two being represented by subgraphs. In comparison with the current system, these hierarchically computed similarity scores between words, verses and epigrams do not only effectively indicate the degree of orthographic similarity between texts but also give a deeper insight into how certain epigrams are in some way related to each other. In fact, the similarity relationships between all the textual elements in the graph allow for more advanced and efficient queries than the DBBE in its current relational database form.

Character-based similarity measures, where the similarity between two character strings is quantified by comparing full character sequences and identifying the amount of edits required to transform one string into the other [9], have extensively been discussed in literature. Some examples of this approach are Levenshtein (-Damerau) [5,14], Longest Common Subsequence [19], Jaro (-Winkler) [10,20] and N-grams [13]. Also, similarity measures for (sub)graphs have been studied by means of the Graph Edit Distance, defined as the cost of the least expensive sequence of edit operations to transform one graph into another [8]. Many different approaches exist to compute this similarity, including probability [15], graph kernel [16], subgraph and supergraph [7] based methods. While these techniques are useful in many applications, the problem at hand requires a more elaborate approach, where string-based and graph-based similarity measures are combined. Furthermore, graph-based text representations based on the semantic nature of texts have been proposed [4,11], but due to the limited availability of Byzantine Greek texts adequate semantic models are not (yet) available. In this paper, we propose a novel approach for combining string-based and graph-based similarity measures, resulting in a novel technique for exploring interconnected (parts of) texts. The relevancy of the approach is demonstrated with a new tool for studying interconnected Byzantine book epigrams.

The remainder of the paper is organised as follows. In Sect. 2 we provide some useful information on (fuzzy) graph databases and the properties of the corpus used in this paper. The design of the graph-based text representation is the subject of Sect. 3. Section 4 describes the hierarchical algorithm used to determine the orthographic similarity between the subgraphs representing (parts of) the epigrams. Next, we describe the experiments performed on this novel similarity measure and discuss the results in Sect. 5. Finally, in Sect. 6 we formulate the conclusions of our work and present some directions for future research.

2   Background

2.1   Byzantine Book Epigrams

Byzantine book epigrams are often (yet not always) small Greek poems found in the margins of manuscripts, which tell the reader more about e.g. the contents of the manuscript, the people involved in its production, or even the emotions felt by the scribe upon finishing a manuscript [17]. These epigrams are typically known to be orthographically inconsistent texts with a complex tradition. That is a tradition, or in other words the transmission of the texts throughout history, in which texts were split-up, (re)combined, or elseways reworked during their copying process. The orthographic inconsistencies these book epigrams display are not only the result of, among other things, spelling and transcription errors, unstandardised punctuation and text wrapping, but are also caused by a phonetic evolution, called *itacism*. The *itacism* indicates the shift of the classical pronunciation of the vowels ι, η, υ and the diphthongs ει, οι to the same pronunciation of *i*, resulting in a corpus where all the previously mentioned vowels and diphthongs are used interchangeably. Due to the inherently complex nature of these Byzantine epigrams, classic orthographic similarity measures fall short, indicating the need for a new approach.

Table 1. An example of two similar epigrams from the DBBE [6]

Epigram 17571:	Epigram 19418:
1. Ὥσπερ ξένοι χαίρουσιν ἰδεῖν πατρίδα,	1. ὥσπερ ξένοι	χαίροντες εἰδεῖν	πατρίδα	
2. οὕτως καὶ οἱ γράφοντες βιβλίου τέλος.	2. οὕτ(ως) (καὶ) οἱ γρά|φοντ(ες) βιβλίου τέλος.

As an example, Table 1 displays two such Byzantine book epigrams which both translate to *"Like travellers rejoice upon seeing their homeland, so too do scribes upon reaching the end of the book."*. Although at first glance there is quite a bit of variation between these two epigrams, most of the differences are minor and relate to itacism, accentuation and capitalisation of certain letters, and punctuation, with the significant variation limited to χαίρουσιν / χαίροντες on verse one. As for the *itacism* in this example, the words ἰδεῖν and εἰδεῖν clearly represent the same word, with ει and ι being used interchangeably. Except for these small differences, the epigrams are in fact very similar which strongly indicates some kind of interconnection between them. Without taking into account any contextual information such as when, where or by whom these texts were written, the possible causes for the interconnection between them are the following: (i.) one of the epigrams is, either directly or indirectly, inspired by the other or (ii.) both epigrams are, again either directly or indirectly, inspired by the same epigram. While the epigrams in this specific example, selected for their simple but all-encompassing nature, are visibly very similar, this is not the case for most of the texts in the corpus of Byzantine book epigrams. Hence the need for a novel approach capable of dealing with such texts.

2.2   Graph Databases

Graph database management systems structure and store data as a graph, consisting of nodes (or vertices) and relationships (or edges) connecting these nodes. Unlike their relational counterparts, where data are modelled and stored by means of relations, graph database systems do not have a fixed database schema. This allows for managing entities with complex, variable data structures [2]. Furthermore, graph-based database systems have shown great performance in handling highly interconnected data, which makes them particularly useful for storing the numerous and intricate interconnections between our data, while their native graph-like structure makes them the ideal tool for performing network analysis on the links between the stored information [3].

Various underlying graph models for graph databases are described in literature, including the (labelled) property graph model where each node and relationship contains a key-value property structure and is associated with a label [1,2]. A formal definition of this graph model is given in Definition 1.

Definition 1. (Labelled Property Graph [1].) *Let L be a set of labels, P a set of property names and V a set of atomic values. A labelled property graph G is a tuple $(N, E, \rho, \lambda_N, \lambda_E, \sigma)$, where N is a finite set of nodes and E is a finite set of edges. The function $\rho : E \to N \times N$ is used to associate each edge in E with a pair of nodes and indicate its direction. Labels are assigned to nodes by the $\lambda_N : N \to \mathcal{P}(L)$ function and to edges by the $\lambda_E : E \to L$ function, where $\mathcal{P}$ is the powerset operator. Finally, the properties are assigned to vertices and edges through the function $\sigma : (N \cup E) \times P \to \mathcal{P}(V)$. In what follows, $N_{l \in L} = \{n | n \in N, l \in \lambda_N(n)\}$ and $E_{l \in L} = \{e | e \in E, \lambda_E(e) = l\}$ are shorthand notations to indicate a set of nodes or edges with a specific label.*

2.3   Fuzzy Graphs

A fuzzy graph, as proposed by Rosenfield [18], is a weighted graph $\tilde{G}(N, \tilde{E})$ with N the set of nodes and $\tilde{E}$ a fuzzy relation indicating the relationships between elements of N, where the membership function $\mu_{\tilde{E}}$ is symmetrical [21,22]. The connectedness of a fuzzy graph is relative to its basic graph $G(N, E)$, with $E = \mathrm{supp}(\tilde{E}) = \{(n_1, n_2) | (n_1, n_2) \in N^2, \mu_{\tilde{E}}(n_1, n_2) > 0\}$. Moreover, the α-cut on the edges of a fuzzy graph is defined as $E^\alpha = \{(n_1, n_2) | (n_1, n_2) \in E, \mu_{\tilde{E}}(v_1, v_2) \geq \alpha\}$.

Small changes are required to the labelled property graph model, described above, in order for it to become a *fuzzy* labelled property graph. A formal definition of a Fuzzy Labelled Property graph is given in Definition 2. In practice, the fuzzy edges are implemented by a **degree** key-value pair, assigned to the relationships. For relationships with a crisp nature, this property can be omitted.

Definition 2. (Fuzzy Labelled Property Graph.) *A fuzzy labelled property graph is a labelled property graph* $\tilde{G}(N, \tilde{E}, \rho, \lambda_N, \lambda_E, \sigma)$, *where* $\tilde{E}$ *is a fuzzy set on* E *with membership function* $\mu_{\tilde{E}}(e), e \in E$ *and* $E = \text{supp}(\tilde{E})$, *indicating the fuzzy edges. The* α-cut *on the graph* $\tilde{G}$ *is* $G^\alpha(N, E^\alpha, \rho, \lambda_N, \lambda_E, \sigma)$, *with* $E^\alpha = \{e | e \in E, \mu_{\tilde{E}}(e) \geq \alpha\}$.

3 Graph-Based Text Model

Before describing our novel similarity measure for the texts in our corpus, we explain how text content is transformed into a graph-based representation. We propose a model where the content of the texts is partitioned into smaller textual units, represented by nodes and subgraphs in the database. For the DBBE corpus, the texts are partitioned into three levels of textual units: individual words, verses, and the actual epigram.

The subgraph representing a single epigram is constructed in a bottom-up manner. First, the text is partitioned into individual words. For each of these words, not yet present in the database, a word node is created, storing the content of that word. Next, for all verses that are not yet stored in the database, verse nodes are created and, instead of storing the verse text inside the newly created vertices, the verse nodes are linked to the related word nodes from which the original verse can be reconstructed. The edge connecting a verse node with related word nodes additionally indicates the position (starting from zero) of a word within that verse. Finally, epigram nodes are added to the graph. In turn these are associated to the verse nodes the epigram consists of, in the same fashion as the edges between verse and word nodes. In order to easily distinguish different epigrams in our graph, all epigram nodes are extended with a unique id. As a result, the distinct verses and epigrams are each represented by a subgraph within the graph database and the content of those textual elements can be reconstructed by traversing the graph down to the individual word nodes.

The same procedure is followed each time new texts are added to the graph. For every epigram, a new epigram node is created, whereas for verses (resp. words) a new node is created only when that exact verse (resp. word) is not yet present in the graph. Definition 3 gives a formal description of the graph model.

Definition 3. (Graph-based Text Model) *The graph model for representing texts is a fuzzy labelled property graph* $\tilde{G}(N, \tilde{E}, \rho, \lambda_N, \lambda_E, \sigma)$, *where* $N(= N_{Word} \cup N_{Verse} \cup N_{Epigram})$ *consists of nodes representing words* (N_{Word}), *verses* (N_{Verse}) *and epigrams* $(N_{Epigram})$. *The edges in* $\tilde{E} \ (= \tilde{E}_{CONTAINS})$ *represent a relationship of containment, indicating what word (resp. verse) nodes are contained in a verse (resp. epigram) node, with* $\mu_{\tilde{E}}(e) = 1.0$. *The* σ *function maps the* text *property on word nodes* $\sigma(n, \textbf{text}) \in W, n \in N_{Word}$ *and* W *the set of all unique words. Furthermore, the* rank *property, indicating the rank of a word (reps. verse) within a verse (resp. epigram), is assigned by* $\sigma(e, \textbf{rank}) \in \mathbb{N}, e \in \text{supp}(\tilde{E})$ *and the* id *property on epigrams is mapped by* $\sigma(n, \textbf{id}) \in \mathbb{N}, n \in N_{Epigram}$.

Due to the orthographic inconsistent nature of the Byzantine book epigrams, as mentioned in Sect. 2.1, it is decided to perform some basic transformations before importing the texts in the graph. By performing these text transformations, we try to reduce the noise in the original textual data by mainly focussing on the underlying Greek characters. Three simplifications are performed on the epigrams. More specifically, (i.) capital letters are removed and replaced by their lowercase counterparts, (ii.) characters that are not part of the Greek alphabet are removed and (iii.) accents and other diacritical marks are omitted.

As an example, consider the two epigrams displayed in Table 1. The graph representation after transforming and importing the epigrams is shown in Fig. 1. The second verse of both epigrams (left) is represented by the same node, meaning that their transformed versions are orthographically equal. The first verses, on the other hand, differ in two words, resulting in a different verse node for every epigram. In fact, when both texts consist of orthographically equal words, the structure of the graph already gives an indication of the similarity between epigrams.

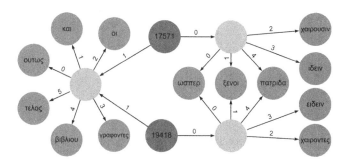

Fig. 1. Graph representation of the epigrams in Table 1. `Word` nodes are indicated in green and display their `text` property, `Verse` nodes are indicated in yellow and `Epigram` nodes in blue, including their numeric `id` property. Values of the `rank` property are shown on the edges.

4   Hierarchical Orthographic Similarity Algorithm

Now that we have a graph model in place representing the entire textual corpus, this section will describe a new hierarchical orthographic similarity measure. Analogous to the construction of the graph-based text representation, the hierarchical similarity computation is performed in a bottom-up manner. We start by calculating the similarity between words in order to subsequently compute the similarity between verses and epigrams. The similarity measure proposed in this paper is based on the concept of edit distances, more specifically the Damerau-Levenshtein (DL) edit distance [5], which we have adapted for hierarchically computing the similarities at different levels of the text. Edit distances are typically calculated between two character strings, as the minimum summed cost of the edit operations required to transform one string into the other. A formal description of the base edit distance, which is extended in the following sections, is provided in Definition 4.

Definition 4. (Base Edit Distance) *Let insertions (I), deletions (D) and replacements (R) of a single character and transpositions (T) between two subsequent characters be the edit operations of the DL edit distance. The base edit distance between two character strings a and b is recursively defined by the function $d_{a,b}(i,j)$, whose value is the minimum distance between the prefix of a up to the i-th character and the prefix of b up to the j-th character.*

$$
d_{a,b}(i,j) = \begin{cases} \max(i,j)c_{I,D} & , \textit{if } \min(i,j) = 0 \\ \min \begin{pmatrix} d_{a,b}(i-1,j) + c_{I,D} & \text{(I)}, \\ d_{a,b}(i,j-1) + c_{I,D} & \text{(D)}, \\ d_{a,b}(i-1,j-1) + \mathbb{1}_{(a_i \neq b_j)}c_R & \text{(R)}, \\ d_{a,b}(i-2,j-2) + c_T & \text{(T)} \end{pmatrix} & , \begin{array}{l} \textit{if } i,j > 1 \\ \wedge\ a_i = b_{j-1} \\ \wedge\ a_{i-1} = b_j \end{array} \\ \min \begin{pmatrix} d_{a,b}(i-1,j) + c_{I,D} & \text{(I)}, \\ d_{a,b}(i,j-1) + c_{I,D} & \text{(D)}, \\ d_{a,b}(i-1,j-1) + \mathbb{1}_{(a_i \neq b_j)}c_R & \text{(R)} \end{pmatrix} & , \textit{otherwise} \end{cases}
$$

The cost for each edit operation is represented by $c_* \in [0,1]$ where $*$ is a placeholder for one of the edit operations $\{(I,D),R,T\}$ and $\mathbb{1}$ is the indicator function.

Additionally, the similarity score between two character strings a and b is obtained by normalising the resulting edit distance over the length of the longest character string and subtracting it from 1.0:

$$
\text{sim}(a,b) = 1.0 - \frac{d_{a,b}(|a|,|b|)}{\max(|a|,|b|)} \tag{1}
$$

In the following sections, we will give a concise description of (i.) how our similarity measure, is computed and (ii.) which parameters can be tuned at the word, verse and epigram levels of the texts. Each step of the algorithm is performed on the graph-based text representation $\tilde{G}(N, \tilde{E}, \rho, \lambda_N, \lambda_E, \sigma)$, as described in Sect. 3.

4.1 Calculating Word Similarities

As a first step, the similarity between each pair of word nodes $(n_1, n_2) \in N_{\text{word}}^2$, $n_1 \neq n_2$ is calculated. At this level, the edit distance in Definition 4 and similarity calculation in Eq. (1) are slightly adapted in order to deal with the *itacism*. As described in Sect. 2.1, the letters ι, υ, and η and diphthongs ει and οι are used interchangeably in this corpus. This is dealt with by handling those letter combinations as one single character, also when determining the length of the word, and by assigning a cost of 0.0 when a replacement occurs between any of these (combinations of) letters. Furthermore, the calculation of the word similarities can be tuned by adjusting the cost of insertion and deletion $c_{I,D}^w$, the cost of replacement c_R^w, and the cost of transposition c_T^w.

As an example, let us take a look at the words εἰδεῖν and ἰδεῖν from Fig. 1 and assume all edit operation costs equal to 1.0. Because ει is seen as a single character, only a single replacement operation is needed in order to transform the first word into the second. Since ει coincides with ι due to the *itacism*, the replacement cost is equal to 0.0 and thus the total edit distance between both words results in 0.0. Consequently, the similarity between both words, following Eq. (1), is sim^w(εἰδεῖν, ἰδεῖν) $= 1.0$, indicating that they are fully similar. Looking at the words χαίρουσιν and χαίροντες, on the other hand, the minimum edit distance is obtained by performing four replacement operations, resulting in a total edit distance of 4.0 and a (rounded) similarity score of 0.56.

At the end of this step, the obtained similarity scores between each word node pair is written back to the graph database, by means of a fuzzy edge e_{new}, $\rho(e_{new}) = (n_1, n_2)$, with label SIMILAR_TO and a membership degree $\mu_{\tilde{E}}(e_{new}) = sim^w(\sigma(n_1, \text{text}), \sigma(n_2, \text{text}))$. Since the edit distance is symmetric, this edge can be interpreted as an undirected edge and can be stored only once.

4.2   Calculating Verse Similarities

Next, the similarity scores between each verse pair $(n_1, n_2) \in N_{\text{Verse}}^2$, $n_1 \neq n_2$ in the graph is computed. The main idea of this algorithm is again based on the edit distance described above, but instead of comparing individual characters in a word, the edit distance is adapted to work on verse nodes. The edit distance between verse nodes is determined by counting the minimum number of edit operations required to transform a sequence of word nodes, representing a verse, into the other. Similar to the previous step, the costs for a transposition between two subsequent word nodes (c_T^v), and insertions and deletions of a single word node $(c_{I,D}^v)$ are fixed and can be tuned for a specific corpus. As a novelty, the cost for replacements is based on the dissimilarity between the two word nodes which are being compared. This dissimilarity is acquired by subtracting the similarity between the word nodes from 1.0. Additionally, we propose to introduce a similarity threshold parameter T^v as a way to deal with the large amount of orthographic inconsistencies in the corpus. Before calculating the dissimilarity, the similarity between both words is assumed to be fully similar (i.e. a similarity score of 1.0) when the similarity is greater than or equal to the threshold T^v, resulting in a greater tolerance for (small) orthographic inconsistencies. This threshold is enforced by means of the Gödel R-implication [12]. A formal definition of this hierarchical distance is provided in Definition 5.

Definition 5. (Hierarchical Verse Edit Distance) *The hierarchical verse edit distance is an extension of the base edit distance, calculated by determining the minimum edit distance between the word node sequences contained in verse nodes n_1 and n_2. The word node sequence contained by a verse node v is the* *ordered list* $W_v = [w_1, w_2, \ldots, w_n]$ *where* $w_i \in N_{Word} \wedge e \in E_{CONTAINS} \wedge \rho(e) = (v, w_i) \wedge i = \sigma(e, \textbf{rank})\}$. *In all cases except replacements (R), the recursive definition* $d^v_{n_1, n_2}(i, j)$ *is identical to Definition 4, whose value is the minimum distance between the first* i *word nodes in* W_{v_1} *and the first* j *word nodes in* W_{v_2}. *In the case of replacements (R), the function is adapted to*

$$d^v_{n_1, n_2}(i - 1, j - 1) + \mathbb{1}_{(W_{v_1,i} \neq W_{v_2,j})}(1.0 - (T^v \Rightarrow_{Go} \mu_{\tilde{E}}(e))) \quad (R),$$

where $e \in E_{SIMILAR\_TO}$ *and* $\rho(e) = (W_{v_1,i}, W_{v_2,j})$ *is the similarity relationship between both word nodes.* $\Rightarrow_{Go}$ *is the Gödel R-implication and is defined by:*

$$p \Rightarrow_{Go} q = \begin{cases} 1 & \text{if } p \le q \\ q & \text{otherwise} \end{cases}$$

The similarity score $\text{sim}^v(n_1, n_2) = 1.0 - \frac{d^v_{n_1,n_2}(|n_1|, |n_2|)}{\max(|n_1|, |n_2|)}$ between both verses is obtained by plugging in the edit distance and the maximum length between both verses in Eq. (1), where the length of a verse node is expressed by the number of contained word nodes. Just like the similarities between word nodes, the resulting similarity score is written back to the graph database.

As an example, let us take a look at the first verses from Fig. 1, with parameter values $c^v_{I,D} = c^v_T = T^v = 1.0$. Taking into account the similarity scores calculated in the previous example, the minimum edit distance between the two verses is obtained by performing a replacement between the word nodes containing ιδειν and ειδειν with a cost of 0.0 and a replacement between χαιροντεσ and χαιρουσιν with a (rounded) cost of 0.44. As a result the total edit distance between the verse nodes is 0.44 and the (rounded) similarity score is 0.91.

4.3 Calculating Epigram Similarities

As a final step, the similarity between every pair of epigram nodes $(n_1, n_2) \in N^2_{Epigram}$, $n_1 \neq n_2$ is calculated. This step is completely analogous to the previous step. The textual units however, compared by the hierarchical edit distance, are verse nodes instead of word nodes, which can be adapted in Definition 5 by changing all Word (resp. Verse) labels to Verse (resp. Epigram) labels. Additionally, the same parameters $c^e_{I,D}$, c^e_T, and T^e can be tuned in function of the similarity calculations between epigrams.

As an example, assuming parameter values $c^e_{I,D} = c^e_T = T^e = 1.0$, we compute the similarity between the two epigram nodes in Fig. 1. The cost of replacement for the first verse is the dissimilarity between both verse nodes which is $1 - 0.91 = 0.09$. Since the second verse is the same in both epigrams, the dissimilarity between these verses is 0.0, resulting in a total edit distance of 0.09 between both epigram nodes. Plugging this value in Eq. (1) as well as the maximum length of an epigram, expressed in the number of verses, results in a (rounded) similarity score $\text{sim}^e(n_1, n_2) = 1.0 - \frac{d^e_{n_1,n_2}(|n_1|, |n_2|)}{\max(|n_1|, |n_2|)} = 1.0 - \frac{0.09}{2.0} \approx 0.96$. To conclude, a subset of the graph database for the epigrams in Table 1, including all similarity scores between its elements, is shown in Fig. 2.

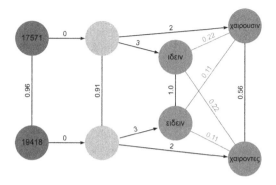

Fig. 2. Subset of the graph representation of Fig. 1. The values of the `rank` property are displayed on the (directed) edges between different levels of the text, `similarity` values are indicated on the (undirected) edges between the same level text elements.

5   Experiments

In order to test the capabilities and usefulness of our similarity measure, we have set up an experiment that compares the resulting similarity scores with a representative subset of groups of similar verses and epigrams that are composed by domain experts and act as a ground truth. Two kinds of such groups exist in the DBBE: the groups composed of similar epigrams called *epigram types* and the groups composed of similar verses called *verse variants*. For each of these groups of similar texts, a representative subset is determined and imported from the DBBE dataset [6]. The subset of verses is composed of the verses contained in the *verse variant* groups with identifiers 6353, 5354, 3949, 10869, 15261, 6342, 9033, 14886, 5840, 445, 2520, 15327, 15681 and 15652, resulting in a subset consisting of 365 verses. Additionally, the subset of epigrams is composed of the epigrams contained in the *epigram type* groups with identifiers 2150, 2148, 5248, 3436, 2965, 4152, 2326, 3147, 4155 and 5030, resulting in a subset consisting of 232 epigrams.

We have implemented our approach using two Neo4j[2] graph databases, one for the verses subset and one for the epigrams subset. The subsets of verses and epigrams have been modelled according to the model defined in Definition 3 and inserted in the databases. The similarity measure is implemented as a Neo4j plugin and executed on the database with the empirically chosen parameter values in Table 2. Since the *epigram type* and *verse variant* groups from the DBBE are defined in a crisp way, we perform a α-cut for different values of α on the graph database at hand. For each of the remaining similarity relationships in the graph (after the α cut) it is checked whether the two verse (resp. epigram) nodes it connects to are part of the same *verse variant* (resp. *epigram type*) group, resulting in a true positive, or not, resulting in a false positive. Likewise, all similarity relationships that were pruned by the α-cut are checked in the same

---

[2] https://neo4j.com/.

manner. All pruned relationships that connect two nodes which are part of the same *verse variant* or *epigram type* group are counted as false negatives, while the others are counted as true negatives. These four values allow us to calculate some quality measures on the performance of the algorithm for individual verses and full epigrams according to some α value.

Table 2. Experiment parameter values

Word parameters		Verse parameters		Epigram parameters	
$c_{I,D}^w$	0.9	$c_{I,D}^v$	0.9	$c_{I,D}^e$	0.95
c_T^w	0.0	c_T^v	0.0	c_T^e	0.0
c_R^w	1.0	T^v	0.9	T^e	0.9

Table 3. Experimental results

	Verse $\alpha = 0.8$	Verse $\alpha = 0.6$	Epigram $\alpha = 0.8$	Epigram $\alpha = 0.6$
Precision	**1.0000**	0.9990	**0.9814**	0.7669
Recall	0.5948	**0.9027**	0.4283	**0.7237**
Accuracy	0.8883	**0.9729**	0.8895	**0.9054**
F1-score	0.7459	**0.9484**	0.5964	**0.7447**

Table 3 shows the results of the calculated quality measures for the *verse variant* and *epigram type* subsets, mentioned above, calculated for two distinct α values. For verses we see an almost perfect score for precision in both cases. Since barely any verses are fully similar, better results for recall, accuracy, and F1-score are achieved by choosing a lower α value, with only a small loss in precision. The quality measures for epigrams show the same trend as for verses. Note that the overall performance is lower in the case of epigrams, indicating that finding similar epigrams is more complex which is explained by the fact that epigrams can vary in more ways than individual verses. Here, careful consideration is required for choosing a α value. A higher α value result in a high precision but a lot of similar epigrams get missed, while a lower α value will find a lot more similar epigrams but has a lower precision. Generally, no ideal α value can be determined. Instead the value should be chosen based on the properties of the (subset of the) corpus and the requirements of the analysis to be performed. Taking into account that not all possible orthographic inconsistencies can be automatically dealt with and that the expert-based similarity groups also include texts that are only partially complete or include versions of the texts where synonyms are used, this orthographic similarity measure shows encouraging results.

6 Conclusions

In this paper, we presented an orthographic similarity measure for texts represented by graphs. First, we proposed a graph-based representation for texts, where textual levels are represented by nodes and subgraphs in a graph database. Next, we described a similarity measure, based on edit distances, which hierarchically computes the similarity score for each level in the text, allowing to discover and/or quantify interconnections between multiple texts. As shown by some examples and an experiment on the capabilities of the similarity measure, the DBBE corpus could clearly benefit from this new system which is not only capable of automatically detecting interconnections between the texts, but also provides a deep and interpretable insight in how and to what degree the texts are related to each other. In fact, combining this hierarchically computed similarity measure with the full capabilities of a graph database system, we proposed a flexible query answering technique ideal for finding similar or duplicate texts and for supporting (in-depth) analysis into the complex interconnections between them. While this paper mainly focusses on the specific corpus of Byzantine book epigrams, we believe that the described approach, except for the specifics for the Byzantine Greek language, is also applicable to the analysis of plagiarism, copyright infringement and even textual data lineage, leading to interpretable results.

In future work, we will investigate the performance of this similarity measure on different, larger ground truths. Furthermore, we will investigate the possibility of extending the idea of a hierarchical similarity measure to other (string-based) similarity measures, the possibility of combining multiple similarity measures at each hierarchical level of the text as well as the possibility of using the resulting similarity scores in clustering algorithms.

Bibliography

1. Angles, R.: The property graph database model. AMW (2018). https://doi.org/10.1109/ICDEW.2012.31
2. Angles, R., Gutierrez, C.: Survey of graph database models. ACM Comput. Surv. (CSUR) **40**(1), 1–39 (2008). https://doi.org/10.1145/1322432.1322433
3. Batra, S., Tyagi, C.: Comparative analysis of relational and graph databases. Inter. J. Soft Comput. Eng. (IJSCE) **2**(2), 509–512 (2012)
4. Bronselaer, A., Pasi, G.: An approach to graph-based analysis of textual documents. In: 8th European Society for Fuzzy Logic and Technology, Proceedings, pp. 634–641 (2013). https://doi.org/10.2991/eusflat.2013.96
5. Damerau, F.J.: A technique for computer detection and correction of spelling errors. Commun. ACM **7**(3), 171–176 (1964). https://doi.org/10.1145/363958.363994
6. Demoen, K., et al.: Database of Byzantine Book Epigrams (2023). https://doi.org/10.5281/zenodo.7682523
7. Fernández, M.L., Valiente, G.: A graph distance metric combining maximum common subgraph and minimum common supergraph. Pattern Recog. Lett. **22**(6–7), 753–758 (2001). https://doi.org/10.1016/S0167-8655(01)00017-4

8. Gao, X., Xiao, B., Tao, D., Li, X.: A survey of graph edit distance. Pattern Anal. Appl. **13**, 113–129 (2010). https://doi.org/10.1007/s10044-008-0141-y
9. Gomaa, W.H., Fahmy, A.A.: A survey of text similarity approaches. Inter. J. Comput. Appli. **68**(13), 13–18 (2013)
10. Jaro, M.A.: Probabilistic linkage of large public health data file. Stat. Med. **14**(5–7), 491–8 (1995). https://doi.org/10.1002/sim.4780140510
11. Jiang, C., Coenen, F., Sanderson, R., Zito, M.: Text classification using graph mining-based feature extraction. Knowl.-Based Syst. **23**(4), 302–308 (2010). https://doi.org/10.1007/978-1-84882-983-1_2
12. Klir, G., Yuan, B.: Fuzzy sets and fuzzy logic: Theory and Applications, vol. 4 (1995)
13. Kondrak, G.: N-gram similarity and distance. In: String Processing and Information Retrieval: 12th International Conference, SPIRE 2005, Proceedings, vol. 12, pp. 115–126, Buenos Aires, Argentina (2005). https://doi.org/10.1007/11575832_13
14. Levenshtein, V.I.: Binary codes capable of correcting deletions, insertions, and reversals. Soviet Phys. Doklady **10**, 707–710 (1966)
15. Neuhaus, M., Bunke, H.: A probabilistic approach to learning costs for graph edit distance. In: Proceedings of the 17th International Conference on Pattern Recognition, ICPR 2004, vol. 3, pp. 389–393. IEEE (2004). https://doi.org/10.1109/ICPR.2004.1334548
16. Neuhaus, M., Bunke, H.: A convolution edit kernel for error-tolerant graph matching. In: 18th International Conference on Pattern Recognition (ICPR'06), vol. 4, pp. 220–223. IEEE (2006). https://doi.org/10.1109/ICPR.2006.57
17. Ricceri, R., et al.: The Database of Byzantine Book Epigrams Project: Principles, Challenges, Opportunities; preprint (2022). https://hal.science/hal-03833929
18. Rosenfeld, A.: Fuzzy graphs. In: Fuzzy Sets and Their Applications to Cognitive and Decision Processes, vol. 1, pp. 77–95. Elsevier (1975). https://doi.org/10.1016/B978-0-12-775260-0.50008-6
19. Wagner, R.A., Fischer, M.J.: The string-to-string correction problem. JACM **21**(1), 168–173 (1974). https://doi.org/10.1145/321796.321811
20. Winkler, W.E.: String comparator metrics and enhanced decision rules in the fellegi-sunter model of record linkage (1990)
21. Zadeh, L.A.: Fuzzy sets. Inf. Control **8**(3), 338–353 (1965). https://doi.org/10.1016/0165-0114(78)90029-5
22. Zadeh, L.A.: Similarity relations and fuzzy orderings. Inf. Sci. **3**(2), 177–200 (1971). https://doi.org/10.1016/S0020-0255(71)80005-1

Applying AI to Social Science and Social Science to AI

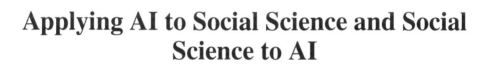

An Unsupervised Approach to Extracting Knowledge from the Relationships Between Blame Attribution on Twitter

Matija Franklin[2] , Trisevgeni Papakonstantinou[2], Tianshu Chen[2],
Carlos Fernandez-Basso[1,2(✉)] , and David Lagnado[2]

[1] Research Centre for Information and Communications Technologies (CITIC-UGR),
University of Granada, 18014 Granada, Spain
cjferba@decsai.ugr.es
[2] Causal Cognition Lab, Division of Psychology and Language Sciences,
University College London, London, UK
{matija.franklin,trisevgeni.papakonstantinou.19,
carlos.basso,d.lagnado}@ucl.ac.uk

Abstract. The present paper suggests and examines a technique for analyzing individuals' public blame attributions on online platforms, with a specific focus on the blame attributions expressed in Twitter 'Tweets' in response to various incidents involving Artificial Intelligence (AI). Twitter was chosen as it offers an 'Academic Research product track, which provides researchers with free historical data of discourse which took place on the platform. AI Incidents were chosen as they are a contemporary topic that is often talked about on Twitter, and currently, the focus of many academic papers due to the nature of "The responsibility gap" present when an AI does something that might be blameworthy [44]. Online experiments have been used to investigate these issues in recent years. However, this paper suggests a more ecologically valid approach that can reproduce findings from this field of research. The benefit of the approach is the potential discovery of novel factors that haven't been traditionally manipulated or measured in experimental settings. The outlined method can also be applied to different online platforms, and research topics within the field of causal attribution [6].

Keywords: Blame · Attribution · Artificial Intelligence · Twitter

1 Introduction

The main objective of this paper is to propose and evaluate a technique for analyzing public blame attributions made by individuals on online platforms, specifically focusing on the blame attributions expressed in Twitter "Tweets" in response to various incidents caused by Artificial Intelligence (AI). Twitter was chosen as the data source due to its "Academic Research product track," which provides unrestricted access to past discourse on the platform. AI incidents were selected because they are a topical issue frequently discussed on Twitter and the

© Springer Nature Switzerland AG 2023
H. L. Larsen et al. (Eds.): FQAS 2023, LNAI 14113, pp. 221–233, 2023.
https://doi.org/10.1007/978-3-031-42935-4_18

subject of numerous academic papers due to the "responsibility gap" inherent when an AI behaves in a potentially blameworthy manner [44]. In recent years, these issues have been investigated empirically using online experiments. This present paper proposes a more ecologically valid method that may replicate findings from this area of research. The benefit of the approach is the potential discovery of novel factors that haven't been traditionally manipulated or measured in experimental settings. The outlined method can also be applied to different online platforms, and research topics within the field of causal attribution [6].

1.1   Blaming Artificial Intelligence

Although an AI may have causal efficacy, it is not clear who should be held responsible when it makes a mistake [24]. Further, it is not clear whether developers should be held responsible as they are not fully capable of predicting an AI's behaviour [36]. In this sense, the responsibility gap is an example of the problem of many hands, where multiple different agents bring about an outcome [45]. Artificial Intelligence as an autonomous agent presents a novel challenge due to the possibility of different principal-agent relationships [26]. A human can have different levels of oversight over an AI agent. Further, the AI agent can carry out the tasks in different ways and may have various ways of responding to the input from the human-in-the-loop.

Recent empirical research has identified certain patterns in how people judge AI. People tend to judge AIs more for the outcomes of their actions, and humans more for their intentions [22]. They also blame AIs more for causing physical harm, and humans more when they treat someone unfairly. This is supported by findings suggesting that discrimination by an algorithm causes less moral outrage than human discrimination [8]. When people judge human-AI teams, they attribute less blame and causality to the AI when both agents make an error [4]. Further, people receiving advice from an AI get more blame than people receiving advice from a human [47].

People's perceptions of artificial autonomous agents' capability influence the way they judge and interact with them. People expect people to make mistakes for automation to be flawless [32]. People will also rely more on algorithmic advice as the difficulty of a task goes up [9]. People are less trustworthy of autonomous artificial agents when dealing with tasks that are subjective [11] or anything that involves emotions [46]. Finally, people prefer not to use artificial autonomous agents for making moral decisions [14]. They expect artificial autonomous agents, to make utilitarian moral choices, and blame them when they don't [35]. These findings may be explained by the fact that people perceive machines as agents that cannot fully think or feel [7], or as agents that are selfish and uncooperative [23].

People's perceptions of artificial autonomous agents' autonomy also influence the way they judge them. Autonomous artificial agents can be viewed as more or less autonomous which in turn is associated with people's intent inferences towards these agents [5]. One study found that when robots were described as autonomous that they received blame attributions that were nearly equal to what a human would receive [17]. Finally, drivers of automated vehicles are seen as having less responsibility than drivers of manually controlled vehicles [37].

Prior cognitive research on how people attribute responsibility[1] has identified factors that influence people's judgments across contexts [28]. [15] have proposed a framework outlining nine factors that influence responsibility attribution - causality, role, knowledge, objective foreseeability, capability, intent, desire, autonomy, and character.

While an agent can cause an outcome but not be blamed for it, causality is a precursor to attributing responsibility [28]. Agents are responsible for carrying out actions according to their role [20] and are blamed more highly for highly foreseeable outcomes, which relates to their knowledge [29]. Objective foreseeability, which represents how likely an outcome is irrespective of what an agent subjectively foresees, also affects blame attributions. Expectations of an agent's capability influence blame attributions. High expectations of capability result in more blame for negative outcomes [19]. Furthermore, intentionality influences blame attributions because they allow one to identify the effects an agent intended [27]. Desire is conceptually different from desire in that intention involves committing to performing an intended action [33] and also influences blame attribution [12]. Finally, people blame more autonomous agents as they have more control over their own decisions [1].

1.2   The Present Study

Previous research studying attribution towards autonomous artificial agents has mostly used vignettes [16] or evidence in the form of images [3]. In such studies, certain aspects of these vignettes or images that pertain to factors that influence blame are manipulated. The present paper proposes a more ecologically valid method that may replicate and contextualize previous experimental findings, or identify new factors that are relevant to people's blame attributions.

Specifically, the goal of the method is to identify the *agents* people are attributing blame to, and the *factors* that have an effect on people's attributions. Agents are often context-specific, thus requiring a bottom-up approach to identifying which ones are relevant. For the present context, this raises the context-specific question of who people blame when an AI makes a mistake. The investigated factors that are highly correlated with blame build on the framework proposed by [15], examining how these factors are used by people making attributions outside the context of an experimental study.

Taking a computational social science approach can provide new data that can enhance our understanding of findings in cognitive psychology experiments. The nature of online data, particularly the fact that they are for a big part written, real-world instances of human behavior, accompanied by personal and network information, makes it possible to put novel technologies in natural language processing to use to gain insights from language about human psychology.

---

[1] Resposibility relates to *outcome responsibility* - people's attributions of blame or praise for actions that have occurred in the past.

The method is able to capture naturally-occurring behaviour, rather than behaviour displayed in an experimental setting. It is open-ended, that is "participants" are not assigned a task -they simply behave as they would. Moreover, it has the ability to capture live reactions to critical events [25].

2 Methods

2.1 Data Collection

To gather the tweets, Twitter's official API was employed with an academic license. Search queries that contained relevant keywords were used to identify the tweets. To minimize the likelihood of obtaining irrelevant tweets, the search was restricted to within one month following the incident.

The study focused on tweets related to several incidents involving AI, including the Ofqual A-levels predictive algorithm, the COMPAS recidivism algorithm, the self-driving Uber and Tesla crashes, the Amazon hiring algorithm scandal, and the use of AI-generated art and text. In addition, we gathered tweets related to similar incidents without AI involvement, such as road accidents involving human drivers and university admission scandals like operation varsity blues, to facilitate a comparison of the occurrence of factors and sentiment in both contexts. Specifically, the study looked at tweets responding to the Ofqual A-levels predictive algorithm (i.e., a computer program designed to predict what grades the students would have received if they had taken exams), the COMPAS recidivism algorithm (i.e., algorithm designed to assess the risk that a given defendant will commit a crime after release), the self-driving Uber hitting and killing someone, the self-driving Tesla crash, the Amazon hiring algorithm scandal (i.e., an algorithm that would assess people's job application that had a bias against female applicants), and the use of AI-generated art and text. We also collected tweets on similar incidents involving human-only systems, where no AI was involved, to enable a comparison of the prevalence of factors and sentiment across the two contexts; we collected tweets on road accidents involving human drivers and university admission scandals (e.g. operation varsity blues). The rationale for selecting these specific contexts is primarily based on the media attention they attracted. Secondly, they represent a combination of factors already known to influence blame attributions, such as physical harm, fairness-related outcomes, intent, role-related obligations, and more.

All tweets and meta-data gathered, as well as the scripts and keywords used for data collection can be found at https://osf.io/t6sw3/view_only=d2b1103711244cea9c2661183d5fb418.

2.2 Analytic Strategy

We followed a hybrid qualitative-quantitative approach to explore blame allocation amongst agents and factors in a bottom-up manner in two stages. The first stage in that process involved manual qualitative coding of the tweets in terms of *blame attribution, agents, factors, and sentiment*. The second stage involved transforming the codes created in the first stage into variables, investigating potential associations between them, and applying an unsupervised classification algorithm to examine how these variables cluster together.

Qualitative Coding. We applied a variation of the framework method [43], a comparative form of thematic analysis that follows a structure of inductively and deductively-created themes. Five trained coders independently coded a sample of 1342 tweets initially according to whether they involved a responsibility attribution for the pre-specified contexts. The subset of tweets that involved an attribution (N=522) was then coded in terms of the agents the attribution was directed at (e.g., the self-driving car), the factors that were involved in making this attribution (e.g., capability), and the sentiment of the attribution, which could have been either positive, negative, or neutral. When for some reason this was not possible, for example, because the tweet was too short or did not contain a judgment, a tweet's agents, factors, and sentiment would get labelled with none. We started with a pre-specified set of codes, based on well-established findings (see: https://osf.io/t6sw3/view_only=d2b1103711244cea9c2661183d5fb418) and through the process of data familiarisation and calibration, we expanded that initial set. Finally, we grouped the codes into themes. 28% (N=465) of tweets were blindly double-coded.

Statistical Approach. Based on the initial qualitative analysis, we employed two quantitative analysis techniques to investigate this dataset. To examine the associations among blame, context, sentiment, agents, and factors in the subset of tweets that included an attribution, we utilized Pearson's r statistic. We employed k-means clustering on the complete dataset that included all corpora, utilizing the coding of agents, factors, sentiment, and blame attributions to identify clusters and verify if they forecast blame attribution. The reason for choosing k-means clustering was that the primary objective of this study was not solely to predict blame, but rather to investigate how agents, factors, and sentiment coalesce to create an attribution from the bottom-up.

3   Results

3.1   Qualitative

We identified 10 agents and 12 factors related to attribution across the different contexts. Table 1 presents the codes and their descriptions, along with their prevalence in the dataset.

Agents with a high proportion of blame attributions were the algorithm (28%), company (13%), government (12%), and system (11%). Factors with a high proportion of blame attributions were bias (20%), negative result (16%), and capability (15%). Figure 1 presents the allocation of blame across factors and agents.

Figure 2 presents the allocation of blame across agents and factors. Incidents involving human-only systems had a higher prevalence of factors relevant to

Table 1. Agents and factors derived through qualitative analysis

Code	N (%)	Description
Agents		
Algorithm	180 (32%)	AI
Company	75 (13%)	Name of a company or representative of a company
Data	6 (1%)	Data the AI is trained on
Developer	44 (8%)	Developer of the AI
Government	79 (14%)	Government as a whole and specific member
Media	17 (3%)	Media source discussing the incident
Person	52 (9%)	A third party discussing the incident
System	72 (13%)	The system around the main agents, enablers, and barriers
User	36 (6%)	User of AI or equivalent system
Victim	6 (1%)	Victim of an incident
Factors		
Bias	118 (21%)	Expression of prejudice for or against an agent or group
Capability	110 (19%)	Capability to fulfill a role, referencing skill or knowledge
Censorship	25 (4%)	Suppression of speech or information
Culpable action	31 (5%)	An act that is in itself blameworthy, regardless of outcome (e.g. bribing)
Employment	87 (15%)	Use of algorithm
Fairness	34 (6%)	Fairness/unfairness explicitly pointed out using relevant language (e.g. "unjust" or "unfair")
Intent/Foreseeability	5 (1%)	Harm that was intended or foreseen
Intellectual property	9 (4%)	Discussion of ownership and intellectual property
Myth	17 (3%)	Misconception about how a system (mainly an algorithm) works (e.g. black-boxing)
Negative result	77 (14%)	An unexpected or negative outcome
Obligation	39 (7%)	A moral obligation or duty, generally attached to a role
Replacement	15 (3%)	Discussion of humans being replaced by AI

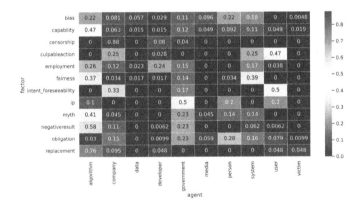

Fig. 1. Percentage of blame attributed to pairs of agents and factors

moral attributions, such as bias (57%), obligation (67%), and intent or foreseeability (67%). On the flip side, incidents involving AI had a higher prevalence of factors relating to performance and use, such as capability (81%) negative result (100%), and replacement (100%).

3.2   Quantitative

Associations. Figure 3 presents the correlation coefficients for all pairwise combinations of blame, context, sentiment, agents, and factors. Blame was most

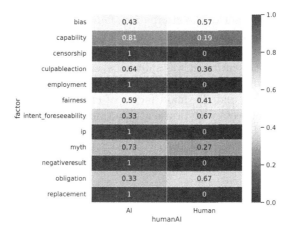

Fig. 2. Prevalance of factors in human-AI and human-only contexts

strongly positively correlated with human-only scenarios ($r(703) = .22$, $p = <.001$), negative sentiment ($r(703) = -.72$, $p = <.001$), and bias ($r(703) = .21$, $p = <.001$). It was strongly negatively correlated with neutral ($r(703) = -.53$, $p = <.001$) and positive ($r(703) = -.49$, $p = <.001$) sentiment, employment ($r(703) = -.28$, $p = <.001$), and replacement ($r(703) = -.20$, $p = <.001$).

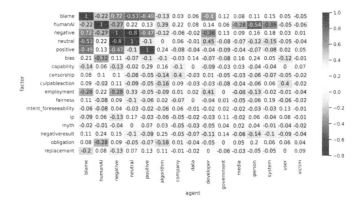

Fig. 3. Pearson's r correlation coefficients for all variables of interest

Cluster Analysis. The k-means cluster analysis grouped the variables into 6 clusters. Clusters 3, 5, and 6 grouped together tweets containing >94% blame attributions. The sentiment in those clusters was almost entirely negative (>93%). The agents blamed in those scenarios ranged across the codes, with no particular agent being prevalent. Cluster 5 grouped together tweets with the negative result as the main factor relevant to the attribution. Cluster 6 grouped together tweets with bias as the main factor. Clusters 2 and 4 both had a low percentage of blame attributions (<15%). In Cluster 2 the main agent receiving the attribution was the algorithm, and the sentiment was split between neutral and positive. Cluster 4 represented a small percentage of observations and grouped together tweets with neutral sentiment and the main factor of employment. Finally, Cluster 1 grouped together all tweets with praise attributions, as well as many with blame attributions (79%). The sentiment was mostly negative and the main factor relevant to the attribution was capability. Table 2 presents the clusters in detail. Figure 4 presents the t-SNE projection of the clustering.

Table 2. Descriptions of clusters

Cluster	Prevalence	Blame	Sentiment
1	21%	79% blame, 16% praise	79% negative
2	20%	12% blame	61% neutral, 19% positive
3	27%	96% blame	94% negative
4	6%	15% blame	100% neutral
5	13%	94% blame	93% negative
6	13%	100% blame	100% negative

Cluster	Agents	Factors
1	69% algorithm	72% capability, 13% employment
2	52% algorithm, 12% government, 12% user	22% bias, 20% replacement, 15% intellectual property
3	43% company, 19% system, 13% government	split across
4	71% developer, 17% company	96% employment
5	69% algorithm, 25% goverment	100% negative result
6	27% person, 26% algorithm, 18% system	100% bias

4   Discussion

Twitter users make attributions towards different agents, including human agents, group agents, and artificial agents (e.g., algorithms or data). They justify or enrich these attributions with different relevant factors in order to praise or blame an agent. We have found that the tweets containing these attributions can serve as a valuable source of data for studying these attributions, the agents they are directed towards, as well as the relevant factors and sentiments contained within them. This adds to the previous research that has used Twitter to research sentiment and opinion [42], and provides a new tool for researching causal attribution [6].

The attributions contained a total of 10 different agents and 12 different factors across different contexts. Arguably, participants were able to grasp the complexity of "the responsibility gap" [44], making attributions toward different agents that brought about the outcome, and factors that were relevant to them.

The most blamed agents were algorithm (28%), company (13%), government (12%), and system (11%), respectively. This replicates the finding that people

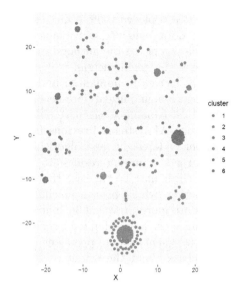

Fig. 4. t-SNE projection of dataset (all corpora)

are willing to make attributions towards algorithms directly [15]. As with past research participants also tend to centralize responsibility [22]. People are also willing to blame the government (e.g., for not regulating the use of AI), which is an agent that is not often considered in experimental settings. Further people are also willing to blame the broader system around the main agents. The way people blame *group agents*, such as governments or companies, has been explored in the literature [31] and discussed in relation to AI [30]. People are willing to view group entities as agents, and this shapes the way they think about and interact with them. Attribution toward systems is an understudied phenomenon in previous research. People are indeed capable of thinking about systems [38], but when, why, and how they blame them remains an open question.

The most commonly used factors to blame were bias (20%), negative result (16%), and capability (15%), respectively. Although bias in AI has been extensively researched by AI Ethics researchers [40], its impact on attribution has been seldom explored. Future research could further explore bias as a factor. Our findings that people focus on negative outcomes when making attributions replicate the findings of previous research [22]. This is also true for capability [18].

The percentage of blame attributed to pairs of agents and factors in Fig. 1 reveals certain patterns. Algorithms are often blamed for causing negative outcomes, in line with research showing that machines are blamed more for the outcomes of their actions rather than their intentions [22]. They are also often blamed for replacing humans, which similarly to bias has often been a topic of research in AI Ethics [2], but less so in attribution research. The companies that make AI were often blamed for using AI to censor certain users, which is adjacent to experimental research on users' judgments of moderation on social media platforms [39]. When data was blamed, it was most likely blamed for the bias contained within it; a topic very often discussed in machine learning research [13]. Although anecdotal evidence is available for people's willingness to blame data as an artificial agent, to the authors' best knowledge this is the first research paper to observe this phenomenon.

The prevalence of the 12 factors in human-AI and human-only contexts is available in Fig. 2. Bias, obligation, and intent/foreseeability were more prevalent for human-only systems, whilst capability, negative outcomes, and replacement was more prevalent for human-AI systems. Previous findings that humans get more blamed for their intent or foresight, and algorithms get blamed more for their role or capability mirror the present results [15]. As bias as such is not explored by previous research, it may be the case that Twitter users view bias in humans as a culpable action, whilst bias in machines is more statistical in nature. Negative outcomes are more prevalent in human-AI contexts is in line with the finding that machines get more blame for their outcomes [22]. Finally, it may be the case that replacement is more prevalent in human-AI contexts as there is a current active debate about the extent to which AIs will be able to perform certain tasks better than humans [10].

Blame was positively associated with negative sentiment and negatively associated with neutral and positive sentiment (see Fig. 3). The stronger positive than negative correlation relates to previous findings showing that blame is more differentiated and more extreme than praise [21]. The rest of the associations mirror the patterns previously discussed in Fig. 1. Overall, blame exhibited strong (i.e., > .02) positive associations with bias and strong negative associations with employment and replacement.

The six clusters also reveal certain unique patterns. Cluster 1 uniquely contains praise attributions, mostly towards algorithms, and mostly for their capability. This was often the case for tweets making attributions towards AI-generated text and art. Clusters 3, 5, and 6 are all large blame clusters (i.e., ¿94%) and are mostly negative in sentiment. Cluster 5 exclusively contains attributions focused on negative outcomes, while cluster 6 only contains attributions focused on bias. Cluster 3 on the other hand contains a range of different factors. Clusters 2 and 4 are low in blame, which is evidenced by their relatively high neutral and or positive sentiment.

This paper's approach has uncovered new agents and factors that individuals consider when faced with the "responsibility gap" of AI. This method can be utilized to explore both new and previous inquiries into people's blame attributions[6], using readily accessible, extensive tweet datasets. Such large-scale research would improve the validity of the proposed models. It is possible that factors that are highly significant in a lab setting may receive little attention in certain public online discourse contexts. Analyzing people's attributions can offer novel insights. Given the novelty of attribution towards AI, the approach outlined in this paper has discovered novel agents and factors people are considering when faced with the AI "responsibility gap". The method can be further used for exploring new and replicating old questions pertaining to people's blame attributions [6]. This can be done with readily available, large-scale datasets of tweets. The large-scale nature of this type of research would give researchers more validity to their proposed models. One may find that a factor that was highly significant in the lab, is barely mentioned in certain contexts of public online discourse. Studying and analysing people's attributions would provide us with novel insights,

4.1 Limitations

This approach however is not without limitations. Even though using naturally-occurring datasets, such as social media, has many advantages such as reducing bias and increasing ecological validity, it also limits the researcher's control and thus the ability to make inferences.

Future research can be directed towards applying and examining this framework using richer datasets that consist of a longer text. Data from similar media such as Reddit or other forum-like websites can be used to further interrogate this model. Additionally, the current dataset can be explored in alternative ways that allow for natural themes to emerge from the text without human direction, such as topic modeling.

5   Conclusion

An issue in cognitive and psychological research is that researchers can only model the factors that get measured. Deciding what gets measured is heavily influenced by the research history of the field [25]. A noteworthy example of this comes from the relationship between people's perceptions of intent, capacity, and blame. Perceptions of the relationship between these factors vary greatly between different academic traditions. The relationship between intent and skill are not features of any known legal concept [12]. In psychological research, on the other hand, actions are seen as more intentful, and thus more blameworthy, if the agent receiving the blame has the necessary skill to execute that action [34]. The approach proposed in this paper can serve as a way of avoiding entrenched measurement bias within a specific field [41]. It does so by allowing one's framework to update itself if this is what is reflected in the analyzed discourse. This study is also a step toward training an algorithm capable of identifying and analysing attributions in social media posts.

References

1. Alicke, M.D.: Culpable control and the psychology of blame. Psychol. Bull. **126**(4), 556 (2000)
2. Ashton, H., Franklin, M.: The corrupting influence of AI as a boss or counterparty (2022)
3. Ashton, H., Franklin, M., Lagnado, D.: Testing a definition of intent for AI in a legal setting. Submitted manuscript (2022)
4. Awad, E., et al.: Blaming humans in autonomous vehicle accidents: shared responsibility across levels of automation. arXiv preprint arXiv:1803.07170 (2018)

5. Banks, J.: A perceived moral agency scale: development and validation of a metric for humans and social machines. Comput. Hum. Behav. **90**, 363–371 (2019)
6. Bender, A.: What is causal cognition? Front. Psychol. **11**, 3 (2020)
7. Bigman, Y.E., Gray, K.: People are averse to machines making moral decisions. Cognition **181**, 21–34 (2018)
8. Bigman, Y.E., Wilson, D., Arnestad, M.N., Waytz, A., Gray, K.: Algorithmic discrimination causes less moral outrage than human discrimination. J. Experim. Psychol. General (2022)
9. Bogert, E., Schecter, A., Watson, R.T.: Humans rely more on algorithms than social influence as a task becomes more difficult. Sci. Rep. **11**(1), 1–9 (2021)
10. Brynjolfsson, E., McAfee, A.: The second machine age: Work, progress, and prosperity in a time of brilliant technologies. WW Norton & Company (2014)
11. Castelo, N., Bos, M.W., Lehmann, D.R.: Task-dependent algorithm aversion. J. Mark. Res. **56**(5), 809–825 (2019)
12. Cushman, F.: Crime and punishment: distinguishing the roles of causal and intentional analyses in moral judgment. Cognition **108**(2), 353–380 (2008)
13. DeBrusk, C.: The risk of machine-learning bias (and how to prevent it). MIT Sloan Manag. Rev. (2018)
14. Dietvorst, B.J., Bartels, D.M.: Consumers object to algorithms making morally relevant tradeoffs because of algorithms' consequentialist decision strategies. J. Consumer Psychol. (2021)
15. Franklin, M., Ashton, H., Awad, E., Lagnado, D.: Causal framework of artificial autonomous agent responsibility. In: Proceedings of the 2022 AAAI/ACM Conference on AI, Ethics, and Society, pp. 276–284 (2022)
16. Franklin, M., Awad, E., Lagnado, D.: Blaming automated vehicles in difficult situations. Iscience **24**(4), 102252 (2021)
17. Furlough, C., Stokes, T., Gillan, D.J.: Attributing blame to robots: I. the influence of robot autonomy. Human Factors **63**(4), 592–602 (2021)
18. Gerstenberg, T., Ejova, A., Lagnado, D.: Blame the skilled. In: Proceedings of the Annual Meeting of the Cognitive Science Society, vol. 33 (2011)
19. Gerstenberg, T., Ullman, T.D., Nagel, J., Kleiman-Weiner, M., Lagnado, D.A., Tenenbaum, J.B.: Lucky or clever? from expectations to responsibility judgments. Cognition **177**, 122–141 (2018)
20. Gibson, D.E., Schroeder, S.J.: Who ought to be blamed? the effect of organizational roles on blame and credit attributions. Int. J. Conflict Manag. (2003)
21. Guglielmo, S., Malle, B.F.: Asymmetric morality: blame is more differentiated and more extreme than praise. PLoS ONE **14**(3), e0213544 (2019)
22. Hidalgo, C.A., Orghian, D., Canals, J.A., De Almeida, F., Martin, N.: How Humans Judge Machines. MIT Press (2021)
23. Ishowo-Oloko, F., Bonnefon, J.F., Soroye, Z., Crandall, J., Rahwan, I., Rahwan, T.: Behavioural evidence for a transparency-efficiency tradeoff in human-machine cooperation. Nat. Mach. Intell. **1**(11), 517–521 (2019)
24. Johnson, D.G., Verdicchio, M.: Ai, agency and responsibility: the vw fraud case and beyond. Ai & Society **34**(3), 639–647 (2019)
25. Kapoor, K.K., Tamilmani, K., Rana, N.P., Patil, P., Dwivedi, Y.K., Nerur, S.: Advances in social media research: past, present and future. Inf. Syst. Front. **20**, 531–558 (2018)
26. Kim, E.S.: Deep learning and principal-agent problems of algorithmic governance: the new materialism perspective. Technol. Soc. **63**, 101378 (2020). https://doi.org/10.1016/j.techsoc.2020.101378, https://www.sciencedirect.com/science/article/pii/S0160791X19306906

27. Kleiman-Weiner, M., Gerstenberg, T., Levine, S., Tenenbaum, J.B.: Inference of intention and permissibility in moral decision making. In: CogSci (2015)
28. Lagnado, D., Gerstenberg, T.: A difference-making framework for intuitive judgments of responsibility. Oxford Stud. Agency Respons. **3**, 213–241 (2015)
29. Lagnado, D.A., Channon, S.: Judgments of cause and blame: the effects of intentionality and foreseeability. Cognition **108**(3), 754–770 (2008)
30. List, C.: Group agency and artificial intelligence. Philo. Technol. **34**(4), 1213–1242 (2021)
31. List, C., Pettit, P.: Group agency: The Possibility, Design, and Status of Corporate Agents. Oxford University Press (2011)
32. Madhavan, P., Wiegmann, D.A.: Similarities and differences between human-human and human-automation trust: an integrative review. Theor. Issues Ergon. Sci. **8**(4), 277–301 (2007)
33. Malle, B.F.: Intention: A folk-conceptual analysis. In: Intentions and intentionality: Foundations of Social Cognition, p. 45 (2001)
34. Malle, B.F., Knobe, J.: The folk concept of intentionality. J. Exp. Soc. Psychol. **33**(2), 101–121 (1997)
35. Malle, B.F., Scheutz, M., Arnold, T., Voiklis, J., Cusimano, C.: Sacrifice one for the good of many? people apply different moral norms to human and robot agents. In: 2015 10th ACM/IEEE International Conference on Human-Robot Interaction (HRI), pp. 117–124. IEEE (2015)
36. Matthias, A.: The responsibility gap: Ascribing responsibility for the actions of learning automata. Ethics Inf. Technol. **6**(3), 175–183 (2004)
37. McManus, R.M., Rutchick, A.M.: Autonomous vehicles and the attribution of moral responsibility. Soc. Psychol. Personal. Sci. **10**(3), 345–352 (2019)
38. Meadows, D.H.: Thinking In Systems: A Primer. Chelsea green publishing (2008)
39. Myers West, S.: Censored, suspended, shadowbanned: user interpretations of content moderation on social media platforms. New Media Soc. **20**(11), 4366–4383 (2018)
40. Ntoutsi, E., et al.: Bias in data-driven artificial intelligence systems-an introductory survey. Wiley Interdisc. Rev. Data Mining Knowl. Dis. **10**(3), e1356 (2020)
41. Oort, F.J., Visser, M.R., Sprangers, M.A.: Formal definitions of measurement bias and explanation bias clarify measurement and conceptual perspectives on response shift. J. Clin. Epidemiol. **62**(11), 1126–1137 (2009)
42. Pak, A., Paroubek, P., et al.: Twitter as a corpus for sentiment analysis and opinion mining. In: LREc, vol. 10, pp. 1320–1326 (2010)
43. Ruhl, K.: Qualitative research practice: a guide for social science students and researchers. Historical Soc. Res. **29**(4), 171–177 (2004). https://doi.org/10.12759/hsr.29.2004.4.171-177
44. Santoni de Sio, F., Mecacci, G.: Four responsibility gaps with artificial intelligence: why they matter and how to address them. Philos. Technol. **34**, 1057–1084 (2021)
45. Slota, S.C., et al.: Many hands make many fingers to point: challenges in creating accountable AI. AI Soc., 1–13 (2021)
46. Waytz, A., Norton, M.I.: Botsourcing and outsourcing: robot, British, Chinese, and German workers are for thinking-not feeling-jobs. Emotion **14**(2), 434 (2014)
47. Westcott, C., Lagnado, D.: The AI will see you now: Judgments of responsibility at the intersection of artificial intelligence and medicine (master's thesis). Unpublished Manuscript (2019)

"Health Is the Real Wealth": Unsupervised Approach to Improve Explainability in Health-Based Recommendation Systems

Bartolome Ortiz-Viso[1,4]([✉]) [ID], Carlos Fernandez-Basso[1,2] [ID],
Jesica Gómez-Sánchez[2,3] [ID], and Maria J. Martin-Bautista[4] [ID]

[1] Research Centre for Information and Communications Technologies (CITIC-UGR),
University of Granada, 18014 Granada, Spain
bortiz@ugr.es
[2] Causal Cognition Lab, Division of Psychology and Language Sciences,
University College London, London, UK
{carlos.basso,jesica.gomez}@ucl.ac.uk
[3] Department of Developmental and Educational Psychology, University of Granada,
18011 Granada, Spain
gomezjs@ugr.es
[4] Department of Computer Science and Artificial Intelligence, University of Granada,
18071 Granada, Spain
mbautis@decsai.ugr.es

Abstract. Nutritional recommendation systems are one of the major challenges in the field of recommendation systems. These systems can be based on various aspects such as individual preferences, group affiliations, or nutritional needs. The latter, known as healthy recommendation systems, aims to offer a menu tailored to the user and their vital needs, as well as having a positive impact on their health. However, although these systems allow for very precise multiple nutritional adjustments, users often do not understand what values are taken into account and why these values matter. This study proposes an unsupervised pipeline that generates nutrient-focused natural explanations, based on the nutritional data of the recommended recipes and nutritional textual guidelines made by experts.

Keywords: Recommender systems · Explainability · Question Generation · Question Answering

1 Introduction

Multi-objective recommender systems are often opaque to the consumer, who is unaware of the number of parameters and the rules used by the recommender to provide a solution. This is especially relevant in nutrition, as the nutritional knowledge and adjustment of the recommender system often exceeds the knowledge of the average user using it. This is even more noticeable in systems such as [23,43] where even the microbiota, genetics or polyphenols in the food are taken into account when generating the recommendation.

© Springer Nature Switzerland AG 2023
H. L. Larsen et al. (Eds.): FQAS 2023, LNAI 14113, pp. 234–246, 2023.
https://doi.org/10.1007/978-3-031-42935-4_19

Moreover, some of those systems are health-based recommender systems [38]. In general, in nutrition recommendation systems, health plays an essential role [39]. However, food is a highly cultural aspect influenced by our knowledge or even mood. If the system prioritizes our health before our tastes, it may generate recommendations that are rejected by the users, as they do not understand them. Thus combining both requirements and preferences is a high active research topic [19,30,35]

Therefore, in multi-objective nutritional systems, focused on health and nutrition, there is a problem still open on what are the best strategies to explain our recommendation. Many institutions [6,44] offer guides and educational material where the information on why these values are adjusted is already written, but few users will read all of them and be able to generalized its information to other situations.

Our work proposes a first approach to how to use this information in an unsupervised way to generate or improve the modules in charge of the explainability of this kind of systems. At the same time, this system can also be used to generate text corpus database useful for training future nutritional Question-Answering systems.

2   Related Work

2.1   Food Recommendation Systems

Health-based recommendations are a type of recommendation system that suggests options or actions to individuals based on their health status, lifestyle, and preferences [40]. These recommendations can help individuals make informed decisions about their health and well-being by providing personalized advice and guidance. There are several types of health-based recommendations, including:

- Lifestyle recommendations: These recommendations provide guidance on several aspects of our daily routines that impact on our health. Those can be focus on physical activity based on their fitness level, goals, and health status [13], improve cardiovascular health [29], or improve sleep habits [12,42]. There are also examples related to managing health mental behaviours like managing stress and improving mental health based on an individual's lifestyle and stressors. They can be used to help individuals reduce anxiety and depression, improve resilience, and enhance overall well-being [25].
- Food recommendations: These recommendations provide guidance on what to eat and how much to eat based on an individual's dietary needs and preferences [14]. They can be used to help individuals maintain a healthy weight, manage chronic conditions such as diabetes or heart disease, or optimize athletic performance. Consequently, current nutritional recommender systems must handle multiple constraints and preferences. On this behalf studies such as [37] incorporate various parameters for ingredient classification. More recently, [36] have focused on recommending food specifically for patients with chronic kidney disease (CKD), ensuring that specific parameters are

fulfilled for their needs. In addition, evolutionary algorithms have also been successfully employed in this domain. Research by [8, 28] has explored the use of evolutionary algorithms to generate bundles or sets of recommendations, including an additional source of recommendation related to physical exercises. In addition to them, other approaches that use Case-Based Reasoning [17] or Fuzzy Rule-Based Systems [15] are a source of recommendation systems that can manage multiple constraints, and at the same time, they are accesible in terms of the rules they use.

Health-based recommendations can be delivered through various channels, including mobile apps, wearables, and online platforms [9, 26]. These recommendations can be personalized based on an individual's health data, such as their blood pressure, heart rate, or sleep patterns, or based on their preferences and goals.

Overall, health-based recommendations can be a valuable tool for individuals looking to improve their health and well-being. By providing personalized advice and guidance, these recommendations can help individuals make informed decisions about their health and achieve their health goals.

2.2 Explainability

Explainable Artificial Intelligence (XAI) is a subset of AI that aims to create models and systems that can provide transparent and understandable explanations for their decisions and actions [21, 27]. The goal of XAI is to increase the trust, accountability, and ethicality of AI systems by making them more interpretable to humans [18, 31]. This is important because AI systems are increasingly being used to make decisions that can have a significant impact on individuals and society, such as in the case of food recommendation systems.

The state of the art in XAI and food recommendation is still in developing, but there has been some research and development in this area [7]. One approach is to use machine learning algorithms, such as decision trees and rule-based systems. This approach can be used to extract a set of rules (that are used by the algorithm) that may be useful to explain the system to the end users (if we preserve the interpretability of the variables used in the rules). In that sense, we can use the inner workings of this models to provide insight into how the system is making its recommendations as some works reflects [18].

Another approach is to develop posthoc explainability techniques [11], which involve analyzing the outputs of a black box AI model to generate explanations for its decisions. These techniques use methods such as local feature importance, surrogate models, and counterfactual explanations to provide insights into how the model arrived at its recommendations.

Overall, XAI and food recommendation is an emerging field that has the potential to improve the transparency and trustworthiness of AI-based food recommendation systems. However, more research and development are needed to create models and techniques that are both effective and explainable to humans.

2.3   User Adhesion

The application of XAI methods is increasingly important in recommender systems to help users understand the basis for recommendations made by the system [21]. Traditional recommender systems rely on machine learning algorithms to make recommendations based on patterns in user data, such as past purchases or browsing history [27]. However, these models can be difficult to interpret and users may not understand why they are being recommended a particular item.

XAI techniques can help to address this issue by providing explanations for the recommendations made by the system. Some of the XAI techniques that can be used in recommender systems include:

– Content-based explanations: This approach provides an explanation for a recommendation by highlighting the content features of the item that are similar to the user's interests.
– Collaborative filtering explanations: This approach provides an explanation for a recommendation by identifying other users with similar preferences and highlighting the items that they have enjoyed.
– Rule-based explanations: This approach uses rule-based systems to generate explanations for recommendations. For example, the system might explain that it is recommending a particular item because it meets a certain set of criteria, such as being on sale or having a high rating.

By providing explanations for their recommendations, recommender systems can help to increase user trust and satisfaction. This is particularly important in domains where the recommendations can have a significant impact on user decision-making, such as in e-commerce, healthcare, or financial services [16,20, 45].

3   Model for the Generator of Explanations

In this section, we will describe all the parts that make up the architecture of the system that we propose for creating explanations for recommendations. A global overview can be found in Fig. 1.

3.1   Data Sources

We begin by highlighting the initial data sources that are used during the generation process: user data, recipe data, and a heterogeneous corpus of text from nutrition experts.

– Recipe data: Recipes are obtained from a RECIPEDB database [10]. In this database, we find the recipe description and the quantities of its ingredients. From them, we can generate the nutritional information for each 100 g of the recipe. This nutritional information is obtained from nutritional databases [22], and the set of nutrients that will be taken into account for the recipe evaluation is selected.

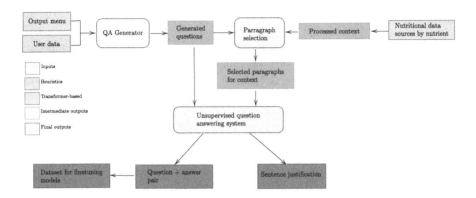

Fig. 1. Overview of the system

- User: The user's biometric values are necessary for obtaining the recommendation but also for the personalization of the explanation. Within it, we can highlight two main sources of data: the user's objective (health, physique) and their health status (i.e. diabetic, smoker). These variations can be an insterenting source for completing the generated questions.
- Finally, in the other hemisphere of the diagram, we find the set of heterogeneous texts that serve as a source of information. To obtain them, two main approaches have been followed: the extraction of web texts from NHI [1] and the extraction of text from PDFs on nutrition guidelines from EFSA as [6].

3.2   Question Generation

The key step of our explanation generation system is to transform a recommendation into a question that reflects the user's doubts. The philosophy behind this procedure is based on the fact that when we want to know why we are being recommended something, the underlying question is what characteristics does the item has that make it better or worse than the rest in my situation. However, not every user is able to understand which question can really help to interpret the results. This is the key novelty of the system, as this step would be transforming the worries of the user in natural language questions. More on expanding options of this approach in Sect. 5.

Particularly, let focus on health-centered systems (multi-objective). In this case, the question underlying a user that want to know why they are being recommended something would be similar to: *What characteristics does this recipe have to make it beneficial for my health?* This question also admits another reading, which is: *what characteristics does this recipe have to help me achieve a certain health-oriented goal?*

However, that question is a generic question that does not add really any value and probably would need a very long answer to fulfill its purpose. In addition, most of the knowledge extraction systems that we can build would result in a less useful explanation. On the contrary, this question can be further transformed if we process the recommended recipe and obtain its main characteristics and how they relate to the rest of the recipes in the dataset (a small selection of them). Thus, if a recipe has been recommended in a multi-objective system, it is because some characteristics make it more desirable than others. These characteristics give specificity to the question:

For example if the recipe stands out for its amount of vitamin C (the reason why the system has recommended it over another), the question would result in: *What benefits on my health/objective does vitamin C provide?* This question is more specific and directly refers to quantifiable aspects of the recipe.

3.3 Paragraph Selection

Once the set of different questions are selected we can choose which one will be used as our objective. Generally, we could prioritize questions based on the following scale: the nutritional pyramid, macro-nutrients, and micronutrients. We focus in the latter two cases. Before searching for important paragraphs in the text, we break down the relevant text chunks into shorter paragraphs. This is because we need specific information to adequately answer the question but also because we need to locate those specific smaller sections, due to the inability of the transformer to support a big number of tokens to be processed.

With the text properly divided, we conduct a semantic search to determine the similarity between the paragraphs related to the nutrient and our question. For this purpose, we used the multi-qa-mpnet-base-dot-v1 transformer model, which maps sentences and paragraphs to a 768-dimensional dense vector space and was specifically designed for semantic search. We deployed it using the sentence-transformers [33,34] library and HuggingFace. The selection of this model prioritizes the size of the embedding and the performance of the benchmark models. This model used the pre-trained mpnet-base model with specific training on 215M (question, answer) pairs. The evaluating function was Multiple Negatives Ranking Loss using CLS-pooling, dot-product as a similarity function, and a scale of 1. More details on their model card [5].

3.4 Question Answering

Having a set of paragraphs that encode the relevant information for answering our question, we then proceed to create a pipeline that processed both the query and paragraphs and produces an answer. For that approach, we use the distilled model of Roberta-base model [41], fine-tuned using the SQuAD2.0 dataset [24]. It's been trained on question-answer pairs, including unanswerable questions, for the task of Question Answering. Specifically, we used the tinyroberta-squad2 model. A further description and training data can be found on its Hugginface card model [3].

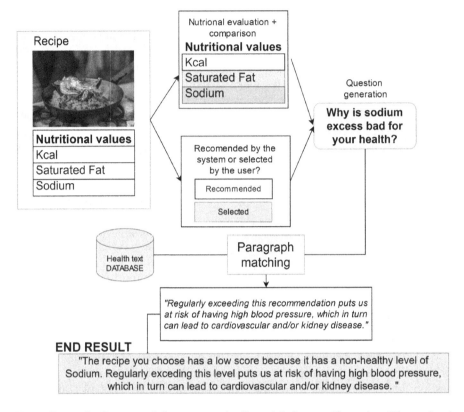

Fig. 2. Example diagram of the system pipeline with for specific recipe. The recipe is evaluated and a explanation on why it is not recommended/has a low score for the recommendation is generated.

4 Results

In this section, we present the main results of the proposed system in the article. Initially, we selected a corpus of medical texts described in Sect. 3. We used NHI [1], EFSA [6] and EUFIC [2,4] as the text corpora.

We selected a representative group of 5 Spanish recipes from RECIPEDB [10] with their nutritional values, and we computed the percentages associated with the chosen nutrients for all the recipes.

For the micronutrients, we made a selection based on three main reasons: the existence of reference material on both pages, the characteristics that differentiate one recipe from another, and finally, a selection that represents different nutrients with different nature (vitamins, minerals, macros, etc.). Finally, the selection is composed of: Calcium, Fiber, Iron, Magnesium, Potassium, Sodium, Vitamin C, and Saturated Fats. The values that determine the generator's preference for one micronutrient or another are based on the recommended daily amounts, the FSA scores in the case of sodium and saturated fats [19], and the comparative amount with respect to the rest of the recipes.

Table 1. Results table for the explainable recommendation based on micronutrient information

Nutrient selected	Generated question	Answers fom the text	Appropiate?
calcium	Why is calcium beneficial to be healthy if you are adult?	calcium is particularly important to growing healthy and strong bones, making it a key mineral during periods of fast growth and development	Educative and specific
fibre	Why is fibre beneficial to be healthy if you are adult?	Improves bowel movements and reduces transit time of food in the digestive tract	Educative and specific
Vitamin C	Why is vitamin c beneficial to be healthy if you are adult?	it helps our bodies make key hormones and neurotransmitters that keep the healthy functioning of our brain and nervous system	Educative and specific
Magnesium	Why is magnesium beneficial to be healthy if you are adult?	One of the key roles of magnesium is to make sure that our cells have enough energy to perform their roles	Educative and specific
potassium	Why is potassium beneficial to be healthy if you are adult?	Potassium is one of the major minerals, which our bodies need in relatively larger amounts to keep healthy	Not specific

We have focused on generate two different type of questions: one centered on obtaining justifications for a given recommendation (Table 1) and the other centered on the specific evaluation of a choice (Table 2). The first case would correspond to a system recommendation, while the second would focus on obtaining a criterion to explain the high or low score of specific changes in a recommended menu. A complete example can be seen in Fig. 2.

Table 2. Results table for the explainable evaluating based on micronutrient information differentiation from deviation up and down from the health average.

Nutrient selected	Generated question	Answers from the text	Appropriate?
Sodium excess	Why is sodium excess harmful for health ?	diets high in salt (sodium chloride) can reduce the levels of calcium in our bodies, even if we regularly include good amounts of calcium in our diets	Educative and specific
Iron deficit	Why is Iron deficit harmful for health?	While iron deficiency can affect our health at any age, it's particularly concerning during pregnancy and childhood, as it can impair the child's growth and development, particularly their cognitive development	Educative and but not specific
Vitamin C excess	Why is vitamin c excess harmful for health ?	Taking too much vitamin C can cause diarrhea, nausea, and stomach cramps	Educative and specific
Saturated Fat excess	Why is saturated fat excess harmful for health?	Evidence supporting a benefit for reducing the amount of saturated fat we eat is based on whether this in turn reduces the levels of LDL cholesterol	Not educative but specific

The process of obtaining the question-answer pairs is the key aspect of our system. As we stated before, the question generation and answers would help users understand the inner working of the system. Therefore, we have added a evaluation on how specific or educative are the answers found.

We checked that there were multiple answers to the questions in the corpus. The system was able to found most of them, except on Iron were the wording of the question and the text were different. Also, some of the answers, like Potassium were too unspecific. Adding more sources to the text database will help to alleviate this issue. As well as evaluate a top-n answers choosing the best one.

Examples for the highlighted micronutrients can be seen in Tables 1 and 2. In all cases except one, the system was able to find one or several educational and interpretable justifications in the text, which could be transformed into final feedback for the user.

5   Conclusions and Future Work

In this paper, we have presented a pipeline that allows us to translate users doubts about recommendations into natural language questions. We then used those question to obtain a corpus of natural-language explanations based on heterogeneous expert's documents. Specifically, we have focused on a case of great relevance: the health-based nutritional recommendation. Not only it a really cultural-driven decision but also because this recommendation is often multi-objective, which further complicates the generation of useful explanations for the user.

We believe that this work constitutes an interesting first step in the use of current NLP techniques to improve the explainability of multi-objective recommender systems. We have focused our work on well-known situations to show that the system can produce valuable output. But as novel approaches in nutrition take place (microbiome-based [23] or genomics [32]) we will need bigger source of scientific ground truth for our explanations. For this reason a non-supervised approach allows us to use a large number of texts of heterogeneous nature that are already available. Finally, we consider this first work as a foundational piece in the necessary next steps to be taken:

1. Recommendation-Justification Corpus. If we look at the natural output of the system, we find recommendation-answer pairs but also nutritional-question-answer pairs. These two corpora can be enlarged to constitute a proper dataset on which to train the appropriate language models or to perform fine-tuning on them, reducing the suggested pipeline.
2. Our results lead us to believe that the model can be integrated into the usual recommendation pipeline with an even larger corpus of recipes or even menus, as well as different characteristics. This is a step that the authors would like to explore as a natural next step, as modern NLP techniques are powerfull enough to produce question-answering systems about our recommendations in chat-based nature.
3. Finally, this process can help us to understand and improve the explanations given to the subjects. This work is the first step to design psychological studies focusing on what kind of explanations are more useful when recommending complete menus based on the health of the user. Similarly, it would be interesting to analyze the level of user satisfaction not only based on the

recommendations provided but also based on the explanations given by the system.

Acknowledgements. We would like to acknowledge support for this work from the Grants: Grant PID2021-123960OB-I00 funded by MCIN/AEI/ 10.13039/501100011033 and by ERDF A way of making Europe and Grant TED2021-129402B-C21 funded by MCIN/AEI/ 10.13039/501100011033 and, by the European Union NextGenerationEU/PRTR.

Funding Information. In addition, this research has been partially supported by the Ministry of Universities through the EU-funded Margarita Salas programme NextGenerationEU and the pre-competitive project of the Plan Propio of the "University of Granada".

References

1. Dietary Supplement Fact Sheets. https://ods.od.nih.gov/factsheets/list-all/
2. Eufic calcium factsheet. https://www.eufic.org/en/vitamins-and-minerals/article/calcium-foods-functions-how-much-do-you-need-more, (Accessed 23 Mar 2023)
3. Eufic fibre factsheet. https://huggingface.co/deepset/tinyroberta-squad2, (Accessed 23 Mar 2023)
4. Eufic fibre factsheet. https://www.eufic.org/en/whats-in-food/article/what-is-dietary-fibre-and-is-it-beneficial, (Accessed 23 Mar 2023)
5. sentence-transformers/multi-qa-mpnet-base-dot-v1. https://huggingface.co/sentence-transformers/multi-qa-mpnet-base-dot-v1, (Accessed 23 Mar 2023)
6. EFSA Panel on Dietetic Products, Nutrition and Allergies (NDA): Scientific opinion on dietary reference values for iron. EFSA J. **13**(10), 4254 (2015). https://doi.org/10.2903/j.efsa.2015.4254, https://efsa.onlinelibrary.wiley.com/doi/abs/10.2903/j.efsa.2015.4254
7. Adak, A., Pradhan, B., Shukla, N.: Sentiment analysis of customer reviews of food delivery services using deep learning and explainable artificial intelligence: Systematic review. Foods **11**(10), 1500 (2022)
8. Alcaraz-Herrera, H., Cartlidge, J., Toumpakari, Z., Western, M., Palomares, I.: Evorecsys: Evolutionary framework for health and well-being recommender systems. In: User Modeling and User-Adapted Interaction, pp. 1–39 (2022)
9. Baclic, O., Tunis, M., Young, K., Doan, C., Swerdfeger, H., Schonfeld, J.: Artificial intelligence in public health: challenges and opportunities for public health made possible by advances in natural language processing. Can. Commun. Dis. Rep. **46**(6), 161 (2020)
10. Batra, D., et al.: RecipeDB: a resource for exploring recipes. Database 2020 (Jan 2020). https://doi.org/10.1093/database/baaa077
11. Beaudouin, V., et al.: Flexible and context-specific AI explainability: a multidisciplinary approach. SSRN Electron. J. (2020). https://doi.org/10.2139/ssrn.3559477
12. Cay, G., et al.: Recent advancement in sleep technologies: a literature review on clinical standards, sensors, apps, and AI methods. IEEE Access (2022)
13. Chen, H.K., Chen, F.H., Lin, S.F.: An AI-based exercise prescription recommendation system. Appl. Sci. **11**(6), 2661 (2021)

14. Comerford, K.B., Miller, G.D., Boileau, A.C., Masiello Schuette, S.N., Giddens, J.C., Brown, K.A.: Global review of dairy recommendations in food-based dietary guidelines. Front. Nutr. **8**, 671999 (2021)
15. Correia, A., Kim, S., Kozak, M.: Gastronomy experiential traits and their effects on intentions for recommendation: a fuzzy set approach. Int. J. Tour. Res. **22**(3), 351–363 (2020)
16. Das, A., Rad, P.: Opportunities and challenges in explainable artificial intelligence (xai): A survey. arXiv preprint arXiv:2006.11371 (2020)
17. Duarte, A., Belo, O.: Blending case-based reasoning with ontologies for adapting diet menus and physical activities. In: Intelligent Systems and Applications: Proceedings of the 2022 Intelligent Systems Conference (IntelliSys), vol. 3, pp. 829–843. Springer (2022). https://doi.org/10.1007/978-3-031-16075-2_60
18. Ehsan, U., Liao, Q.V., Muller, M., Riedl, M.O., Weisz, J.D.: Expanding explainability: towards social transparency in AI systems. In: Proceedings of the 2021 CHI Conference on Human Factors in Computing Systems. ACM (6 May 2021). https://doi.org/10.1145/3411764.3445188
19. Elsweiler, D., Trattner, C., Harvey, M.: Exploiting food choice biases for healthier recipe recommendation. In: Proceedings of the 40th International ACM SIGIR Conference on Research and Development in Information Retrieval, SIGIR 2017, pp. 575–584. , Association for Computing Machinery, New York (2017). https://doi.org/10.1145/3077136.3080826
20. Fernandez-Basso, C., Gutiérrez-Batista, K., Morcillo-Jiménez, R., Vila, M.A., Martin-Bautista, M.J.: A fuzzy-based medical system for pattern mining in a distributed environment: application to diagnostic and co-morbidity. Appl. Soft Comput. **122**, 108870 (2022)
21. Gade, K., Geyik, S.C., Kenthapadi, K., Mithal, V., Taly, A.: Explainable AI in industry. In: Proceedings of the 25th ACM SIGKDD International Conference on Knowledge Discovery &; Data Mining. ACM (25 Jul 2019). https://doi.org/10.1145/3292500.3332281
22. Haytowitz, D.B., et al.: Usda national nutrient database for standard reference, legacy release. Database (17 Mar 2023). https://data.nal.usda.gov/dataset/usda-national-nutrient-database-standard-reference-legacy-release
23. Hinojosa-Nogueira, D., et al.: Development of an unified food composition database for the European project "Stance4Health". Nutrients **13**(12), 4206 (2021). https://doi.org/10.3390/nu13124206, https://www.mdpi.com/2072-6643/13/12/4206
24. Hulburd, E.: Exploring bert parameter efficiency on the stanford question answering dataset v2. 0. arXiv preprint arXiv:2002.10670 (2020)
25. Lin, Q., Li, T., Shakeel, P.M., Samuel, R.D.J.: Advanced artificial intelligence in heart rate and blood pressure monitoring for stress management. J. Ambient. Intell. Humaniz. Comput. **12**, 3329–3340 (2021)
26. Matheny, M., Israni, S.T., Ahmed, M., Whicher, D.: Artificial intelligence in health care: The hope, the hype, the promise, the peril. National Academy of Medicine, Washington, DC (2019)
27. Mittelstadt, B., Russell, C., Wachter, S.: Explaining explanations in AI. In: Proceedings of the Conference on Fairness, Accountability, and Transparency. ACM (29 Jan 2019). https://doi.org/10.1145/3287560.3287574
28. Ortiz Viso, B.: Evolutionary approach in recommendation systems for complex structured objects. In: Proceedings of the 14th ACM Conference on Recommender Systems, pp. 776–781 (2020)

29. Patil, A., Rao, D., Utturwar, K., Shelke, T., Sarda, E.: Body posture detection and motion tracking using AI for medical exercises and recommendation system. In: ITM Web of Conferences, vol. 44, p. 03043. EDP Sciences (2022)
30. Pecune, F., Callebert, L., Marsella, S.: A recommender system for healthy and personalized recipes recommendations. In: HealthRecSys@ RecSys, pp. 15–20 (2020)
31. Preece, A.: Asking 'Why' in AI: explainability of intelligent systems - perspectives and challenges. Intell. Syst. Account. Finan Manag. **25**(2), 63–72 (2018). https://doi.org/10.1002/isaf.1422
32. Rajesh, S., Varanavasiappan, S.S.V.R.: Nutrigenomics: insights and implications for genome-based nutrition. In: Conceptualizing Plant-Based Nutrition: Bioresources, Nutrients Repertoire and Bioavailability, pp. 207–230. Springer (2022). https://doi.org/10.1007/978-981-19-4590-8_10
33. Reimers, N., Gurevych, I.: Sentence-bert: sentence embeddings using siamese bert-networks. In: Proceedings of the 2019 Conference on Empirical Methods in Natural Language Processing. Association for Computational Linguistics (Nov 2019). http://arxiv.org/abs/1908.10084
34. Reimers, N., Gurevych, I.: Making monolingual sentence embeddings multilingual using knowledge distillation. In: Proceedings of the 2020 Conference on Empirical Methods in Natural Language Processing. Association for Computational Linguistics (Nov 2020). https://arxiv.org/abs/2004.09813
35. Reinders, M.J., Starke, A.D., Fischer, A.R.H., Verain, M.C.D., Doets, E.L., Van Loo, E.J.: Determinants of consumer acceptance and use of personalized dietary advice: a systematic review. Trends Food Sci. Technol. **131**, 277–294 (2023). https://doi.org/10.1016/j.tifs.2022.12.008, https://www.sciencedirect.com/science/article/pii/S0924224422004782
36. Shandilya, R., Sharma, S., Wong, J.: Mature-food: food recommender system for mandatory feature choices a system for enabling digital health. Int. J. Inform. Manag. Data Insights **2**(2), 100090 (2022)
37. Toledo, R.Y., Alzahrani, A.A., Martinez, L.: A food recommender system considering nutritional information and user preferences. IEEE Access **7**, 96695–96711 (2019)
38. Tran, T.N.T., Felfernig, A., Trattner, C., Holzinger, A.: Recommender systems in the healthcare domain: state-of-the-art and research issues. J. Intel. Inform. Syst. **57**, 171–201 (2021)
39. Trattner, C., Rokicki, M., Herder, E.: On the relations between cooking interests, hobbies and nutritional values of online recipes: Implications for health-aware recipe recommender systems. In: Adjunct Publication of the 25th Conference on User Modeling, Adaptation and Personalization, pp. 59–64 (2017)
40. Visser, M., Gosens, I., Bard, D., van Broekhuizen, P., Janer, G., Kuempel, E., Riediker, M., Vogel, U., Dekkers, S.: Towards health-based nano reference values (HNRVS) for occupational exposure: recommendations from an expert panel. NanoImpact **26**, 100396 (2022)
41. Warstadt, A., Zhang, Y., Li, H.S., Liu, H., Bowman, S.R.: Learning which features matter: Roberta acquires a preference for linguistic generalizations (eventually). arXiv preprint arXiv:2010.05358 (2020)
42. Watson, N.F., Fernandez, C.R.: Artificial intelligence and sleep: advancing sleep medicine. Sleep Med. Rev. **59**, 101512 (2021)
43. Wilson-Barnes, S., et al.: Personalised nutrition for healthy living: the protein project. Nutr. Bull. **46**(1), 77–87 (2021)

44. World Health Organization: Vitamin and mineral requirements in human nutrition. Tech. rep., World Health Organization (2004), https://apps.who.int/iris/handle/10665/42716, iSBN: 9789241546126 number-of-pages: 341
45. Zhang, Y., Weng, Y., Lund, J.: Applications of explainable artificial intelligence in diagnosis and surgery. Diagnostics **12**(2), 237 (2022)

Are Textual Recommendations Enough? Guiding Physicians Toward the Design of Machine Learning Pipelines Through a Visual Platform

Andrea Vázquez-Ingelmo[1]([✉]) [iD], Alicia García-Holgado[1] [iD],
Francisco José García-Peñalvo[1] [iD], Pablo Pérez-Sánchez[2] [iD], Pablo Antúnez-Muiños[2],
Antonio Sánchez-Puente[2] [iD], Víctor Vicente-Palacios[3] [iD],
Pedro Ignacio Dorado-Díaz[4] [iD], and Pedro Luis Sánchez[5]

[1] GRIAL Research Group, Computer Science Department, Universidad de Salamanca, Salamanca, Spain
{andreavazquez,aliciagh,fgarcia}@usal.es

[2] CIBERCV and Biomedical Research Institute of Salamanca (IBSAL), University Hospital of Salamanca, Salamanca, Spain
{pperezsanc,pantunezm,asanchezpu}@saludcastillayleon.es

[3] Philips Clinical Science, Western Europe, Valencia, Spain
victor.vicente.palacios@philips.com

[4] Biomedical Research Institute of Salamanca (IBSAL) and University of Salamanca, Statistics Department, Salamanca, Spain
acho@usal.es

[5] University Hospital of Salamanca, CIBERCV, Biomedical Research Institute of Salamanca (IBSAL) and University of Salamanca, Cardiology Department, Salamanca, Spain
plsanchez@saludcastillayleon.es
https://ror.org/02f40zc51

Abstract. The prevalence of artificial intelligence (AI) in our daily lives is often exaggerated by the media, leading to a positive public perception while overlooking potential problems. In the field of medicine, it is crucial to educate future healthcare professionals on the advantages and disadvantages of AI and to emphasize the importance of creating fair, ethical, and reproducible models. The KoopaML platform was developed to provide an educational and user-friendly interface for inexperienced users to create AI pipelines. This study analyzes the quantitative and interaction data gathered from a usability test involving physicians from the University Hospital of Salamanca, with the aim of identifying new interaction paradigms to improve the platform's usability. The results shown that the platform is difficult to learn for inexperienced users due to its contents related to AI. Following these results, a set of improvements are proposed for the next version of KoopaML, focusing on reducing the interactions needed to create the pipelines.

Keywords: Information system · Medical data management · Artificial Intelligence · Health platform · HCI · Usability · SUS

© Springer Nature Switzerland AG 2023
H. L. Larsen et al. (Eds.): FQAS 2023, LNAI 14113, pp. 247–255, 2023.
https://doi.org/10.1007/978-3-031-42935-4_20

1 Introduction

Artificial intelligence is present in our daily lives, however media coverage is not always realistic and exacerbates its capabilities [1, 2]. This media attention makes the public's perception of AI positive and overlooks the problems it can cause [3].

It is certain that AI is becoming increasingly present in our daily lives, and medicine is no exception [4]. For this reason, it is important to provide future medical students and healthcare professionals with adequate education in this regard [5]. And despite the fact that future doctors are not afraid of being replaced by AI [6], it is important to let them know its pros and cons [7]. It is also important for clinicians to be aware of the importance of using or creating models that are fair [8], ethical [9] and reproducible [10].

In order to train inexperienced users in all the above-mentioned points, the KoopaML platform was created [11–13]. The main objectives of this platform are (1) to provide a visual and intuitive interface and (2) to offer an educational AI experience. To develop the platform to the needs of inexperienced users, their feedback is necessary.

This work presents the quantitative and interaction analysis results of KoopaML of a usability study involving physicians from the University Hospital of Salamanca. The analysis of the results aims at identifying new interaction paradigms to solve the issues arisen during the usability test.

The rest of this work is organized as follows. Section 2 provides an overview of the KoopaML platform. Section 3 describes the methodology followed for the usability test and analysis. Section 4 presents the test results, while Sect. 5 discusses the results and proposes new methods to interact with the ML pipelines to address the encountered issues.

2 Background

KoopaML [11–13] is conceived as a platform with two main goals; (1) to ease and automate the generation and execution of ML pipelines, and (2) to offer a learning experience to non-expert users on the basics of ML while leveraging its benefits.

These goals are tackled through a graphical interface inspired in building blocks, in which users can add, connect, and execute ML tasks transparently, without programming expertise. Figure 1 shows a pipeline example in which a Logistic Regression algorithm is trained with an input dataset (in dark blue).

Although the platform has allowed the automatization of ML pipelines visually, it is still complex to address their design with no expertise. For these reasons, in previous works, we have included a new feature: a textual recommendation engine that yields information about the potential steps to take given the current state of the workspace (type of ML nodes included, current connections, etc.).

This recommendation engine was included in the workspace in the form of a modal box (Fig. 2, bottom), and the textual recommendations can be easily modified by privileged users (experts) to include new heuristics or explanations.

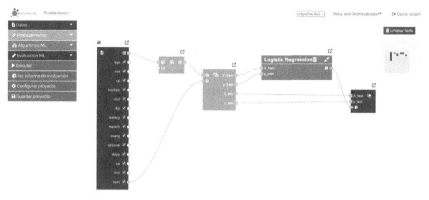

Fig. 1. The KoopaML platform (contents in Spanish).

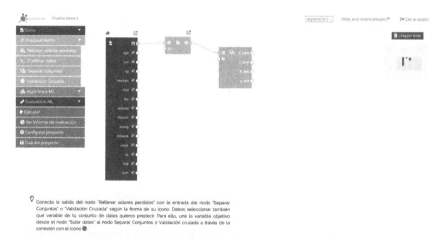

Fig. 2. Recommendation engine (contents in Spanish). In this case, the textual recommendation is explaining how to use the "Test/Train Split" node, and what is the goal of splitting the input dataset.

3 Methodology

A user testing was conducted to test the usability and find issues related to the user experience in KoopaML. The study was conducted with **8 physicians** (with low or no expertise in ML) by using the **think-aloud method** [14, 15], with the goal of analyzing the interactions performed by the users while using KoopaML.

Every participant was introduced to the tool and to the basic concepts of ML through the following video (contents in Spanish): https://www.youtube.com/watch?v=JeQrz2 I20TY. The think-aloud method was complemented with a quantitative analysis of the perceived usability.

3.1 Interaction Analysis

The user interactions were captured through Hotjar (https://hotjar.com), a digital data analysis tool that allows the visualization of heatmaps and even recordings of the interactions carried out by the users during the testing. The analysis of interaction allows to better understand the decisions taken by the users while carrying out simple tasks in the platform.

3.2 Perceived Usability Evaluation

For the quantitative analysis, the System Usability Scale was selected as the instrument to assess the platform's perceived usability (SUS). The SUS questionnaire offers a practical, reliable, and valid [16, 17] method for rating a system's usability, and it can be used with different categories of systems [18].

The items of the questionnaires are positive and negative alternated and rated on a 1 to 5 Likert scale [19].

The instrument was implemented using a customized version of LimeSurvey (https://www.limesurvey.org), an Open-Source on-line survey web application.

The interpretation of the results is guided by the System Usability Scale benchmarks [20, 21] which allow SUS score comparisons and provide useful insights about the perceived usability of the system.

4 Results

The qualitative results provided beneficial insights into the current interface of KoopaML. The interaction heatmaps obtained from Hotjar enabled us to understand the parts of the interface that were more prone to interactions and the differences between users that had the textual recommendations enabled and those who did not.

Figure 3 shows one of these heatmaps. In this case, the participant did not have textual recommendations during the study. It is possible to observe that the participant spent more time navigating through the side menu than interacting with and constructing the pipeline. The evaluation shown the same pattern for almost every user, as they were unsure about which node needed to be included into the workspace in order to complete the ML pipeline.

Figure 4, on the other hand, also shows a high number of interactions on the side menu. But in this case, with the textual recommendations enabled, participants could interact more with the pipeline as the system guided the process through the suggestions. However, although a difference between the participants with the recommendation engine can be identified, most participants did not finish the task successfully, leaving the pipeline incomplete despite the system support.

Regarding the quantitative results, six participants that took part in the think-aloud evaluation answered the survcy. Although a small samplc, it allows to complement the analysis of the results obtained in the qualitative assessment and to get deeper insights.

The guidelines from [19] were followed to compute the SUS score. In this case, the score contributions from each item were added. Given that each item's score must range

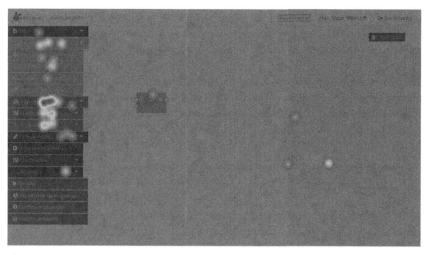

Fig. 3. Heatmap of the interactions made by a participant with the recommendation engine disabled. Obtained through Hotjar.

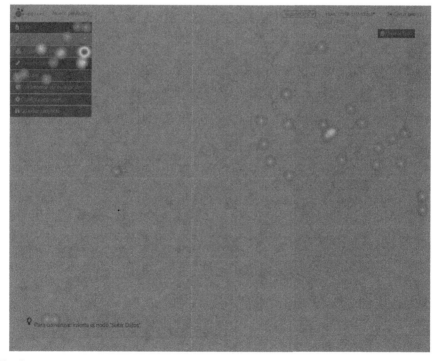

Fig. 4. Heatmap of the interactions made by a participant with the recommendation engine enabled. Obtained through Hotjar.

from 0 to 4, the positive items of the questionnaire were subtracted 1 point, while the negative items' scores were subtracted from 5, to normalize the sample. The sum of the scores is finally multiplied by 2.5 to obtain the overall value of the SUS between 0 to 100.

The SUS score was calculated following the scoring instructions [19] for every participant's responses. The SUS questionnaire also enables the computation of a learnability score (from items 4 and 10) and a usability score (from questions 1, 2, 3, 5, 6, 7, 8, and 9). Both scores were also calculated and transformed to fit a scale from 0 to 100. The following results were obtained for the KoopaML platform (Fig. 5):

- The average perceived usability of the KoopaML platform is **62.5**, which is considered a borderline acceptable SUS score (interpretation based on the studies done in [20, 21]).
- On the other hand, the perceived usability is significantly higher (**70.31**) than the learnability (**31.25**), which indicates that the platform is complex to learn.

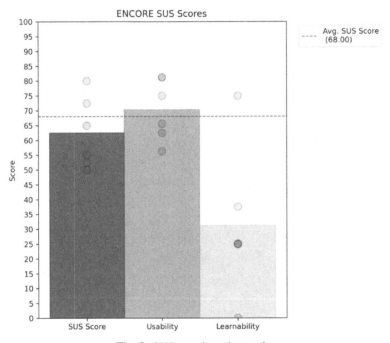

Fig. 5. SUS questionnaire results.

5   Improvements Proposal and Conclusions

Based on the previous qualitative validation and following the SUS results, it is possible to affirm that, although textual recommendations offer support to some extent, the platform is still complex, especially for non-expert users.

This issue is confirmed by the learnability score obtained from the SUS questionnaire. In fact, the usability score (70.31) is considered a "good" score following the SUS interpretation guidelines, however, the learnability (31.25) of the system is poor and not acceptable, which has impacted the overall SUS score (62.5).

The consequences of the learnability score can be observed in the interaction analysis. As shown in Figs. 3 and 4, although the users that had the textual recommendations enabled (Fig. 4) performed more interactions in the workspace and more actions with the nodes, they were not able to create a functioning ML pipeline.

One of the theories of this performance is the location and format of the recommendations. The modal box containing the next steps to perform is at the bottom of the screen, which may provoke it to be overlooked. On the other hand, the textual recommendations can be lengthy even broken down into individual steps due to the complexity of the topic, so they can be considered hard-to-follow.

Regarding the side menu containing the toolbox for creating the ML pipelines, most of the users' interactions were concentrated in this area, meaning that users spent more time searching for the proper nodes than designing the pipeline. In addition, participants were confused about finding the right node to add to the pipeline.

Finally, even if participants included the right nodes to carry out the training of the ML algorithm, they could not properly connect the nodes to create the pipeline, resulting in errors.

After this evaluation, there is a list of improvements to be included in the new version of KoopaML (Fig. 6). The proposal is to provide the recommendations visually by constraining the nodes that can be connected to a specific ML task. This way, the connections can be made almost automatically, saving time for users from connecting each socket in each node.

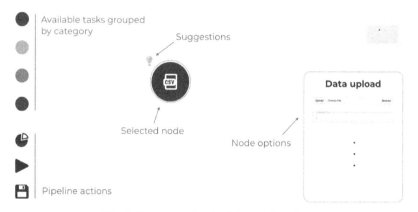

Fig. 6. Prototype sketch of the new interface.

Moreover, by using this graphical approach, the time spent on the side menu would be reduced due to the downsizing of the available nodes to connect. In this sense, nodes can be directly included through the selected node instead of going back and forth to the menu (Fig. 7).

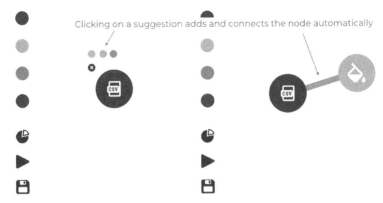

Fig. 7. Automatic connection of nodes based on suggestions.

These improvements are in the prototype phase. Future research lines will involve the implementation of the improvements in KoopaML and further testing to compare and measure the performance of the new version of the platform.

Acknowledgments. This research was partially funded by the Ministry of Science and Innovation through the AVisSA project grant number (PID2020-118345RB-I00). This work was also supported by competitive community grants (GRS 2033/A/19, GRS 2030/A/19, GRS 2031/A/19, GRS 2032/A/19) from the SACYL, Junta Castilla y León; by competitive national grants (PI14/00695, PIE14/00066, PI17/00145, DTS19/00098, PI19/00658, PI19/00656, PI21/00369) from the Institute of Health Carlos III, Spanish Ministry of Science and Innovation and co-funded by ERDF/ESF, "Investing in your future" and; by the CIBERCV (CB16/11/00374) from the Institute of Health Carlos III, Spanish Ministry of Science and Innovation.

References

1. Nemitz, P.: Constitutional democracy and technology in the age of artificial intelligence. Philosophical Trans. Roy. Soc. A Math. Phys. Eng. Sci. **376**, 20180089 (2018)
2. Brennen, J.: An industry-led debate: How UK media cover artificial intelligence (2018)
3. Fast, E., Horvitz, E.: Long-term trends in the public perception of artificial intelligence. In: Proceedings of the AAAI Conference on Artificial Intelligence (Year)
4. Secinaro, S., Calandra, D., Secinaro, A., Muthurangu, V., Biancone, P.: The role of artificial intelligence in healthcare: a structured literature review. BMC Med. Inform. Decis. Mak. **21**, 1–23 (2021)
5. Kolachalama, V.B.: Machine learning and pre-medical education. Artif. Intell. Med. **129**, 102313 (2022)
6. Pinto dos Santos, D., et al.: Medical students' attitude towards artificial intelligence: a multicentre survey. Europ. Radiol. **29**, 1640–1646 (2019)
7. Carbone, M.R.: When not to use machine learning: A perspective on potential and limitations. MRS Bulletin 1–7 (2022)
8. Pfohl, S., Xu, Y., Foryciarz, A., Ignatiadis, N., Genkins, J., Shah, N.: Net benefit, calibration, threshold selection, and training objectives for algorithmic fairness in healthcare. In: 2022 ACM Conference on Fairness, Accountability, and Transparency, pp. 1039–1052 (Year)

9. Prabhakaran, V., Mitchell, M., Gebru, T., Gabriel, I.: A Human Rights-Based Approach to Responsible AI. arXiv preprint arXiv:2210.02667 (2022)

10. Kapoor, S., Narayanan, A.: Leakage and the reproducibility crisis in ML-based science. arXiv preprint arXiv:2207.07048 (2022)

11. Vázquez-Ingelmo, A., et al.: Bringing machine learning closer to non-experts: proposal of a user-friendly machine learning tool in the healthcare domain. Ninth International Conference on Technological Ecosystems for Enhancing Multiculturality (TEEM'21), pp. 324–329. Association for Computing Machinery, Barcelona, Spain (2021)

12. García-Peñalvo, F.J., et al.: KoopaML: a graphical platform for building machine learning pipelines adapted to health professionals. International Journal of Interactive Multimedia and Artificial Intelligence (In Press)

13. García-Holgado, A., et al.: User-centered design approach for a machine learning platform for medical purpose. In: HCI-COLLAB 2021, pp. 237–249. Springer, Cham (2021). Doi: .https://doi.org/10.1007/978-3-030-92325-9_18

14. Jääskeläinen, R.: Think-aloud protocol. Handbook of translation studies **1**, 371–374 (2010)

15. Van Someren, M., Barnard, Y.F., Sandberg, J.: The think aloud method: a practical approach to modelling cognitive. London: AcademicPress 11, pp. 29–41 (1994)

16. Brooke, J.: SUS: a retrospective. J. Usability Stud. **8**, 29–40 (2013)

17. Tullis, T.S., Stetson, J.N.: A comparison of questionnaires for assessing website usability. In: Usability Professional Association Conference, pp. 1–12 (Year)

18. Bangor, A., Kortum, P.T., Miller, J.T.: An empirical evaluation of the system usability scale. Intl. J. Human-Comput. Inter. **24**, 574–594 (2008)

19. Brooke, J.: SUS-A quick and dirty usability scale. Usability Evaluation Ind. **189**, 4–7 (1996)

20. Bangor, A., Kortum, P., Miller, J.: Determining what individual SUS scores mean: adding an adjective rating scale. J. Usability Stud. **4**, 114–123 (2009)

21. Sauro, J.: A practical guide to the system usability scale: Background, benchmarks & best practices. Createspace Independent Pub, Scotts Valley, CA, US (2011)

Who Is to Blame? Responsibility Attribution in AI Systems vs Human Agents in the Field of Air Crashes

Jesica Gómez-Sánchez[1,2(✉)] (iD), Cristina Gordo[3] (iD), Matija Franklin[2] (iD),
Carlos Fernandez-Basso[2,4] (iD), and David Lagnado[2] (iD)

[1] Department of Developmental and Educational Psychology, Faculty of Psychology,
University of Granada, Granada, Spain
`gomezjs@ugr.es`
[2] Causal Cognition Lab, Division of Psychology and Language Sciences,
University College London, London, UK
`{jesica.gomez,matija.franklin,carlos.basso,d.lagnado}@ucl.ac.uk`
[3] Department of Psychology, Campus Universitario Las Lagunillas,
University of Jaén, Jaén, Spain
`cggordo@ujaen.es`
[4] Research Centre for Information and Communications Technologies (CITIC-UGR),
University of Granada, 18014 Granada, Spain
`cjferba@decsai.ugr.es`

Abstract. This study aims to explore how adults assign responsibility to different agents-both Artificial Intelligence (AI) systems and human beings-in the context of an airplane crash, based on factors of criticality and pivotality. Criticality is related to the perceived importance of an agent's actions in achieving an outcome (prospective judgements), while pivotality examines the degree to which the agent's actions contributed to the actual outcome (retrospective judgements). Our results replicate previous findings, demonstrating that participants are sensitive to both factors. They rate agents involved in a conjunctive structure as more critical than those in a disjunctive one. Similarly, agents are held more responsible when their errors are completely pivotal to the crash. Interestingly, participants attribute more responsibility to human beings than to AI systems, but this trend is only observed in trials where the pivotality is reduced.

Keywords: AI Responsibility · Causal Cognition · Pivotality · Criticality

1 Introduction

As artificial intelligence (AI) permeates various aspects of society, it has become increasingly crucial to examine the ethical implications of AI-driven decision-making [18]. One particularly important aspect of this discourse is the attribution of blame and responsibility when AI agents cause harm or make morally significant decisions [8]. This article delves into the dynamics of blame attribution towards AI agents - autonomous artificial agents capable of making decisions, often unpredictable by their creators and users [6]. AI today is being used in many domains,

© Springer Nature Switzerland AG 2023
H. L. Larsen et al. (Eds.): FQAS 2023, LNAI 14113, pp. 256–264, 2023.
https://doi.org/10.1007/978-3-031-42935-4_21

including hiring [19], health care [4], parole [17], and autonomous vehicles [20]. Some of today's examples include Artificial Intelligence (AI) contributing to decisions on parole [17], hiring [19], and health care [4].

By dissecting the intricacies of blame allocation and exploring the dimensions of the AI Responsibility Gap, this research seeks to provide critical insights into the moral and ethical landscape of AI, ultimately contributing to the development of robust frameworks for accountability in an increasingly AI-driven world.

The diverse spectrum of AI systems encompasses an array of categories, extending from narrow or weak AI, which is tailored to execute specialized tasks such as image recognition, to general or strong AI, characterized by its capacity to undertake a broad scope of assignments and exhibit human-like cognitive capabilities [10]. As the intricacy of these AI systems augments, so too does the propensity for unforeseen ramifications, including but not limited to prejudiced decision-making processes, inaccuracies, or even detrimental consequences that may impact individuals or the broader societal fabric.

In instances where an artificial intelligence (AI) system engenders harm, the attribution of responsibility becomes a multifaceted endeavor encompassing a multitude of potential culpable parties [1,12]. These may comprise the AI system's developers, the organization responsible for its deployment, the end-users interacting with the system, and the regulatory entities that sanctioned its utilization. Moreover, an array of issues may arise, encompassing the data employed for training the AI system, the underlying algorithms instantiated within the system, and the methodologies governing its deployment and maintenance. These complexities contribute to the emergence of the AI Responsibility Gap, a phenomenon that underscores the challenges in ascertaining and allocating responsibility in the context of AI-driven outcomes [16].

The ascription of responsibility in AI-related incidents is rendered increasingly intricate by the inherent opaqueness or "black-box" nature of certain AI systems, signifying that the elucidation of decision-making processes or actions undertaken by the system frequently proves elusive [5]. This absence of transparency exacerbates the challenge of discerning culpability in instances where harm is engendered by the system [2], further accentuating the necessity for a comprehensive examination of responsibility allocation within the rapidly evolving sphere of artificial intelligence [7].

1.1   Related Work

Establishing causation is a fundamental prerequisite for the assignment of responsibility. Nevertheless, an agent might instigate a result without being held accountable for it. For instance, although an AI system may induce an event, the blame may be attributed to the AI user. One theoretical framework posits that, during the attribution of blame, individuals prospectively assess an agent's criticality, which refers to the degree of dependency of a particular outcome on the agent's action [13]. Additionally, individuals retrospectively evaluate an agent's pivotality, which denotes its causal contribution to the outcome. In the context of multiple agents, blame attributions are influenced by an agent's pivotality [9].

Ultimately, an agent's position within a causal chain affects causal inference, with agents provoking later events perceived as more causally significant and deserving of blame [14].

Despite the capacity of AI systems to exhibit causal potency, engendering various states of affairs, the question of who ought to bear responsibility remains nebulous [11]. In contemporary years, this conundrum has been subject to empirical scrutiny and analysis.

Studies indicate that both role and causality influence the attribution of blame. In situations where a vehicle is under the shared control of a human and an AI driver, the machine is attributed with less blame and causality when both drivers commit an error [3]. This discrepancy in blame attribution remains absent in scenarios where one driver is assigned the driving task while the other is permitted to intervene. A congruent observation arises when an AI assumes the position of an advisor; physicians guided by AI advisors were deemed more culpable compared to those advised by human counterparts [21]. This trend persisted even when the AI advisor had the capacity to interfere with the doctor's decisions. Lastly, AI agents, in contrast to human agents, were anticipated to opt for utilitarian moral decisions and faced increased blame for not adhering to such choices [15].

1.2 This Study

The concept of pivotality in the attribution of responsibility vis-à-vis AI cases emerges from the growing incorporation of AI systems into consequential decision-making processes. For instance, AI applications permeate domains such as loan approvals, recruitment procedures, and even criminal justice sentencing. Should these systems be developed or deployed irresponsibly, they harbor the potential to perpetuate and exacerbate pre-existing biases and discriminatory practices, culminating in inequitable outcomes for individuals and collective entities.

Furthermore, the criticality of assigning responsibility in AI scenarios is underscored by the challenge of identifying and rectifying the harm engendered by AI systems. Consider, as an example, a biased hiring decision facilitated by an AI system; detecting the inherent bias might prove arduous, with the mitigation of the harm inflicted upon the unfairly rejected applicant presenting an even more formidable task. Consequently, ensuring that culpable parties are held accountable for AI-induced harm is paramount in preempting future harm and guaranteeing the administration of justice.

This study seeks to scrutinize the manner in which individuals attribute responsibility to various agents based on whether a human or an AI application bears responsibility for an airplane crash.

2 Method

2.1 Participants

A total of sixty-one students (12 male and 49 female) from the University of Jaén (age: M = 21.20; SD = 3.71) took part in the experiment. They participated in exchange for course credits. Participants were split into two experimental groups with thirty-two participants (6 male and 26 female) attributing responsibility to human agents, while the remaining twenty-nine participants (6 male and 23 female) attributing responsibility to AI agents.

2.2 Materials

To explore the attribution of responsibility in aviation mishap scenarios contingent upon whether human actors or AI applications are accountable for the operation, we devised two distinct questionnaires, diverging solely in the agent implicated in the plane crash (human beings vs. AI systems). Participants were provided with detailed information delineating the contributions of each human or AI system to the ultimate outcome of the flight.

There were four agents involved in each case. For the human condition, they were: 1) Plane A's pilot, 2) Plane B's pilot, 3) Air traffic controller, and 4) Radar technician. For the AI condition, they were: 1) Plane A's autopilot, 2) Plane B's autopilot, 3) AI air traffic control system, and 4) AI anti-collision system.

Participants were prompted to consider a specific agent, wherein the contributions of each agent were manipulated to demonstrate varying degrees of criticality and pivotality concerning the outcome. This approach allowed for an in-depth examination of how alterations in an agent's causal influence impacted the attribution of responsibility within the given context. In order to avoid a collision between both airplanes (A and B):

1. Either the anti-collision AI system or the air traffic control AI system (the radar technician or air traffic controller in the human being condition), must detect the risk of collision (with at least one of the two fulfilling this role) and provide instructions to the involved aircraft to adjust their positions accordingly.
2. The autopilots of the two aircraft (the pilots in the human being condition) must accurately implement the provided instructions in order to adjust their positions and thereby avert a collision. If either party commits an error, the airplanes will collide.

Consequently, the dual autopilots-or pilots-assume a fully critical role ($C = 1$) within a conjunctive structural relationship. In the event that either party fails to fulfill its duties, the aircraft will collide. Conversely, the AI anti-collision system and the AI air traffic control system (radar technician and air traffic controller in the human being condition), are situated within a disjunctive structural relationship ($C = 1/2$), highlighting the distinct causal dependencies in these complex aviation scenarios. Even if one of these fails in its duties, the collision can be avoided because its counterpart can correct the error.

Participants made two different judgments: 1) prospective judgments (criticality), which required them to estimate the level of importance of an agent's contribution in preventing the collision of the airplanes, and 2) retrospective judgments (pivotality), where they were asked to rate the level of responsibility of an agent for the crash.

During prospective judgment trials, the criticality of an agent's contribution was manipulated by asking participants about an agent embedded in either a conjunctive structure (C = 1), where its contribution was necessary to avoid the crash (pilots or autopilots in both planes), or a disjunctive structure ($C = \frac{1}{2}$), where its contribution was sufficient but not necessary to avoid the crash (the anticollision AI system and the air traffic control AI system or the radar technician and air traffic controller in the human condition).

In the retrospective judgements, we manipulated the agent's criticality and its pivotality for the outcome. Criticality was manipulated as in the prospective trials. Pivotality was manipulated by varying the number of agents that failed in their duties in each trial. In all trials, participants were informed that the two airplanes crashed, as negative outcomes are known to trigger causal reasoning.

Each questionnaire included twelve prospective (criticality) judgements trials and twelve retrospective (pivotality) judgements trials. Although the criticality judgements were prior to the pivotality judgments, the order in which each of the agents was asked about was randomized.

Participants used scales to provide their responses, with labels at the endpoints, ranging from "no important at all" to "very important" for criticality judgments and "no responsible at all" to "very responsible" for pivotality judgments. The scales ranged from 0 to 10.

2.3 Procedure

The study was conducted utilizing an online platform, where participants were randomly allocated to one of two experimental conditions (human beings vs. AI systems). The instructions provided in both conditions were identical, with the sole exception being the categorization of the four agents involved, thereby ensuring methodological consistency and the ability to make valid comparisons between conditions.

Participants were told that their task will be to assess and evaluate the importance and responsibility of each agent involved, considering their respective roles and contributions to the outcome, in order to discern the extent of accountability attributed to both human and AI agents.

Participants initially engaged in the criticality judgments, followed by an assessment of pivotality judgments, effectively examining the nuanced causal relationships and the extent of each agent's influence on the final outcome.

During the criticality judgments, participants were prompted to evaluate the significance of a particular agent in ensuring the successful completion of the flight. Subsequently, in the pivotality judgments, they were asked to assess the extent to which a specific agent was responsible for the occurrence of the crash.

3 Results

3.1 Prospective Judgements

Participants' responses to prospective judgements trials were submitted to an ANOVA 2 (criticality's value: 1, $\frac{1}{2}$) x 2 (agent: human being, AI system) with the first factor manipulated within participants and the second between groups. Results are shown in Table 1. The analysis revealed a main effect for criticality's value, $F(1, 59) = 10.74$, $p = .002$, $\eta2 = .15$. Participants rated as more critical the agent contribution in conjunctive ($C = 1$) than in disjunctive ($C = \frac{1}{2}$) condition trials. Neither the agent factor, $F(1, 59) = 0.01$, $p = .906$, $\eta2 = .01$, nor the interaction, $F(1, 59) = 0.01$, $p = .972$, $\eta2 = .01$, were significant.

Table 1. Participants means ratings in prospective and retrospective judgements in the function of the criticality and pivotality's value.

	Prospective judgements		Retrospective judgements		
	$C = 1$	$C = \frac{1}{2}$	$C = 1, P = 1$	$C = 1, P = \frac{1}{2}$	$C = \frac{1}{2}, P = 1$
Human	9.67 (0.88)	9.10 (1.41)	9.35 (1.25)	8.53 (1.24)	8.01 (2.08)
AI	9.65 (0.62)	9.07 (1.47)	9.30 (1.77)	7.11 (2.46)	7.12 (2.05)
Total	9.66 (0.76)	9.09 (1.42)	9.32 (1.51)	7.86 (2.04)	7.59 (2.09)

3.2 Retrospective Judgements

In order to check whether participants' retrospective judgements were sensitive to pivotality's value, we submitted their responses to constant condition ($C = 1; P = 1$) and pivotality reduced condition ($C = 1; P = 1/2$) to an ANOVA 2 (pivotality's value: 1, $\frac{1}{2}$) x (agent: human being, AI system) with the first factor manipulated within participants and the second between groups. Results are displayed in Table 1. The analysis showed a main effect of pivotality's value, $F(1, 59) = 47.59$, $p < .001$, $\eta2 = .44$: participants held the agent as more responsible in the trials where her/its error was pivotal to the plane crash than in those where a change was required to make her/it pivotal to the crash. Interestingly, the interaction between both factors was significant, $F(1, 59) = 10.16$, $p = .002$, $\eta2 = .14$. It was due to the fact that participants provided higher ratings when the target of judgements was a human being than when it was an AI system, but only in the pivotality reduced conditions trials, $t(59) = 2.88$, $p = .005$. In the constant condition trials there were no significant differences, $t(59) = 0.12$, $p = .899$. Nevertheless, it is important to note that in both tasks participants were sensitive to target pivotality's value: human task, $t(32) = 4.24$, $p < .001$, and AI task, $t(59) = 0.12$, $p = .899$.

Finally, to check the effect of criticality in participants' retrospective judgments, we performed the same analysis but now include their ratings to constant condition $(C = 1; P = 1)$ and criticality reduced condition $(C = \frac{1}{2}; P = 1)$. The analysis revealed an effect of criticality's value factor, $F(1, 59) = 43.61$, $p < .001$, $\eta 2 = .42$: participants held the target as more responsible when its contribution was necessary $(C = 1)$ than when it was sufficient $(C = \frac{1}{2})$ in spite of being pivotal for the crash in both cases $(P = 1)$. Neither the agent factor, $F(1, 59) = 1.52$, $p = .221$, $\eta 2 = .02$, nor the interaction, $F(1, 59) = 2.51$, $p = .118$, $\eta 2 = .04$, were significant.

4   Discussion

The results of the study offer valuable insights into participants' prospective and retrospective judgments concerning the criticality and pivotality of both human and AI agents in aviation scenarios.

In the prospective judgments, the main effect of criticality's value was found to be significant, indicating that participants regarded the agent contribution as more critical in conjunctive (C = 1) trials than in disjunctive (C = 1/2) trials. However, the agent factor and interaction were not significant.

For retrospective judgments, participants' responses revealed sensitivity to pivotality's value, with the agent being deemed more responsible when their error was pivotal to the crash. Notably, the interaction between pivotality's value and the agent was significant, attributable to higher ratings for human pilots in pivotality-reduced condition trials. Participants' sensitivity to target pivotality's value was observed in both human and AI tasks.

Lastly, an analysis examining the effect of criticality in retrospective judgments demonstrated a significant effect of criticality's value factor, with participants holding the target more responsible when its contribution was necessary (C = 1) than when it was sufficient (C = 1/2), despite being pivotal for the crash in both cases (P = 1). Neither the agent factor nor the interaction was significant.

The results of this study further our understanding of the factors that influence the attribution of responsibility in both prospective and retrospective judgments. In line with the theoretical framework proposed by [13], the findings indicate that participants indeed take into account the criticality of an agent's contribution when making prospective judgments. The significance of the main effect of criticality's value suggests that the degree to which an outcome depends on an agent's action plays a crucial role in the attribution of responsibility.

Moreover, the results support previous research by [9] on the influence of pivotality in retrospective judgments. Participants were found to be sensitive to pivotality's value, deeming an agent more responsible when their error was pivotal to the crash. This suggests that an agent's causal contribution to the outcome is an important factor in determining responsibility.

Interestingly, the significant interaction between pivotality's value and the agent in retrospective judgments, particularly with higher ratings for human pilots in pivotality-reduced condition trials, highlights a potential bias towards human agents. This finding implies that people may be more inclined to hold human pilots responsible for their errors as compared to AI systems, even when both agents have a reduced causal contribution to the outcome.

The last analysis further reinforces the importance of criticality in retrospective judgments. Participants held the target more responsible when its contribution was necessary rather than sufficient, even though it was pivotal for the crash in both cases. This finding is consistent with [14] work on causal inference and the perception of agents provoking later events as more causally significant and deserving of blame.

5   Conclusion

In conclusion, this study sheds light on the nuanced manner in which participants attribute responsibility to human and AI agents in complex aviation scenarios, underscoring the importance of understanding causal attributions in relation to criticality and pivotality. These findings have implications for the ongoing discourse surrounding AI ethics and accountability.

References

1. Ashton, H., Franklin, M.: The corrupting influence of AI as a boss or counterparty (2022)
2. Ashton, H., Franklin, M., Lagnado, D.: Testing a definition of intent for AI in a legal setting. Unpublished Manuscript (2022)
3. Awad, E., et al.: Blaming humans in autonomous vehicle accidents: shared responsibility across levels of automation. arXiv preprint arXiv:1803.07170 (2018)
4. Bates, D.W., Saria, S., Ohno-Machado, L., Shah, A., Escobar, G.: Big data in health care: using analytics to identify and manage high-risk and high-cost patients. Health Aff. **33**(7), 1123–1131 (2014)
5. Castelvecchi, D.: Can we open the black box of AI? Nat. News **538**(7623), 20 (2016)
6. Franklin, M., Ashton, H., Awad, E., Lagnado, D.: Causal framework of artificial autonomous agent responsibility. In: Proceedings of the 2022 AAAI/ACM Conference on AI, Ethics, and Society, pp. 276–284 (2022)
7. Franklin, M., Awad, E., Ashton, H., Lagnado, D.: Unpredictable robots elicit responsibility attributions. Behav. Brain Sci. **46**, e30 (2023)
8. Franklin, M., Awad, E., Lagnado, D.: Blaming automated vehicles in difficult situations. Iscience **24**(4), 102252 (2021)
9. Gerstenberg, T., Lagnado, D.A.: Spreading the blame: the allocation of responsibility amongst multiple agents. Cognition **115**(1), 166–171 (2010)
10. Gutierrez, C.I., Aguirre, A., Uuk, R., Boine, C.C., Franklin, M.: A proposal for a definition of general purpose artificial intelligence systems. Available at SSRN 4238951 (2022)
11. Johnson, D.G., Verdicchio, M.: AI, agency and responsibility: the vw fraud case and beyond. AI Soc. **34**(3), 639–647 (2019)

12. Köbis, N., Bonnefon, J.F., Rahwan, I.: Bad machines corrupt good morals. Nat. Hum. Behav. **5**(6), 679–685 (2021)
13. Lagnado, D., Gerstenberg, T.: A difference-making framework for intuitive judgments of responsibility. Oxford Stud. Agency Respons. **3**, 213–241 (2015)
14. Lagnado, D.A., Channon, S.: Judgments of cause and blame: the effects of intentionality and foreseeability. Cognition **108**(3), 754–770 (2008)
15. Malle, B.F., Scheutz, M., Arnold, T., Voiklis, J., Cusimano, C.: Sacrifice one for the good of many? people apply different moral norms to human and robot agents. In: 2015 10th ACM/IEEE International Conference on Human-Robot Interaction (HRI), pp. 117–124. IEEE (2015)
16. Matthias, A.: The responsibility gap: Ascribing responsibility for the actions of learning automata. Ethics Inf. Technol. **6**(3), 175–183 (2004)
17. Perry, W.L.: Predictive policing: The role of crime forecasting in law enforcement operations. Rand Corporation (2013)
18. Rahwan, I., et al.: Machine behaviour. Nature **568**(7753), 477–486 (2019)
19. Richtel, M.: How big data is playing recruiter for specialized workers, pp. 1–7, New York Times (2013)
20. Ruggeri, K., et al.: In with the new? generational differences shape population technology adoption patterns in the age of self-driving vehicles. J. Eng. Tech. Manage. **50**, 39–44 (2018)
21. Westcott, C., Lagnado, D.: The AI will see you now: Judgments of responsibility at the intersection of artificial intelligence and medicine (master's thesis). Unpublished Manuscript (2019)

Artificial Intelligence Law
and Regulation

Methodology for Analyzing the Risk of Algorithmic Discrimination from a Legal and Technical Point of View

Javier Valls-Prieto(✉) ⓘ

University of Granada, 18008 Granada, Spain
jvalls@ugr.es

Abstract. Artificial intelligence has been shown in different cases to produce discriminatory situations against vulnerable groups, be it based on gender or race. Analysing discrimination in real-life situations is already complicated, as there can be direct and indirect discrimination, which is not entirely clear, but there can also be discrimination that is justified. European legislation is developed ad hoc for different areas, but there are no homogeneous criteria for all cases. This, in addition to the fact that different technical and data processing factors increase the factors of discrimination, makes it very difficult to analyse whether discrimination has occurred.

So far, the analysis has focused on legislative and technical analysis to determine whether there has been algorithmic discrimination. However, the human factor in the development and use also plays a role. This is why a methodology of analysis is proposed that takes into account all these factors to ensure respect for the right to equality from the beginning of the creation of artificial intelligence, taking into account the technology to be applied, the context in which it is used, the operational phase of artificial intelligence and the subject that interacts with it, in order to respect the future European regulation of this technology and the ethical guidelines of the European Commission.

Keywords: Discrimination · Artificial Intelligence · Impact assessment · Equality right

1 Introduction

Equality and non-discrimination right is recognized since the French Revolution. Internationally, it has been enshrined in the International Convention on Civil and Political Rights in Article 26 of 1966. In Europe, the European Convention of Human Rights includes, in its article 14, the right to non-discrimination in particular cases: sex, race, color, language, religion, political, or other opinion, national or social origin, association with a national minority, property, birth or other status. Later, the European Union has introduced by the Treaty of Amsterdam in Article 13, which is now Article 19 of the TFEU, the non-discrimination principle, which reads as follow "Without prejudice to the other provisions of the Treaties and within the limits of the powers conferred by

© Springer Nature Switzerland AG 2023
H. L. Larsen et al. (Eds.): FQAS 2023, LNAI 14113, pp. 267–278, 2023.
https://doi.org/10.1007/978-3-031-42935-4_22

them upon the Union, the Council, acting unanimously in accordance with a special legislative procedure and after obtaining the consent of the European Parliament, may take appropriate action to combat discrimination based on sex, racial or ethnic origin, religion or belief, disability, age or sexual orientation". On this basis, the development of this right has been developed in several regulations that have tried to harmonize its content throughout the EU. Thus, we can find a variety of legal texts that regulate within a specific scope the content of this fundamental right, such as Council Directive 2000/43/EC of 29 June 2000 implementing the principle of equal treatment between persons irrespective of racial or ethnic origin, Council Directive 2000/78/EC of 27 November 2000 establishing a general framework for equal treatment in employment and occupation, Directive 2006/54/EC of the European Parliament and of the Council of 5 July 2006 on the implementation of the principle of equal opportunities and equal treatment of men and women in matters of employment and occupation (recast) [1] and Council Directive 2004/113/EC of 13 December 2004 implementing the principle of equal treatment between men and women in the access to and supply of goods and services [2]. If we add to this the jurisprudence of the ECtHR and the CJEU, we find ourselves with a very fragmented system of protection adapted to the specific field in which discrimination occurs, making it difficult to find a generalized solution [3].

The use of artificial intelligence, in certain contexts, presents a major challenge to the protection of equal and non-discriminatory treatment in today's world. Amazon's use of an intelligent system for hiring employees resulted in discrimination against women because the historical data used by the company was mostly male, in the engineering sector [4]. Something similar occurs with price discrimination. As Angwing et al. point out, in the case of Princeton Review, a company that offers tutoring services at a cost depending on the area in which one lives, areas with a higher population of Asians had to pay higher prices for the same service, having a clear racial bias [5].

But it is not only in the private sector, in the public administration there are also situations of discrimination through algorithms. An automated system for prioritizing access to housing for the homeless that was implemented in Los Angeles in 2013. The idea was to create a list of homeless people and classify them in order to sort the order in which housing solutions would be distributed. The vulnerability index was used as part of the prioritization tools. The system was fed with administrative data such as name, date of birth, immigration and residence information, and medical data on mental health. Once the information is managed with other social services databases, the candidates are classified with a level from 1 to 17 points. On the other hand, another system performs a count of the room opportunities that are free. A second algorithm identifies which people are at high risk of needing a specific solution. In the case of a waiver of the housing situation, a situation that does not always occur due to a voluntary waiver by the subject, the subject is scored downward to obtain a second housing solution. The program ended with a lack of resources for the houses and rooms, however, the data were kept. Over time, data was used by the Los Angeles police in the fight against crime, increasing the information on homeless people as possible criminals [6]. This brings us to the use of intelligent systems by the police to fight crime. The cases of COMPAS [7] and HART [8], in the USA and UK respectively, are well known for predicting crime and its consequences in the discrimination of racial groups and underprivileged classes. But it also discriminates against the victims of these crimes, as has been seen in the VIOGEN system [9]. A system that determines which women should be given police protection because of their risk of aggression when they have filed a complaint for domestic violence. Apart from the unreliability of the system, which has been in place for ten years and has not managed to reduce the number of assaults resulting in death, the use of the economic factor variable and the zip code to determine whether the risk is high and can be assigned surveillance stands out.

As we can see, discrimination by algorithms is possible, although data-driven decision making is considered to be fairer [3], and this leads us to analyze in the following point why it occurs.

2   Algorithmic Discrimination

To understand how more sophisticated artificial intelligence techniques, such as ML or deep learning, can produce discrimination, we will focus on two papers that describe it. The first is the work of Barocas and Selbst, where, based on the data feeding the system, they find five levels of bias. They start with the concepts of target variables and class labels. The first ones are a subjective exercise by the person in charge of determining the objectives of the intelligent system. With these target variables, the system will proceed to execute the system to achieve the objectives. The definition of these initial target variables is complicated, especially when the problem to be solved is not binary. Concepts such as good employee are not easy to transfer since "good" will depend on a subjective interpretation of the person in charge of making the decision. In this case, the person may want to define the target variable using other variables, for example, employee ratings over the past five years, to see what is good and what is not. These new variables connected to the target variable are called class labels. These choices may be more or less reasonable, what is clear is that they result in discrimination in their choice, which is not always desired [10]. The second level would come in the learning phase with training data that may be biased in its collection or because the data itself is biased [10]. Biases will be found in labeling the data, as a reproduction of the data scientist's biases, and in data collection, which may be because the data are purchased or because the protected groups are underrepresented. There is a third phase that determines the features selection; organizations determine which elements they consider important for their decisions. In this phase, the protected groups may understand that the features that determine decision making are less important to them than to the beneficiary groups [10]. Proxy data are data considered key to belonging to a class or group with similar characteristics. The choice of these proxies usually depends on obvious historical reasons but at other times they simply increase stereotypes to the detriment of the groups to be protected. This decision making does not intentionally pursue this objective. In many cases they derive simply from prejudices that come from society [10]. Finally, Barocas and Selbst consider that intentional discrimination can be masked by using one of the methods mentioned above. Discriminating against a particular group can be done by using a proxy that has a strong link to that group [10]. For example, using the zip code of neighborhoods where there is a high concentration of that minority group.

This approach to the problem of discrimination focuses exclusively on the data that feed into the system and from an American perspective. From a European perspective,

Hacker's examination is based on exchange market law. For him discrimination by algorithms can occur in two main ways: the training data used and the unequal ground truth [11]. For ML systems to learn, they need to be trained with data. This training data allows the system to learn with examples, allowing it to refine the model with right answers. At the end of the process, allowing the system to make "correct" decisions based on the data it receives. The problem arises when training data is misused, for example in supervised learning when the results are poorly assessed by supervisors, or when training data do not represent underrepresented groups well [11]. Another possibility of discrimination is when the data set has a historical origin. In contexts where there has historically been a misrepresentation of discriminated groups the datasets that feed artificial intelligence systems are going to produce discriminatory results [11]. Hacker includes a second form of discrimination consisting of unequal ground truth. We can consider ground truth as a system that is statistically validated by data [12].

These two solutions, focused on the technique, provide an interesting analysis of discrimination by means of algorithms, but forget an important factor such as the human factor. From a technical point of view, developers and industry can improve many of their algorithms to avoid discrimination. However, once they put them in the hands of professionals, biases unrelated to their work may occur. Thus, in creating artificial intelligence for crime prediction, the police can feed the algorithm with biased data. This situation is similar to the case of historical data in that the criminal history, if biased, will reinforce this bias. The algorithm may be well developed and implemented by manufactures or developers, however, because of the data or the interpretation of the results by professional users, algorithmic discrimination may occur [13]. In algorithmic discrimination it is important to put into context what technology is applied, in what situation [14] and by whom it is used, in order to correctly analyze discrimination situations.

We currently have the legal tools to analyze these discriminations, although there is room for improvement.

3 Legal Protection Against Discriminatory Uses of Artificial Intelligence

We have analyzed some real cases of discrimination and where is the cause from a technical point of view that makes discrimination with the use of artificial intelligence so special. The European regulation on artificial intelligence is currently under discussion and is expected to come out later this year. However, this does not mean that there is no legal recourse to give due protection. As mentioned above, the European Convention of Human Rights includes, in its article 14, the right to non-discrimination in particular cases: sex, race, colour, language, religion, political, or other opinion, national or social origin, association with a national minority, property, birth or other status. Following the latest reform of the European Union treaties, known as the Treaty on the Functioning of the European Union, Article 19 establishes the principle of non-discrimination, with powers to legislate on the subject [15], as we have seen before.

Two concepts can be distinguished in this right: direct and indirect discrimination. Direct discrimination can be understood as "one person is treated less favuorably than other is, had been or would be treated in a comparable situation" (Art. 2(2)(a) Directive 2000/43/EC). This discrimination has to be directly motivated and is on the individual, not a group [11]. Thus, for instance, if an employer do not give a job to an applicant because certain feature that is not related to the job [16], this should be considered discrimination. This kind of discrimination is rare within the use of artificial intelligence. This cases only happened when the models are not neutral [2, 11]. Indirect discrimination is more common in the use of artificial intelligence [17]. It should be understood as "where an apparently neutral provision, criterion or practice would put persons of one [protected group] at a particular disadvantage compared with [other persons], unless that provision, criterion or practice is objectively justified by a legitimate aim and the means of achieving that aim are appropriate and necessary" (Art. 2(b) Directive 2004/113). The case law of the European Court of Justice, in case C-17084 Bilka-Kaufhaus GmbH v. Weber von Hartz, establishes three requirements for discrimination to be acceptable. The first is that it must be based on a legitimate interest. The second is that the measure adopted pursues that interest. And the third is that the measure be proportionate [1].

This indirect discrimination focuses on groups, as opposed to direct, which focuses on individuals. For this to occur, there must be formal equal treatment, disparate outcomes, and a justification as to why this decision was made. In order to test indirect discrimination, statistical models must be used to prove it [18]. There are already statistical models applied to intelligent systems to try to prove differential treatment in these cases [3]. The *prima facie* cases that fall within this indirect discrimination will be favored by the possibility of proving discrimination by means of statistics [2], and this in intelligent systems where there is a clear problem of being able to prove discrimination because of the black box [19], which makes difficult, if not impossible, particularly in machine learning systems, to prove differential treatment.

Of particular interest is the General Data Protection Regulation (GDPR) which, although not designed for artificial intelligence, does provide solutions that can be applied to solve the problem of discrimination through Article 1(2), which states that the rights and freedoms of citizens shall be protected [18]. More precisely, GDPR recital 71 states that fair data processing necessitates securing personal data to prevent "discriminatory effects", which opens the possibility of protecting equality through this regulatory framework.

The GDPR establishes seven principles to be respected for the correct processing of data, which are: a) use of data should be lawfulness, fairness and transparency, b) data can be collected only for a purpose that is specified in advance, and should not be used for unrelated purposes, c) data should be limited to what is necessary for the processing purpose, d) data should be accurate and up to date, e) data should not be retained for an unreasonably long period, f) data should be secured against data breaches, illegal use, etc., and g) data controller is responsible for compliance.

The list is too long to be able to focus on this paper, but even so, we will present some of the solutions proposed by the doctrine. One of the solutions provided by the GDPR is that of transparency. As we have seen above, the need for the aggrieved party to prove the situation of discrimination implies an extremely complicated burden of proof. Only through the obligation to provide such information by respecting the principle of transfer, which is also included in the ethical guidelines of the High Level Experts Group on artificial intelligence of the European Commission [20], will it be feasible to allege discriminatory treatment. Thus, the principle of transparency implies that organizations must provide information on data processing. Obviously, it will not be fully detailed information, but it can be useful for the data subject (Access right, article 15 GDPR). For example, it will be possible to request information on what data is held on individuals and what data is used as proxies, thus giving an idea of where the discrimination lies.

Another good tool is the Data Privacy Impact Assessment (DPIA). Mandatory by the GDPR, it is a form of self-regulation, by which, you are going to be able to be aware of where the risks are in data processing, in our case by artificial intelligence, and establish prevention measures. *Privacy impact assessment* is a "methodology for assessing the impacts on privacy of a project, policy, programme, service, product or other initiative which involves the processing of personal information and, in consultation with stakeholders, for taking remedial actions as necessary in order to avoid or minimise negative impacts" [21].

Wright and Friedewald perform a structuring of the privacy impact assessment in which 15 points could be established to ensure the correct use of the three processing areas.

The first step is the analysis of whether an impact assessment plan is necessary or not, provided that it is going to have an influence on the design of the project to which it is going to be applied, which we understand that in our object of study is essential.

A second one is to determine a work team to carry it out. Although the person responsible for carrying out the impact assessment is the one in charge of data processing, the task of control is not easy to perform, so it has to be carried out by a multidisciplinary team composed of technical, legal and ethical personnel, representatives of end users and citizens.

Drawing up a strategic impact plan, with the issues, the people who are going to work on them, the distribution of tasks, a timetable and the consultation of external experts. It is also necessary to describe the project to be analyzed, how it will be developed with a designed work schedule, as well as to analyze who are the potential users of the project.

In direct relation to how the project will be developed, it is necessary to determine how the information flow will be transmitted, what data will be requested, for what purpose, who will collect it, how it will be stored, how it will be protected and distributed, and how it will be processed.

It is essential to seek the advice of end users in order to determine precisely what their needs are and how it will be used in practice. It is at this point that a legislative analysis of the adequacy of the project to current regulations will be necessary.

Once the infrastructure has been created, the risks and possible solutions must be identified hand in hand with the users, as well as the magnitude of the impact in case they occur. Recommendations will then be formulated, which must be written in a report that must be made public so that it can be discussed with the interested parties and the recommendations suggested and approved can be implemented. In the event that some of the measures provided are not to be implemented, it must be explained why this has not been done and the decision must be adequately justified in order to keep the arguments in mind for future assessments of the same privacy risk situations.

In addition, it must be reviewed and evaluated by outsiders, so that the impact assessment and possible measures to be implemented to avoid risks are not exclusively controlled by internal project personnel. This analysis by outsiders may imply the need to update its content either because of their comments or because of changes that may occur during the execution of the mass data processing project. Finally, a training plan is necessary for those who, within their competencies and tasks, will perform activities related to data processing [22].

For Oetzel and Spiekerman, based on the German experience, the impact assessment would have seven steps: a) description of the processing system in an understandable and detailed way to be able to detect the problems with privacy; b) definition of the privacy targets, that there are already risk catalogs where many of them are collected, does not imply that in that particular system there are all of them or that there are new ones, therefore, that analysis is necessary keeping in mind the first point; c) an evaluation of the degree of protection that each of the detected privacy targets demands, not all data are equal nor have the same impact on Fundamental Rights therefore by degrees of high, medium and low impact; d) identification of the threats of each of the privacy objectives, the different forms of privacy attacks can be classified and once determined it is necessary to study and identify the possible threats of each of them; e) identification and control recommendations, technical or non-technical, adopted to protect against these threats, can be classified into three levels satisfactory, strong and very strong, depending on how it mitigates the particular risk; f) assessment and documentation of residual risks, even when controlling the security measures to be implemented and how they solve the privacy problems, there may still be residual risks arising from the cost benefit of the measure, the impossibility of achieving complete security, etc. and g) documentation of the entire privacy impact assessment system, as long as there are no standards, it is necessary to document the entire assessment process in order to be able to demonstrate how it has been carried out in the event of an audit [23].

Regardless of the methodology of these two examples, we can affirm that the DPIA allows us to access relevant information to a) know if there has been data that facilitates discrimination and b) if the organization has taken the appropriate measures to avoid it.

Connecting GDPR's fairness duty with the creation of DPIAs, Hacker believes that the data protection authority will be able to ensure, through the DPIA, that non-discrimination measures are taken, allowing to have a prevention system from the training phase of the system, ensuring an equal treatment by design [11].

This risk prevention methodology is the prevailing one in the European Union's digital strategy, with the GDPR being the first regulatory step to be joined by the Artificial Intelligence Act (AIA) and the Digital Market Act (DMA). This leads us to the new approach of risk prevention through technology. This brings us to the new approach to risk prevention through technology, especially when we try to implement it in a democratic society.

The proposed regulation on artificial intelligence, in its latest version, stipulates that high-risk systems will require a fundamental rights impact assessment before being placed on the market (Article 16 AIA). Although the proposed regulation seeks to impose prevention by design when developing artificial intelligence systems, this requirement is only mandatory for so-called high-risk systems (Article 43 AIA). For the rest of the systems not considered as such, it will only be voluntary to carry out these evaluations, which leaves many artificial intelligence systems that produce discrimination without this preventive evaluation and, therefore, only at the mercy of the mechanisms that we have pointed out above that regulate the GDPR. We should understand high-risk systems as are mentioned in the Annex III of the AIA by areas. Thus, the following will be considered as such when they operate in biometric identification and categorization of natural persons, management and operation of critical infrastructure, education and vocational training, employment, workers management and access to self-employment, access to and enjoyment of essential private services and public services and benefits, law enforcement, migration, asylum and border control management, and administration of justice and democratic process.

The list clearly states the environments and functions in which they are to be used, but it is true that it does not specify any specific technology, which may generate uncertainty among operators. Even so, it is true that cases of discrimination in the workplace or in the relationship between the citizen and the administration [6] would be covered by this regulation.

Title III, Chapter Two of the IA Act stipulates the elements that these high-risk systems must comply with. Many of the requirements are already outlined in the European Commission's HLEG ethical guidelines. Thus, a risk management plan, a data governance system, technical documentation, record-keeping, transparency and provision of information to users, and human oversight, accuracy, robustness and cybersecurity are necessary. The risk management plan in the GDPR was compulsory, but in the AIA has a relevant role.

Although risk systems may have different methodologies, the AI Act identifies at least four points to take into consideration. First, identification and analysis of the known and foreseeable risks associated with each high-risk AI system. Second, estimation and evaluation of the risks that may emerge when the high-risk AI system is used in accordance with its intended purpose and under conditions of reasonably foreseeable misuse. This means that a proactive role of the developers should be in consideration. Third, evaluation of other possibly arising risks based on the analysis of data gathered from the post-market monitoring system, as it is stablished in article 61 of the AIA. And finally, it will be needed the adoption of suitable risk management measures in accordance with the provisions of the AIA in article 9. To identifying the most appropriate risk management measures, three points should be ensured: a) elimination or reduction of risks as far as possible through adequate design and development; b) where appropriate, implementation of adequate mitigation and control measures in relation to risks that cannot be eliminated; and c) provision of adequate information pursuant to Article 13, in particular as regards the risks referred to in paragraph 2, point (b) of Article 9, and, where appropriate, training to users.

One important point to consider when eliminating risks is literacy. An especial consideration shall be given to the technical knowledge, experience, education, training to be expected by the user and the environment in which the system is intended to be used.

In risk management, testing is of particular relevance. Items 5, 6 and 7 of Article 9 describe a testing system in which the objective is to ensure the best possible risk avoidance measures, in compliance with the provisions of Article 9, with a system, so to speak, by design.

Undoubtedly, even if discrimination is not specified as a risk, there is no doubt that in certain uses and contexts, equality will be affected and, therefore, an analysis methodology will be necessary. Our proposal will be developed in the following section.

4 Improvements to Achieve Artificial Intelligence that Respects Fundamental Rights

The HLEG Guidelines focus on the protection of human rights. It has therefore developed two pillars on which to build the concept of trustworthy AI. The first is respecting human rights, and the second is seven ethical principles that underpin the idea of good use of artificial intelligence. Some of these, such as privacy and data governance, security and safety, diversity, non-discrimination and fairness, and transparency, are already included in the GDPR. But there are others that are completely new to intelligent systems, such as human supervision, social welfare, environmental protection, and accuracy in the AIA [20].

The European Union, in its digitisation policy, has opted for prevention systems as a strategy to address the problems arising from digitisation. As we have seen in the case of the GDPR, the risk prevention methodology is the basis for respecting fundamental rights. We encounter problems in approaching the analysis. On the one hand, we have different contexts in which discrimination can be affected and different groups, as we have seen. But we also have different models of technology, different contexts in which they are used and different objectives.

The delimitation and classification of the use of artificial intelligence is a complicated task. Fortunately, we are not starting from scratch, as advances have been made in this area in the philosophy of technology in the past, with the aim of carrying out an ethical assessment of the use of technology through a phased analysis. The Brey's methodology on anticipatory ethics in technology [14] proposes three phases of study to adequately resolve the assessment: a) the technology assessment level, which defines which particular technology is to be used, understanding technology as a collection of techniques that are related to each other by common purpose, domain or formal or functional characteristics; b) the artefact development level, which is the physical configuration that operates in the appropriate way and environment and produces the desired development; and c) the application level, which focuses on the use of the artefact and the problems that may arise from that specific use.

This is a good starting point for the legal analysis. But we need to introduce more detail into the legal analysis. We propose an analysis methodology that will allow us to determine where we are going to find implementation failures and who is responsible for them, influenced by this predictive analysis of ethical problems, at three different levels and having, first, determined the need for the use of an intelligent system to perform a task instead of a human, the field in which it is going to be applied and the objectives that are intended. Thus, we can distinguish three important moments to determine inappropriate and irresponsible use from the point of view of the specific use of artificial intelligence: in data collection, in data processing and in the interpretation of the final results. As we have seen, the great advance in artificial intelligence in recent years has been in those intelligent systems that are fed with data, which implies that we must know how the data have been obtained, what data are going to be used, for what purpose and for how long they are going to be used, who has access to the data and how they are secured, similar to what Hacker [11] and Barocas and Selbt [10] said earlier. In the next phase, the data processing, it is necessary to understand how the system works (algorithm and the models on which decisions are made), who has access to it, security measures in place, among others. If the processing cannot be explained, it is necessary to understand the processes and procedures involved in the creation and implementation of the use of these systems. Thus, black box paradox should be not an unsolvable problem. Finally, in the third phase of analysis of the outcomes extracted from the machine, it is necessary to analyse whether the results are of good quality, whether they show any negative impact on rights and whether they justify the use of intelligent systems. The results are not always reliable, not least because artificial intelligence is not a crystal ball [24]. These three phases will give us a closer understanding of the system to understand where the attack on the legal good will arise.

As noted above, algorithmic discrimination is not only a technical problem, but also the human factor plays an important role. It is therefore necessary to analyse these three phases in the use of technology from the perspective of the relationship between the subject and the intelligent system. Errors of the subjects involved in the whole life cycle of artificial intelligence can be produced by the creators and developers, by the professionals who use it and, finally, by the recipients/end users. Limiting it exclusively to developers or manufacturers or manufacturers does not cover the full spectrum of possibilities. It is the professional user who uses the artificial intelligence for a certain purpose that may lead to the commission of a crime, but the system itself has no fault that leads to the injury of the legal good. It is a machine that is not defective from a product point of view. From this methodology we will be able to carry out an appropriate risk management system to determine from the beginning of the construction of the intelligent system whether or not there is a risk of discrimination, being able to detect and analyse the risks from a human and technological perspective.

Acknowledgments. This work is carried out under the funding of the GOIA project: The governance of Artificial Intelligence based on citizenship. Ref.TED2021-129402B-C22. Call 2021 of projects oriented to the ecological transition and digital transition, of the state plan for scientific technical and innovation research 2021–2023, in the framework of the recovery, transformation and resilience plan of ministry of science and innovation's National State Agency, and as a member of the project "Los mercados para el interncamibo de datos o data market. Situación jurídica y restos tecnológicos y empresariales".

References

1. Allen, R., Masters, D.: Artificial intelligence: the right to protection from discrimination caused by algorithms, machine learning and automated decision-making. ERA Forum. **20**, 585–598 (2020). https://doi.org/10.1007/s12027-019-00582-w
2. Xenidis, R., Senden, L.: EU non-discrimination law in the era of artificial intelligence: mapping the challenges of algorithmic discrimination. Kluwer Law International (2020)

3. Žliobaitė, I.: Measuring discrimination in algorithmic decision making. Data Min. Knowl. Disc. **31**(4), 1060–1089 (2017). https://doi.org/10.1007/s10618-017-0506-1
4. Dastin, J.: Amazon scraps secret AI recruiting tool that showed bias against women, https://www.reuters.com/article/us-amazon-com-jobs-automation-insight-idUSKC N1MK08G (2018)
5. Larson, J.A., Mattu, S., Jeff: The Tiger Mom Tax: Asians are nearly twice as likely to get a higher price from Princeton review. https://www.propublica.org/article/asians-nearly-twice-as-likely-to-get-higher-price-from-princeton-review
6. Eubanks, V.: Automating inequality: how high-tech tools profile, police, and punish the poor. St. Martin's Press, New York, NY (2017)
7. Mattu, J.A., Larson, J., Kirchner, L., Surya: Machine Bias. https://www.propublica.org/art icle/machine-bias-risk-assessments-in-criminal-sentencing?token=-LWC0UDWQ7X23iLE OqYYQFkDs9mlu7vg
8. European Commission for the Efficiency of Justice (CEPEJ): european ethical charter on the use of artificial intelligence in judicial systems and their environment. Council of Europe, Strasbourg (2018)
9. Valdés, M.G.P., Isabel: VioGén: visita a las tripas del algoritmo que calcula el riesgo de que una mujer sufra violencia machista. https://elpais.com/tecnologia/2022-04-10/viogen-vis ita-a-las-tripas-del-algoritmo-que-calcula-el-riesgo-de-que-una-mujer-sufra-violencia-mac hista.html
10. Barocas, S., Selbst, A.D.: Big Data's Disparate Impact. SSRN J. (2016). https://doi.org/10.2139/ssrn.2477899
11. Hacker, P.: Teaching fairness to artificial intelligence: Existing and novel strategies against algorithmic discrimination under EU law. COLA **55**, 1143–1185 (2018). https://doi.org/10.54648/COLA2018095
12. Veale, M., Binns, R.: Fairer machine learning in the real world: mitigating discrimination without collecting sensitive data. Big Data & Soci. **4**, 205395171774353 (2017). https://doi.org/10.1177/2053951717743530
13. Valls Prieto, J.: Sobre la responsabilidad penal por la utilización de sistemas inteligentes. Revista electrónica de ciencia penal y criminología. 27 (2022)
14. Brey, P.A.E.: Anticipatory Ethics for Emerging Technologies. NanoEthics **6**, 1–13 (2012). https://doi.org/10.1007/s11569-012-0141-7
15. Gerards, J., Zuiderveen Borgesius, F.: Protected grounds and the system of non-discrimination law in the context of algorithmic decision-making and artificial intelligence. SSRN J. (2020). https://doi.org/10.2139/ssrn.3723873
16. Heinrichs, B.: Discrimination in the age of artificial intelligence. AI Soc. **37**, 1–12 (2021). https://doi.org/10.1007/s00146-021-01192-2
17. Hildebrandt, M.: Smart Technologies and the end(s) of Law: Novel Entanglements of Law and Technology. EE Edward Elgar Publishing, Cheltenham, UK Northampton, MA, USA (2016)
18. Zuiderveen Borgesius, F.: Discrimination, artificial intelligence, and algorithmic decision-making. Council of Europe, Directorate General of Democracy, Strasbourg (2018)
19. Pasquale, F.: The Black box society: the secret algorithms that control money and information. Harvard University Press, Cambridge, Massachusetts London, England (2015)
20. High-Level Expert Group on Artificial Intelligence: Ethics Guidelines for Trustworthy AI. European Commission (2019)
21. Wright, D., De Hert, P.: Introduction to privacy impact assessment. En: Priv. Impact Assess. 3–32 (2012)
22. Wright, D., Friedewald, M.: Integrating privacy and ethical impact assessments. Sci. Public Policy. **40**, 755–766 (2013). https://doi.org/10.1093/scipol/sct083

23. Oetzel, M.C., Spiekermann, S.: A systematic methodology for privacy impact assessments: a design science approach. Eur. J. Inf. Syst. **23**, 126–150 (2014). https://doi.org/10.1057/ejis.2013.18

24. Dignum, V.: Responsible Artificial Intelligence: How to Develop and Use AI in a Responsible Way. Springer International Publishing, Cham (2019). https://doi.org/10.1007/978-3-030-30371-6

Data as Wealth, Data Markets and Its Regulation

José Antonio Castillo Parrilla(✉) ⓘ

(Civil Law Department), Ramón y Cajal Fellow at University of Granada, 18071 Granada, Spain
castillop@ugr.es

Abstract. The onerous exchange of data is a reality that needs to be regulated by the European Union. Despite the reluctance expressed by EDPS and EDPB during the debate on the current EU Directive 2019/770, the scientific literature is beginning to accept and demand that the rules take into account the reality that data are another economic asset. An example of data functioning as an economic asset is the existence of data marketplaces. In these data marketplaces, different parties exchange data packages in the same way as they exchange goods and services in other markets. Data marketplaces face two major regulatory challenges. On the one hand, the aforementioned need for regulations to accept that data functions as an economic asset; on the other hand, their adaptation, like other digital markets, to the rules established by the Digital Market Act.

Keywords: data · personal data protection · data marketplaces · Digital Markets Act · GDPR

1 Data as Wealth and Its Possible Onerous Exchange

Since 2014, a regulatory sector known as data economy has developed strongly within the European Union. In the words of the European Commission itself, the data economy can be defined as an ecosystem where different market players collaborate to ensure that data is accessible and usable, in order to extract value from it through, for example, the creation of an increasing variety of applications with great potential to improve everyday life. The value of the data economy surpassed the €400 billion threshold in 2019 for the EU27 plus the UK, growing at 7.6% per year; while the value of data markets in the same timeframe reached €75 billion, growing at 5% per year.

These economic data justify the growing regulatory concern in the European Commission, with regulations that in one way or another affect the economic traffic of data (the one that most directly does so for the moment, the Data Act Proposal) or that aim to consolidate or accelerate the construction of a European Digital Single Market. Along with all this, it is important to take into account the tension between the EDPS and

This publication is part of RYC2021-031430-I, financed by MCIN/AEI/10.13039/501100011033 and by European Union «NextGenerationEU» and the result of the Research Project entitled "Data market places. Legal situation and technological and business challenges", funded by the Research Excellence Unit SD2. Digital society: security and protection of rights, whose PI is Dr. José Antonio Castillo Parrilla.

H. L. Larsen et al. (Eds.): FQAS 2023, LNAI 14113, pp. 279–289, 2023.
https://doi.org/10.1007/978-3-031-42935-4_23

the EDPB, and some national Competition Commissions of Member States around the possibility of paying for certain digital goods and services with one's own personal data.

This debate had its regulatory echo in the replacement of Recital 13 of the Proposal for Directive 634/2015 by Recital 24 of the current Directive 2019/770. Recital 13 of the Proposal for Directive 634/2015 states the following: "In the digital economy, information about individual is often and increasingly seen by market participants as having a value comparable to money. Digital content is often supplied not in Exchange for a Price but against counter-performance other tan money i.e. by giving Access to personal data or other data". Consecuentemente, el Considerando 14 de dicha Propuesta de Directiva afirma que "this Directive should apply (also) to contracts where the supplier requests and the consumer actively provides data". Recital 24 of Directive 2019/770 is the equivalent of the previous Recitals 13 and 14 of Proposal 634/2015; and is less clear on the use of data as a means of payment in certain digital contracts to the point of stating that data cannot be considered as a commodity: "Digital content or digital services are often supplied also where the consumer does not pay a price but provides personal data to the trader (…) While fully recognising that the protection of personal data is a fundamental right and that therefore personal data cannot be considered as a commodity, this Directive should ensure that consumers are, in the context of such business models, entitled to contractual remedies".

As can be seen, while in 2015 it was stated that data represent a value comparable to money, in 2019 it is maintained that they cannot be considered as a commodity (the main function of money). The change of position does not go into detail insofar as the articles remain practically unchanged in this aspect between 2015 and 2019, and in Recital 24 of Directive 2019/770 itself we can see that while it is stated that data cannot serve as a commodity, at the same time it is said that in certain digital contracts the consumer consents to the processing of his data after receiving the digital good or service (i.e., he uses his data as a commodity). The reason for the apparent change of approach is to be found in Opinion 4/2017 of the European Data Protection Supervisor, where it strongly recommends avoiding any reference to the use of data as a commodity.

The debate on whether or not data can be used as a commodity remains latent. For example, the Spanish transposition of Directive 2019/770 has led to a reform of the Spanish Consumers Act reforming an important part of its articles or including new articles. One of these new articles is Article 119 ter, which states in its paragraph 2 that "termination (of the contract) will not proceed when the lack of conformity is of minor importance, except in cases where the consumer or user has provided personal data as consideration". However, recent publications in this area suggest an acceptance by the doctrine that the rules should reflect (and regulate) the reality of the onerous use of one's own personal data in digital environments.

2   Can Data Be Considered as Goods from a Legal Point of View?

If we understand that the debate we have just summarised about understanding data as a commodity from a legal point of view has been overcome and we accept this reality, there are still legal difficulties regarding the possibility of exchanging data in the same way as other types of goods are exchanged. It is precisely a question of assessing whether we can understand data as a specific type of goods from a legal point of view. This aspect is not free of difficulties, although we advance our positive judgement: data can be understood as economic goods from a legal point of view, despite their specific legal characteristics and the difficulties that these characteristics entail.

Private property law is based on two main categories: goods and services. Whereas goods are the object of exchange, services are activities that are performed for the benefit of a person. The circulation of property centred on services has given rise to what RIFKIN calls the "economy of speed"[1], which channels patrimonial relations through licensing, access or leasing contracts and which, ultimately, does not allow wealth to circulate as easily as it does in an "economy of scale", which is the one based on sale and purchase contracts. Contracts of sale (and similar) favour the circulation of goods, and not their mere use or economic exploitation at a specific moment in time, however prolonged this may be.

In order to understand data as goods, we must begin with a brief review of the theory of goods that allows us to propose a definition of goods in which data could be framed. In Europe there are at least two models for dealing with the legal treatment of goods: the German model and the French model. The German model has its point of reference in § 90 BGB, according to which "things in the legal sense are only tangible objects", and is followed, for example, in Austria (cf. § 250 ABGB). The French model, of which Spain is a part, understands that goods are "all things that are or can be the object of appropriation" (Art. 333 CC)[2]. The fundamental divergence between the two models lies in: (1) the term chosen (goods vs. things) and (2), above all, the requirement of corporeality. While the German model does not admit the category of incorporeal things, the French model does admit the concept of intangible property and operates with it[3]. The flexibility of the French model or legal theory of property would make it possible to accept the idea of digital property with less difficulty, as well as the consideration of data as property in the property law sense[4].

The functional concept of property that we propose is the following: property in the property-legal sense will be understood as meta-legal entities of a static nature and whose economic value determines their legal relevance or, in other words, the need for the law to recognise their existence and their own legal status[5]. When we speak of meta-legal entities we refer to realities that do not belong to or are not created by law (e.g. contracts), but are recognised by law because of their legal relevance (e.g. property, life

---

[1] Rifkin, J.: La era del acceso: la revolución de la nueva economía, 1st edn. Paidos, Barcelona (1999), p. 135.

[2] Cf. Also Art. 516 of the Code civil (France). A broader definition, always within this model, is that of Art. 810 of the Codice civile (Italy), according to which goods are those things that can constitute the object of rights.

[3] Cf. GAYO's Instituta, II. 13 and 14, which distinguishes between corporeal and incorporeal things (Domingo Oslé, R.: Textos de Derecho Romano, 1st edn. Aranzadi, Navarra (2002), p. 81).

[4] It must be said, however, that in recent years German authors have proposed revising the rigidity of § 90 BGB, precisely in order to be able to admit the consideration of data as property (Becker, Stevens & Bossauer).

[5] As we will see below, there are differences between the idea of digital goods and the legal consideration of data as goods (whether digital or otherwise), mainly due to the difficulty of delimiting the quantity and characteristics of the data that would constitute a "data-good".

or privacy)[6]. Goods (legally relevant things ex art. 333 CC) are, moreover, static if we compare them with services (dynamic). By constructing this dichotomy (static goods vs. dynamic services) we intend to show that services are rendered or performed for the benefit of their recipient in the course of a period of time and that, as activities or facere[7], their existence is exhausted with their execution. Goods, on the other hand, remain before and after the contract; they are not performed for the recipient, but are given to him: they are given to him. Finally, the economic value of both things and activities means that the law must pay attention to them. Those things whose economic value makes them worthy of legal attention and, in accordance with Article 333 CC, susceptible of appropriation[8] will have the legal classification of goods.

With all that said, could the data fit into the functional category of goods that we have proposed? We also believe so.

Digital wealth is composed of three broad categories of goods: (1) digitised intangible goods, (2) digital goods and (3) digitised informational goods or "data as goods". Digitised intangible goods serve as a bridge[9], as a criterion to trace a proper application of the principle of functional equivalence[10]: if when I buy a physical copy of a book I can read it wherever I want or resell it, why can't I do the same with a digital copy if it is the same book, i.e. the same good? The answer is simple: the contracts through which one and the other are marketed are different[11], one allowing the physical good to circulate and the other preventing the digitised good from doing the same. A computer program is always digital (even if it is also an intellectual property work), but the reasoning is equally applicable in your case: it is a (digital) good that can therefore circulate contractually in the same way as a physical good. All possibilities would thus be open (online distribution of computer programs both through sale and purchase contracts and through license contracts), without a sale of a computer program (i.e. of a copy) being confused with the sale of the exploitation rights of the protected work[12].

---

[6] Castillo Parrilla, J. A.: Bienes digitales. Una necesidad europea, 1st edn. Dykinson, Madrid (2018).

[7] It should be stressed that the term "services" is used ambivalently, referring both to the (service) contract and to the specific activity to be performed. This is a confusion of planes, as a type of contract (service contract) should not be confused with the meta-legal reality on which it is projected (the concrete activity on which it is projected).

[8] Or of any other rights as stated in Art. 810 CC-IT, which serves in this case as a valid interpretative criterion of Art. 333 CC insofar as he who can do the most (appropriation) can do the least (all other rights).

[9] We understand digitised real estate as intellectual property works converted into digital format, such as a novel in pdf format.

[10] On the principles of electronic commerce, Illescas Ortiz, Madrid Parra, Castellani, Finocchiaro (see references).

[11] In the case of a physical book, commercialisation is always through sale and purchase; in the case of a digital book, it is more common to enter into licensing contracts, although there is nothing to prevent sale and purchase.

[12] As far as the right of distribution is concerned, for the time being, we understand that it would be necessary to make a modification or, at least, a functional interpretation (contra legem) of art. 19 Spanish Act on Intellectual Property, according to which distribution of an intellectual property work is understood as "the making available to the public of the original or copies of the work, on a tangible medium" (italics added). If the physical copy and the digital copy

As far as data are concerned, they have gone from being a projection of the personality of the person with whom they are associated to being seen as a commodity (i.e. a good in the property-legal sense) on a par with any other. Data is, according to the Commission[13] and ISO/IEC 2382–2015, "any interpretable representation of information in a formalised form suitable for communication, interpretation or processing" or, in other words, encoded and machine-readable information[14]. There are two important classifications of data: one distinguishing between personal and non-personal data, and one distinguishing between raw data, structured data and derived or inferential data. Data will be personal or non-personal depending on whether or not they are associated with an identified or identifiable natural person (Art. 4 GDPR). The distinction is fundamental, as only to the former is the GDPR (cf. Cons. 26) and the LOPDGDD (Arts. 1.a and 2.3) applicable. The distinction between raw data, structured data and derived data is based on a syntactic analysis of the data[15]. Raw data are data that are not structured according to any sort criteria, while structured data are data that are structured (e.g. through their incorporation into databases, association of metadata, etc.). Finally, derived or inferential data are those that can be obtained through the study of already structured massive data (Big Data). This last classification of data is particularly useful in this study as it looks at data not so much as a projection of the personality of its owner (as it encompasses both personal and non-personal data), but as products or commodities, i.e. as goods[16]:

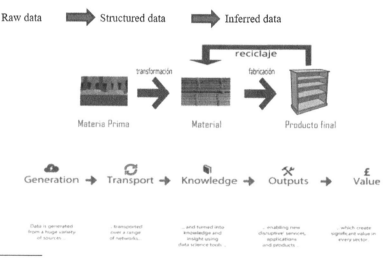

of an intellectual property work are functionally equivalent, it will be necessary to (1) delete the reference to the tangible medium or (2) understand tangible medium as a durable medium. On the other hand, this could no longer be the distinguishing criterion between the right of distribution and the right of public communication of an intellectual property work, but the distinction between one and the other would lie in the possibility that an indeterminate plurality of persons may have access to the work (public communication) or not (distribution), regardless of the medium of the copy.

[13] European Commission (2014), pp. 4–5.

[14] Sartor, Zech (2017), p. 54, Becker, pp. 322–323.

[15] Zech (2017), pp. 53–54.

[16] Castillo Parrilla (2019), p. 294.

With all this normative background, what are the difficulties faced by data to be considered as goods from a property law point of view? The main challenge lies, in our view, in finding a prior paradigm of property with which to compare it. Data cannot be understood as goods in the same way as a tangible movable good (i.e., a book); but they do resemble goods that need to be bottled or packaged in order to be marketed (i.e., water or electricity).

3   Data Market Places or Platforms for Data Exchange

Data, as an economic asset, can be monetised through its exchange and sharing between organisations[17]. Data market places are platforms that provide infrastructure for the exchange or sharing of data. These platforms provide parties with a common (virtual) place where they can meet and exchange or share data, and simplify their interaction by bringing them into contact with each other.[18] These platforms act as neutral inter-mediaries that allow their customers to upload and sell or share their data (understood as products) through access contracts, usage contracts or even exchange contracts (data trading). Data markets and data sharing can bring benefits for business, social creativity and technological progress[19]. Data analytics requires continuous storage and exchange of data, and these activities are part of data marts and essential for the near future of business according to Pauer et al[20]. The following diagram by Spiekerman[21] provides a clear explanation of the different roles in a data marketplace:

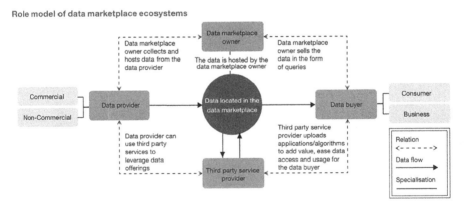

Data providers act as de facto 'owners' of data and offer it to others, either for a fee or for free. For the time being, companies do not trust each other to share or exchange

[17] Navas Navarro (2018), p. 101.

[18] Spiekermann (2019), p. 209, defines data marketplaces as electronic marketplaces where data is traded as a commodity; and in turn, electronic marketplaces as infrastructures that allow participants to meet and transact in a secure electronic environment.

[19] Demchenko et al. (2018), pp. 3–4.

[20] Pauer et al. (2018), p.11.

[21] Spiekermann (2019), p. 210.

their data[22], so the data market has been dominated by privately managed commercial platforms that operate within closed systems and sell or share their data through bilateral exchange relationships. However, the trend seems to be changing as legal certainty for data transactions increases and multilateral and open data markets become increasingly important[23].

Data markets can be classified according to various criteria. We will use two: (1) the number of economic actors on each side of the negotiation and (2) the type of data being exchanged or shared. Regarding the number of economic actors, a first division can be made: bilateral markets and multilateral markets. In bilateral markets, data interaction (i.e. data exchange or sharing) takes place between two distinguishable user groups or market parties; whereas in multilateral markets, interaction between market parties is facilitated by platforms that are not directly involved[24]. Stahl et al.[25] have published a classification framework for multi-sided data markets taking into account three sub-criteria: hierarchy level, data ownership and business model.

Depending on the type of data being exchanged or shared, we can distinguish between (1) personal, non-personal or mixed data markets; (2) specific or generalist data markets; and (3) raw data markets and structured or processed data markets.

Non-personal data markets are an emerging sector at present as these data are not regulated by the GDPR, but by the EU Regulation 2018/1087 of 14 November 2018 on a framework for the free movement of non-personal data in the EU, to which we must add the Data Act Proposal that is currently under discussion. As far as personal data markets are concerned, it should be stressed at the outset that they are a reality, however uncomfortable that may be. We are all familiar with the Cambridge Analytica scandal, for example. To note the existence of personal data markets does not mean stating that they are legal (or that they are legal in all cases); it is simply a factual observation. In any case, it seems risky to qualify a data market as illegal just because it facilitates the exchange or sharing of personal data. It will depend on specific compliance with the GDPR.

There is a wide range of data marketplaces which, as we have seen, can be generic or specific depending on the type of data you focus on. Dawex or Qlik DataMarket are generic data marts. Here are three examples of specific data markets that present specific problems depending on the type of data traded through them[26]:

- Climpact-Metnext focuses on the sale of weather data to farmers[27]. Climpact-Metnext does not only act as a marketplace: it provides operational tools and services to

---

[22] According to the European Commission, in an overwhelming majority of cases (78% of the companies surveyed) data is generated and analysed internally by the company or by a sub-contractor. In other words, the data remains within the companies themselves, which do not usually transfer it to third parties (European Commission (2017), p. 15).

[23] Spiekermann (2019), p. 210.

[24] Spiekermann (2019), p. 209.

[25] Stahl et al. (2016), p. 141.

[26] Other marketplaces are the following: Advaneo (https://www.advaneo.de/en/#), Caruso (https://www.caruso-dataplace.com/), Qlik DataMarket (https://www.qlik.com/us/products/qlik-sense/data-sources) o Dawex (https://www.dawex.com/en/).

[27] European Commission (2017), p. 13, footnote 43.

measure the impact of weather on economic activity and to model future activity based on weather forecasts, as well as tools and expertise to create and structure weather risk management products to brokers, banks, insurers and reinsurers[28].

- AAAData started as a specific marketplace for automobile number plate data sold to automobile insurance brokers[29]. They have now expanded the categories of data, although it is still automobile data[30]. This is a good example of a "quasi-personal" data market: in principle, car-related data are non-personal data, but if it is possible to trace the driver and/or the owner of the car, these data become personal data. It goes without saying that this is relatively easy to do.
- Cerved has also expanded its business model. It started as a marketplace for credit rating data sold to banks[31]. It is a clear example of a specific data marketplace that works with both personal and non-personal data, as we can see in this graphic on its website[32]:

Reliable, detailed and easy to find information

Credit Direct covers every Business Information need with immediate and effective solutions

Information on businesses	Information about people	Information on foreign companies
Collect all the data you need to know and evaluate customers, partners and suppliers	Obtain essential data to learn more about individuals and business persons	Explore the databases of Cerved and its partners to get data and news on foreign companies
Find out more	Find out more	Find out more

Most of the concepts related to data markets (data provider, data buyer, data owner, buying and selling data...) conflict with the categories and spirit of personal data protection rules[33].

It is difficult to distinguish personal data from non-personal data, except for data that cannot in any way refer to individuals (e.g. weather data). This difficulty is manifested in the reluctance of the GDPR to speak of anonymisation of data (see Recital 26, which uses the term pseudonymisation). This circumstance is even more delicate if one takes into account that pure raw data markets do not exist in practice, and that the line separating a personal profile from a non-personal profile is even thinner than the line separating personal data from non-personal data.

---

[28] https://www.crunchbase.com/organization/climpact-metnext. Other weather data are: Api-Agro (https://api-agro.eu/en/) o Graniot (https://graniot.com/).

[29] European Commission (2017), p. 13, footnote 43.

[30] https://www.aaa-data.fr/

[31] European Commission (2017), p. 13, footnote 43.

[32] https://www.cerved-online.com/credit-direct/?utm_campaign=2018_CervedOnline&utm_medium=Banner&utm_source=SitoCerved.

[33] Wendehorst (2018), p. 353.

4 Impact of the Digital Market Act on Data Markets

The main objective of EU Regulation 2022/1925 of 14 September 2022, better known as the Digital Markets Act, is to contribute to the smooth functioning of the internal market by establishing rules to ensure contestability and fairness in markets in the digital sector in general (Recital 7). In short, it is a rule that aims to prevent unfair commercial practices and monopolistic behaviour in the EU Digital Single Market.

Digital markets should not be confused with data markets. The DMA defines digital markets as platform services, such as online intermediation services, online search engines, online social networking services, video-sharing platforms, personal communications services, operating systems, web browsers, virtual assistants, cloud computing services or online advertising services (art. 2.2). This is a list of the main "digital markets" covered by the DMA, among which we can of course include data market places.

One of the main concerns of this regulation is to regulate the activity of what it calls "gatekeepers" (art. 3). Gatekeepers are platforms whose pre-eminent characteristics in the market require them to comply with specific rules developed by the DMA with the intention of reducing this pre-eminence. A gatekeeper is a gatekeeper if: (1) it has a significant impact on the internal market; (2) it provides a core platform service which is an important gateway for business users to reach end users; and (3) it enjoys an entrenched and durable position, in its operations, or it is not forseeable that it will enjoy such a position in the near future.

In any event, a gatekeeper will be presumed to be present if (1) it achieves an annual Union turnover equal to or above EUR 7,5 billion in each of the last three financial years, or where its average market capitalisation or its equivalent fair market value amounted to at least EUR 75 billion in the last financial year, and it provides the same core platform service in at least three Member States; (2) it provides a core platform service that in the last financial year has at least 45 million monthly active end users established or located in the Union and at least 10 000 yearly active business users established in the Union; (3) where the previous thresholds were met in each of the last three financial year.

An access guardian may not, with respect to end users: (1) process personal data of end users who use the platform as a means of intermediation to reach another service; (2) combine and cross-reference personal data from the core services with data from third party services; nor (3) log in end users to other services of the access guardian to combine data. These prohibitions shall not apply if the end user has given his or her consent, which may only be requested by the gatekeeper once a year if the end user has requested or withdrawn it. Nor may they, irrespective of the end-user's consent, require them to use a particular identification service, browser engine or payment service, or to subscribe or register for any additional service.

With respect to professional users, gatekeepers must apply fair, reasonable and non-discriminatory general conditions of access to their shops, search engines and social networks, and allow the communication of professional offers free of charge; and they may not prevent professional users from offering the same products and services through other services or through their own channel, nor may they use data that is not publicly accessible and generated by professional users.

This entire legal regime outlined above could be applicable to some of the data markets discussed above, not so much because of their level of turnover, but because they meet the basic requirements of Article 3(1) DMA. An example of this could be the generalist data market place DAWEX, arguably the most important data market place to date in the EU area.

5 Conclusions

There is a basic problem, and that is precisely the legal acceptance of the reality of the exchange of data for a fee. This debate is still ongoing within the European institutions (not only the European Commission, but also the EDPB and EDPS). At the same time, however, data on the importance of the data economy in the euro area and the number of data markets and companies that in one way or another orientate their business model around the data economy are growing steadily.

The main problem facing data marketplaces is precisely their small number. Despite the considerable increase in the number of platforms dedicated to data exchange in recent years, there are still very few of them, and those that have started in this sector run the risk of an undesirable hegemony, considering that excessive market dominance is not in the interest of even the most advantageous market players.

On the other hand, the number of data market places is likely to continue to increase in the coming years and the high barriers to entry in this sector are likely to be lowered. This will come about as legal certainty increases, both in terms of the possibility of exchanging data for valuable consideration and in terms of the regulation of digital markets that will be brought about by the Digital Market Act.

References

1. Becker, M.: Rights in Data – Industry 4.0 and the IP Rights of the Future. In: Zeitchrift für Geistiges Eigentum – Intellectual Property Journal, núm. 3, band 9, pp. 253–265. Mohr Siebeck, Tübingen (2017)
2. Castán Tobeñas, J.: Derecho Derecho Civil español común y foral. Tomo I. Introducción y parte general. Vol. 2. Teoría de la relación jurídica. La persona y los derechos de la personalidad. Las cosas. Los hechos jurídicos, 15 edn. Reus, Madrid (2007)
3. Castellani, L.: I testi dell'UNCITRAL in materia di comercio elettronico. In: Finocchiaro, G., Delfini, F. (coords.) Diritto dell'informatica, pp. 43–62. UTET, Milano (2014)
4. Castillo Parrilla, J. A.: Bienes digitales. Una necesidad europea, 1st edn. Dykinson, Madrid (2018)
5. Castillo Parrilla, J. A.: Economía de datos y datos entendidos como bienes. In: Castaños Castro, P., Castillo Parrilla, J. A. (dirs.) El Mercado digital en la Unión Europea, 1st edn. Reus, Madrid (2019)
6. Demchenko, Y., Los, W., De Laat, C.: Data as economic goods: definitions, properties, challenges, enabling technologies for future data markets. In: ITU Journal: ICT Discoveries, special num. 2 (2018)
7. Díez-Picazo y Ponce de León, L.: Fundamentos del Derecho Civil Patrimonial, Vol. III, 5th edn. Civitas, Madrid (2008)
8. Domingo Oslé, R.: Textos de Derecho Romano, 1st edn. Aranzadi, Navarra (2002)
9. European Commission: Towards a thriving data-driven economy. Brussels, 2.07.2014. https://eur-lex.europa.eu/legal-content/EN/TXT/PDF/?uri=CELEX:52014DC0442&from=EN. Accessed 21 Apr 2023

10. European Commission: on the free flow of data and emerging issues of the European data economy Accompanying the document Communication Building a European data economy. Brussels, 10.01.2017, https://eur-lex.europa.eu/legal-content/EN/TXT/?uri=CELEX%3A52017SC0002. Accessed 21 Apr 2023
11. Finocchiaro, G.: La Convenzione sull´uso di comunicazioni elettroniche nei contratti internazionali. In: Finocchiaro, G., Delfini, F. (coords.) Diritto dell´informatica, 1st edn, pp. 63–70. UTET, Milano (2014)
12. Illescas Ortiz, R.: Derecho de la contratación electronica, 2nd edn. Civitas, Madrid (2009)
13. Madrid Parra, A.: Contratos electrónicos y contratos informáticos. In: Revista de la contratación electronica. num. 11, pp. 5–35. Dykinson, Madrid (2011)
14. Navas Navarro, S.: El valor de los datos personales en el mercado. In: Kindl, J., Arroyo Vendrell, T., Gsell (coords.) Verträge über digitale Inhalte und digitale Dienstleistungen, 1st edn. pp. 101–122. Nomos, Baden-Baden (2018)
15. Pauer, A., Nagel, L., Fedkenhauser, T., Fritzsche-Sterr & Resetko, Y.: Data exchange as a first step towards data economy, https://www.pwc.de/en/digitale-transformation/data-exchange-as-a-first-step-towards-data-economy.pdf. Accessed 21 Apr 2023
16. Rifkin, J.: La era del acceso: la revolución de la nueva economía, 1st edn. Paidos, Barcelona (1999)
17. Sartor, G.: L´informatica giuridica e le tecnologie dell´informazione, 2nd edn. Giappichelli, Torino (2012)
18. Spiekermann, M.: Data marketplaces: trends and Monetisation of data goods. Intereconomics 54(4), 208–216 (2019). https://doi.org/10.1007/s10272-019-0826-z
19. Stahl, F., Schomm, F., Vossen, G., et al.: A classification framework for data marketplaces. In: Vietnam Journal of Computer Science. num. 3, pp. 137–143 (2016)
20. Stevens, G., Bossauer, P.: Technical prospects: big data in the digital world – dealing with personal data in the age of big data economies. In: Zeitchrift für Geistiges Eigentum – Intellectual Property Journal. núm. 3, band 9, pp. 266–278. Mohr Siebeck, Tübingen (2017)
21. Wendehorst, C.: Of Elephants in the room and paper tigers: how to reconcile data protection and the data economy. In: Lohsse, S., Schulze, R., Staudenmayer, D. (eds.) Trading data in the Digital Economy: Legal Concepts and Tools, 1st edn., pp. 227–355. Nomos, Baden-Baden (2018)
22. Zech, H.: Data as a Tradeable Commodity. In: De Franceschi, A. (ed.) European Contract Law and the Digital Single Market. The implications of the Digital Revolution, 1st edn. pp. 51–79. Intersentia, Cambridge (2016)
23. Zech, H.: Building a European Data Economy – The European Commission´s Proposal for a Data Producer´s Right. In: Zeitchrift für Geistiges Eigentum – Intellectual Property Journal, núm. 3, band 9, pp. 317–330. Mohr Siebeck, Tübingen (2017)

ADM in the European Union: An Interoperable Solution

Francesca Tassinari[(✉)] [iD]

Juridical Science, European Commission, 1049 Brussels, Belgium
francescatassinari92@gmail.com

Abstract. Regulations (EU) 817 and 818 of 2019 establish a framework for the interoperability of six large-scale IT systems within the Area of Freedom, Security, and Justice. These Regulations bring significant changes to these systems' infrastructure by introducing four main components. This paper focuses on the analyse of a specific one, namely the Multiple-Identity Detector (MID) and the procedure thereto. The MID compares individuals' biometric, identity, and travel document data stored in the shared Biometric Matching Service (sBMS), the Common Identity Repository (CIR), and the Schengen Information System (SIS) according to probabilistic matching. The comparison might result in the automated generation of white or yellow links: White links indicate that the data belong to the same person; yellow links call for the human verification of the competent authority to establish a white, green, or red link. To date, it is not clear if the MID triggers decisions based solely on automated processing and, if so, to what extent they impact individuals. By shedding light on its functioning, this paper analyses whether data subjects could claim the right not to be subject to such links.

Keywords: Automated-Decision Making · Multiple-Identity Detector · Interoperability · Area of Freedom · Security and Justice

1 Introducing the Interoperability Framework of Regulations (EU) 817 and 818 of 2019

Regulations (EU) 817[1] and 818[2] of 2019 (or IO Regulations) establish a framework for the interoperability[3] of six large-scale IT systems currently in existence or that are soon to be implemented within the European Union's (EU) Area of Freedom, Security and

---

This paper proceeds from the reflections the author developed in her Ph.D. thesis —Tassinari, F.: The external reach of the interoperability of large-scale IT systems in the AFSJ. University of Granada. Granada (2022). https://hdl.handle.net/10481/77708— while considering updated literature and case-law. Any opinions, even possible errors, must be attributed to her, and not to the institutions she is affiliated to (i.e., the European Commission).

[1] OJ L 135, 22.5.2019, p. 27–84.

[2] OJ L 135, 22.5.2019, p. 85–135.

[3] On the implementation of interoperable solutions as part of the eGovernment strategy see, for example, Sołtysik-Piorunkiewicz, A., and Banasikowska, J.: Interoperability and Standardization of e-Government Ubiquitous Systems in the EU Member States. In: Castelnovo, W., and

© Springer Nature Switzerland AG 2023
H. L. Larsen et al. (Eds.): FQAS 2023, LNAI 14113, pp. 290–303, 2023.
https://doi.org/10.1007/978-3-031-42935-4_24

Justice (AFSJ). The sister Regulations[4] aim at interconnecting systems that fall under the General Data Protection Regulation[5] (GDPR), the Law Enforcement Directive[6] (LED), and/or the EU Data Protection Regulation[7] (EUDPR). These systems are the Schengen Information System[8] (SIS); the Visa Information System[9] (VIS); the Entry/Exit System[10] (EES); the European Travel Information and Authorization System[11] (ETIAS); the European Dactyloscopy Database[12] (Eurodac), and the European Criminal Records Information System for Third-Country Nationals[13] (ECRIS-TCN).

The IO Regulations ensure fast, seamless, systematic and controlled access to the information[14] —mainly personal data— by the Member States' authorities and Union agencies with access to the underlying IT systems. The need for this assurance finds its rationale in the new infrastructure[15] the IO Regulations provide for EU large-scale IT systems. From the studies conducted by the EU Agency for the Operational Management

Ferrari, E. (eds.). Proceedings of the 13th European Conference on eGovernment, ECEG 2013, pp. 481–490. Academic Conferences and Publication International Limite, Varese (2013), and Wiese Schartum, D.: Sharing Information between Government Agencies: Some Legal Challenges Associated with Semantic Interoperability. In: Van der Hof, S., and M. Groothuis, M. (eds.) Innovating Government: Normative, Policy and Technological Dimensions of Modern Government, pp. 347–362. Springer, The Hague (2011).

[4] As renamed by the Opinion of the EDPS No. 4/2018 on the Proposals for two Regulations establishing a framework for interoperability between EU large-scale information systems, Brussels, 18.04.2018, 9, available at www.edps.europa.eu.

[5] OJ L 119, 4.5.2016, p. 1–88.

[6] OJ L 119, 4.5.2016, p. 89–131.

[7] OJ L 295, 21.11.2018, p. 39–98.

[8] OJ L 312, 7.12.2018, p. 14–55, and OJ L 312, 7.12.2018, p. 56–106.

[9] OJ L 218, 13.8.2008, pp. 60–81.

[10] OJ L 327, 9.12.2017, p. 20–82.

[11] OJ L 236, 19.9.2018, p. 1–71.

[12] OJ L 180, 29.6.2013, p. 1–30.

[13] OJ L 135, 22.5.2019, p. 1–26.

[14] For the different shades of the concept 'interoperability', cfr. Santusuosso, A., and Malerba, A.: Legal Interoperability as a Comprehensive Concept in Transnational Law. Law, Innovation and Technology. **6**, 51–73 (2014). https://doi.org/10.5235/17579961.6.1.51.

[15] Lanzara, G. F.: The Circulation of Agency in Judicial Proceedings: Designing for Interoperability and Complexity. In: Contini, F., Lanzaraat, G. F. (eds.) The Circulation of Agency in E-Justice. Interoperability and Infrastructures for European Transborder Judicial Proceedings, pp. 3–32. Springer, Heidelberg (2014), 15: 'Thus, an information infrastructure consists of a set of standards, protocols and gateways that link the running applications, programs and systems […]'.

of Large-Scale IT Systems in the AFSJ[16] (eu-LISA), we understand that the interoperability architecture should have been chosen among three options, and unification was the preferred one[17].

IO Regulations[18] largely consist[19] of dispositions regulating the interoperability components, of which there are four: the ESP (European Search Portal); the sBMS (shared Biometric Matching Service); the CIR (Common Identity Repository), and the MID (Multiple-Identity Detector). The CRRS (Common Repository for Reports and Statistics) must be added even though it is not catalogued as a component. The IO Regulation set down each component's purpose rather than defining its functioning, which raises doubts about their impact on individuals' fundamental rights[20]. This paper focuses on the MID (1.1) and addresses its purposes (1.2) together with the procedure stemming from it (2.1). Afterward, it analyses whether data subjects could claim a right not to be subject to a MID decision by virtue of Articles 22(1) of the GDPR, 11(1) of the LED, 24(1), and 77(1) of the EUDPR (2.2).

1.1 One of the New Components: The Multiple-Identity Detector

The MID may be defined as a complementary database in charge of creating, establishing, and storing the links tying the data stored in the CIR and the corresponding categories in the SIS, for which purpose it acts through the ESP and the sBMS[21]. The MID is made up of a central infrastructure, storing links and references to EU information systems, and a secure communication infrastructure to connect the MID with the SIS and the central infrastructures of the ESP and the CIR. It is therefore connected with the SIS, the CIR, and the ESP.

---

[16] Tassinari, F.: La institucionalización de la competencia operativa de la Unión Europea para la gestión y la interoperabilidad de los sistemas informáticos de gran magnitud del Espacio de Libertad, Seguridad, y Justicia: eu-LISA. La Ley Unión Europea. **111**, 1–38 (2023).

[17] eu-LISA: Elaboration of a Future Architecture for Interoperable IT Systems at eu-LISA. Tallin (2019), 11. The three options were: continuation; integration, and unification, www.eulisa.eur opa.eu, last accessed 2023/03/25.

[18] See Article 1 of the IO Regulations.

[19] Additional elements are directed at regulating data protection rights, responsibilities of the EU agencies and the Member States, the amendments brought to the legislative instruments affected by interoperability, and the final provisions.

[20] Šarf, P.: Automating Freedom, Security and Justice: Interoperability of AFSJ Databases as a Move Towards the Indiscriminate Mass Surveillance of Third-Country Nationals. In Završnik, A., and Badalič, V. (eds.) Automating Crime Prevention, Surveillance, and Military Operations, pp. 85–108. Springer, Switzerland (2021); Curtin, D., and Brito Bastos, F.: Interoperable Information Sharing and the Five Novel Frontiers of EU Governance: A Special Issue. European Public Law. **26**, pp. 59–70 (2020). https://doi.org/10.54648/euro2020004, and Hartmut, A.: Interoperability Between EU Policing and Migration Database: Risks for Privacy. European Public Law. **26**, 93–108 (2020). https://doi.org/10.54648/EURO2020006.

[21] According to the Proposal for a Regulation of the European Parliament and of the Council, COM(2017) 0794 final, Brussels, 13.12.2017, 19: 'The fourth interoperability component proposed in this draft Regulation (the multiple-identity detector) was not identified by the high-level expert group, but arose during the course of additional technical analysis and the proportionality assessment conducted by the Commission'.

The MID contains an identity confirmation file that gathers: the links referred to in Articles 30 to 33 of the IO Regulations —i.e., red, green, and white links; an alphanumeric code of reference to the EU information systems in which linked data are held; an alphanumeric code of a single identification number allowing the retrieval of the linked data from the corresponding EU information systems; an alphanumeric code of reference for the authority responsible for the manual verification of different identities, and the date of creation, or update, of the link.

The possibility to save the links established among the identity files —i.e., the identity data, travel document data, and biometrics belonging to the same person, but stored across large-scale IT systems— allows users to see prior identity checks carried out on the individual. Consequently, where the circumstances surrounding a specific individual change —because of the changing of personal data and/or when these are newly registered in another system— then, existing links are updated, or a new one/s created[22]. The identity confirmation file and the data stored therein, including the links, are stored in the MID only as long as the linked data is stored in two or more EU information systems[23]. Afterward, it must be erased from the MID in an automated manner.

1.2 Accessing the Common Identity Repository for Detecting Multiple Identities

The detection of multiple identities and the fight against identity fraud were among the main reasons against the silo approach followed by the development of large-scale IT systems[24]. Article 21 of the IO Regulations leads the procedure for the detection of multiple identities and, in a nutshell, enables the finding of discrepancies between declared identities, increasing the ability to identify identity fraudsters[25].

Article 21 adds a data processing activity to the personal data stored in the CIR and the SIS, and the corresponding templates held in the sBMS. This Article focuses on yellow and red links as these provide new access rights to the data already stored in the systems and the CIR. Yet, the multiple-identity detection procedure —or linked detection process[26]— must be interpreted in light of Articles 25–36 of the IO Regulations. These

---

[22] See below the analysis on the access to the CIR for the detection of multiple identities.

[23] Article 55 of Regulation (EU) 2018/1862; Article 40 of Regulation (EU) 2018/1861; Article 14 of Regulation (EU) 2018/1860; Article 23 of Regulation (EC) No 767/2008; Article 34 of Regulation (EU) 2017/2226; Article 54 of Regulation (EU) 2018/1240; Article 16 of Regulation (EU) No 603/2013, and Article 8 of Regulation (EU) 2019/816.

[24] Commission Staff Working Document Impact Assessment, SWD(2017) 0473 final, Strasbourg, 12.12.2017: 'Repeated and separate storing of personal information in separate and unconnected systems makes it possible that people are recorded under different identities, without this being detected. Ultimately, as it has been reported, one person may end up having different identities recorded in SIS, Eurodac and VIS, while national authorities are unable to distinguish the cases where the difference points to identity fraud or to a regular situation (e.g. change of name, multiple nationalities etc.)'.

[25] Note that large-scale IT systems already contemplate internal forms to manage third country nationals' identities: SIS has alerts; Eurodac has links; VIS has dossier reference numbers; EES has traveler files; ETIAS has 'linked applications' with the exception of identical travel documents, and ECRIS-TCN has data records.

[26] European Commission: Feasibility study on a Common Identity Repository (CIR). Brussels (2017), www. op.europa.eu, last accessed 2023/03/25, 57.

Articles clarify that such a procedure is triggered: as soon as a large-scale IT system is added to the interoperability architecture, and each time an identity file is created or updated in one of the underlying IT systems[27]. The former situation is expected to occur as soon as existing or future systems migrate into the interoperability infrastructure. The latter, instead, occurs as soon as the interoperability components enter into operation.

In any case, the multiple-identity detection procedure pursues two main objectives: first, it seeks to facilitate the controls over bona fide travellers, and second, it aims to detect identity frauds used to access the Schengen area. Identity frauds consist of two phenomena: identity thefts and false identities[28]. Identity theft is the unlawful stealing of someone's identity, which results in an individual becoming a victim of the crime; identity fraud is the usage of a bogus identity that hides the individual's true one while undermining the State. For this reason, detecting multiple identities is crucial to the fight against organised crime, terrorism, migrant smuggling, and trafficking in human beings[29].

2   The Multiple-Identity Detection Procedure

The multiple-identity detection procedure is comprised of two phases, where the former is an automated procedure, and the latter consists of a manual verification.

2.1   The Multiple-Identity Detection Procedure in a Nutshell

The creation, or updating, of an individual/application file or alert[30] in one of the IT systems launches an automatic order to the MID that must compare the newly added data with the biometric data stored in the sBMS and the identity and travel document data stored in the CIR and the SIS through a *one-to-many* comparison[31]. Notably, the comparison occurs within the same category of data (fingerprints against fingerprints;

---

[27] Article 27(1) of the IO Regulations.

[28] Note that the SIS stores 'aliases' and information on 'misused identity': 'alias' occurs when a person uses a false or assumed identity; 'misused identity', instead, happens where a person, subject to an alert in SIS, uses the identity of another real person, in particular when a document is used to the detriment of the real owner of that document.

[29] Hoffberger-Pippan, E.: The Interoperability of EU Information Systems and Fundamental Rights concerns. Spanish Yearbook of International Law. **23**, 426–250 (2019), and European Migrant Smuggling Center: 4th Annual Activity Report. The Hague (2020), www.europol.eur opa.eu, last accessed 2023/03/25.

[30] Article 27(1) of the IO Regulations.

[31] European Commission: Feasibility study on a Common Identity Repository (CIR). Brussels (2017), www. op.europa.eu, last accessed 2023/03/25, 3: 'In probabilistic matching, several field values are compared between two records and each field is assigned a weight that indicates how closely the two field values match. The sum of the individual fields weights indicates the likelihood of a match between two records'.

facial images against facial images; identity data against identity data[32], and travel document data against travel document data)[33] and identity data is the sole category that must always be present. Moreover, the comparison occurs among data belonging to different systems and not within each system[34] and must terminate before the new record is created or updated. Only one link can be established between two individual/application files or alerts, including when a person has more than one individual/application file or alert stored within a single system[35]. Thus, the MID supports the CIR[36] in determining the type of links to be generated among the systems' individual/application file or alert and stores the links in the identity confirmation file for future use[37].

From this comparison, either no link or an automated white/yellow link would be created. Thus, the MID functioning might be assimilated to the one of a supervised[38] machine learning[39] based on pre-defined outcomes. If no match is found, the procedure must continue according to the instrument governing it. The generation of links,

---

[32] Thus: names will be compared with names (including surname and first name); date of birth will be compared with date of birth; gender will be compared with gender, nationality and place of birth will be compared with nationality and place of birth.

[33] These are not the identity data contained in the document but the type, number, expiring date, and issuing country of the travel documents.

[34] Article 27(5) of the IO Regulations.

[35] If a person is known under several identities within a sole IT system, and only one link has to be generated with the data eventually present in the other IT system, we don't know which identity will be compared.

[36] The CIR detects new identities and decides whether a white/yellow link should be created. The CIR itself instructs the MID of the links created in the identity confirmation file. However, the competent authority in charge of the manual verification procedure interacts with the MID to convert the yellow links as explained below.

[37] It also stores the reference to that authority in charge of the manual verification – i.e., the one that decide to turn a yellow link in a specific color as explained below – the date and hour s/he did it.

[38] ADM systems are supervised or not, that is, they may need human intervention to pre-establish the result or not. If supervised machine learning is required, a training phase is deployed before it is made operational as the dataset provided by 'the designer' must be tested. After this stage, the machine is 'ready' to be used: When it is fed with new data, it can make predictions according to the trained model. In other words, the individual chooses both the set of data to be matched and the outcome pursued as a result of the analysis of that data. The machine, in turn, finds patterns and correlations among the data.

[39] Cfr. Gupta, R., Gupta, H., and Mohania, M.: Cloud Computing and Big Data Analytics: What Is New from Databases Perspective?. In: Srinivasa, S., and Bhatnagar, V. (eds.) Big Data Analytics. Lecture Notes in Computer Science, pp. 42–61. Springer, Berlin, Heidelberg (2012), 42.

instead[40], considers two different scenarios of multiple justified identities (white) or unclear identities (yellow).

Automated White/Yellow Links

Coloured links depend on predetermined thresholds that define "matches"[41] among identity data, travel document data, and biometrics similarities[42]. If compared data are the same or similar[43], a white link should be generated in an automated manner[44]. Same and similar identities do not require a 100% match: the former requires that only some data is equivalent —e.g., the surname and first name; the latter might occur when transliteration or inversions are detected.

In case of unclear identities, a yellow link is generated in an automated manner. Here, the automated decision-making (ADM) procedure is not able to establish whether the data belongs to the same person or not as there are significant discrepancies[45] among biometrics, identity data, and/or travel document data. As a general norm, the ESP notifies the generation of a yellow link to the authority that inputted or modified the file triggering the multiple-identity detection procedure. Therefore, yellow links are established in an automated manner like white links. Yet, yellow automated links are "provisional" and support the activity of the competent authorities in charge of taking the final decision as explained below.

Manually Established White/Green/Red Links

As its label suggests, the manual verification procedure calls for human intervention[46]. As a general rule, the authority responsible for resolving a yellow link is the same one that created or modified the individual/application file or alert in one of the systems[47] —i.e.,

---

[40] Article 28(7) of the IO Regulations establishes that the procedure is laid down by the European Commission with an implementing act together with eu-LISA.

[41] Article 4(18) of the IO Regulations establish that match 'means the existence of a correspondence as a result of an automated comparison between personal data recorded or being recorded in an information system or database'.

[42] European Commission: Feasibility study on a Common Identity Repository (CIR). Brussels (2017), www. op.europa.eu, last accessed 2023/03/25, 58.

[43] Article 33(1)(a),(b),(c) of the IO Regulations.

[44] According to Article 28(5) of the IO Regulations, the definition of the same or similar data should be concretised by the European Commission in a delegated act. This is enabled by an algorithm programmed to detect the similarity between identity data from data fields belonging to different systems. The algorithm would point out when the identity data can be considered similar according to thresholds of similarity previously defined —see the EDPS: Formal comments of the EDPS on the draft Commission Delegated Regulations supplementing Regulation (EU) 201997 and Regulation (EU) 2019/818 of the European Parliament and Council with regard to cases where identity data may be considered as same or similar for the purpose of the multiple identity detection. Brussels (2021), www.edps.europa.eu, last accessed 2023/03/25.

[45] Article 30(1) of the IO Regulations.

[46] Article 29 of the IO Regulations.

[47] Article 29 of the IO Regulations.

a Member State's competent authority[48]— which is kept reflected in the identity confirmation file[49]. Several authorities are involved at this stage: border guards, competent visa authorities, and immigration authorities for the EES; visa authorities and authorities competent for the issuance of residence permits as far as the "new VIS" is concerned; the ETIAS Central Unit and ETIAS National United for ETIAS; the SIRENE Bureau of the Member State that creates or updates an SIS alert, and the central authorities of the convicted Member State competent for entering data in ECRIS-TCN[50]. Conversely, Union agencies cannot enter or modify files in the underlying systems, or the CIR and their staff is not competent to conduct the manual verification procedure, for the time being[51]. An important exception is made in cases where the link involves one or more SIS sensitive alerts according to Regulation (EU) 2018/1862, for: persons wanted for arrest for surrender or extradition purposes[52]; missing or vulnerable persons[53]; persons sought to assist in a judicial procedure[54], and persons that are sought for discreet checks, inquiry checks or specific checks[55]. Here, the authority competent for the manual verification is always the SIRENE Bureau of the Member State that created the alert[56].

The resolution of yellow links allows the verifying authority to access the 'linked data contained in the relevant identity confirmation file and to the identity data linked in the CIR and, where relevant, in SIS'[57]. In practice, to "resolve" a yellow link the competent authority should have access to the sets of linked data stored in the CIR and, in case of updating a file, to the links already recorded in the MID. All in all, the verifying authority must turn the yellow link into a white, green, or red one:

---

[48] European Commission: Feasibility study on a Common Identity Repository (CIR). Brussels (2017), www. op.europa.eu, last accessed 2023/03/25, 32. Therefore, Member States discarded the possibility to establish a Central Link Verification Unit (CLV unit) in charge of resolving all the links alone or together with the Member States with the exception of the ETIAS Central Unit in the terms analysed below.

[49] Article 71(1) of Regulation (EU) 2019/817 and Article 67(1) of Regulation (EU) 2019/818 establish that the national authorities using or accessing the MID and the CIR are notified to eu-LISA that must publish —and update— a list on the OJ three months from the date on which each interoperability component commenced operations. The European Commission, then, is in charge of notifying the Member States and the public through the website.

[50] Article 26(1) of the IO Regulations. Note that during the negotiations of the IO Regulations, more authorities were contemplated by virtue of Regulation (EU) No 603/2013 —Council of the EU: Proposal for a Regulation of the European Parliament and of the Council on establishing a framework for interoperability between EU information systems (police and judicial cooperation, asylum and migration) - Presidency revised text of provisions specific to this Regulation, 6551/18. Brussels (2018), 9–12.

[51] OJ L 185, 12.7.2022, p. 1–9 finally turned down the possibility for Europol directly enter alerts into SIS directly.

[52] Article 26 of Regulation (EU) 2018/1862.

[53] Article 32 of Regulation (EU) 2018/1862.

[54] Article 34 of Regulation (EU) 2018/1862.

[55] Article 36 of Regulation (EU) 2018/1862.

[56] Article 29(2) of the IO Regulations.

[57] Article 29(3) of the IO Regulations.

- A white link is established if that authority considers that the data belongs to the same person[58], thus allowing the retracing of an individual's dispersed identity data that are lost in different systems;
- A green link is established if s/he considers that the data belongs to two different persons that have similar identities[59], and
- A red link refers to a person using different identities in an unjustified manner, or a person using someone else's identity in an unjustified manner[60], without distinguishing between the perpetrator and the victim[61]. Because of their relevance from a security perspective, the authorities responsible for the linked data should be notified of the creation of a red link —that is, the authorities responsible for the pre-existing data against which a red link has been established— in an automated manner[62].

2.2 Is There a Right Not to be Subject to the MID Links?[63]

Articles 22(1) of the GDPR, 11(1) of the LED, 24(1) and 77(1) of the EUDPR set forth the right not to be subject to a decision based solely on automated processing, including profiling[64]. These provisions are not equally formulated, as rules ensuring the protection of personal data in the judicial and criminal law domains are generally less stringent[65]. Notably, the fact that automated white/yellow links are generated by an EU central component (the MID) implies that the processing activity could be assigned to a Union's body instead of the Member States[66], with the consequent application of the EUDPR and not the GDPR/LED. Overall, the application of these provisions requires analysing: first, whether the multiple-identity detection procedure gives rise to a profiling technique or not; second, if MID decisions are based solely on automated processing and, third, if the ADM at issue 'produces [adverse] legal effects' on or '[similarly] significantly affects' data subjects.

---

[58] Article 33(1)(d) of the IO Regulations.

[59] Article 31(1) of the IO Regulations.

[60] Article 32 of the IO Regulations.

[61] Article 32(2) of the IO Regulations.

[62] Article 32(6) of the IO Regulations.

[63] For an in-depth analysis on individuals', especially third-countries nationals', rights to be informed, access, rectify, and erase personal data and to restrict the processing, see Tassinari, F.: La interoperabilidad de los sistemas de información de gran magnitud de la Unión Europea y la detección de identidades múltiples: garantías y responsabilidades. In: Garrido Carrillo, F. J. (ed.) Lucha contra la criminalidad organizada y cooperación judicial de la UE: instrumentos, límites y perspectivas en la era digital, pp. 291–338. Thomson Reuters Aranzadi, Navarra (2022).

[64] Article 4(4) GDPR, Article 3(4) LED, and Article 3(5) EUDPR define profiling as '[…] any form of automated processing of personal data consisting of the use of personal'. Cfr., for example, Kleinberg, J., Lakkaraju, H., Leskovec, J., Ludwig, J., and Mullainathan, S.: Human decisions and machine predictions. The Quarterly Journal of Economics. **113**, 237–293 (2018). https://doi.org/10.1093/qje/qjx032.

[65] Tassinari, F. The European Union's external competence in the data protection field: is mixity the only way out? Revista de Derecho Comunitario Europeo **75**, 247–291 (2023).

[66] Tassinari, F.: The role of eu-LISA in the implementation of the interoperability framework. ADiM Blog, Analyses & Opinions (2023), www.adimblog.com, last accessed 2023/03/25.

First, the generation or establishment of links between personal data could help evaluate certain aspects relating to natural persons[67]. In particular, MID links would help analyse or predict aspects concerning the reliability, behaviour, location, or movements of the persons concerned[68]. White links hint at whether the same person is known under different systems and would suggest that s/he is a visa-exempt traveller or not. Besides, if a white link is generated with the ECRIS-TCN data stored in the CIR, this would point out that the third-country national has been convicted previously. In practice, white links generated with SIS would catch police and judicial authorities' attention toward "bad travellers" —i.e., investigated and wanted people— and persons in need of protection[69]. Green links, instead, are expected to facilitate external border crossing to bona fide travellers[70] by detecting "false positives"[71] matches and, consequently, they would enhance the reliability of the persons involved. Similarly, red links would flag individuals using false or fraudulent identities in an unjustified manner and, consequently, could provide clues on the subject at stake —being s/he the perpetrator or the victim.

Second, Articles 22(1) of the GDPR, 11(1) of the LED, 24(1) and 77(1) of the EUDPR require that the decision is taken only on an automated processing basis. According to Advocate General (AG) Pikamäe, and in the absence of any legislative guidance, the term 'decision' should be broadly interpreted to encompass 'a multiplicity of acts that may affect the person concerned in different ways'[72]. Hence, a 'decision' would require an examination on a case-by-case basis of the circumstances and the seriousness of the effects on the individual's legal status[73]. Applied to our concrete case, whether MID links and the acts undertaken on its basis are decisions or not depends on 'the way the decision-making process is structured'[74]. As we explained above, the multiple-identity detection procedure is made of different phases and the generation or establishment of coloured links is prodromic to the adoption of follow-up actions. Although national authorities are in charge of the decision-taking process, the MID has been delegated

---

[67] According to the Committee of Ministers of the Council of Europe: The protection of individuals with regard to automatic processing of personal data in the context of profiling. Strasbourg (2010), www.rm.coe.int, last accessed 2023/03/25, 25, profiling consists of three stages: data warehousing, data mining, and variable deduction.

[68] Leese, M.: Fixing State Vision: Interoperability, Biometrics, and Identity Management in the EU. Geopolitics. **27**, 113–133 (2020). https://doi.org/10.1080/14650045.2020.1830764.

[69] Cfr. Regulation (EU) 2018/1862.

[70] Recital (39) of IO Regulations.

[71] Note that the IO Regulations do not contemplate cases of false negatives that according to the international standards of the ISO/IEC: Information technology—Vocabulary—Part 37: Biometrics, 2382–37 (2017), are '[...] of rejecting a biometric claim that should have been accepted in accordance with an authorities statement on the origin of the biometric probe and the biometric reference'.

[72] Opinion of Advocate General Priit Pikamäe, *OQ v. Land Hessen*, C-634/21, 16 March 2023, EU:C:2023:220, para. 38. The Opinion is not available in the English language and its translation is ours.

[73] *Ibid.*, para. 39.

[74] *Ibid.*, para. 40.

specific tasks to accomplish freedom, security, and justice purposes[75]. Thus, we should wonder whether MID links might end up pre-determining an authority's action[76]. If and only if such an authority acts based on a MID link, without checking it further, then, the MID link could be seen as a 'decision' in the light of Articles 22(1) of the GDPR, 11(1) of the LED, 24(1) and 77(1) of the EUDPR. It is now easy to understand how automated white links fall within the scope of these ADM provisions, but that verified white, green, or red links do not. Specifically, as long as an automated white link '[...] have negative repercussions on the person concerned, i.e. significantly restrict him in the exercise of his freedoms, or stigmatise him in society, it seems justified to qualify it as a 'decision' within the meaning of the aforementioned provision [...]'[77].

Provided that only automated processing must be taken into account under Articles 22(1) of the GDPR, 11(1) of the LED, 24(1) and 77(1) of the EUDPR, automated white links must be the only element upon which an authority justifies his/her action[78]. Notably, according to AG Pikamäe, '[t]his condition would be fulfilled in the presence of human intervention in the process, which, however, could not intervene in the causal link between the automated processing and the final decision'[79]. Therefore, if the MID will *de facto* take the final decision, without leaving a margin of discretion to the relevant authority, then, its procedure should be deemed to be fully automated. In *OQ v. Land Hessen*, AG Pikamäe found that the evaluation should have been conducted at the national level,[80] but also noted that the delegated agency had such a decisive weight on the decision with which the loan would be granted, that its scoring calculation could be understood as pre-determining the final decision generally[81].

A third, final, element to consider for assessing the application of Articles 22(1) of the GDPR, 11(1) of the LED, 24(1) and 77(1) of the EUDPR concerns the effects — adverse, in the specific case of the LED— produced on individuals or, in short, the fact that automated white links should significantly affect the data subjects. In the absence of a definition of 'legal effects' in the Union's legislation, the consequences stemming from the generation of automated white links should again be assessed in light of the applicable national law on a case-by-case basis[82]. From a border management perspective, the multiple-identity detection procedure is expected to legitimise the entry to or exit from

---

[75] Blasi Casagran, C.: Fundamental Rights Implications of Interconnecting Migration and Policing Databases in the EU. Human Rights Law Review. **21**, 433–457 (2021). https://doi.org/10.1093/hrlr/ngaa057.

[76] Opinion of Advocate General Priit Pikamäe, *OQ v. Land Hessen*, C-634/21, 16 March 2023, EU:C:2023:220, para. 42.

[77] *Ibidem.*

[78] *Ibid.*, para. 44.

[79] *Ibidem.*

[80] *Ibid.*, para. 45.

[81] *Ibid.*, paras. 46 and 47.

[82] Shortcomings in national implementation have been highlighted by Duic, D., and Rošić, M.: Interoperability between the EU information systems -from an idea to the realization. Polic. Sigur. (Zagreb), godina. **31**, 118–148 (2022).

the Schengen area, or to resolve its refusal[83]. However, the hybrid nature[84] of the IT systems involved suggests that the multiple-identity detection procedure will be triggered for purely police and criminal judicial cooperation purposes too. As we mentioned above, the IO Regulations specify that there could be no legal consequence for the person concerned based on a verified red link[85]. Nevertheless, the co-legislators are silent concerning automated white links, meaning that the range of the (eventually adverse) effects produced on individuals is not known beforehand.

3 Final Remarks

IO Regulations establish a framework for the interoperability of six large-scale IT systems within the AFSJ. These Regulations introduce four main components. The current paper analysed the MID that will compare data stored in the sBMS, CIR, and SIS to detect identity fraud. The comparison might result in automated white/yellow links. White links hint at the same person known across different IT systems and must be considered as 'decisions' taken in an automated manner if the authority acts without checking them. Differently from verified red links, the IO Regulations do not provide for the (adverse) effects produced by automated white links on individuals/data subjects concerned. Therefore, the consequences stemming from the generation of automated white links should be assessed on a case-by-case basis by virtue of the applicable national law. If the latter condition is also satisfied, then, Articles 22(1) of the GDPR, 11(1) of the LED, 24(1) and 77(1) of the EUDPR would apply. However, individuals' right not to be subject to an ADM might be restricted by virtue of the derogation clauses set down under Articles 22(2) and (3) of the GDPR, 11(1) and (2) of the LED, 24(1) and (2) and 77(1) and (2) of the EUDPR, which might prevent individuals from claiming a right not to be subject to an automated MID white link.

---

[83] Article 6(1)(d) of the Schengen Border Code, OJ L 77, 23.3.2016, p. 1–52, and Article 24(2)(a) or (b) of Regulation (EU) 2018/1861.

[84] Vavoula, N.: Immigration and Privacy in the Law of the European Union. Brill, The Netherlands (2022), and Quintel, T.: Interoperable Data Exchanges Within Different Data Protection Regimes: The Case of Europol and the European Border and Coast Guard Agency. European Public Law. 26, 205–226 (2020). Urn:nbn:se:uu:diva-421838.

[85] Article 32(2) and recital (63) of the IO Regulations.

Bibliography

1. Blasi Casagran, C.: Fundamental rights implications of interconnecting migration and policing databases in the EU. Hum. Rights Law Rev. **21**, 433–457 (2021). https://doi.org/10.1093/hrlr/ngaa057
2. Committee of Ministers of the Council of Europe: The protection of individuals with regard to automatic processing of personal data in the context of profiling. Strasbourg (2010). www.rm.coe.int. Accessed 25 Mar 2023
3. Curtin, D., Brito Bastos, F.: Interoperable information sharing and the five novel frontiers of EU governance: a special issue. Eur. Public Law **26**, 59–70 (2020). https://doi.org/10.54648/euro2020004
4. Duic, D., Rošić, M.: Interoperability between the EU information systems -from an idea to the realization. Polic. sigur. (Zagreb), godina. **31**, 118–148 (2022)
5. EDPS No. 4/2018 on the Proposals for two Regulations establishing a framework for interoperability between EU large-scale information systems, Brussels, 18.04.2018. www.edps.europa.eu. Accessed 25 Mar 2023
6. EDPS on the draft Commission Delegated Regulations supplementing Regulation (EU) 201997 and Regulation (EU) 2019/818 of the European Parliament and Council with regard to cases where identity data may be considered as same or similar for the purpose of the multiple identity detection, Brussels, 27.04.2021. www.edps.europa.eu. Accessed 25 Mar 2023
7. eu-LISA: Elaboration of a Future Architecture for Interoperable IT Systems at eu-LISA. Tallin (2019). www.eulisa.europa.eu. Accessed 25 Mar 2023
8. European Commission: Feasibility study on a Common Identity Repository (CIR). Brussels (2017). www.op.europa.eu. Accessed 25 Mar 2023
9. European Migrant Smuggling Center: 4th Annual Activity Report. The Hague (2020). www.europol.europa.eu, last Accessed 25 Mar 2023
10. Gupta, R., Gupta, H., Mohania, M.: Cloud computing and big data analytics: what is new from databases perspective?. In: Srinivasa, S., and Bhatnagar, V. (eds.) Big Data Analytics. Lecture Notes in Computer Science, pp. 42–61. Springer, Heidelberg (2012) https://doi.org/10.1007/978-3-642-35542-4_5
11. Hartmut, A.: Interoperability between EU policing and migration database: risks for privacy. Eur. Public Law **26**, 93–108 (2020). https://doi.org/10.54648/EURO2020006
12. Hoffberger-Pippan, E.: The interoperability of EU information systems and fundamental rights concerns. Span. Yearb. Int. Law **23**, 426–250 (2019)
13. ISO/IEC: Information technology — Vocabulary — Part 37: Biometrics, 2382–37 (2017)
14. Kleinberg, J., Lakkaraju, H., Leskovec, J., Ludwig, J., Mullainathan, S.: Human decisions and machine predictions. Q. J. Econ. **113**, 237–293 (2018). https://doi.org/10.1093/qje/qjx032
15. Lanzara, G. F.: The Circulation of Agency in Judicial Proceedings: Designing for Interoperability and Complexity. In: Contini, F., Lanzaraat, G. F. (eds.) The Circulation of Agency in E-Justice. Interoperability and Infrastructures for European Transborder Judicial Proceedings, pp. 3–32. Springer, Heidelberg (2014)https://doi.org/10.1007/978-94-007-7525-1_1
16. Leese, M.: Fixing state vision: interoperability, biometrics, and identity management in the EU. Geopolitics **27**, 113–133 (2020). https://doi.org/10.1080/14650045.2020.1830764
17. Quintel, T.: Interoperable data exchanges within different data protection regimes: the case of europol and the european border and coast guard agency. Eur. Public Law. **26**, 205–226 (2020). urn:nbn:se:uu:diva-421838
18. Santusuosso, A., Malerba, A.: Legal interoperability as a comprehensive concept in transnational law. Law Innov. Technol. **6**, 51–73 (2014). https://doi.org/10.5235/17579961.6.1.51

19. Šarf, P.: Automating Freedom, Security and Justice: Interoperability of AFSJ Databases as a Move Towards the Indiscriminate Mass Surveillance of Third-Country Nationals. In Završnik, A., and Badalič, V. (eds.) Automating Crime Prevention, Surveillance, and Military Operations, pp. 85-108. Springer, Switzerland (2021) https://doi.org/10.1007/978-3-030-73276-9_5
20. Sołtysik-Piorunkiewicz, A., Banasikowska, J.: Interoperability and Standardization of e-Government Ubiquitous Systems in the EU Member States. In: Castelnovo, W., and Ferrari, E. (eds.). Proceedings of the 13th European Conference on eGovernment, ECEG 2013, pp. 481–490. Academic Conferences and Publication International Limite, Varese (2013)
21. Tassinari, F.: La interoperabilidad de los sistemas de información de gran magnitud de la Unión Europea y la detección de identidades múltiples: garantías y responsabilidades. In: Garrido Carrillo, F. J. (ed.) Lucha contra la criminalidad organizada y cooperación judicial de la UE: instrumentos, límites y perspectivas en la era digital, pp. 291–338. Thomson Reuters Aranzadi, Navarra (2022)
22. Tassinari, F.: La institucionalización de la competencia operativa de la Unión Europea para la gestión y la interoperabilidad de los sistemas informáticos de gran magnitud del Espacio de Libertad, Seguridad, y Justicia: eu-LISA. La Ley Unión Europea. 111, 1–38 (2023)
23. Tassinari, F.: The European Union's external competence in the data protection field: is mixity the only way out? Revista de Derecho Comunitario Europeo 75, forthcoming (2023)
24. Tassinari, F.: The external reach of the interoperability of large-scale IT systems in the AFSJ. University of Granada, Granada (2022). https://hdl.handle.net/10481/77708
25. Tassinari, F.: The role of eu-LISA in the implementation of the interoperability framework. ADiM Blog, Analyses & Opinions (2023). www.adimblog.com. Accessed 25 Mar 2023
26. Vavoula, N.: Immigration and Privacy in the Law of the European Union. Brill, The Netherlands (2022)
27. Wiese Schartum, D.: Sharing Information between Government Agencies: Some Legal Challenges Associated with Semantic Interoperability. In: Van der Hof, S., and M. Groothuis, M. (eds.) Innovating Government: Normative, Policy and Technological Dimensions of Modern Government, pp. 347–362. Springer, The Hague (2011). https://doi.org/10.1007/978-90-6704-731-9_19

Author Index

© Springer Nature Switzerland AG 2023
H. L. Larsen et al. (Eds.): FQAS 2023, LNAI 14113, pp. 305–306, 2023.
https://doi.org/10.1007/978-3-031-42935-4